The Grand Old Man

The Grand Old Man

OF PURDUE UNIVERSITY AND INDIANA AGRICULTURE

A Biography of William Carroll Latta

FREDERICK WHITFORD
AND ANDREW G. MARTIN

Purdue University Press
West Lafayette, Indiana

Design by Dawn L. Minns
Illustrations by Mary Louise Jones

Library of Congress Cataloging-in-Publication Data

Whitford, Fred, 1955–
    The grand old man of Purdue University and Indiana agriculture: a biography of William Carroll Latta/Frederick Whitford and Andrew G. Martin.
      p. cm.
  Includes bibliographical references and index.
  ISBN 1-55753-395-4 (alk. paper)
  1. Latta, W. C. (William Carroll), 1850–1935. 2. Agriculture teachers—Indiana—Biography. 3. Agricultural extension workers—Indiana—Biography. 4. Agriculture—Study and teaching (Higher)—Indiana—History. 5. Agricultural extension work—Indiana—History. 6. Purdue University—Faculty—Biography. I. Martin, Andrew G. II. Title.
  S417.L36W55 2005
  630'.92–dc22

2005005896

DEDICATION

*This book is dedicated to all of Purdue University's
Extension specialists, educators, administrators, and volunteers—
past and present—who, after devoting their lives to Extension work,
rest knowing that there will be others to carry on the tradition
of serving the people.*

CONTENTS

ACKNOWLEDGMENTS

Biographies are not written in a vacuum. The work involved in the compilation of information is more than just what the authors write. It involves many people to make such a book possible about someone who lived so long ago. The authors were indeed fortunate to have had the assistance of so many people who all helped and provided much encouragement on this long journey.

While it is impossible to name everyone, the authors would like to acknowledge a few who helped pave the road to the completed biography of William Carroll Latta.

The authors wish to thank Irwin Weiser, professor and head of the Purdue University Department of English, for his insightful analysis of William Carroll Latta's poetry and short stories; Katherine M. Markee, the Special Collections librarian for Purdue University, who contributed significantly to the successes in assembling the supporting materials for the book; Roger Wood, a historian from the University of California and a Purdue University alumnus, whose dissertation on Purdue history proved a valuable resource; and Paul Schueler and Kim Wainscott, from the Tippecanoe County Historical Association, who were crucial in the development of this biography. Special thanks to Keith Johnson and Robert Nielsen for reviewing and commenting on the thesis written by William Latta.

We are also grateful to the family of William Carroll Latta. Several individuals contributed family stories, letters, notes, and most of all pictures from an era long ago. They helped to shape the book and, for their efforts, made the book more interesting because of their ties to Professor Latta. Therefore, a special thanks goes to Larry Sullivan and Bettie Gordon, descendents of James Latta; Phyllis and Arthur Webster, descendents of the Wood family; and Kim Sharpe, the great-granddaughter of William Carroll Latta.

We are indebted to our editor, Carolyn A. McGrew, for all of her efforts in improving the readability of the book. Our thanks to Dawn L. Minns for designing the dust jacket and the layout of the book. All the beautiful black-and-white sketches are original drawings by Mary Louise "Lou" Jones.

And finally, thank you to the many others who helped in one way or another: Robert Mitchell, who rescued the book when the computer decided to erase it; Ken Mueller, the editor of the *Latta Newsletter;* the Veterans of Foreign Wars of the United States for assistance in helping to connect the authors with the sailors of the SS *W. C. Latta;* and Bob Gagen, Noble County historian, who helped us find the land that Robert Latta and his son, William Carroll, farmed.

INTRODUCTION

THIS BOOK TAKES AS ITS SUBJECT the life of William Carroll Latta, a figure instrumental in the development of agricultural Extension, teaching, and research at Purdue University during the late nineteenth and early twentieth centuries. However, he would be the first to admit that he was a part of Purdue's success, not its cause. Latta would surely point to the many dedicated Purdue men and women who were pioneers in their efforts to improve the lives of rural people.

Professor Latta and his colleagues were trailblazers. Where previously the science and practice of agriculture operated independently of each other, these men forged a connection, bringing into fraternity Indiana's land-grant institution and the people of the state. Agriculture, in general, and farmers, in particular, took time to accept the ideas and information that Latta and others had to offer, but once Indiana's agricultural community recognized that research and education could improve their lives, the pattern was set for the future. Farmers would come to want and then expect Purdue University to direct its resources toward developing and disseminating, in print and in person, the latest research information about all aspects of farming, from using the latest mechanical device to increasing efficiency and yields.

Those that followed in the footsteps of Latta and his contemporaries built on the early successes, extending research-based educational opportunities to an ever widening circle of Indiana citizens. Each new generation of Purdue University's Extension professionals have reached back to the previous generation to use those programs and methods that worked—modified where necessary—or to serve as the inspiration for new ideas about Extension work. Tomorrow's Extension educators will no doubt continue the tradition of paving over old roads and designing new highways of ideas on which the current generation never imagined traveling.

Why William Carroll Latta? What drew us into an exploration of the life of this remarkable individual? We are Extension specialists with the Purdue University College of Agriculture, where Latta devoted more than five decades of professional service. This biography is an opportunity to reflect on the life of a man who has influenced our careers in ways he could never have imagined. Each article, book, and reference that yielded information on this agricultural visionary inspired a sense of excitement and discovery.

Professor Latta's name resonates at Purdue University to this day, but his work is largely unknown. It has been seventy years since he strolled across the West Lafayette campus, where he is still known variously as the founder of Extension and the founder of the Experiment Station. Some recall that a World War II Liberty Ship, the SS *W. C. Latta*, was named in his honor, and it is fitting to remember that Indiana 4-H youth nominated his name to that ship. Others know of his portrait, painted by the Hoosier artist Robert Grafton and presented to Purdue University on Latta's eightieth birthday, March 9, 1930. A few recognize his book titled *Outline History of Indiana Agriculture* as the only one ever written on the subject.

But ask those who recognize William Carroll Latta's name about his specific accomplishments, and it becomes clear that the details of his life are forgotten. How is it that the work of this noted teacher, researcher, Extension worker, editor, administrator, and community leader has been lost in history? Why has his life never been the subject of a comprehensive inquiry by the institution where he figured so prominently?

It is unfortunate that the memory of Professor Latta, the thirteenth faculty member at Purdue University, is fading into obscurity. So it was our desire to know this man, to document the surviving fragments of his life and weave them into a coherent whole.

William Carroll Latta, from his boyhood on a northern Indiana farm to his work as a university professor, was deeply concerned with the rural issues of his day. Information leaped from the pages of old manuscripts, dusty reports, and yellowed newspaper clippings as we dug deeper and deeper into his past. And out of the shadows the man emerged.

This biography offers a clear understanding of why William Latta was so important to Purdue University, Indiana agriculture, and rural life. We hope that our book on this unique university agriculturist will bring knowledge of his work to those who serve in Extension today. His mission then is our mission now: helping others help themselves.

It is our sincere wish that Latta's descendants will appreciate this book as an accurate portrayal of his life and his work on behalf of Purdue University. We wish them to feel honored that others may come to know Professor Latta through the pages of this biography. His impact—through Purdue education, research, and Extension, as well as Indiana agriculture—lives on in these pages. If Professor Latta were alive today, we would hope that he might read this work and say, "Well done!"

The Education of William Carroll Latta:
His Early Years

CHAPTER  ONE

O radiant childhood's morn, thy marvels
In round-eyed wonderment beheld!
Each mirror pool or rippling stream
Allures to splash, swim, fish, or dream.
Each vale, flower-decked, the eye's delight;
Each rising hill or mountain height
A challenge to ascend and see beyond.
Roseate morn, purple eve, and glowing noon
Blue sky, bright star, or brilliant moon
All vie to charm, inspire. In truth
We say, O glorious day of youth.

—William Carroll Latta
"Yesterday" from "Yesterday, Today, Tomorrow," 1925

THE YOUNG MAN HAD WORKED HARD all day weeding the corn patch, cutting red clover for hay, feeding the animals, and clearing a few more trees from the pioneer farm in northern Indiana. His muscles were tired and aching from the heavy labor of a well-established routine. Work started at sunup and finished at sunset if he was lucky.

It was lonely for a fifteen-year-old in 1865 working the fields and doing a man's job. But his spirits began to rise as the sun set and the buzzing of the night insects filled the evening air. Tomorrow would be Sunday, his favorite day of the week. William Carroll Latta would gladly rise the next morning to feed the animals, take a quick breakfast, part his hair just so, put on his Sunday best, and then hustle himself to the church down the road. He always looked forward to God's day, where he could hear the gospel as preached by his father, sing out loud, read the Bible, and talk to others of his own age. He welcomed the temporary respite from his grueling farm labors.

William Carroll Latta's early experiences living on an isolated farm and being the son of an itinerant minister would direct his life's work. He chose agriculture as his profession to improve farmer productivity, encourage farm family education, and promote community improvement. Over the course of time, he would direct the attention of diverse groups—Purdue University, public schools, rural churches, business and civic organizations, government agencies—to the plight of rural people living in small towns across Indiana. He believed this was his calling. Agriculture and church became the compass by which he would set the course of his life. But to appreciate his accomplishments means understanding the role of previous generations of Lattas as agricultural, civic, and spiritual leaders in their rural communities.

The Latta Family Tree

Robert Latta (1773–1851) m. **Isabella Johnston** (1768–1853)

Children

Jane, William, Margaret, Samuel, Mary, Johnston, Sarah, Achsa,

and

James Latta (1796–1855) m. **Elizabeth Seegar** (1800–1839)

Children

Milton, William, Samuel, James, Jabez, Eden,

and

Robert Seegar Latta (1826–1900) m. **Mary Tumbleson** (1828–1907)

Children

Sarah, Milton, Mary, James, Margaret, George, Charles,

and

William Carroll (1850–1935) m. **Alta E. Wood** (1854–1940)

Children

Bertha, Robert, Pauline, Mary

William Carroll Latta's early ancestors were of Scotch-Irish stock. His great-grandfather was Robert Latta (1773–1851), the son of William Latta, an immigrant to Great Britain's North American colonies in the mid-eighteenth century. As a young man, Robert was apprenticed to a saddle maker named Robert Galloway in Washington County, Pennsylvania. The relationship between master and apprentice was difficult, and in 1795 Galloway advertised a reward in the *Pittsburgh Gazette* for the return of Robert, who had allegedly run away:

> Nine Pence Reward. Ranaway from the subscriber an apprentice boy, named Robert Latta, 19 years of age, well made, fair complexion, has very long black hair, very large black eye brows, and gray eyes, has a very lofty walk, takes short steps, not exceeding four inches, when in company is very polite, and talks of paying his addresses to ladies of a superior rank; he is very much addicted to drinking spirituous liquors; and is a most abandounded liar. I suppose him to be gone to Fayette county. Whoever shall apprehend him shall have reward but no charges paid.[1]

As an apprentice, Robert was contractually obligated to perform work for Galloway. Robert's father signed the papers agreeing that his son apprentice to Galloway for a certain number of years, provided that the master tradesman teach the boy the business of making saddles and repairing leather. In addition, the contract would obligate Galloway to provide Robert with lodging, clothing, and food in return for his labor. Robert Latta was, in fact, bound by legal contract.

However, this was no simple runaway. On February 15, 1796, a letter written by Robert Latta in an attempt to clear his name appeared in the same newspaper:

> Whereas a certain Robert GALLOWAY, saddler, of Washington county, advertised me in the *Pittsburgh Gazette* the 29th October last as having ran away from him as an apprentice, offered the generous reward of 9 pence for apprehending me and bringing me home, but no charges. As my time was precious to one of his business he would give a reward equivalent for the loss he was like to sustain, but know, impartial reader, that said Galloway had been down at Yorktown and reported, that he had furnished his apprentices with arms and ammunition, and that they had been at the burning of General Neville's house, and if he had not made a precipitate retreat he would have been apprehended. On his return home he sent me down to bring up some property he had neglected in his hurry, and I got as far as Getty's town, in York county, where I was apprehended, on his

report, and taken to Chambersburg and there confined in jail, after some time I was admitted to jail, and when a examination took place I was honorably acquitted, and said Galloway proved to be a liar. After my return home he gave me my indentures, and employed me as a journeyman for 4 months, at 5 pounds per month, to superintend his business, during which time he went to Kentucky; when he came back, being vexed at paying so much money, he reported that I had stolen some of his money in the month of November, at which time, I have made it appear before William Boyd, Esq., that I was not on the west side of the Allegheny mountains. He then sued me for the clothes he was to give during my apprenticeship, I also cast him in this action—he then swore before Squire Boyd, the second time, that I had stole his money and that it was done in December; I also proved that false—I threatened to prosecute him, he then produced a deposition of a minor boy, taken before a magistrate in Washington county. Squire Boyd then asked him how he knew I had taken the money, he replied, that the boy had told him so, and took up the boy's deposition, and swore to the contents of it, (amazing it is to think that a man would swear to a boy's deposition without a certainty) and then apprehending his danger, and being armed by some of his friends that James Paul, Esq., sheriff of Fayette county, was waiting to take him, he took a quick departure, giving Ohio Bail to all his creditors, and like all evil disposed persons with hasty strides flying from justice for fear of being detected in their villainy. ROBERT LATTA, Fayette county, Feb. 15, 1796. N. B. He carries on the saddler business in Fayette county, Bullskin twp.[2]

What Galloway had failed to disclose was that Robert Latta was in jail after being arrested while doing what he was told to do by Galloway himself. The backdrop of this unfortunate event was the Whiskey Rebellion, an incident in which Pennsylvania farmers rose up in armed revolt against the federal government. The burning of the Neville home mentioned in Robert Latta's newspaper ad was the most dramatic and final act of the Whiskey Rebellion. What role Robert Latta played in the revolt is unclear, but it seems obvious that he was a confident, articulate, and resourceful young man.

At the age of twenty-two, Robert Latta married Isabella Johnston on December 22, 1795. They built a new log house in the town of Greensburg, Pennsylvania, but "[t]he first night they spent in their newly erected log house the ridge pole fell down between them as they sat at the fire. They took that as an evil omen, packed up their effects and moved to Bellefontaine, Ohio."[3]

Robert Latta, newly settled in Ohio, was a member of the Presbyterian Church when he changed religious denominations. Family lore holds that a Methodist minister, the Reverend Strange, had greatly offended Mrs. Latta. Robert and Isabella decided to go down to his church one Sunday and settle matters. When Robert confronted the Reverend Strange, he found a person who was frail and sick. He took pity on the minister, and he and Isabella sat down with the congregation to listen to the sermon. Afterward, Robert Latta was overheard to say that he "had heard the truth for the first time,"[4] and both he and his wife joined the Methodist Church.

The Lattas had a son, Johnston, practicing medicine in Indiana. Robert had brought medicine and supplies to him in Goshen, Indiana, and found the area to be as good for farming as any he had ever seen. Although he had a good farm around Urbana, Ohio, Robert was so enthralled with this new area that he moved to what would become the famous farming region known as the Haw Patch. In 1820, just four years after Indiana had been admitted as a state, Robert Latta moved to LaGrange County, Indiana, becoming one of the first to settle the area.

He purchased eighteen 80-acre tracts of land (1,440 acres) from the federal government and built a log house in Section 26. The Haw Patch encompassed thousands of acres of relatively treeless, flat, very productive land straddling several townships in LaGrange and Noble Counties.

The following gives an idea of Robert Latta's investment and income:

Prairie land costs $1.25 an acre, and the cost of breaking the land is $1.50 an acre. Timber land could be had for $3 an acre. Fencing a quarter section would take 960 rods of fence. With 15,366 rails at one cent and 3,846 stakes at one-half cent, the fence would cost $173. A well with pump would cost $30; with bucket, $15. A log cabin would cost $50. Livestock prices in 1842 were low. Horses, $40 to $60; six-year-old oxen, $35 to $50; three-year-old steers, $6 to $10 each; year-old steers, $5 each; sheep, $1.25 to $1.70; and cows, $6 to $10 each. Berkshire and Improved Breeds at $1 to $1.75 per hundred pounds. Chickens could not be priced singly, because we have no silver coin small enough to express their value. In Chicago wheat brought 60 cents a bushel; corn, 21 cents; oats, 19 cents; timothy seed, $1.50; flax seed, 87.5 cents; beans, 56 cents; peas, 62.5 cents; barley, 37.5 cents; potatoes, 12.5 cents; onions, 37.5 cents.[5]

Robert Latta was a man of remarkable physical stature and social status. He was prominent in local and state politics, favoring candidates affiliated with the Whig Party. He was known as a sharp administrator, shrewd businessman, and civic contributor. He offered men of all trades and professions eighty acres of land free of charge if they lived on the land for an agreed upon number of years, and if he needed their expertise, they would work for him at no charge. Robert Latta made sure that his family's needs would be met.

Latta also erected a large church and built a schoolhouse for the community. The first Methodist services were conducted in Robert Latta's home, frequently presided over by his son James. In 1842, a church called the Eden Chapel was built on Robert Latta's property. To the west of the chapel, land was set aside for a cemetery on additional property donated by Robert Latta. He also paid the salary of the man who was both minister and schoolmaster, and he established an endowment that would create scholarships for the children of his tenants to attend college.

Robert Latta died in LaGrange County, Indiana, in 1851, when his great-grandson, William Carroll, was just one year old. While the great-grandfather would have no direct influence on William Carroll, he had established a pattern of civic responsibility that would be followed by the next three generations of Lattas.

James Latta (1796–1855), William's grandfather, was one of nine children born to Robert Latta. He was just seventeen years old when he served in the Ohio Militia as a first sergeant in Captain Andrew Hemphill's company in the War of 1812.

As a young man, James Latta had moved from his parent's home in Ohio to Bloomington, Illinois. He was one of the first settlers in that area, where he farmed and preached. James held various positions in county government and in 1827 he was appointed one of several commissioners to organize the nearby county of Tazewell, Illinois.

In the fall of 1832 James moved his family to the Haw Patch in Indiana, close to where his father and mother lived. He was later to become a judge, a poet, and one of the area's first Methodist ministers. James, who was a lay minister in his father's household, was an itinerant preacher who made the preaching circuit. He was in fact the "first minister of the gospel in Ligonier."[6]

Like his father, James Latta also was a public servant. According to his obituary, he served as county treasurer for two years, was a township assessor and deputy assessor for seventeen years, and was a member of the Noble County Council for four years.

Robert Seegar Latta (1826–1900) was born in McLean County, Illinois, to James and Elizabeth Latta. He married Mary Tumbleson (1828–1907) on

December 22, 1848, in Eden Township in LaGrange County, Indiana. They, too, were among the early settlers of that particular township. Less than two years later, their first son, William Carroll Latta, was born.

Robert Seegar Latta appears in the 1860 U.S. Census as a farmer by occupation. But his avocation, the joy of his life, was traveling the back roads of northern Indiana hosting revivals for rural churches as a circuit-riding Methodist minister.

> For several years after his marriage R. S. Latta was engaged in the work of the ministry, his labors taking him to LaPorte, Jay, and Noble counties. His labors in the cause of religion were quite successful, being productive of much good in the communities in which he served.[7]

Robert Seegar Latta, an "earnest Bible student,"[8] was much in demand as a minister and left much of the farming to his oldest son, William Carroll Latta. Robert Seegar Latta preached at a church known as Buzzard's Glory, which later became known as Spring Hill Church. Describing his father in 1906, William said, "while owning [a] farm, [he] devoted much of his time to church work as an itinerant Methodist Episcopal preacher,"[9] a respectful way of saying that his father was gone many days out of the month, leaving him the responsibility of the farm.

In the late 1850s, Robert moved his wife and three children, William, Sarah, and Milton, to Olmstead, Minnesota. Here Mary Tumbleson Latta delivered Mary Caroline Latta on October 15, 1856, and twins James Theodore and Margaret Elizabeth on September 23, 1858. Margaret died at birth.

By 1860 Robert had moved back near Ligonier, Indiana, where he purchased an eighty-acre farm one mile north and one mile west of Ligonier. The home was located at the south end of the farm near a railroad line, about a quarter of a mile from the Elkhart River. Robert Seegar Latta estimated the value of his land in Ligonier at $1,000 and his personal property at $500. Another son, George, was born in 1862 in Perry Township, later followed by Charles Lewis, born in 1864 in Ligonier, Indiana.

Robert and most of the family would eventually leave Indiana and move to Loup County, Nebraska, where the family farmed and he continued to preach. William Carroll, who remained in Indiana, seldom saw his parents in Nebraska. According to a letter dated July 3, 1894, on one occasion fourteen years passed between visits.

William Carroll was born March 9, 1850, at Union Mills in LaPorte County, Indiana. He indicates that he was "born in country, early years spent there. Lived in town about 2 yrs. moved to country again about age of 10 and grew to manhood there."[10] William Carroll's return to the country as a ten-year-old was to the farm near Ligonier, a prosperous place to settle.

William Carroll grew up from the age of ten in a small house built on a hill overlooking the road in the front of their home. It was close to the main railroad tracks and within sight of the Elkhart River. All that remains of the home are a small foundation and an old rusty well pump because the house was torched by an arsonist. Life on the farm must have been rough for young William. Since his father spent much of his time spreading the Methodist gospel across northern Indiana, William Carroll was expected to assume a full workload. He modestly wrote, "From 10 to about 18 I lived and worked on a farm doing the work incidental to cleaning up a farm in timberland."[11] His experience of hands-on farming, with its failures and successes, would forever be incorporated into his adult work in research, teaching, and Extension. He learned at a young age what it took to be a farmer, which would serve him well in his professional career at Purdue University.

The Latta farm was small, had little in the way of farm implements, and used very little hired help.[12] It was a pioneer farm that required endless hours of work just to harvest crops sufficient to feed his family and livestock. William and his father raised wheat and corn as their primary crops. The farm consisted of 80 acres of land, with half in woods. The remaining forty acres were divided into 4 acres of corn, 16 acres of wheat, 1 acre of oats, and 5 acres of red clover and timothy mix hay. There was an acre around the house for gardens, farm buildings, and animal stalls, leaving about 13 acres for pastures. In 1870, the cash value of the farm was given as $4,000 with an additional $200 worth of farm implements and machinery. Robert Latta spent $100 for labor. They grew 175 bushels of wheat, 150 bushels of Indian corn, 25 bushels of oats, 30 pounds of Irish potatoes, and 5 tons of hay. They even sold $10 worth of orchard products.

Forty acres of improved ground meant that, without hired hands, the Lattas depended on livestock to work the ground. Robert had access to five horses, which provided all of the power they would need to plow, plant, and harvest the crops. Other animals raised on the farm provided meat, milk, and wool. They had two dairy cows to supply their milk, which was used to make 250 pounds of butter a year. They slaughtered about $150 worth of meat that would have been raised from the three cows, two swine, and sheep. About ten pounds of wool were produced from one or two sheep. The total value of all of the livestock that the Lattas owned in 1870 amounted to $450.

Tending animals was a round-the-clock job. Relying on them as the only source of power was slow and back-breaking work. First, William and his father had to clear the land. Harvesting trees for firewood was a simpler task. The greater challenge was ridding the area of stumps before they could effectively plow, plant, and process their crops. Realistically, only a few acres could be cleared in any given year.

William Carroll learned how to grow winter wheat, Indian corn, oats, Irish potatoes, fruit, and hay. He and his father also made a small amount of maple syrup and sugar from the woods they owned. In addition to providing ample game, such as squirrel, deer, rabbit, and turkey, the woods were a source of firewood for their stoves and for the fence rails that separated the pastures and the animals from the gardens.

🌾 🌾 🌾

William Carroll attended the common schools of Noble County from 1858 to 1868. Prior to 1851, the schools were supported by the parents, who paid a subscription for their children's education. By the time William Carroll went to first grade, the schools were free to all children who could be spared from farm work. The schools in many of the townships were often located so that the children from nearby farms would not have to walk more than two miles to get there. Rural children would attend these local schools until they were consolidated into larger county schools, bringing an end to the one-room schoolhouses.

Just having a school nearby did not necessarily mean that the children attended. In the late nineteenth century, boys and girls were expected to work alongside their families, preparing the fields for planting, tending the crops, and harvesting the grain, vegetables, and fruit. Boys old enough to work in the fields would miss school during most of the spring, summer, and fall months. Indeed, William Carroll once noted that he attended the common schools during "chiefly winter terms."[13] During the warm months, the schools were mainly attended by girls and taught by young women. When the boys arrived for the winter term, it was generally thought that they were best taught by male teachers.

William Carroll grew up near three 1-room schoolhouses: Buzzard's Glory School, Goodhope School, and Independence School. While these rural schools and their records no longer exist, anecdotal evidence suggests that he probably attended Goodhope and Independence.

William Carroll received his secondary education at Ligonier High School from 1867 to 1869. After graduating from high school, he taught the summer term at Goodhope near the family home. He continued on at Goodhope from 1869 to 1871 while continuing to farm with his father.

William Carroll and his brother James would be the only sons of Robert Seegar Latta to remain in Indiana to farm after their father moved the family to Nebraska. Plat maps from that era indicated that James Latta owned a forty-acre farm that he inherited from his wife's family. The farm was adjacent to Robert Seegar Latta's eighty-acre farm to the southwest, and the homes were about a mile apart. William Carroll owned a twenty-eight-acre tract abutting his brother's farm to the east and their parents' farm to the south. James farmed both his and William Carroll's land as a single operation.

🌾 🌾 🌾

When William Carroll turned twenty-two years old, he left the farm with all intentions of becoming a public school teacher. He headed to Lebanon, Ohio, where he attended National Normal School, also called Holbrook Normal School in honor of Alfred Holbrook, its principal.

National Normal University—as it was later renamed—was a school for training high-school graduates to become teachers and was, by all accounts, one of the earliest teachers' colleges in the region. In fact, during the time that William Carroll attended the school, National Normal graduated 7 in the classics, 34 in science, 60 in business, and 94 in engineering, indicating that the courses offered a great deal in addition to teacher education.[14] The school even had a model grade school—what would today be called a laboratory school—that could be used by the students learning the process and principles of teaching.

Alfred Holbrook was an influential teacher educator. In 1857, he published *Normal Methods*, which was said to have "had a very wide sale, perhaps as large as any other educational work published in America. It has been translated into

Japanese.... It has contributed much to the growth of the school by its use as a text-book in the training class, and by attracting pupils from all parts of the nation."[15]

Holbrook also published *School Management* in 1872 and *The New Method of School Expositions* in 1881. Under the direction of Alfred Holbrook, National Normal was a hotbed for the development of new ideas on how to properly manage a school and how best to teach students. This made it an appealing place for students from around the country who were looking for an exciting place to learn how to be teachers and school administrators.

National Normal School would have been an interesting and confusing place for young Latta. Having grown up attending one-room schools, he must have been stunned by the size of this school. At that time, National Normal employed 14 teachers to instruct 1,506 students, and it boasted a large library of 2,000 volumes and laboratories filled with the most modern scientific equipment.[16] The university is said to have graduated more than 80,000 students during its time.[17]

A fundamental difference between the teaching methods at National Normal and William Carroll's experiences in rural schools was the school's rejection of recitation as a means of mastering a subject. William Carroll would be indoctrinated in a new way to teach and train students in the public schools.

> From the first [days the school was opened], no memorizing of definitions, rules, or any other matter contained in the text-book has been required. That kind of thoroughness which recognizes only the mastery of the precise words of the text-book, in preparation for recitations and examinations, we have ever held as abominable. It is incompatible with genuine love of study, and subversive of that general class interest which makes hard work exciting, fascinating, easy.... We have ever discarded that kind of thoroughness, so prevalent in most schools and colleges, which makes the verbal knowledge of a text-book a test and a standard.[18]

The 1872 catalog of National Normal indicated that the total expenses per week were four dollars, which included tuition, books, room rent, meals, bedding, and bed washing.[19]

For whatever reason, William Carroll attended the school for about eight months and did not earn a degree there. Nonetheless, he surely would have learned how to be an effective teacher using the progressive methods of National Normal School. Alfred Holbrook would also have taught him the "value of mental and spiritual liberty and the value of religious freedom,"[20] which would later in life become trademarks of William Carroll.

William Carroll returned to Indiana for a short time to farm and teach in the rural schools. Then in the summer of 1873, he moved to Michigan to work and earn enough money to attend Michigan Agricultural College. He worked a summer job in a Michigan sawmill during 1873 and that next winter taught one winter term in a country school west of Saginaw, Michigan. He wrote about "having taught country schools and boarded round,"[21] which meant living with the families whose children he taught. The more children a family sent to school, the longer they would have to feed and house the teacher.

In 1874, William Carroll enrolled at Michigan Agricultural College, today known as Michigan State University at East Lansing. It was the first land-grant college in the United States. Michigan Agricultural College would offer William Carroll Latta and other students wanting to specialize in agriculture a place to study and to learn the practical aspects of science-based agriculture. For decades thereafter, graduates from Michigan Agricultural College were in great demand throughout the country to serve as faculty at other land-grant institutions. Purdue University administrators also looked to Michigan Agricultural College graduates to staff their own faculty positions.

Neither William Carroll nor his parents had the means to fund a college education, so he had to support himself while taking classes. During his early years at the college, he worked in the school greenhouse and for the president of the college. He also established a pattern of opting out of the winter terms to teach in the rural schools in order to help finance his college education.

The list of classes he took included:

Freshman Classes in 1874	Sophomore Classes in 1875
Agriculture, 1st	Botany, 2nd
Algebra, 1st	Chemistry, analytical
Algebra, 2nd	Chemistry, elementary
Book Keeping	Geometry, 2nd
Botany, 1st	Horticulture
Composition	Rhetoric
Geometry, 1st	Surveying
History	Trigonometry

Junior Classes in 1876	Senior Classes in 1877
Anatomy	Agriculture, 2nd
Chemistry, agricultural	Astronomy
Drawing	Civil Engineering
Economic Entomology	Constitution
Entomology	Geology
French, 1st	Landscape Gardening
French, 2nd	Logic
Literature	Mental Philosophy
Mechanics, 1st	Moral Philosophy
Mechanics, 2nd	Physiology
Meteorology	Political Economy
Physics	Zoology[22]

The Morrill Act of 1862 required at that time that the land-grant schools offer military science, training, and drills. Latta was an Army cadet who was listed as a captain in the spring term of 1876 and a lieutenant in the fall of the same year. Often, officers were either elected by their fellow cadets or by their instructors. In 1877, he would earn his bachelor of science degree from Michigan Agricultural College. After teaching in the rural schools for a few years after his graduation, he returned to his alma mater for a master's degree.

Prior to pursuing a graduate degree, William Carroll found employment during the spring of 1878 working for Amos Wood as a farmhand. Wood owned a farm that was located about ten miles southeast of Michigan Agricultural College near the town of Mason. It was here that the young, college-educated William Carroll learned how science could help farmers improve production and the importance of bringing farmers and their families together to discuss life on the farm.

Amos Wood (1824–1905) was a New Yorker who had moved to Michigan in October 1866 and developed what today would be called a showcase farm, named Maple Ridge Farm. He was highly esteemed in farming and livestock-breeding circles in central Michigan. William Carroll was familiar with the 300-acre farm as "the College often brought students out to the Wood farm to show them the latest ideas being put to use."[23]

A Michigan Agricultural College professor wrote a brief account of the Wood farm after visiting the farm and speaking with Amos Wood. This is what William Carroll would have observed while working at Maple Ridge Farm:

> Near the city of Mason, Ingham county, is located the farm and home of Mr. Amos F. Wood. The farm contains nearly 300 acres, the greater part of which is, at present, under cultivation. The public road leading westwardly from Mason divides the farm, thus not only furnishing facilities for transportation but adding materially to the value of the land.
>
> Mr. Wood differs somewhat from the average farmer, and upon this point I wish more particularly to speak. Leaving Jefferson Co. N. Y., some 15 years ago, Mr. Wood shaped his course to the Wolverine State, to practically introduce into Michigan the "short-horned" breed of cattle, or at least to prepare the mind of the farmer for a new departure in stock raising. This was his central idea.
>
> Mr. Wood's present herd numbers over 50 "short horned" and "grades." He has also a very fine flock of the Leicester breed of sheep. He considers them superior to "fine wools," as they have a quiet disposition, mature much quicker, and are well adapted to the cultivated fields of Michigan. Last year the flock averaged 10 lbs. of wool, per head. Mr. Wood was the first man to practically introduce the Essex swine into Central Michigan.
>
> As a man Mr. Wood's character is above reproach. His sterling integrity and scrupulous honesty in public as well as in private life proves that he is a man of the first necessity. He has long been connected with the "State Agricultural Society," one of the stalwart few who have made the Central Michigan Agricultural Society a permanent success. For many years he was the President of the Ingham County Farmer's club. Any one intending to visit Maple Ridge Farm on business or for the pleasure it affords, will meet with that kindness and hospitality which only a generous host can give. Were there more such men in the world "man's inhumanity to man" would be the exception, and not the order of the day.[24]

Wood's influence on furthering the education of William Carroll cannot be underestimated. At Maple Ridge Farm, William Carroll would see the impact that the application of science could have on improving the productivity of farmers and the lives of farm families.

And there is every reason to believe that Amos Wood and William Carroll continued to talk about the state of agriculture and carry on this conversation throughout Wood's lifetime as Wood assumed another important role in

William Carroll's life, that of his father-in-law. On July 10, 1879, William Carroll married Wood's daughter, Alta E. Wood, in Mason, Michigan. Alta was born in Woodville, New York, on March 16, 1854. She was a well-educated woman who had graduated from Mason High School in 1875, taught in the local school system, and also worked at Michigan Agricultural College. After they married, the couple would live at Maple Ridge Farm for a while, then later they would routinely visit the farm, bringing their children to visit their grandparents during the summer.

Amos Wood also influenced William Carroll's outlook in numerous other areas of agricultural improvement and rural development. Wood initiated several agricultural associations and lent his name by membership to others. He was one of the organizers of the Michigan Shorthorn Breeders' Association and also of the State Association of Breeders of Improved Live Stock. Wood was also a member of the Michigan State Fair Board for sixteen years. In addition, he served for nearly a quarter of a century as president of the Ingham County Farmer's Club.

The Ingham County Farmer's Club enjoyed a reputation as one of the best in Michigan. It was founded on January 27, 1872. Wood was elected as president during the club's second year. His daughter, Nettie Wood Tanswell, served as secretary for twenty-seven years, and another daughter, Myra Wood Cheney, would also be elected president. This farmer's club was definitely a family affair. During the more than five decades of its existence, it had only five presidents and four treasurers. The members, it was said, "are strong believers in independence and they practice it to the last letter. Their association has no tie to bind it to other farm organizations."[25]

Later in life, William Carroll would also start many organizations and remain with most of them for his whole life. And he enjoyed a lifelong connection in the Ingham County Farmer's Club. During his stay at the Wood's farm and afterward while a professor at Purdue University, he would continue to attend the meetings when in Michigan, where club members would discuss agriculture and family life. For a brief period he served as club secretary, probably before he married Alta Wood.

In the beginning, the Ingham club membership was confined to men only, and meetings were held on Saturdays in town during the winter and in the homes of its members in the summer. In 1898, whole families were allowed to become members, and the meetings were held in member families' homes each month.

The purpose of the club was "to promote improvement along agricultural and horticultural lines and every phase of farm life is represented on the programs."[26] Wood wrote in his history of the club that meetings included "discussing topics of the day and better methods of agriculture, having many addresses from outside as well as fruit exhibitions, vegetable and garden seeds, poultry shows, etc."[27]

Meeting attendance ranged from 50 to upwards of 200. Managing the larger crowds was often a struggle:

> It [the Ingham County Farmer's Club] met a real need in those days, although it frequently taxed the capacity of some of the largest of the county's remaining old farm houses to accommodate the crowds that met—for, since 1898 meetings have been held at homes of members—and many a time when the family entertaining the farmers' club at one of its monthly meetings, there was considerable hustling to take down the beds and store them temporarily in attic or woodshed so that even the bedrooms might be utilized for space for seating of the members and their families during the program which always followed the potluck dinner at the noon hour. Chairs were rented and borrowed, saw horses with planks across them were utilized, and all sorts of make-shifts made to accommodate the crowd.[28]

The general order of business was a discussion of market reports, what the latest experiments from Michigan Agricultural College were finding, what farmers were doing to improve their farm production, and discussions of current events. Eunice Brewster Wood, the wife of Amos, reported at the November 1906 meeting, "Market reports were given much attention, practical subjects were discussed and everything done to encourage the growth of two blades of grass where but one grew before."[29]

Mrs. Wood also wrote, "Occasionally we met at the homes during the summer months and the whole family enjoyed a day's outing and the visits to the M.A.C. [Michigan Agricultural College]. The members of the faculty at the college have always been helpful and ready to meet and address the club at any regular meeting."[30] And, "Memory recalls many pleasant meetings all with the tendency of more culture and better education."[31]

Governors and judges, heads of university departments, United States senators, college presidents, and other officials spoke at meetings of the Ingham County Farmer's Club. Topics addressed in the 1870s and 1880s included: poultry raising, farm building, farm fencing, the horse, dairying, pinning and grafting, political economy, wintering stock, farm gardening, agricultural improvements, dairying and dairy products, the process of drying fruit, sheep husbandry, the influence of agriculture, and how to live on a farm.

The club also provided a means of communicating with neighbors. Eliza Melton remembered,

> In December, 1898, there was a meeting of the Club members at Maple Ridge, and there they voted to take the wives and families into the Club and meet the second Saturday of each month at the homes of the members, and from that time it is a pretty bad day that will keep us home from a Club meeting. We enjoy them—we need them. The Club has been a help to us in a good many ways. Farmers always can find enough to do to stay at home all the time, but it is not profitable. One grows to be narrow-minded and soon will lose all interest in the world outside of his own home. We have spent many happy days visiting different places of interest and getting acquainted with people outside of our own home town. We enjoy meeting them in their own homes and become better acquainted.[32]

Members were regular competitors at the State Fair in Detroit, Michigan. Myra Wood Cheney reported on the fortieth anniversary of the club noting, "In passing, I just want to mention that $25 prize won by this body at the state fair at Detroit in September, 1880, when Nettie Wood [Tanswell] put into shape for exhibition 100 samples of wool of different breeds furnished by 10 men."[33]

Amos Wood was a frequent livestock exhibitor at county and state fairs. One of William Carroll's jobs was to show the fine livestock that Amos raised. In the autumn of 1878, he wrote:

> Dear Friends All.
>
> This has been a busy day and somewhat eventful as several awards have been made and we have a fair share. I feel particularly well satisfied with the two "blues" which the colts took off this noon.
>
> We have not shown further but the work will go on at 9 a.m. tomorrow. There is great competition among the cows. Am inclined to think we'll get no prize in that line. The fair in full blast today. We get along well except for the water supply of which is insufficient.
>
> We stand bunk life well. Am afraid I'll make myself sick by too much eating. Cannot write much of the fair in general as I have as yet seen very little of it outside of the stock dept. Heard Lawrence Barrett play "haunted" last eve. The play was excellent. A.B.P. was there and came home with me. He bunks here again to-night. There will be only nine of us this eve.

Provisions are lasting quite well. Pie went to-day. The sauce will depart tomorrow. We shall fare all right though as fruit is plenty and our barrel is not yet exhausted.

I s'pose Dan is about half way to China with that ditch.

You will excuse a short letter. I know as I am needing a good sleep. Will try to drop a line about starting when I learn about it.

Cordially
Will C. Latta[34]

The Ingham County Farmer's Club disbanded as an association in 1936. The death of its founding members, competition with other rural organizations, and the inception of the Extension Service with "a county agricultural agent to study and meet with the farmers and discuss the modern farm life problems"[35] spelled the end of the club.

Poor health would eventually force Amos Wood to sell Maple Ridge Farm in 1896 to his son-in-law, John E. Tanswell. He lived out the rest of his life at the farm, remaining active in agriculture and his community.

In 1880 William Carroll and Alta were living at Maple Ridge Farm while he was pursuing his master's degree at Michigan Agricultural College. That same year, he became a foreman in the Horticultural Department and an assistant in the Agricultural Department at Michigan Agricultural College. William Carroll and his wife were also teaching. In the 1880 U.S. Census, he and Alta listed their occupations as "Teacher" and "Teaching School," respectively. William Carroll was repeating his earlier pattern of teaching winter terms, most likely north of Grand Rapids, Michigan, in a country school located in the town of Pierson.

William Carroll was among the first fifty people to earn an advanced degree from Michigan Agricultural College (M.S., 1882). However, there is no evidence that he ever took any graduate classes. Either the records have been lost or, more likely, William Carroll was simply not required to take advanced coursework in agriculture to receive his master's degree.

Catalog announcements for the college specified what it took for a student to earn an advanced degree:

The requirements that a student had to meet to earn a master's degree varied depending on what year they enrolled at Michigan Agricultural College. From 1861–1878, the degree of Master of Science was conferred upon those graduates of three years' standing, who made a proper proficiency in scientific studies. From 1879 to 1882, in addition to the above, the graduates were required to present an acceptable thesis upon some topic assigned by the faculty. Since 1882, the graduates have been required to spend at least one year in this college in a course of post-graduate study, presenting at the close an acceptable thesis. Study in absentia was permitted under certain conditions until 1898, since which time the residence of study has been strictly insisted on.[36]

If this policy was applied to William Carroll Latta, he had only to complete a research thesis for his graduate degree program while his time as an undergraduate sufficed for three years' standing.

What were his research skills and his aptitude for analytical thinking? Based on his master's thesis, "Feeding Value of Ensilage," one could surmise that his understanding of research methodology was not well developed. However, his later Purdue University Experiment Station bulletins provide a very different viewpoint, showing a man who understood what it took to perform agricultural research at a high level of proficiency and professionalism.

His thesis is seventeen pages in length and professionally handwritten by someone other than himself; his own penmanship was distinctively poor. The subject of his research into silage and animal nutrition was not surprising considering his work with Wood, one of Michigan's most respected Shorthorn breeders. In the opening statements of his thesis, William Carroll wrote:

> It is worthy of note, however, that, almost without exception, those who have tried ensilage [silage] both private feeder and public experimenters— pronounce in its favor. And the decreasing opposition to ensilage, as well as the more steady current of public sentiment in its favor indicate that it will have a permanent place among foods for our domestic animals.
>
> While its great bulk adapts it to ruminates especially, ensilage has been fed with good results, and no observed ill effects, to horses, swine, and poultry. Ensilage has been fed to cattle of all ages and conditions, and the results obtained may be summed up as follows. It is a palatable and wholesome food, is, alone, hardly sufficient for maintenance, but, where supplemented by nitrogenous foods, produces excellent results in growth, milk, butter, etc.[37]

So what did Latta present as evidence that silage had potential? Actually not much in the way of facts, figures, tables, and graphs. His research evidence included the following types of casual observations:

> Cattle subsisting wholly on ensilage have an irregular, capricious appetite. At times the full allowance is eaten eagerly. Frequently the animals eat mincingly, and, now and then, one-third to one-half of the feed remains (uneaten). They will sometimes pick over their own bedding and, if allowed to do so, will eat considerable quantities of the stained litter of the horse stable. They generally lose a trifle in weight, and occasionally seem a little dejected, though generally in good spirits. The eyes are bright, skin soft, coat glossy, bowels open and regular, and the excreta appears to be normal.
>
> When ensilage constitutes one-third to two-thirds-in-the-bulk of the rough feed of a mixed ration, the animals are exceedingly well nourished, and have a very gratifying satisfied look. The appetite is keen and regular. Young stock grow rapidly, older ones take on flesh readily. Their milk is rich, abundant and wholesome, and the butter is improved in color and flavor. To the close observer, the unmistakable verdict of cattle is in favor of ensilage as an ingredient in a mixed ration.[38]

By today's standards, Latta's thesis is remarkably brief and written in a familiar, off-hand manner. Most notably, there is no attempt at experimentation. Rather, his thesis offers numerous observations but lacks citations, references, etc. And while the thesis addresses the then new technology of silos and ensilage, he chose not to discuss how silage is produced.

However, he did demonstrate a progressive approach to livestock production through his use of the concept of "relative feeding value." This term reappears a hundred years later in the agronomy literature as a unitless index that encompasses intake and digestibility into a number that can be used to value the worth and use of conserved forages. Latta's thesis also demonstrates his commitment to the practical applications of academic work by emphasizing the need for an economic analysis to ensure that the cost of implementing new technology is justified.

The brevity of Latta's thesis is, in all likelihood, explained by the timing of a job offer with Purdue. A position became available just prior to the completion of his graduate work, and there was only a short timeframe to relocate from Michigan to Indiana. He probably put in just enough effort to pass review by Michigan's agricultural faculty. So he left Michigan after working his way through school from 1880 to 1882 as a horticultural assistant, caretaker of gardens and orchard, garden foreman, and assistant in agricultural experiments. And in 1882, after nearly two years of study, William Carroll Latta earned his master's degree in agriculture from Michigan Agricultural College.

Two months after completing his advanced degree, Latta's next and final career move would take him to Purdue University's School of Agriculture, where he began as an instructor and farm superintendent. His timing for earning a master's degree was ideal. Purdue University had need of a person with his experience to assist the current professor of agriculture in managing the Purdue farm, teaching, and conducting research. Latta was also well positioned to step in as a professor himself when the opportunity arose a short time later.

William Carroll Latta's upbringing in a religious family and his personal experience of tilling the ground with plow and horse undoubtedly influenced his long-term career in agriculture and his personal interest in helping to improve the lives of rural people. When reflecting back on his life in 1906, Latta wrote that "the Bible and the various works on agriculture" were most beneficial in helping him to shape his life, and that he "also owe[d] much to the Sunday School and Church." [39] He stated also that home, school, and private study were important in his success in life.

Latta's religious upbringing and the importance of the church in his early life produced a desire to help underprivileged children, women, and minorities. His work with the precursors of 4-H and his dedication to improving rural life may have also stemmed from the fact that he worked so hard at an early age in near isolation. He knew firsthand how hard rural people had to work to scratch out a living and that their comings and goings were largely unknown to city people, civic organizations, politicians, and government agencies. Concern for rural people would remain a driving force for this man.

William Carroll Latta was a strong advocate of using science to improve agricultural production. Michigan Agricultural College at that time was the country's leader in training agricultural scientists. Their graduates were in great demand across the country, and the college prepared him well on the techniques and tools needed to set up an effective agricultural research program at Purdue University.

What principally determined his choice of occupation? William Carroll's emphatic answer was, "My education at an agricultural college."[40] He would later say that expanding farm production was the only way to offer a better standard of living to rural people. Maple Ridge Farm is where Latta would realize the importance of an education and the prominent role that education and science could have on improving the technical skills of farmers. Amos Wood offered Latta the opportunity to see how a well-organized farm could improve the lives of farm families. It would provide Latta with the practical experience in which to place the facts and figures he learned at Michigan Agricultural College and a comparison with how he had farmed as a younger man. He would see the worst and the best of farming by the time he was thirty years old.

It is probably during this time that Latta learned also how important long-term experiments were in improving agricultural practices. And, just as importantly, he witnessed the value of bringing together farmers to share failures and successes.

Amos Wood was a father-in-law and mentor to William Carroll Latta. This Michigan farmer deserves credit, in large measure, with helping Latta become an important figure in Indiana agriculture. William Carroll Latta would come to Purdue University in 1882, ably prepared, well experienced, and with a zeal and passion for work that he would express for the next fifty-three years of service to the university and state.

William Carroll Latta, age 27, in 1877. Courtesy of Purdue University Libraries Special Collections.

Alta E. Wood, age 21, in 1875. Courtesy of Phyllis Webster.

Marriage certificate of William Latta and Alta Wood. The couple was married on July 10, 1879, in Mason, Michigan. Courtesy of Purdue University Libraries Special Collections.

William Carroll Latta's parents, Robert Seegar Latta (1826–1900) and Mary Tumbleson Latta (1828–1907). Courtesy of Larry Sullivan.

Amos and Eunice Wood on July 5, 1898, at Maple Ridge Farm. Courtesy of Phyllis Webster.

The home of Amos Wood, William Latta's father-in-law, circa 1920. Courtesy of Kim Sharpe.

The Maple Ridge Farm near Mason, Michigan, circa 1900. The farm was well known for its large and modern barns, which can be seen at the far right. Courtesy of Phyllis Webster.

Alta Wood Latta (back left) with her family, circa 1890. Seated are her sister, Nettie Wood Tanswell (left), and her mother, Eunice Wood. Standing in the back row are Alta's sisters, Myra Wood Cheney (center) and Flora Wood Sprout. Courtesy of Kim Sharpe.

Amos Wood (right) with his son-in-law, John Tanswell (center), circa 1898. At the far left is one of Wood's prized shorthorn cows held by a farmhand. Courtesy of Phyllis Webster.

THESIS

Feeding + feeding stuff

Feeding Value of Ensilage,

by

William Carroll
W. C. Latta.

Michigan Agricultural College,

1882.

M.S. 1882

The front cover of William Carroll Latta's master's thesis, "Feeding Value of Ensilage," dated 1882. Courtesy of Larry Olsen and Michigan State University.

Building an
Agricultural University:
Politics, Vision, and Perseverance

CHAPTER  TWO

As months to years will lengthen,
May hope, faith, courage, strengthen,
To bring to glad fruition
Each laudable ambition.

—William Carroll Latta
from "Remembered," 1935

Events INSTRUMENTAL IN MAKING universities such as Purdue a reality unfolded back when Latta was still a child and continued in the years leading up to the Civil War. How a few acres of prairie in the small community of Chauncey became the home of Purdue University is a tale of community competition, political wrangling, and one man's quest to have a university bear his name.

In the late nineteenth century, the concept of an agricultural college proved to be somewhat popular with farmers, some of whom understood that they would no longer have to invest in and gamble on new ideas. Instead, university researchers would be paid to take new concepts and production practices to the field and, from their research, filter out those that didn't work or were economically unfeasible. By letting the university cull those ideas that didn't work from those that did, farmers could take the "tried and true" ideas to the home, field, pasture, and market.

In the 1850s, Jonathan Turner, a Yale-educated college professor and Illinois farmer, gained a reputation for his outspoken remarks about the need for the United States government to promote the establishment of state colleges that would open their doors to young men and women from the working classes of

American society. Turner became a well-known lecturer and writer, traveling across the United States to discuss his thoughts on the federal government's responsibility to promote higher education.

He argued persuasively that the children of the working class should have the same opportunity to attend college and improve their lives through education as did the children from affluent families, who could attend expensive private schools. He and others believed that the students for whom they were speaking needed a classical education supplemented with courses in agriculture, engineering, military science, and commerce. Students educated in industry and the arts would have a greater opportunity to better their lives economically and socially.

Professor Turner found agreement among farming associations and the editors of trade magazines and newspapers. Their voices captured the attention of Justin Morrill, an influential and tenacious Vermont congressman. Morrill, a Republican, had a distinguished career serving in the United States Congress for forty years as both a representative and a senator from the Green Mountain State. This legislator, who came to champion the need for agricultural and industrial colleges, was himself forced to quit school early in order to support his family.

Justin Morrill introduced a bill, later signed into law by President Abraham Lincoln, referred to as the Morrill Act of 1862, or the Land Grant College Act. The Morrill Act would help each state set up an endowment that could be used to create an agricultural and engineering school. Today, the colleges established by the Morrill Act are collectively called land-grant schools, because the endowment given to each state was based on the sale of federal land. Each state was given public land to sell, amounting to 30,000 acres for every representative and senator in Congress, based on the representation established by the 1860 United States population census.

Morrill had actually submitted his bill previously, only to be vetoed by President Buchanan in 1857. Congressional opponents of the original bill, especially those representing the southern states, did not want education to be controlled by federal bureaucrats. They argued that it had always been the states' prerogative to promote public education. In addition to the states' rights issue, some congressmen from the West opposed the legislation because the sale of federal land—the money used to endow these universities—would largely come out of their states, where the majority of public lands were held. But by 1862, with the southern states having seceded from the Union, opposition to the federal government's role in education had all but dissolved, assuring successful passage of Morrill's bill.

The Morrill Act was just one bill President Lincoln signed into law that would have a lasting impact on the development and expansion of the land-grant school system. With the southern states no longer present in Congress, President Lincoln signed two additional laws that created the United States Department of Agriculture and implemented the Homestead Act, which opened public lands in the American West for agricultural development. Thus, placing public lands into the hands of farmers, establishing a government agency devoted to farm productivity and farm health, and promoting universities to educate young men and women in the ways of agriculture, production, and processing would forever change the role of the federal government in U.S. agriculture.

In many ways, Michigan Agricultural College was the model for what Professor Turner must have envisioned. It opened its doors in 1855, after the state legislature appropriated a rather sizable sum of money. Michigan Agricultural College laid claim to being the first school of its kind to specifically focus on attracting students to study agriculture and engineering.

⁂

The sign that greets visitors traveling west across the Wabash River onto the university campus reads *Purdue University Founded 1869*. Behind these simple words is a colorful history of what it took to create this institution. Numerous developmental problems were actually caused by the Morrill Act, which set specific, targeted deadlines for the states to act upon in order to obtain the federal land that would help fund their land-grant schools.

In 1863, the Indiana General Assembly began a contentious six-year debate on the state's future land-grant school. Many of the deliberations focused on where to build the college. It was only in the last days of 1869, with a federal deadline looming, that a deal to establish Purdue University was completed.

The story of Purdue University, where William Carroll Latta would make his career, begins in 1863, when the General Assembly agreed in principle that Indiana would accept the terms and conditions of the Morrill Land Grant Act. The endowment created by the Morrill Act could not be used to construct buildings, which meant that the state would have to provide additional funding to support the school. And with the numbers of dead and wounded from the

Civil War mounting and the cost of the war escalating, a commitment of scarce funds for a new university must have been a difficult decision for the state legislators.

In 1865, the General Assembly formally accepted another provision of the Morrill Land Grant Act when it approved a governing board for the Indiana Agricultural College. The college now had legal standing and a board of trustees to manage its affairs.

One of the first actions by the board of trustees was to sell Indiana's share of public land. Under the Morrill Act, Indiana's thirteen members of Congress meant that the state would get 390,000 acres of public land to sell on the open market. Individuals wanting to submit bids to purchase the land were given scrip, which they could redeem to purchase federal land available for sale anywhere in the United States.

Indiana Governor Oliver P. Morton received a letter of transmittal from the commissioner of the General Land Office for 2,438 pieces of scrip:

> . . . each for one quarter section [160 acres], except the last number which
> is for a half quarter [80 acres], to make up the exact quantity of 390,000
> acres, being the amount in full to which the State of Indiana is entitled
> under the Act of Congress.[1]

The treasurer for the board of trustees made a motion on August 28, 1866, "to authorize to place the Scrip upon the Market by advertising the same in such papers as he might select, at the minimum price of 75 cents per acre."[2] But the trustees soon found out that their asking price of 75 cents per acre was too high to generate much interest by the public. They placed another set of ads in various papers, including the *Indianapolis Daily Journal, Indianapolis Daily Herald, Cincinnati Daily Gazette, Cincinnati Daily Commercial, Chicago Tribune, New York Tribune,* and *Wabash Express:*

> Notice is hereby given that sealed proposals will be received by mail or
> otherwise for the purchase of the Indiana Agricultural College Scrip in
> quantities not less than one section, and refer to 390,000—the whole
> amount owned by the State. That said proposals shall be sealed and
> directed to Conrad Baker, Governor of the State of Indiana, and endorsed
> "Bids of College Scrip."[3]

The bids were opened on April 9, 1867, at two o'clock in the governor's office with the Indiana Agricultural College trustees present to view who had purchased the land and for how much. Twenty-four bids were submitted, and five were selected.

Robert Cox	4 sections	60 cents per acre	$1,536.00
John Morrison	2 sections	55 cents per acre	704.00
Lay Noble	5 sections	55 cents per acre	1,760.00
D. E. White	1 section	55 cents per acre	352.00
Gleason Lewis	597 sections	54 cents per acre	207,885.50
	609 sections/ 390,000 acres		$212,238.50 [4]

Gleason Lewis, who purchased most of the land, was by profession a land scrip broker.

The federal land sale yielded more than $200,000 for the trustees of the Indiana Agricultural College. They then purchased bonds from the First National Bank of Indianapolis in the name of Indiana Agricultural College.

The money that Indiana and other states received from the sale of public land was much less than what Justin Morrill expected. Unfortunately, with millions of acres available in the western states after the Civil War, the value of federal land was depressed. Morrill tried to remedy the problem in 1872 by introducing legislation that provided additional federal funds to the states, but his efforts were defeated in Congress when two well-known educators, Charles W. Eliot of Harvard University and James McCosh of Princeton University, opposed his bill on the grounds that the United States did not need agricultural colleges. [5]

The next step for the Indiana General Assembly was to resolve the issue of where to build the agricultural college. The pressure on state legislators became intense as public officials and private citizens weighed in and made their opinions known.

Politicians, community leaders, and college presidents all offered advice on where best to situate the school. But the General Assembly had until January 1, 1870, to make its final selection.

Existing institutions vied for the agricultural college. Indiana University administrators made it known early on in the legislative debate that they believed that the agricultural school should be housed at their Bloomington campus. Where better to establish a school of agriculture than at a school that was already the state's premier educational institution? In fact, Indiana University had an agricultural department, but due to a lack of state funding, it existed only on paper with no faculty or students. While Indiana University would be considered on and off for the next several years, some legislators worried that the Indiana University administrators had no real commitment to building an agricultural and engineering school.

Another proposal, which had a strong patriotic appeal for the public, was to build a college for the children of Civil War veterans. Others wanted to divide the proceeds from the endowment among all colleges in the state, with one or two additional professors being hired at each school to teach engineering and agriculture. A variation on the idea of multiple locations involved locating the main agricultural college at the Indiana University Bloomington campus in conjunction with the development of eleven satellite campuses to correspond to the eleven congressional districts in the state.

However, the debate began to focus more on a single, new university devoted to teaching agriculture and engineering principles. Communities became deeply involved in trying to lure the university to their area. They began offering land, buildings, and money to entice the state legislature to select their community. For instance, Stockwell Collegiate Institute and Battle Ground Institute, both located in Tippecanoe County, offered their colleges and land as the site for the land-grant school. Stockwell offered its buildings and 160 acres of land, while Battle Ground had buildings and lands valued at $100,000.

Then the individual players began to find partners. The city of Greenfield teamed up with Hancock County to offer $125,000 worth of land and buildings. Monroe County offered a farm valued at $50,000 to locate the new school at Indiana University, while Marion County presented 27 acres and $75,000 to site the college at Butler University. Tippecanoe County extended 320 acres, and cash and bonds in the amount of $100,000 in support of the Stockwell and Battle Ground plans.

The debate was intense and the vote close in the 1867 General Assembly when two competing plans from Tippecanoe County and Indianapolis came to the floor. The Tippecanoe County proposal fell just 6 votes short of the required 26 votes in the Senate. Thus, by 1867 the state legislators were still unable to resolve their differences as to where Indiana's agricultural college should be built.

Two more years of legislative debate followed. With the General Assembly still deadlocked over where to site the university and facing a federal mandate under the Morrill Act to name the school's location, the Indiana State Board of Agriculture tried to gain control of the agricultural school but failed.

Then, on March 3, 1869, a sixty-seven-year-old Tippecanoe County merchant, John Purdue, entered the fray in the closing days of the Indiana session. He offered $100,000 of his own money if the land-grant school was built at Battle Ground and the name of the school changed from Indiana Agricultural College to Purdue University. The General Assembly flatly turned down his offer.

Governor Conrad Baker called a special session of the General Assembly on April 8, 1869, to continue the discussion and, hopefully, to come to a consensus once and for all. The General Assembly had to make a final decision about where to locate the school and purchase the land before December 31, 1869.

Even though the state legislature spurned John Purdue's first offer, he again entered the debate with an updated proposal that substantially sweetened the pot. This time John Purdue dropped his requirement that the school be built in Battle Ground and insisted only that it be located in Tippecanoe County. Purdue also increased his financial offer to $150,000 and agreed to donate 100 acres of land for the campus and a farm. In addition, he wanted the General Assembly to appoint him to the board of trustees for life. He remained insistent that the college bear his name. The battle over the agriculture school came to a close on May 6, 1869, with a favorable Senate vote of 32–10 and a House vote of 76–19 that accepted the terms of John Purdue.

But the board of trustees still had to formally acquire the land to meet the terms of the Morrill Act. John Purdue began searching for 100 acres of land in Tippecanoe County on which to place his namesake university. He selected prairie land located less than two miles west of the Tippecanoe County courthouse in the town of Chauncey (later renamed West Lafayette). The 100 acres that he promised in his proposal to the General Assembly consisted of outright gifts by donors and land purchased at prices well below market value.

The original 100 acres were located south of State Street (State Road 26), which runs through the Purdue campus today. Rachel and Hiram Russell gave a gift of 10 acres of land that formed the western limit of campus, and two other parcels of land comprising 51.25 and 38.75 acres, which ran east of the Russell tract, were purchased from the Marsteller and Steely families.

On December 22, 1869, the board of trustees received the deed to the 100 acres from John Purdue. One week later, Indiana officially accepted the property, just days before the December 1869 deadline. Indiana would be the twenty-first state to accept the terms of the Morrill Act, the twenty-fourth to pick a site for a campus, and the thirteenth to open its doors to students.

The first campus building was started in 1871 near the area occupied today by Smith Hall. For some unknown reason, it was abandoned soon after the initial construction project started. In 1872, the Purdue board of trustees decided that 200 acres of land north of State Street should be purchased on which the main campus buildings would be constructed. However, land prices being much higher than what the trustees had anticipated, only 84 acres were purchased. This additional land was bounded roughly by present-day University, Grant, and Seventh Streets. It was here that the first university buildings were built.

❦ ❦ ❦

The board of trustees needed to hire a president to help them get the university off the ground, find funding, construct buildings, attract students, and hire faculty. Their first selection was William S. Clark of Massachusetts Agricultural College. Unfortunately, Clark reneged, so the trustees instead named Richard Owen, who would serve as president from 1872 to 1874.

The trustees were literally forced to open the university with a thrown-together session from March to June 1874 in order to meet yet another statutory deadline under the Morrill Act. They were taught by John S. Hougham, who was the first professor hired by the trustees in early 1872. Professor Hougham taught higher arithmetic, algebra, physical geography, natural science, physiology, and chemistry in the makeshift three-month session.[6]

There were no women among the first students admitted to Purdue University. Eight women who wanted to enroll in March 1874 were all denied admission.[7] On March 10, 1874, the trustees put the matter into their official record:

> On motion of Mr. Coffrast the report was received and it was ordered that
> the Sec'y certify to Prof. Hougham that the University is not now prepared
> to receive female students, and that the question of the admission of such
> is reserved for consideration and future determination.[8]

Just a year later, the university reconsidered its position on allowing women to attend the college. Purdue University would continue to tout the openness of the school for many years thereafter with proclamations of equal opportunities for both sexes.

The students enrolling for the start of classes in September 1874 are generally credited as the first official class of Purdue University. By this time, the trustees had staffed the university with five professors and one assistant professor, including Abraham Shortridge, who taught in the classroom in addition to succeeding Richard Owen as president. By the end of 1874, sixty-four students were enrolled, with "13 in regular college classes, 2 in special or advanced courses, and the remaining 49 were in preparatory class."[9] In terms of class standing for the 13 students who were determined ready for college work, "one was registered as a Senior, three as Sophomores, and nine as Freshmen."[10]

Purdue University held its first commencement in May 1875, with John Bradford Harper, a transfer student from Northwestern Christian University in Indianapolis, as the sole graduate. By 1877, the new university would graduate the first students to complete their entire coursework at Purdue, including Eulora Miller from Lafayette, who would be the first female graduate, and Franklin Pierce Clark from Baltimore, Ohio, who holds the distinction as the first out-of-state graduate conferred a bachelor of science degree. Five years later, in 1882, the School of Agriculture would award its first bachelor of science degrees to Henry A. Beck, William E. Driscoll, and Elwood Mead. In 1890, George W. Lacey would become Purdue's first African-American graduate, and Genzo Murata of Japan would become the first international student to graduate.[11]

※ ※ ※

The requirements for enrolling at Purdue University for much of the nineteenth century focused on moral character, age, and satisfactory entrance examination scores. The incoming freshmen were to be of good moral character and have attained an age of sixteen years. Students wishing to apply for admission were instructed to apply directly to the university president.

Soon thereafter, the Purdue *Annual Register* suggested that Purdue would admit incoming students younger than age sixteen if they could pass the entrance examination. The college entrance examination focused on grammar, United States history, geography, natural science, physiology, arithmetic, algebra, and geometry.

Initially, the school year was divided into three terms until 1901, when the university switched to the semester system. The projected cost for attending Purdue University in 1876 was listed in the *Annual Register* as follows:

> The students' expenses for 38 weeks in the Academy or College will be $169.
> Tuition of residents: free
> Tuition for residents of other states: $20 per year
> Enrollment fee: $10
> Room, rent, fuel and light per term: $5
> Janitor's fee: $5
> Board per week: $3.50
> Washing per dozen: $0.75 [12]

While a twenty-five-dollar tuition fee would not be assessed to Hoosier students until 1901, the fees for room and board in the 1870s and 1880s were often prohibitive for many of the students wanting to attend college. Money was hard to come by for those who farmed, and many families could not afford to send their children to Purdue University.

Purdue tried hard at first to attract potential students by offering them work on the farm and college grounds, and in the vegetable garden. They could work for two to three hours per day to help them offset at least part of their expenses. Students were paid ten cents an hour for their work. [13]

The Indiana General Assembly passed a law in early 1877 that offered scholarships to Purdue University. The law authorized the board of commissioners in each Indiana county to select two students who, once admitted, would have their entrance fees, some incidental fees, and the cost for room, heat, and light waived. The savings to each student amounted to $33 a year, which helped to defray the cost of attending Purdue by 20 percent.

The trustees had to change their position on student work programs as the Purdue budget could not support all of the students requesting work. They limited work to students majoring in agriculture, perhaps, in part, to help the university's recruitment efforts in the School of Agriculture.

※ ※ ※

Purdue University in the early years seemed to constantly be revamping its educational programs. At first, the trustees and the president agreed to an organization that encompassed five schools with specialization within those schools: Agriculture and Horticulture, Chemistry, Engineering, Industrial Design, and Natural History. [14]

This organizational model was changed in 1876, when the curriculum was divided into three departments with students having the option of majoring in special schools.

    I. The University Academy
   II. The College of General Science
  III. Special Schools of Science and Technology
     1. School of Agriculture and Horticulture
     2. School of Civil Engineering
     3. School of Industrial Design
     4. School of Physics and Metallurgy
     5. School of Natural History[15]

The University Academy would take those students with low college entrance examinations who could not qualify to start college classes. These students were admitted to the academy, but they still had to pass a lesser qualifying examination that measured their understanding of English, arithmetic, geography, and spelling.

The University Academy required students to devote two years of study to subjects such as math, English, reading, spelling, geography, history, zoology, and physiology. For many students, the academy was their first step toward getting into the regular classes that Purdue University offered in the College of General Science or in the special schools. For many years, enrollment figures for the University Academy were higher than in the other two Purdue University departments combined. The University Academy operated until 1894, when the remedial program was phased out.

The School of Agriculture and Horticulture designed special courses for students who had completed their first year of classes in the College of General Science. The School of Agriculture and Horticulture would pronounce that its mission was to teach "practical and theoretical agriculture, horticulture and veterinary science."[16]

The student's three-year plan of study was prescribed with few electives provided. The agriculturally related courses that students would take were:

First Year
   First Term
      livestock, 10 weeks
      dairying, 3 weeks
      farm experiments, 3 weeks
   Second Term
      livestock breeding, 8 weeks
      veterinary obstetrics, 4 weeks

Third Term
> veterinary obstetrics, 4 weeks
> entomology, 6 weeks

Second Year
First Term
> horticulture, floriculture, and greenhouse management, 16 weeks

Second Term
> diseases of animals, 12 weeks

Third Term
> market gardening, 7 weeks
> drainage, 3 weeks

Third Year
First Term
> landscape gardening, 8 weeks
> history of agriculture, its development, etc., 8 weeks

Second Term
> rotation of crops, farm management and economy, etc., 6 weeks
> meteorology, 6 weeks

Third Term
> agricultural chemistry, 10 weeks[17]

Students were allowed to complete their agricultural courses in the College of General Science and earn the bachelor of science degree. This meant they also had to take additional language requirements. Those students who enrolled in any of the three-year special schools received a diploma instead of the degree. A candidate for either the bachelor of science degree or the diploma was required to "present themselves at the annual examination, before commencement."[18]

However, students in those first years were not interested in the program of study offered by the agricultural school.

> It is a suggestive fact that, though systematic and well-arranged courses
> of instruction in agriculture were announced, not a student applied for
> such instruction. The nominal students in agriculture (one or two) were
> in the first year's course—common to the other schools.[19]

The trustees recognized that the university's mission was, in part, to teach students about agriculture. They wrote:

These [agricultural] courses will soon be revised, with a view of making them more acceptable and successful. To this end, the experience of the older agricultural schools will be consulted, and the feasibility of teaching the details of farming by actual practice will be earnestly considered. It is expected that the new courses in Agriculture and Horticulture will be arranged before the opening of the University in September next [1876].[20]

Little changed over the next few years, as agricultural science failed to become popular with students. The board of trustees tried to improve the situation by hiring a professor of agriculture who could focus attention on building the agricultural program into one that would at least attract enough students to make it respectable. The trustees passed this resolution at their October 22, 1878, meeting:

Mr. Wells there upon moved that the suggestions in said Report relative to establishing a School of Agriculture be adopted and that a Professor of Agriculture for the head of such School be appointed. Vote was 6 to 0 in favor. This in reference to President E. E. White's plan for reorganization.[21]

The vote to hire a professor of agriculture came after President Emerson E. White at this same meeting made a very persuasive speech in which he spoke about the need for a strong School of Agriculture. His suggestions would become the blueprint for developing the School of Agriculture for years to come:

The University has, from the first, announced special courses of instruc-tion in agriculture, but, until recently, there has been no demand for such instruction. The present demand happily comes when we are prepared to organize the School of Agriculture, both for instruction and experiment. The demand for systematic instruction may be small for several years to come, but the wide field of experiment will furnish full employment for the professor in charge of the school.

The first step in the organization of the school is the selection of a competent man to take charge of it. This will require time and care, for the men in the country qualified to fill such a position, are few in number. I repeat the remarks made in my inaugural address that a superficial empire in such a person would do more harm than good. What is needed is a first-class scientific man—one not only competent to teach the sci-ence of agriculture, but also competent to conduct a series of observations and experiments in a scientific manner.

The next step is to provide the professor of agriculture with necessary facilities for conducting experiments; and this involves the whole question of the management of the farm. In the light of the experience of other institutions, I put the plan suggested in my inaugural address, into the form of a recommendation, believing that it is the best possible solution of the problem before us. Set apart from five to ten acres of the farm for such agricultural experiments as can be made on a small scale, and make this an *agricultural laboratory* [White's emphasis], under the charge of the professor. The experience of the agricultural schools of Europe shows that such a laboratory can be made to cover most of the important questions in agriculture, with a small expenditure of money—a very important consideration.

Let the rest of the land owned by the University, about 150 acres, be conducted as a model farm as an illustration of scientific and business farming. To this end the farm should be made to pay not only its running expenses but all ordinary improvements. There will necessarily be some land on the farm for experiments which can best be conducted on a large scale, including experiments in the feeding of stock, the rotation of crops, etc.—experiments requiring great care but little expense. We have an illustration of this fact in the recent experiment relating to the quantity of seed wheat to be sown to the acre. This experiment promises valuable results, but its value would be increased by analyses of the soil in the different sections to determine their comparative fertility, a very important fact, determining the comparative height of the stalk measurement; by comparing the weight of the straw, etc. These and other inquiries repeated with the experiment for several years, with a careful record of the results will throw much light upon the practical question involved—at least as far as our soil and climate are concerned. These experiments should be made under the supervision of the professor of agriculture; they should be repeated on different soils and in different parts of the State.[22]

Later on in his address, President White made the following remarks to the board of trustees:

There will also be a demand on the farm for practice for those students in agriculture who are not familiar with the details of farming. Nearly all the applicants for admission to the School of Agriculture have been made by young men who have not been brought up on a farm. The Japanese youth, who made the first application for admission to this school, did not enter, because I could not promise him practice on the farm, and I have been obliged to give a similar answer to all applicants—a necessity under the present system.

I have said enough to show that there must be a close connection between the School of Agriculture and the model farm. If divorced, the success of the school will be greatly lessened, and the value of the farm, as one of the appliances of the University, will be nearly, if not quite, destroyed.

How can this necessary connection be made? I have given this important question long and careful consideration, and, as a result, the following plan is recommended: Let the management of the farm be entrusted to a committee of the Board of Trustees, and let the professor of agriculture submit to this committee, from time to time the experiments he wishes to be made on the farm. If the committee approves, let it order the experiments made under the supervision of the professor of agriculture, all extra expense involved to be charged to the experiment fund. When students wish and require practice on the farm, let application be made to the same committee, and such practice be provided under its orders.

This arrangement for the management of the model farm will relieve the Faculty of all responsibility for the results. I have no desire to assume any such responsibility, and I shall be glad to have this duty entrusted to a committee of the Board, composed of experienced and successful farmers. The President of the University will, by virtue of his office, be the dean of the School of Agriculture, as he is of all schools and departments, and all applications for experiments and practice will be made with his approval.

It is my opinion that this arrangement will avoid the complications which have so seriously crippled the schools of agriculture in several other institutions. The vital condition is that the farm be at all times under the immediate control of the Board of Trustees. It is impossible to determine beforehand how much land will be needed for experimental purposes; where it should be situated; what assistance the farm must render, etc. These and many other important questions can be wisely settled only after consultation with the professor to be selected and appointed, and to enter upon his duties not earlier than March 1st, 1879.[23]

By June 1879, a motion to create a committee to hire a professor of agriculture was passed. By September, the selection committee made their decision to hire Charles L. Ingersoll, who was, at that time, the professor of agriculture and farm superintendent at Michigan Agricultural College, for a salary of $1,600.

In many ways, Purdue University was fortunate to attract someone with his experience, both as a professor and the superintendent of a college farm. President White would offer these remarks about Professor Ingersoll:

There are very few men in the country fitted by education and experience to take charge of such a school. This fact made the selection of a person for the position here a difficult task. A wide correspondence pointed to only two available men whose employment we could confidently recommend. The Board was fortunate in securing one of these men, Prof. Charles L. Ingersoll, then Professor of Agriculture in the State Agricultural College of Michigan, one of the oldest and most successful institutions of its class in the country.

He is a graduate of the college, and has successfully filled the positions of foreman and superintendent of the farm, and of instructor in agriculture.

He was induced to accept the position, not by the salary offered (the salaries of the professor in Purdue being small), but by the opportunity presented to do a successful work as an instructor and experimenter. Professor Ingersoll entered upon his duties here in September, and has given daily instruction to a class of deeply interested students. [24]

Charles L. Ingersoll secured his place in Purdue agricultural history as the first professor of agriculture and horticulture. President White hired Ingersoll to "teach agriculture, perform experiments, manage a farm, deal with farmers, and accept a comparatively low salary when the demand for professors of agriculture was much greater than the supply." [25] He was one of eleven faculty and instructors employed by Purdue University at that time.

Enrollment in the Special School of Agriculture and Horticulture jumped from zero to eleven students in the first year of Ingersoll's appointment, and he is given credit for beginning the process of building an agricultural degree program at Purdue. Professor Ingersoll would change the original curriculum somewhat by adding courses dealing more with science than those focusing on practical agriculture. His additions included biology, botany, chemistry, comparative anatomy, forestry, physics, veterinary science, and zoology. Ingersoll did leave behind a few details of what it was like to teach in 1880 and 1881:

The year covered by this report [1880–81] was the second year of the instruction in Agriculture and Horticulture, and my time was occupied for two hours each day in the classroom, and for nearly the same time during the Fall and Spring terms in the practical work of the Department. The classes, as a rule, did excellent work and fully met my expectations. The total number enrolled in the classes during the year was twelve. During the Winter term the students in this course took a short course in Carpentry in the machine shop, as was previously contemplated. The class in Drainage made a complete survey of a set of drains, and each member was required to submit a plat with working specifications as to depth of excavation, grade of fall, etc. This gave the complete work of drainage engineer in the matter of land drainage.

At the close of this year the course of study was slightly changed. The Landscape Gardening and Forestry of the third or Junior year was made to change places with the Veterinary Science of the Sophomore year. This harmonizes the work in the separate years of the course much better, and also brings the work in better conjunction with the work in other departments.[26]

Professor Ingersoll would see the first agriculture students graduate. At the June 1881 graduation ceremonies, four students were listed as having completed their coursework: three were awarded bachelor of science degrees for having completed their program in the College of General Science with an emphasis in agriculture, while one student received a diploma for having completed the three-year agriculture program in the Special Schools of Science and Technology.

President White's dreams for a strong agricultural program at Purdue University took an unexpected turn when, in 1882, the man he had hand-picked to lead that effort resigned to become president of the Colorado Agricultural College.

Professor Charles Ingersoll laid a solid foundation for Indiana's new agricultural college. His departure, untimely as it was, offered his successor the challenge of building on good work. As the second professor of agriculture and horticulture, William Latta would meet that challenge. Latta would move to Purdue University when the School of Agriculture was just beginning the uphill battle to engage Indiana farmers to send their children to Purdue for a college education in agriculture, not engineering. He would make the job his own and successfully deliver the Purdue University School of Agriculture into the twentieth century.

The College Professor:
Fulfilling a Dream of Teaching (1882–1911)

CHAPTER THREE

Can one achieve more open mind,
Yet larger, richer truth to find;
Push back the walls of ignorance
To realms of wider cognizance.

—William Carroll Latta
from "A Better New Year," 1930

WITHIN SIX MONTHS OF ARRIVING on campus for his new job, William Carroll Latta was asked to deliver a speech to the Indiana State Board of Agriculture (today known as the Indiana State Fair Board). This was a quasi-governmental organization that represented members of different agricultural associations, and its main purpose was to serve as a clearinghouse for agricultural information. The board lobbied the Indiana General Assembly for money to fund various agricultural programs, while working with legislators to develop positions, policies, and laws of interest to the farming community. Consequently, it wielded tremendous influence.

In his speech to the board, the thirty-two-year-old Latta pointed out the benefits of getting an agricultural education at Purdue University. Having been at Purdue for only a short time, his remarks dealt with the benefits of an agricultural college education in general.

While new to Purdue University, he was well equipped to deliver a speech touting the value of an agricultural education. He was college educated and had farmed. His relatives, going back many generations, were farmers. His brother James still farmed the family homestead in north central Indiana. And Latta himself was a native-born Hoosier. He had also learned from his father-in-law, Amos Wood, how successful a farm could be if it were properly managed. That experience taught him that science could be used to improve many aspects of farm life. Through work and education, trial and error, Latta had gained a deep appreciation of farm issues and farm people.

As he got up to the podium to speak, he must have been concerned about how the audience would interpret his remarks. In fact, the young professor's blunt comments would have resulted in a serious breach of trust had they been made by someone other than a university professor and a fellow Hoosier farmer.

Latta's ideas about why an agricultural education was good for Indiana's sons and daughters would become a theme that he would return to during the next fifty years. His speech, "Agricultural Education: Its Practical Value," outlined much of his philosophy on research, Extension, and education. (See Appendix 1 for selected text from Latta's speech.) It offers a historical perspective of the challenges faced in 1883 by the agricultural faculty at Purdue University.

In his address, he spoke honestly and frankly to the board members, stating that farmers were not well equipped to use the technical information that was being developed by Purdue, nor were they readily able to distinguish among solid advice, unproven speculation, and the outright fraudulent claims that were appearing in farm magazines and agricultural newspapers.

He reminded them that educated farmers were assets to the community. He also emphasized the financial value of an agricultural education for their children. He spent much of his time talking about how young men and women who used the facts and principles they learned at school would be more successful, adapt more readily to a changing marketplace, and provide a better living for their families. His speech was designed to walk a fine line between staying within and breaking away from acceptable rural traditions of criticism and praise.

A decade later, Latta published an article called "Culture and Agriculture," in which he once again articulated many of the same arguments that he had made to the Indiana State Board of Agriculture. In it, he bluntly offered his opinion that "most of the farmers of to-day are deficient in education—the very foundation of all liberal culture; and for the fundamentals of an education we must ever look to the schools."[1]

Professor Latta's trademark was his lifelong commitment to educating farmers in sound agricultural practices and promoting Purdue University as the place for them to receive that education. Fifty years later, in his book *Outline History of Indiana Agriculture*, Latta wrote:

That the school of agriculture is also doing a great work for the farmers of Indiana may not, at first, be so apparent. It should be remembered, however, that while the station and extension workers are dealing with matter, the school of agriculture is preparing men who are to control matter and harness nature's forces, both animate and inanimate, for the service of man. More than this, the school of agriculture is training men to become the inspirers and leaders of other men in the great wide field of agriculture. Purdue agriculture graduates are not only demonstrating on their own farms the methods of successful agriculture, but they are also becoming community leaders who are helping to lift agriculture to its rightful place among the callings of men. . . .

In view of the good record made by its former students, may we not regard the product of the Purdue School of Agriculture as the crowning work of the University in behalf of agriculture? In view also of its growing material equipment and the increasing number and efficiency of its teaching staff, may we not rightfully expect that Purdue's School of Agriculture will continue to turn out an unbroken succession of scientific farmers and public-spirited agricultural leaders who will help to put and keep Indiana among the foremost agricultural states of the Union?[2]

From that first speech to the Indiana State Board of Agriculture in 1883 until his death in 1935, Professor Latta helped shape what eventually would become a major educational institution known worldwide for its diverse student body, quality education, and wide assortment of agricultural majors and specializations. He would live to see how his contributions helped to dramatically change the way Indiana's farming community viewed a Purdue education in agriculture.

William Carroll Latta came to Purdue in 1882 as an instructor in agriculture. He was hired to help Charles Ingersoll teach some of the agricultural courses and also serve as farm superintendent, responsible for managing the farm on the southwestern part of campus. Latta would report to Professor Ingersoll.

However, when Professor Ingersoll announced in July 1882 that he was leaving Purdue to become the president of Colorado Agricultural College, Latta found himself quickly promoted to professor of agriculture and horticulture. In an August 30, 1882, press release in the *Indianapolis News*, the following passage appears:

> Professor Wm. C. Latta, of the State Agricultural College of Michigan, has
> been appointed to fill the vacancy in the chair of Agriculture at Purdue
> University, caused by the resignation of Professor C. L. Ingersoll. The col-
> lege opens September 7.[3]

With Professor Ingersoll leaving so close to the start of the fall term,
Purdue University was in immediate need of someone to teach the agricultural
courses and to take charge of the agricultural department. Latta, in a very short
period of time, went from graduate student to Purdue professor.

Professor Latta saw that the School of Agriculture had few students,
employed a single agricultural professor (himself), and was poorly regarded in
comparison to the School of Engineering. He began a slow and deliberate
process of transforming the School of Agriculture to give the program visibility and traction. To do this, he would need to increase student numbers, hire
new faculty, and draw the attention of the Indiana General Assembly to fund
new agricultural programs and buildings.

The first year must have been a difficult and tiring time for Latta. Not only
did he have to teach classes, but he also had to get the harvest in from the farm
and finish many of the research projects initiated by Ingersoll. Latta did not
have an assistant at that time and was consequently performing two jobs as
teacher and farm manager.

With the start of school looming, Latta would have been hard-pressed for
time to develop any original lectures to teach all of his agricultural classes on
opening day. It is possible that Latta would have used his own class notes from
Michigan Agricultural College or perhaps Ingersoll left his course notes behind
for Latta.

> Until 1884, according to a report by President [James H.] Smart, Latta did
> all the teaching in the School of Agriculture. He taught agriculture, stock-
> raising, veterinary science, forestry, drainage, landscape gardening, etc.
> He was thus compelled to teach a greater variety of subjects than any
> other instructor in the Institution.[4]

Even though Professor Latta was the sole member of the agriculture
faculty for a number of years, he began asking the president for additional help
within a year of his appointment. Asking for more of everything would become
a lifelong trademark of Latta:

> The Agricultural Course has been recast and several new subjects added.
> And, while it is believed the course of study has thus been strengthened,

the duties of the Professor of Agriculture have been greatly increased. Hence additional teaching force is urgently needed in this department in order to make the course in Agriculture and Horticulture more thorough and practical.[5]

President Smart in 1883 would second the comments made by Professor Latta and offered the following remarks about the agricultural program:

It is no longer possible for one man to do the work in the Department of Agriculture and Horticulture. For a year past, I have rendered some assistance by taking the immediate oversight of the horticultural work within the college grounds, and I realized more than ever before, the possibility of attaining a success in this department, which we have not yet approached. A competent person should be at once employed to take charge of this work, including horticultural experiments, and practical instruction in floriculture, fruit culture, forestry and landscape gardening. This will leave for the Professor in Agriculture [Latta] the instruction of two, and after this year, three classes in agriculture proper, the planning and direction of all agricultural experiments, and the supervision of the farm—certainly as much as any one man can do in a creditable manner.[6]

These pleas led to the hiring of James Troop in 1884 as professor of horticulture and entomology. Troop took charge of these areas of study, while Latta would focus his teaching efforts in the agronomy, livestock, veterinary, economics, and agricultural engineering courses.

Troop and Latta were colleagues for more than fifty years at Purdue University. Both men would long be remembered as the professors who taught those first agricultural students everything they would need to know about farm management. In fact, the idea of "farm" was central to almost all of the classes that Latta taught, as documented by his course titles: Farm Crops, Farm Stock, Stock Breeding, Farm Economy, Farm Buildings and Utensils, Farm Roads, Farm Implements, Farm Management, Farm Drainage, Principles of Feeding and Dairying, Agriculture, Farm Architecture and Implements, Agricultural Experimentation, Agricultural Physics and Chemistry, Farm Engineering, Evolution of Agriculture, and Science and Art of Agriculture.

Professor Latta wrote brief descriptions about his teaching responsibilities and student contacts between 1882 and 1883:

In this third year [his first] of the work in the Agricultural department, there were three daily recitations to conduct: the Freshman class of eight students, the Sophomore of three, and Junior class of nine students. The work done in all classes was excellent, and would have done credit to students in any institution. In the winter term, by reason of sickness and other causes, the Sophomore class was abandoned, so that after February 1, there were only two recitations daily. This class contained five Seniors, of whom one left and one graduated in the Agricultural course in addition to the Scientific course, and one received a diploma in Agriculture. Thus four left the University with credit, having completed the Agricultural course. This marks an era in the history of Purdue University—the graduation of students in the industrial departments.[7]

Throughout the year I have met with Freshmen and Sophomore students in agriculture in daily recitations. The classes, though small to begin with, remained undiminished through the year, with the exception of one student who temporarily dropped out of college to assist on the farm. The subjects taught were history of stock, stock breeding, veterinary hygiene, farm management, farm drainage, and meteorology.[8]

One of his first classes was to teach three terms—a whole school year— of general agricultural principles to the freshmen. This was described as:

Agriculture.—Thirty-eight weeks. Fall term, fifteen weeks, four hours per week. Winter term, twelve weeks, three hours per week. Spring term, eleven weeks, four hours per week. Subjects in sequence for year: History, Development and scope of agriculture, Soils, Tillage, Manures, Crops and rotation.[9]

In 1884, Professor Latta gave another speech, "The Agricultural College: Its Missions and Needs," to the Indiana State Board of Agriculture. In many ways, it was a continuation of the same themes in his speech "Agricultural Education: Its Practical Value" given the year before to the same group. In it he outlined his views on what an education from Purdue University meant to the student:

Others have the mistaken notion that the chief work of the agricultural college is to give manual training in the art, the practice of agriculture; to teach boys how to plow and sow and reap. Men of this class will say: "Our boys know how to do farm work now; why send them to college to learn what they already know?" This reasoning is good enough, but it is based on a false assumption. These colleges do not aim to teach the "how," so much as the "why." If the student is made to clearly understand the objects to be secured by plowing, and the importance of thorough work; if he is made familiar with the mechanical principles involved in the construction and working of the plow, he will readily learn how to adjust and use the tool to accomplish the desired purpose. While the training of the hand is not lost sight of, the aim is rather to train the head, which is to guide the hand. Instead of sending out "crack" plowmen, "boss" teamsters, and "champion" wheat stackers, the agricultural college aims to so train its men as to fit them—except in the matter of experience—to take charge of the farm, either as manager or foreman, and wisely conduct its many operations. Another misapprehension is that these colleges are mere schools of agriculture, designed to turn young men into farmers as uniformly as the miller turns his wheat into flour. The agricultural college is not a special school. Almost without exception these colleges have full four-year courses of study, the aim being to impart a broad, a liberal education, if you please, which shall at the same time, be a thoroughly practical one.[10]

One of Professor Latta's first significant moves was to expand the agricultural program from a three- to a four-year course of study. This measure was significant in that it enhanced the scholarly standing of the School of Agriculture within the larger college. By 1883, Purdue announced that it was a College of Science, Agriculture, and the Mechanic Arts. It embraced four special schools—the School of Agriculture and Horticulture, School of Mechanics and Engineering, School of Science, and School of Industrial Art. The course description read as if the School of Agriculture and Horticulture required extra work of its students:

> These courses of instruction in the four special schools are so arranged that they include, with few exceptions, the same instruction in general science, mathematics, English, history, political and mental science, and industrial drawing. In addition to these branches, common to the four schools, the School of Agriculture adds four years of daily instruction and practice in agriculture and horticulture.[11]

Latta wrote the following description in 1883 for the *Annual Register*. He once again pointed out that a student pursuing an agricultural education would have to take other courses that would make them "intelligent citizens."[12]

But knowing that three-fourths of their class time would be in other areas, he made sure that the students also understood that they would always be taking an agriculture course:

> It will be observed that the special [agriculture], as well as the general studies, continue throughout the course. It is believed that this arrangement will tend to keep the student constantly in close sympathy with agricultural pursuits. As far as possible, the special subjects are taken up at the most favorable time of the year, and in their proper relation to the purely scientific studies. The work of the classroom is supplemented by field instruction; and the shop work gives a degree of mechanical skill of great value to the farmer. As far as practicable, labor will be furnished to students taking the Agricultural Course, whenever it is desired. Students receive pay for all work not instructional.[13]

Latta began altering the curriculum so that the students would learn to run an efficient, effective, and productive modern farm. He added more practical courses to the student's plan of study: Farm Implements, Shop Work, Bridges and Roofs, Fruit Culture, Roads and Railways, Canals and Rivers, Economic Botany, and Veterinary Hygiene. His new four-year plan of study also required students to take more English and logic courses to introduce culture to prospective young farmers. Professor Latta believed it was the college's obligation to mold well-rounded students.

New faculty members also brought change to the curriculum. However, while agricultural courses were added to and dropped from the school's listings, the basic premise of the course of study remained constant—practical knowledge that could be used in the market, field, barn, and later on, in the home.

The following plan of study provides a glimpse of what the agricultural student of the late nineteenth century would have taken at Purdue University:

Freshmen Class
First Term
Farm Crops, Farm Stock, English Composition
and Rhetoric, Geometry, Botany
Second Term
Stock Breeding, English Composition
and Rhetoric, Geometry, Botany
Third Term
Model and Object Drawing, English
Composition and Rhetoric, Algebra, Botany

Sophomore Class

First Term

Logic, Higher Algebra, Trigonometry,
Farm Implements, Farm Management, Zoology

Second Term

English Literature, Trigonometry, Physics, Shop Work

Third Term

English Literature, Surveying, Floriculture,
Vegetable Gardening, Physics

Junior Class

First Term

Veterinary Hygiene, General History,
Entomology, Meteorology, Chemistry

Second Term

General History, Meteorology, Building
Materials and Masonry, Chemistry, Shop Work

Third Term

Farm Drainage, Landscape Gardening,
General History, Bridges and Roofs,
Agricultural Chemistry

Senior Class

First Term

Human Physiology, Political Economy,
Development of the English Language, Oratory,
Fruit Culture, Forestry, Principles of Agriculture

Second Term

Human Physiology, Geology, United States
Constitution, Psychology, Oratory, Roads and
Railways, Principles of Agriculture, Principles
of Feeding and Dairying

Third Term

Geology, Psychology, Canals and Rivers,
Economic Botany[14]

Course descriptions were created or updated by Professors Latta and Troop for the agricultural classes. Class synopses offer an idea about what early educators thought was important to teach their agricultural students:

Farm Crops—staple and special; planting, cultivating, harvesting, feeding and selling; crop rotation.

Farm Stock—history and characteristics of the various improved breeds of domestic animals, with their adaptations to soil, climate, etc.

Stock Breeding—principles underlying the art; laws of heredity; causes of deterioration and means of improvement.

Farm Implements—study of their mechanism, adaptations, strength and durability, with hand practice in taking them apart, putting them together, and adjusting them for use.

Farm Management—various questions relating to the care of crops, stock, manure, buildings, fences, implements, etc.; farm help; farm accounts; buying and selling.

Shop Work—practice with carpenter's tools in plain wood work.

Floriculture—propagation and culture of flowers.

Vegetable Gardening—preparation of soil, planting, transplanting, cultivation, harvesting, and winter preservation.

Veterinary Hygiene—symptoms, causes, preventives and treatment of diseases of farm stock; sanitary arrangement of farm buildings; disinfection.

Entomology—beneficial and injurious insects; means of preventing or mitigating insect ravages.

Meteorology—climate in relation to agriculture; laws of storms; means of forecasting the weather.

Shop Work—forging, giving practice with blacksmith's tools in plain work in iron.

Farm Drainage—location, planning, leveling, construction and repairing of farm drains and sewers.

Landscape Gardening—ornamentation of the home with trees, shrubs, flowers, lawns, etc.

Agricultural Chemistry—chemistry of soils; chemistry of the germination, growth, ripening and decay of plants; chemistry of curing crops; chemistry of feeding, and of the dairy.

Fruit Culture—propagation, transplanting and cultivation of fruit trees; harvesting, packing, storing and shipping of fruits; orchard sites, orchard management, etc.

Forestry—effects of removing forests; reasons for forest tree planting; trees of various locations, and methods of growing the same.

Principles of Agriculture—effects of tillage, manures, mulching, drainage, irrigation; nature and needs of soils and crops; soil exhaustion, renovation of soils, etc.

Principles of Feeding and Dairying—laws of animal nutrition; feeding rations for young, fattening, and work animals; effects of dry, succulent, concentrated and bulky foods; economy in feeding; effects of food, exposure and treatment on the quantity and quality of milk; milk setting, butter and cheese making; utilization of the by products of the dairy.

Economic Botany—study of noxious and useful plants of the farm, their characteristics, propagation, rate of increase and conditions of growth; time and manner of destroying weeds; cross fertilization and selection as means of improving grains, vegetables, fruits and flowers.[15]

Professor Latta provided a list of books that the students used with their agricultural classes in 1900. The students were asked to buy their books together to get a better price.

Text Books and Reference Books Used in Agricultural Courses
Soils and Crops: Five Principles of Agriculture by Voorhees
Feeds and Feeding by Henry
The Soil by King
Land Drainage by Miles
Manure and Manuring by Aikman
Fertilizer by Voorhees
Milk and Its Products by Wing
Veterinary Anatomy by Strangeway
Veterinary Physiology by Smith
Veterinary Medicine by Dana
Pathology and Therapeutics by Friedberger & Prohnor
Stock Breeds by Miles
How Crops Grow and How Crops Feed by Johnson
New Manual of Botany by Gray
Economic Entomology by Smith
American Fruit Culturist by Thomas
Soils and Crops by Morrow & Hunt
Chemistry of the Farm by Warrington
Agriculture by Storer

Principles of Fruit Growing by Bailey
The Spraying of Plants by Lodeman
Manual of Cattle Feeding by Arms[16]

In 1887, Professor Latta was further assigned governance of the graduate programs in the School of Agriculture. He was continuing to take on more responsibilities in teaching and research. The *Annual Register* summarized the graduate program in agriculture:

> *In Agriculture.*—History of agriculture; laws relating thereto, in this and in other countries; its relations to other pursuits, and to the general prosperity of communities and nations; thus banding the varied sources of fertility; economic and profitable production; social relations of the agricultural classes; needed legislation in behalf of agriculture. Directed by Professor Latta.[17]

During the school year beginning in 1898, Latta expanded the graduate requirements to include research. A faculty member, under Latta's supervision, would direct the student's class work and research. The student had to pass a qualifying examination in front of a special committee, and research, in the thesis form, had to be acceptable to the school.

🌾 🌾 🌾

The development of the Winter Short Course was a milestone in Purdue agricultural history. The 1895 catalog described the Winter Short Course in agriculture as:

> designed for those who feel the need of more thoroughly preparing for their work, but can devote only the winter season to such preparation. The course has been planned, therefore, to give the largest amount of scientific and practical information possible during the winter months and allow the students to return to the farm for the busy season.[18]

In many ways, the Winter Short Course changed how the school interacted with the farm population. Graduates of this course soon became the most vocal supporters of Purdue University.

The short courses entailed eight to eleven weeks of intensive lectures about soils, crops, and livestock. Scheduling the instruction time during the winter months made it more convenient for farmers to spend time learning the latest ideas in agriculture. For some students, the Winter Short Course offered them a chance to work while attending school. Lecturers included faculty and guest speakers, such as stockmen, farmers, and horticulturists. Under the direction of faculty members, the students also made visits to farms in the vicinity of Lafayette. Soil physics and livestock judging were two of the more popular topics covered at many of the short courses, but the 1900 catalog illustrates the depth and breadth of educational winter topics offered:

For Men and Women
1. Livestock husbandry and veterinary hygiene
2. Farm dairying
3. Soils, crops, manures and farm buildings
4. Horticulture, economic botany and entomology
5. Agricultural chemistry, farm sanitation, vegetable parasites and rural law
6. Shop work in wood or iron
7. Special lectures by stockmen, farmers and horticulturists

For Women
8. Floriculture
9. Household chemistry
10. House sanitation
11. Domestic economy
12. Botany
13. Drawing
14. Studies in literature[19]

By 1902, the general design of the Winter Short Course was changed to meet the need for specialization. Instead of learning about the complete field of agriculture by studying general principles, students were allowed to specialize in general agriculture, horticulture, dairy, and animal husbandry.

The Winter Short Courses became enormously popular. The first class numbered 43 students, and by 1909, that number topped 1,000. While the School of Agriculture only had six staff members in the first decade of the twentieth century—compared to 56 in the rest of the university—the short course required hiring 13 temporary nonfaculty members to meet the demands of a rural audience wanting a Purdue education.

The Winter Short Courses provided Latta with an opportunity to say that the School of Agriculture was attracting more students each year. He spent considerable effort building up the enrollment because he knew he could then urge students to continue their studies in the four-year agricultural curriculum. The short courses became his primary recruiting tool for the School of Agriculture.

🌾 🌾 🌾

As the primary recruiter for the School of Agriculture, Professor Latta came under tremendous pressure to increase student enrollment. Quite frankly, the university had invested a lot of time and money in the agricultural program with little apparent gain. The workload assumed by Purdue professors was such that even in 1894, Latta knew that things were still not where he had hoped they would be.

> I have frequently heard Pres. Smart say that more money was expended per capita upon the agricultural students than upon those in any other department in the institution. If this be true, I do not know that farmers have just cause of complaint as to the apportionment of funds. The simple fact is that agricultural education is not very popular with farmers themselves as yet and this, I believe, more than any other thing accounts for the comparatively small attendance in the department of agriculture. Prof. C. L. Ingersoll, now of Nebraska, who was my predecessor here and later president of the Colorado Agricultural College, said to me a few days ago that if absolute freedom of choice were allowed, not over 15 percent of the young men who enter college would choose the agricultural course. I believe he is not very far from the truth and I am sorry for it because I think that the farmers should think enough of their calling and be sufficiently ambitious to take rank with other callings to educate their children properly for this pursuit.[20]

In 1896, Latta wrote to his colleague, Charles W. Garfield at Michigan Agricultural College, about the lower than hoped for enrollment in the schools of agriculture across the United States:

> Judging from the people in our own State, I think you have a tremendous problem to solve. If it is possible to enthuse the farmers generally over agricultural education with a view of preparing their sons for the practical pursuit of agriculture, I would give a good-deal to know just how to arouse them. I believe the time is coming, however, when the farmer will appreciate an education for its own sake and for its helpfulness in the every-day business of farming. I must confess that I think the conditions for working

out this great question are more favorable at M.A.C. than elsewhere and I therefore, with many other alumni, am watching with much interest and solicitude the progress of events there.[21]

He began an appeal for student applications by offering scholarships to the Winter Short Course and to the regular two- and four-year programs. This funding proved to be key in attracting more students to the school.

With reference to the free scholarships to county farmers' organizations, I would say that each organization is permitted to elect two young persons to any of the agricultural courses. Persons so appointed will save ten dollars in the winter course and twenty-five to thirty-five a year in the 2-year and 4-year courses.[22]

As part of his recruitment effort, Professor Latta carried on a letter-writing campaign with many students who wished to come to Purdue University.

Infer that the whole of plane geometry is included among the requirements for admission to the advanced freshmen class. If you are able to pass examination in part of geometry and are especially bright in mathematics and well equipped in other lines you might be permitted to go into the advanced course and make up the delinquencies out of class. . . . [23]

As to the expenses of a Short Course I would say that board and room would cost you about $3.00 to $3.50 per week. Washing would perhaps cost from 30 to 50 cents per week. There are not other items of expenses that would amount to anything. Of course you would want a few notebooks, but these are very cheap. You will see, therefore, that the expense of a course of eight weeks [Winter Short Course] would not be great. For such a course your expense ought not to exceed $40 outside of your traveling expenses and for those who live nearby, $40 ought to cover all the expenses of such courses. [24]

Prof. Plumb informs me that there is always more or less work to be done in the way of chores, and those who are both willing and handy can earn quite a little towards meeting their expenses. The pay is small—not over twelve and one-half cents an hour—so that you could not expect to earn very much while keeping up your studies. You are not so old but that you might wait a year and save up a considerable sum before starting. For your encouragement I will say that I started at the age of twenty-four and even then had to earn my way to a considerable extent. [25]

Professor Latta wrote to parents as well to answer their questions and provide advice about educating their children at Purdue:

> Now, a few words with reference to your son. He is doing good work and we think he should continue in the regular course. You perhaps recall that he consented to enter the four-year course last Fall, with the understanding that he would be permitted to enter the two-year course the second year, if he should think it best to do so. I have no doubt he will be governed by your advice in the matter, and I believe you wish to know my views. It is for this reason that I bring up the matter now. [26]

> I beg to submit some reasons why a young man who expects to farm should seek an agricultural education in some good college of agriculture.

> *1st.* It would give a knowledge of the sciences that have a most intimate bearing upon agriculture and also of their applications to this great calling.

> *2nd.* It would awaken a new interest in the farm and its problems, and thus do much to mitigate the monotony of farm life.

> *3rd.* It would inspire one to earnest effort to lift up the calling and standing of the farmer to their rightful level.

> *4th.* It would sharpen the mental faculties, make one more resourceful and give greater breadth of view.

> *5th.* The contact with other bright young people would have a most wholesome, enlarging and broadening effect.

> *6th.* It would add to one's financial success as well as to one's social, business and political standing. This is being amply demonstrated in our own state. [27]

It should be remembered that the students wanting to attend Purdue University at this time may or may not have graduated from a high school. Professor Latta would advise parents on whether or not a student needed to finish high school prior to attending Purdue:

> With reference to your inquiry about having your son complete High School before coming to Purdue, I beg to say that this depends upon several things. If your son is still young and growing, I think it will be better for him to remain in High School, especially if he can be at home. While we admit at the age of 16, we think it decidedly better that the student

should be, at least, 18 on entering.... In my judgment, it is better for a young man not to come to Purdue until he has practically attained his growth and become pretty well established in his habits and character. Then, he should also be amply qualified in this point of scholarship to carry the work, which is arduous, and keep fully abreast of the best in his class.[28]

In addition to using his letters to recruit students, Latta used his correspondence to support the students after they had arrived at the university. He was, for all intents and purposes, the person who would serve as a guidance counselor and advisor to the agricultural students. As such he often wrote letters on behalf of his students, including letters of recommendation:

I take pleasure in recommending to your consideration Mr. H. C. Mills, a senior who completes his work here the first week in June. He has had the regular instruction in dairy work, and has made a special study of dairy work this last year, and has taken as the subject for his thesis, "Study of the Moisture Content of Butter." In this work he has done a large amount of churning, using the factory size churn. I believe he has the ability to grow into a good man, able to handle considerable responsibility. He is careful—painstaking in his work, and quick to "catch on." I have asked him to write you.[29]

He was also the person to whom parents could write when they needed information about their child:

Your daughter is well and happy. I think you need feel no alarm. We are taking every precaution to isolate the sick students. No new out-breaks reported. Only two are sick. P.S. Since writing the above this morning, I saw Una at noon. She is looking very well indeed. We feel no alarm here.[30]

In 1893, Professor Latta and his colleague, Charles Plumb, professor of animal industry and dairying, coauthored a handbook titled "Course of Instruction, Equipment and Method of Instruction in the School of Agriculture, Purdue University." Its purpose was to introduce Purdue University and, more particularly, the School of Agriculture to prospective students. By the time this document was written, the School of Agriculture consisted of six faculty members, each holding a special chair. The School of Agriculture had become more organized and better focused all within the span of eleven years since Professor Latta had arrived at Purdue University and taken charge of the department. With this organization came more sophisticated advertising to recruit and attract new students to the school. The Plumb and Latta booklet was such a document:

> The purpose of the following pages is to enlighten the reader concerning the scope and work of the School of Agriculture of Purdue University. Six different persons in this school instruct in studies pertaining to the science and practice of agriculture in its various branches. The special chairs in the Agricultural School are those of (1) Agriculture, (2) Agricultural Science, (3) Horticulture, (4) Veterinary Science, (5) Agricultural Chemistry, and (6) Vegetable Physiology and Pathology.
>
> In the course of instruction, laboratory methods are employed in so far as is practicable, and to a very considerable extent, and these are supplemented by syllabi, lectures and references to literature on the subject. This laboratory work involves instruction in the horticultural grounds, on the farm proper, in the dairy and barns, chemical and botanical laboratories, and veterinary hospital.
>
> The work at the farm is not to be associated with ordinary farm labor; it is strictly educational and involves the principles underlying practical work. In the senior year the student takes up experimental work at the farm, some subject of which may form his thesis work.[31]

In this same booklet, Latta offers a syllabus of instruction in farm drainage. It is likely the only surviving record of Professor Latta's teaching goals for one of his favorite classes. His syllabus describes the purpose of the class, identifies how the course would be taught, and provides an outline of the course. It was clear that the students were expected to do a field project that would help them better learn how the materials taught to them in class could be applied to real-world problems. The teaching methods identified in this publication include the typical recitation from textbooks, lectures, and hands-on work. The syllabus reads as follows:

> *The purpose of the instruction in Farm Drainage is*
> 1. To impart a thorough knowledge of the nature of the subject and its relations to the amelioration and improvement of soils.
> 2. To emphasize the very general need and great importance of drainage in successful farming.

3. To give practical directions which will enable the student to perform or supervise the work of thoroughly, economically, and permanently draining his land.

The instruction includes:
1. Study of a text book, with daily quiz and discussion upon the same;
2. References to other authorities;
3. Supplemental lectures by the Instructor; and
4. Field and laboratory work by the student illustrating many of the details in actual practice.

The general trend and scope of the instruction is set forth in outline in the accompanying syllabus and illustrated by students' drawings and photographs showing students at work in class room and field.

I. Introductory
    1. Definition of drainage
    2. Purpose of artificial drainage
    3. Branches of the subject considered
    4. History of drainage
II. Principles of Drainage
    1. Relation of drainage to the soil
    2. Relation of drainage to rainfall and evaporation
    3. Relation of drainage to expenditure and conservation of energy
    4. Relation of drainage to crops
    5. Relation of sub-drainage to soil fertility
    6. Sanitary relations of drainage
III. Soils That Need to Be Drained
    1. Retentive soils
    2. Lowlands
    3. Slopes and basins
IV. Indications of Need of Drainage
    1. The presence of free water
    2. The condition of the soil
    3. The presence of foreign growths
    4. The appearance of cultivated crops
V. Opened and Covered Drains
    1. Relative merits of each
    2. Conditions governing the use of each
    3. Relation to each other

   VI. Size, Depth, Frequency and Efficiency of Drains
         1. Size of drain
         2. Depth of drain
         3. Frequency of drains
         4. Efficiency of drain
  VII. Location of Drains
         1. Conditions governing
         2. Method of determining
 VIII. Construction of Drains
         1. Best time for doing the work
         2. Order of procedure
         3. Steps of the process
         4. Necessary appliances
         5. Materials to be used
         6. Method of performing the work
   IX. Construction of Farm Sewers
         1. The outlet
         2. The conduit
         3. The upper end
         4. Precautions against discharge of sewer gas into house
    X. Repairing of Drains and Sewers
         1. Evidence of defective working
         2. Locating defect or obstruction
         3. Removal of obstruction
         4. Renewing or reconstructing outlet[32]

Class notes from Almon Mace, a 1901 Purdue graduate who eventually worked with Purdue researchers on regional agricultural research, reveal the practical and fiscal orientation of Latta's courses. For example, when Professor Latta talked about farm fences, he would describe the different types of materials from which fences could be constructed—rail, board, patent wire fence, hedge, and stone. The students would learn about building a fence and how to hang a gate. They were expected to do some problem-solving, too. The "fence problem" required the student to select the materials needed and calculate the costs associated with building a wire fence, a board fence, and a rail fence:

An 80 A[cre] farm divided into 4 20 A[cre] fields. Galvanized barb wire with staples $2.25 per hundred. Posts oak split 10 cents each; stapling and stretching wire at 1.5 cents per panel. Posts two rods apart.

A 160 A[cre] farm divided into 6 fields with 26 2/3 A[cre] in each field. Find cost of five board fence, posts 8 feet apart.[33]

Students were also given quizzes and major examinations. Professor Latta provided examples of test questions he expected his students to answer:

History of Stock: How did the Ayrshire cattle originate? Give a brief sketch of the American Merino in the United States. When, where, and how did the Poland-China breed of swine originate? Give five desirable points of the beef animal? What breed of cattle would you recommend for Indiana: a, for milk; b, for beef; c, for butter; d, for general purpose? Compare the Clydesdale and Percheron-Norman: a, for heavy draft; b, for general farm work?

Veterinary Hygiene: Give five causes of indigestion connected with the care and treatment of the animal. Give preventives of tympany and impaction of the rumen—how to treat each? How to prevent scours in young animals? Give five preventable causes of diseases of the urinary organs. How to locate a lameness?

Farm Management: Give objects of tillage. Give the adaptation of the tillage to the character of the soil. Define "manure," and give three sources of the same. Compare the dung and urine of each class of farm animals. Why is the urine more valuable than the dung weight for weight? How to avoid loss of farm-yard manures? Give eight points on the feeding of farm animals.

Farm Drainage: What soils will it pay to drain? Name five advantages of the tile drain over other kinds. Name three points that will affect the size of the tile. Where is it best to have the "main" branch into two "sub-mains"? Give brief directions for road drainage—for house drainage.

Meteorology: What do fluctuations of the barometer indicate? On what does climate depend? Give the proper exposure of the thermometer. Of what use are the wet and dry bulb thermometers in weather predictions? On what two conditions does the per cent. of humidity depend? Give the relations of dew and cloud to frost and rain.

Farm Management: Name ten points to consider in buying a farm. To what extent should farm buildings be combined? Name ten points to consider in deciding upon the kind and amount of fencing. Name five things to consider in buying farm machinery. Give five points on the care of farm machinery. What things should you consider in deciding whether to sell a crop or feed it to stock?[34]

Professor Latta also liked to give the students practical, hands-on instruction. One of Latta's contributions was a laboratory model on which so-called "evener studies" showed how hitches should be made with different numbers of horses. He used this instruction for more than forty years. He also seemed excited about taking students out of the classroom into the field. [35]

> Care has been taken to supplement and enforce the teaching of the class room with outside instruction, the field crops, experiment plats and stock of the college farm being freely used for this purpose. My aim has constantly been to impress upon the students the true dignity and importance of agriculture, and to assist them to become intelligent, successful farmers.[36]

> Last spring I took the sophomore and freshman agricultural students into the orchard, and did considerable pruning. Each student was provided with pruning tools, and how to do the work in a proper manner. The students appreciated this field instruction, and were benefited by it. There should be ample provision for much more field instruction, which would greatly enhance the practical value of the course of study. [37]

When appropriate he would allow his students to deliver talks on their undergraduate research. In one such case, Professor Latta wrote about a junior who had done research on the Hessian fly:

> One of our junior students, Mr. Taylor Fouts has been invited by Mr. W. G. Vandever, chairman of the Farmers' Institute in your County to attend the first session of the annual Farmers' Institute to be held at Lebanon Feb. 8–9. Mr. Fouts will come to discuss the "Hessian Fly" and as his name is not on the program, I would be glad to have you announce the subject in your paper that the farmers may come to hear him.
>
> Mr. Fouts has been making a study of the Fly and has conducted some interesting experiments to determine the time when the eggs are laid to the greatest numbers and the effectiveness of decoy strips as traps for the insect. Mr. Fouts will present charts showing the Hessian Fly in the various stages of its growth and give some very interesting data obtained in field observations last fall on the Experiment Station Farm. Every wheat grower who hears Mr. Fouts will be interested and will be amply repaid for coming to the opening session. Mr. Fouts is a son of one of Carroll County's best farmers. He is quite young and a very modest young man, but he has a message that wheat growers should hear and heed.

Please make such mention in your paper of the subject as will draw out your farmers in large numbers to the opening session of the Institute.[38]

The earlier agricultural students at Purdue University were required to complete a senior thesis on original research, and their work would have to be accepted by the faculty before they were allowed to graduate. The 1895 catalogs would tell the students that "[e]arly in the Senior year each student is assigned a subject for study and investigation. A minimum time of two hours per week during the winter and spring terms is required for this work, which must be performed under the direction of the instructor in charge."[39] By 1901, that requirement had been increased to a minimum of four hours per week the first semester and six hours per week the second semester. The *Purdue Agriculturist* published the names of the agricultural graduates for June 1907 along with their senior theses:

Earl J. Lowe, Butler, Indiana. An Orchard Survey of Wabash Township, Tippecanoe County, Indiana.

William F. Madaus, Valparaiso, Indiana. Experiments in Testing Butter for Moisture Content: A Study of the Comparative Efficiency of the Existing Methods.

Walter G. Neptune, Thorntown, Indiana. Experiments to Determine Causes of Mottles in Butter.

William H. Klepinger, Lafayette, Indiana. Experiments to Determine the Causes of Mottles in Butter.

Walter E. Joseph, Hayden, Indiana. An Experiment to Determine the Effect of Succulents Upon Pregnant Ewes.

Arra C. Howe, Shelbyville, Indiana. Fitting Swine for Show.

John F. Frain, Winamac, Indiana. Composite Samples vs. Single Samples of Cream: Their Effect on the Accuracy of the Babcock Test Vaccine for Hog Cholera.

Clare N. Arnett, New Richmond, Indiana. Vaccine for Hog Cholera.[40]

The editors noted, "Our seniors, only eight in number it is true, but we feel confident they will make a good showing in the battle of life."[41]

The faculty closely monitored classroom performance. Every student's grades, attendance, and classes taken were reviewed at faculty meetings called to order by the university president.

> Each instructor shall report to the President after each examination the grade of all students examined by him. Each instructor shall report to the President at the close of each month of four weeks, the names of all students in his classes who have unexcused absence or tardiness, or who have failed to maintain the prescribed minimum class standing. He shall also report at the close of each term the attendance and class standing of each student during that term.[42]

Excerpts from the faculty meeting records illustrate the intensive oversight of university and student affairs by the faculty during the first twenty-five years of Purdue University. These records provide an account of how student requests and class attendance were handled by the faculty:

> That, a vote of censure be recorded against [two students] for repeated absence from the recitations in Mechanics last term without permission, and without applying to the President for an excuse.[43]

> The request of [student] to take the subject of Farm Management in the Sophomore Class, was refused. [44]

By 1878, the university had begun to publish rules of conduct for its students to provide moral guidance. By today's standards, the rules laid down by the university were strict:

> Students in the Academy and members of the Freshman class, occupying rooms, are not permitted to visit the city of Lafayette in the evening, except by permission.[45]

> The frequenting or visiting of saloons, or other places where intoxicating liquors are sold, is forbidden, and any student who violates this rule, or becomes intoxicated, may be suspended or expelled from the University.[46]

> Students who desire to be absent from any recitation, or other exercise, are expected to obtain leave of absence. Students absent without previous permission, can only be excused by the President or the Faculty, and they

are permitted to recite but twice in any class before producing a written statement that their absence has been reported to the President.[47]

A few years later, students were required to agree to the following terms prior to being admitted to Purdue University:

As a condition of admission to the University, or any department therein, or of re-entrance, students are required to subscribe to all regulations of the University relating to the obligations and duties of students, and promise a faithful compliance therewith during their connection with the University; that is until dismissed or graduated. The pledge prescribed is as follows: I hereby subscribe to all the regulations of Purdue University which relate to the duties and obligations of students, and I promise on my honor a faithful compliance therewith during the University year ending June, _____, next.[48]

The faculty meeting minutes are full of instances whereby students were dismissed or reprimanded by the faculty and the Purdue president for failing to meet the university's standards of conduct. For example:

[Student] reported for gambling was suspended for remainder of second term. [Student] suspended from University for neglect of class work. [49]

—

Inefficient in work and "boyish" in conduct was temporarily remanded to Preparatory department until such time as he shows himself more of a man.[50]

—

President reported that following seniors were either absent from Baccalaureate service or failed to occupy the assigned seats in either case being guilty of a gross breach of courtesy. . . . By vote of the Faculty a record of censure is hereby made against the above named persons and they are required as a condition precedent to graduation to file with the President suitable apologies for their conduct. The President was authorized to withhold diploma degree from any member of the senior class failing to appear upon Commencement day.[51]

One of the more serious aspects of being a faculty member during this period was participation on committees to investigate students accused of misbehavior. At the May 31, 1883, faculty meeting, Professor Latta was serving on a disciplinary committee to look into the problems between two students. At this meeting it was "resolved that [student] be suspended from the Dormitory for the remainder of the term for keeping firearms in his room."[52] Attached to the minutes was the following disciplinary report:

> *To the Faculty:—*
> Your committee appointed to investigate the [two students'] disturbance beg leave to submit the following report and recommendations. We have investigated the trouble between [the two students] as thoroughly as possible.
>
> *We find*
> 1. That a serious disturbance occurred in room no. 17 of the Dormitory on Thursday night, May 24, and that in the several cases [the first student] assumed the offensive;
>
> 2. From the evidence before us, that the charges against [the second student] are not substantiated;
>
> 3. That we are unable to determine anything in regard to the disappearance of [the first student's] Journal;
>
> 4. That [a third student] has, for some time, kept firearms in his room, and that he played a conspicuous part in the disturbance of Thursday night.
>
> From the facts above set forth, your committee recommend that [the first student and the third student] be deprived of their respective rooms in the Dormitory for the remainder of the year.
>
> Signed by the Committee,
> Goss, Latta, Barnes[53]

During the 1890s, Professor Latta began to share teaching responsibilities with other colleagues. For instance, in 1895, juniors could take a class called Agricultural Physics and Chemistry, which was offered by Latta and Professor Henry A. Huston, who was professor of agricultural chemistry. This course, which ran eight hours per week for thirty-seven weeks, provided students an opportunity to study soil chemistry and fertility.

Latta would also work with the associate professor of engineering design, James A. Hoffman, to teach a class called Farm Buildings, Farm Engineering. It was offered for sophomores who were required to meet three hours per week.

The description of the class indicated it would focus on farm machinery and road construction and repair.

Professor Latta even offered special electives. One such course was the Evolution of Agriculture, available to seniors only. It was described as the "comparative study of the agriculture of different countries, latitudes and climates; agriculture in relation to other industries; conditions of progress in agriculture."[54] This course suggests that Professor Latta was beginning to spend time thinking about more than just agriculture. He was considering farming in the larger context of rural development. The class documents his transitioning interest from agricultural research and education to community development and Extension outreach to farm families.

The year 1888 would be the beginning of a low point in the career of Professor Latta as he became embroiled in a controversy that led him to temporarily sever his ties with Purdue University. Professor Latta's problems started with the creation of the Agricultural Experiment Station at Purdue. In 1887, the United States Congress passed the Hatch Act, which funded and directed the development of agricultural experiment stations in the various land-grant institutions across the country. The establishment of the Purdue University Agricultural Experiment Station in 1888, in response to the Hatch Act, set in motion a series of events that almost left Professor Latta a mere footnote in the university's history.

With the creation of the new station came the need to hire a director to oversee it. This would include all of the responsibilities for conducting research, creating the station bulletins that described the results of the experiments, and disseminating the new findings to the press. After discussing the matter, the trustees assigned President James Smart to form a committee to "negotiate with a competent person to fill said positions."[55] Just weeks later, the committee

> . . . appointed to select a Professor of Agriculture and Director of Experiment Station report that they have secured the services of J. W. Sanborn of the Missouri Agricultural College, at a salary of $2500 and to have the use of the Farm House at a rental of $100 per annum; also a garden patch, and the milk from one cow free of charge.[56]

President Smart informed the press in early 1888 that Jeremiah Sanborn from the Missouri Agricultural College would begin work in June of that year. This news was not likely well received by Purdue insiders, including Professor Latta, who were passed over for the appointment.

Sanborn and Smart began a dialogue that lasted many months concerning what it would take to get Sanborn to come to Purdue. Sanborn demanded that he and not Latta be the professor of agriculture and have control over the Experiment Station's research on field crops as a condition for accepting the administrative position. This created a dilemma for President Smart, for there was no precedent for having two professors of agriculture. If he gave in to Sanborn, then Latta would have to be demoted in title, and if he refused Sanborn's request, his choice for director would likely decline. And Sanborn wanted more from Smart than just mere titles. He wanted to be directly in charge of the field crops research program begun and managed by Professor Latta since 1882. Latta stood to lose prestige, power, and position.

The president decided that enticing Sanborn to accept the directorship of the Agricultural Experiment Station was more important than accommodating Professor Latta. He asked Professor Latta to give up his title of professor of agriculture and to turn over the field crops research to Sanborn. Latta responded by submitting his resignation to President Smart and the Purdue Board of Trustees.

At their April 18, 1888, meeting, the trustees accepted Professor Latta's resignation. They added the following paragraph about Professor Latta into the minutes:

> The resignation of Prof. W. C. Latta as Professor of Agriculture was received and accepted, to take effect July 31st, 1888. The following was unanimously adopted. Resolved, that in accepting the resignation of Professor W. C. Latta we desire to place on record our appreciation of his value as a professor, his character as a gentleman and his industry in his particular field of labor, and in severing his connection with us he will carry with him the best wishes of the Board. The Secretary is directed to forward a copy of this resolution to Professor Latta.[57]

Sanborn, however, in spite of all of the president's concessions, decided to remain at Missouri. Professor Latta was allowed to withdraw his resignation letter.

When arrangements with Sanborn failed, Smart once again turned to an outsider and selected Dr. Horace E. Stockbridge in December 1888 as the director of the Agricultural Experiment Station and professor of agriculture at Purdue University. Stockbridge's appointment put Latta in the same precarious position that previously had led him to submit a letter of resignation.

But Stockbridge had just come back from Japan, where he had worked as a chemist, and he had limited experience with conducting agricultural field experiments. Smart worked to keep Latta on the payroll for an additional six months to give Stockbridge an opportunity to acclimate to his new position. Latta would be instrumental in helping Stockbridge learn what experiments were being conducted, the ins-and-outs of the Experiment Station, the personalities of the researchers, and people in positions outside of Purdue who might be helpful to him.

In a dramatic turn of events, Latta's name was no longer listed as the professor of agriculture in the School of Agriculture in 1889. In fact, his name was conspicuously absent from the faculty listing in that year's *Annual Register*. Instead, the prestigious and very important title of professor of agriculture was transferred to Dr. Stockbridge, the new Experiment Station director. Stockbridge accepted the job of director of the Experiment Station, but he also wanted to be the professor of agriculture. While we will never know what actually transpired, Latta had been in many ways demoted in rank, title, and prestige within the School of Agriculture. He did retain his title as the agriculturist in the Experiment Station under Stockbridge, but more than likely, ex-Professor Latta would once again resign.

But now President Smart faced a political dilemma. Latta had become the face of Purdue agriculture and was Purdue's most publicly visible professor. He had made a reputation for his applied research, his bulletins, and the students in his agricultural classes. He also attended most of the annual meetings of the Indiana State Board of Agriculture, where he was very outspoken. If President Smart allowed or forced Professor Latta to resign, it might cause a revolt in the agricultural community.

It seems that Smart recognized the political consequences of forcing the increasingly popular Latta to resign. Smart decided to change the rules of the game. The problem facing President Smart was that there could not be more than one faculty person with the same title. Thus, an easy fix was to change the title of Director Horace Stockbridge to professor of agricultural science and to make Latta once again the professor of agriculture.

But the silver lining of his reinstatement as professor was accompanied by dark and ominous clouds. Whatever Latta had done to regain his title must have been a battle of wills, but that power struggle where Latta "won" his title did not bring to an end the problem that he would have with Stockbridge. One could argue that being a professor of agricultural science and a professor of agriculture were one in the same. So who would teach the agricultural courses? Who would take charge of the graduate program in the School of Agriculture? Stockbridge decided that he would be the one to teach the agricultural classes that Latta had previously taught. The *Annual Register* listed Professor Stockbridge as the course instructor for Soils, Farm Crops, Farm Management, Farm Economy, Farm Drainage, the Science of Agriculture, and the Principles of Feeding and Dairying. It appears that without the appointment as a faculty member or instructor in the School of Agriculture, Latta for the first time would not teach that year but would instead focus on his research. Is this why Latta was omitted from the 1888–89 *Annual Register?*

In all probability, President Smart would have to once again intercede and decide who would teach which courses. Professor Latta must have been stunned when he was "permitted" to teach only one of his old classes on farm drainage. Stockbridge, on the other hand, kept control of the other agricultural classes that he had previously taught. Stockbridge was also allowed to retain management of the School of Agriculture's graduate program that Professor Latta had previously managed.

Stockbridge resigned his appointment to Purdue on June 1890 to become the first president of North Dakota Agricultural College. Following his departure, Professor Charles Plumb, Latta's longtime friend, assumed the directorship of the Experiment Station. With Stockbridge gone, Latta's professional life stabilized as he once again assumed a major role in teaching and in the management of the School of Agriculture for decades to come.

The year 1900 brought a new president to Purdue. Winthrop E. Stone, who had been raised on a farm, "had deeper attachments to agricultural students—real Purdue students—than others."[58] Consequently, he was concerned about enrollment in the School of Agriculture. The number of students was slowly increasing: 1896–97, 45; 1897–98, 60; 1898–99, 92; 1899–1900, 128. While Stone was encouraged, he also knew the numbers were inflated by enrollment in the popular Winter Short Course.

However, President Stone and the board of trustees spent considerable time worrying about the state of agriculture at Purdue:

The facilities and expenditures per capita of student attendance have always been far greater in the School of Agriculture, both here and elsewhere, than in any of the other schools, and our policy towards the students in that department has always been more liberal. In spite of the fact that this policy has been open to direct criticism and complaint among students and members of the faculty, who would naturally be somewhat partisan in the interest of their own departments, I believe that it has been a wise one. It seems to me to be necessary in this field to aid, develop and educate a public sentiment, whereas in other industries it is only necessary to follow indicated courses of action.[59]

Failure to recruit more agriculture students after all of their work to boost enrollment frustrated both the president and the trustees. The answer to the low enrollment in the School of Agriculture was to spend more money, build new buildings, and hire additional faculty.

It has been for a number of years the policy of the University to make special efforts to induce students to enroll in the agricultural courses. To this end, special courses of study have been offered; the entrance requirements and restrictions upon special students applying to other University schools have been modified for the School of Agriculture; special arrangements have been entered into with county agriculture societies, permitting the granting of free scholarships, so that practically all students of agriculture are exempt from the payment of fees; and probably more effort has been expended to distribute information through the State with regard to the School of Agriculture than for any other department.

Purdue's School of Agriculture, if it expects to lead other schools in the University, must do as they have done in their respective fields, viz., command the attention of the industry by its work and facilities. To do this, it must have the best buildings and equipment, and on a far more extensive scale than at present. It needs a building of modern characteristics, equipped with the best of laboratories for instruction in dairying, soils, stock judging, veterinary hygiene, botany, entomology, and all of the special forms of farm practice. It needs additional instructors; it needs more and better specimens of the breeds of live stock; prominent attention should be given to instruction in those branches of farm and domestic economy of interest to women, a branch of instruction which has as yet been hardly touched upon. In short, the entire plant and equipment of the School of Agriculture should be of a character to inspire the pride and confidence of Indiana farmers.[60]

A 1901 question-and-answer brochure described the agricultural program at Purdue University. It conveys to the agriculture community the value of an agricultural education at Purdue University. Near this time the School of Agriculture consisted of Science and Practice of Agriculture, Horticulture, Entomology, Agricultural Chemistry, Veterinary Science, Dairying, and Animal Husbandry.

What Is the School of Agriculture? The department of the University which gives instruction in the principles and approved practices of Agriculture and in the Sciences relating thereto.

What Agricultural Courses Are Offered? THREE:—A four years' course; a two years' course; and a Winter Course of two terms.

What Is the Purpose of Each Course? The four years' course seeks to impart both a general and technical training, and is the best preparation for both practical and scientific Agricultural pursuits. The two year course seeks to give a good training for practical Agriculture. The Winter Course aims to give instruction in the care, cropping and fertilization of the soil, fruit growing, gardening, farm dairying, commercial butter and cheese making, rearing and feeding live stock, stock judging, plant and animal diseases, farm sanitation, etc.

Who Should Attend the School of Agriculture? Every farmer's son and daughter who expects to follow farming as a vocation, and who wishes to be in the highest degree successful and, also, any who seek training for scientific agriculture, or supervision of large Agricultural enterprises.

What Are the Requirements of Admission? Candidates for the four years' course must possess a good knowledge of English, United States History, Geography, Arithmetic and Algebra, as set forth in the University Catalogue. The requirements for the two years' course are the same as for the regular course referred to above, except Algebra, which is not required. Anyone, not less than sixteen years of age (18 is better), who has a common school education, may enter the Winter Course without examination.

What Is the Cost of Tuition? Tuition is free to Indiana Students. No fees are charged those holding Agricultural Scholarships. Those having no Scholarships pay library, laboratory and other fees, ranging from $27.00 to $36.00 per year, in the two years' and four years' course, and $10.00 per term in the Winter Course.

What Are the Expenses for Board, Room, Books, etc.? These expenses need not exceed $175.00 to $200.00 for the year, or $60.00 per term, for the Winter Course.

How Can Agricultural Scholarship Be Secured? Through the various Farmers' Organizations. Those desiring information should consult the undersigned.

Can Students Earn Any Money While Taking the Course, as a Means of Reducing Expenses? The student has little time for work after giving proper attention to his studies. Some students earn small amounts by doing odd jobs. The farm can furnish but little work, which is given, by preference, to Agricultural students.

Do Those Who Complete the Courses Receive Certificates or Diplomas? Everyone who completes the four years' course in Agriculture, receives a diploma, and the degree of Bachelor of Science in Agriculture [first offered in 1897–98]. A suitable certificate is issued to everyone who completes the two years' course, or the Winter Course.

What Do Graduate and Under-Graduate Students of Agriculture Do After Leaving Purdue? Most of them return to the farm. A number have taken good positions as scientific experts, teachers of Agriculture and Experiment Station workers. Several are creamery managers and many are successfully managing farms of their own, or others.

What Are the Opportunities of Profitable Employment for Agricultural Graduates? We are unable, at the present time, to meet the demand for bright, thoroughly trained, energetic men for positions as superintendents and specialists. This is especially true for the higher positions that command the best salaries.

Does the University Guarantee Positions to Those Who Complete the Required Courses in Agriculture? No, but it cheerfully recommends those who have done the best work, and has been able to place many of the best equipped students in good positions.

What Subjects Are of Especial Interest to the Young Women? Dairying, Horticulture, Floriculture, Domestic Economy, Botany, Household Chemistry, House Sanitation, Rhetoric, Literature, History, Music, and Art.

When Does the Next Term Open? The school year will open September 11th. Examinations will begin September 9th. Those intending to take the regular work can best enter at that time. The next term for the Winter Course will begin January 7th, 1902.

How Can Further Information Relative to the School of Agriculture Be Obtained? By addressing W. E. Stone, President of the University, or W. C. Latta, of the School of Agriculture, Lafayette, Ind.[61]

Professor Latta was now at the peak of his career—on par with President Stone as primary contact regarding enrollment in the School of Agriculture. Professor Latta promoted Purdue by writing news columns about requests by businesses for more college graduates in agriculture:

Perhaps never before in the history of agriculture has there been so urgent and so general a demand for young men especially trained for agricultural pursuits. Certainly never before in the history of Purdue University have so many inquiries come for young men fitted to be farm managers, farm foremen, farm tenants, stockmen, dairymen, agricultural teachers and experimenters. Only one inference can be drawn from the fact that so many of these inquires come to Purdue. It is that men who are engaged in practical agriculture are coming to recognize the importance of the Agricultural College in fitting young men for everyday agricultural pursuits. We are quite unable to supply the demand for these trained young men. First, because so very few young men are seeking adequate and thorough preparation for the positions named. Second, because most of the young men who do come, return to the home farm, and thus find a place waiting for them on completing their work at the Agricultural College.

I wish it were possible for the young men of our good state to recognize the fact that the door of opportunity stands wide open to young men who have the pluck and perseverance to prepare themselves for useful positions in scientific and practical agricultural lines. We are again and again reminded that the young people of the state do not know of the splendid opportunities for preparation which the Indiana Agricultural College affords. It will, therefore, be proper to state again that Purdue University offers several courses in agriculture.[62]

The School of Agriculture was eager to attract more traditional students, i.e., high school graduates, to Purdue agriculture. But in addition to the Winter Short Course, Purdue offered a two-year program for students who could not or did not wish to invest four years in the full degree program. The two-year course, developed in 1895, placed more emphasis on practical studies in a shorter time span.

However, by 1902, the two-year course was falling out of favor with the faculty. The catalog urged prospective students to choose the four-year course instead. Latta himself foreshadowed the demise of the two-year program in a 1901 letter:

> Here-to-fore the requirements for admission to the two year course in Agriculture have not required a knowledge of Algebra or Geometry. In all other respects, the requirements are the same as any of the other four year courses. It is quite likely that the two year course will not be continued as it is of doubtful utility. . . . My advice is, that you prepare to enter the regular four year course as this is the best thing we have to offer in the line of Agricultural Education.[63]

Indeed, by 1907 the two-year course was no longer an option for students seeking an agricultural education. It would cease to be advertised in future catalogs.

⚘ ⚘ ⚘

The year 1907 marked the beginning of one tradition and the end of another. That year, President Stone offered the following recommendations to the board of trustees:

> *1st.* That the branches of instruction in the University be grouped in the following divisions: Engineering, Agriculture, Science and Pharmacy; and that there be a head or dean of each division who shall serve as an executive officer for his division under the immediate direction of the President.

> *2nd.* That the Experiment Station and the Farmers' Institute be regarded as divisions or departments of the University coordinate with the above named divisions of instruction, the heads of the same to have equal rank with the deans.

> I recommend further, that to complete the organization the following appointments be made viz Professor J. H. Skinner, to be dean of the School of Agriculture; Professor Stanley Coulter is the dean of the School of Science, including the departments of English, History, Modern Languages, and Mathematics. Also that Professor Latta, Head Professor

in the School of Agriculture, and at present Superintendent of the Farmers' Institutes be relieved from all formal connection with the School of Agriculture, beyond a minimum teaching assignment, in order to give the major portion of his time to the management of the Farmers' Institutes.[64]

The October 1907 issue of the *Purdue Agriculturist* would also make public the changing of the guard at Purdue University when the fifty-seven-year-old Latta gave up most of his teaching responsibilities—but retained his title, professor of agriculture—to focus more on the heavy demands of an increasingly popular program over which he had management responsibilities, the Farmers' Institutes:

> After many years of strenuous labor, having always the good of Purdue's School of Agriculture at heart, Prof. W. C. Latta has finally resigned in favor of a younger man. Prof. Latta came to us from the Michigan Agricultural College in days when little was thought of an agricultural education. He has seen the gradual growth of our own school and its sudden impetus of later years. He has always worked for our advantage and the best wishes of every student go with him as head of the Farmers' Institute workers of the State.[65]

In the editorial of that same issue were details about the man who would take charge of the School of Agriculture from Professor Latta:

> The coming of a new year has marked several changes in the agricultural faculty. Chief of these changes is the appointment of Prof. J. H. Skinner to succeed Professor W. C. Latta as Dean of the School of Agriculture [while Latta was in charge, he was never officially made dean].
>
> Professor Skinner was born and reared on a farm within twelve miles of Purdue University and first came here as a student in 1893, taking the short course. He then entered the regular course and graduated in 1897. After graduating, Prof. Skinner returned to his home farm and managed it until March, 1899. At that time he accepted a position in Purdue University as assistant in agriculture under Prof. Latta.[66]

John Skinner worked at Purdue until September 1901, when he headed off to the University of Illinois to become an assistant professor in animal husbandry for one year. Latta thought highly of Skinner. In a letter to Professor Thomas L. Lyon of Lincoln, Nebraska, he wrote:

> . . . permit me to say that I consider Mr. J. H. Skinner a very efficient assistant. His work has been chiefly in the Station line. He has however, had

charge of the Laboratory Instruction in Soil Physics and has proved entirely competent to direct classes in this line of work so far as it has developed here. He has also occasionally taken my class room work in my absence and conducted it satisfactorily. He is a man of force, with a strong practical bent. He is also a good student and will I believe, prove highly successful both as a Station worker and Instructor. He is a man of excellent character, steady habits, and has proved a very agreeable, prompt and efficient subordinate officer. With additional experience and the broadening influence that will come from contact with another Institution, he will become, in my judgment, a strong effective man. I believe he is now considering a proposition to go to the Illinois University. I think he will accept a position there. If anything should change his decision, I would of course be open to an offer from your Institution. We should be glad to have him remain with us at least another year, but it is our policy to send our graduates, who desire to engage in Station and College work, elsewhere, as much as we can because we believe that is the best way to insure their larger growth and usefulness.[67]

Skinner returned to Purdue to continue his work in animal husbandry, being promoted to professor of animal husbandry in 1906 and then chosen as the first dean of the School of Agriculture. It must have pleased Latta to read the following comments by Dean Skinner in the January 1908 *Purdue Agriculturist:*

This is a day of exceptional educational opportunities. Never in all of the past has it been so easy to acquire a partial or complete education. In recent times special attention has been given to the practical in education, and now the opportunity is quite as good to get an education for industrial pursuits, as for professional lines of work, and industrial education is proving even more profitable to its possessor than a purely academic training.[68]

It was obvious that Skinner felt Professor Latta had left the agricultural program in a far better position than what he had inherited twenty-five years earlier.

Professor Latta would be listed from 1907 until his death in 1935 as a faculty member in the Department of Agronomy. The only class he continued to teach was the Science and Art of Agriculture. No longer a required course after 1910, it was offered as an elective. Due to a lack of Purdue records, it is unclear how often he actually taught the class, but probably by 1911, he was no longer teaching college classes.

Employment as professor of agriculture at Purdue University during the late nineteenth and early twentieth centuries was not a lucrative endeavor. However, Latta managed a comfortable lifestyle. The Purdue personnel files list the official positions Latta held at Purdue University and the salaries that accompanied those positions:

Year	Title	Regular Salary
1882	Instructor/Farm Superintendent	$1,200
1883	Professor of Agriculture	$1,200
1885	Professor of Agriculture	$1,600
1888	Director of the Experiment Station	$1,600
	Professor of Agriculture	
1889	Agriculturist and Professor of Agriculture	$1,600
1901	Superintendent of Farmers' Institutes	$2,800
	Professor of Agriculture	
1907	Superintendent of Farmers' Institutes	$2,500
	Professor of Agriculture	
1911	Farmers' Institutes, Specialist	$2,000
	Professor of Agriculture	
1924	Consulting Specialist, Farmers' Institutes	$2,000
	Professor of Agriculture	
1930	Consulting Specialist	$2,000
	Professor of Agriculture	
1933	Consulting Specialist	$1,800
	Professor of Agriculture	
1935	Consulting Specialist	$1,800 [69]
	Professor of Agriculture	

Although not recorded in his personnel file, Latta was also appointed as the director of the School of Agriculture in 1895 at an annual salary of $1,800. Purdue University President Smart informed the Purdue Board of Trustees in 1895 that Director Plumb had asked to be relieved of his duties as chief of the School of Agriculture to allow him to focus his attentions on managing the affairs of the Experiment Station, teaching his classes in animal husbandry, and spending more time on his research. The trustees agreed and turned over the directorship of the School of Agriculture to Professor Latta. For a short time in 1883, he had also been in charge of the State Volunteer Weather Service.

At one point, Professor Latta had to make sure that he received what was promised by the board of trustees. He wrote in early 1894 to President Smart:

Permit me to remind you of our promise to recommend an increase in my salary to eighteen hundred dollars for the current year if not inconsistent with any previous action of the Board. You will find upon consulting the secretary's records that the Board ordered the payment of one hundred dollars extra last year on account of Farmers' Institutes. That money was paid wholly from the Institute fund. I have received only the regular salary this year thus far. I would suggest that whatever increase may be decided upon the salary should be apportioned as heretofore—one-third to the University, one-third to the Experiment Station and one-third to Farmers' Institutes—as I believe that is as nearly as I can estimate it, the time given to the several lines of work.[70]

He earned his highest income between the years 1901 and 1907. The most he ever made was $2,800, with $1,800 dollars coming from the proceeds of the Farmers' Institutes and the university picking up the remainder. In fact, for much of his career, the Farmers' Institutes would pay a significant portion of his salary.

A 1914 contract between Purdue University and Professor Latta outlined the terms for his appointment at the university:

Except where appointment is for a specific term, it shall continue from year to year without further notice. Members of the Corps of Instructions are entitled to vacations during the summer months when the University is not in session, but in exceptional cases their services may be required in connection with the needs of their departments during any or all of the period without extra compensation. Members of the Station and Extension staffs are entitled to thirty days annual vacation after one years' service at a time to be mutually agreed upon.[71]

Obviously, Purdue professors did not have tenure at this time. This appointment on a yearly basis is still practiced with the non-tenured Extension staff on campus and the field staff. In addition, university contracts often stated that jobs were linked to the availability of funds from state, federal, and other sources, as well as available income from the Agricultural Extension Department.

By 1911 Latta's salary was reduced to $2,000. The Agricultural Extension Department provided $1,600, and the university lowered its contribution to $400. His salary would eventually drop to $1,800 in his final years at Purdue University. Contracts indicated that war, economic downturns, and reductions in state appropriations caused Purdue staff salary reductions.

During the 1930s, Professor Latta was hired under special conditions by the president of the university. These contracts, titled "Special Appointment Memorandums," all contain very similar language. For example, the memorandum for the fiscal year 1935–36 states:

> The Trustees of the University have confirmed your appointment as Consulting Specialist in the Department of Agricultural Extension for the fiscal year 1935–1936, at an annual salary of $1600.[72]

The contract was footnoted to indicate "$200 ad. Univ in ten installments." In effect, the university would add $200 dollars to what the Department of Extension was paying him.

Professor Latta was frequently passed over for the more visible administrative positions at Purdue. In 1907, President Stone ignored Latta and three other senior members of the Purdue staff—James Troop, Joseph Arthur, and William Goss—and selected John Harrison Skinner for the number one position in the School of Agriculture: dean of agriculture. Four years later those same senior professors were again passed over when President Stone selected Professor George I. Christie to head up the new Department of Agricultural Extension.

There is no record as to why Latta and the others were not selected, nor does Professor Latta express his opinions on the matter in any of his surviving documents. At the time, he was the most senior member of the School of Agriculture, only sixty-one years old, and directing the highly successful Farmers' Institutes. He was the logical choice for the Extension administration position. Was he too old for the position? Had he and Stone had a falling out? Had he not excelled in other administrative positions? Was he too useful to Purdue in his role of superintendent of the Farmers' Institutes? Did he just want to be a full-time superintendent of the Farmers' Institutes? Intriguing questions that today have no answers.

Latta's longevity at Purdue University may also be partially explained by the lack of a pension plan for those working in the university's School of Agriculture. This difficulty originated with activities by the Carnegie Foundation for the Advancement of Teaching. Andrew Carnegie was "concerned by the proliferation of American colleges, declining standards, and inadequate faculty salaries."[73] And clearly, the Carnegie Foundation had its attention focused squarely on improving the agricultural colleges created by the Morrill Act.

The Carnegie Foundation offered a carrot to college administrators: a retirement program in which universities could enroll if the educational institutions agreed to have their schools reviewed and, where appropriate, to change their programs to meet Carnegie standards. President Stone provided details to the board of trustees about the Carnegie plan and urged them to approve it. The Purdue trustees responded favorably.

Purdue's President Stone applied for admission to the Carnegie retirement program in 1909, but his first application was rejected. The foundation responded to Stone that Purdue's admission requirements were weak, e.g., a student needed the equivalent of only two years of high school to be accepted; that the courses being offered in the public schools did not mesh with what was needed to enter college; and that Purdue was not part of any association of colleges.[74]

President Stone was very persuasive in rebutting each charge levied against Purdue. In 1910 the Carnegie Foundation relented and decided to grant Purdue University an opportunity to join its retirement program. However, an unfortunate string was attached to Purdue's eligibility. The stipulation attached to inclusion in the retirement program was "with the exception of the agricultural department."[75]

Stone was faced with a personal and professional dilemma. He had after all worked hard with and taken a personal interest in the faculty members of the agricultural school. But Stone hesitantly agreed for the sake of Purdue University. He hoped that plans for the development of a new Extension department would eventually persuade the Carnegie Foundation to include Purdue's School of Agriculture in the retirement program.

Stone's gamble failed. The foundation never reconsidered its decision, and it was not until the late 1930s that Indiana established a state retirement plan for all employees of Purdue University.

For all practical purposes, Latta's official research, teaching, and Extension duties came to a close in 1924 when, at the age of seventy-four, he relinquished control of the Farmers' Institutes. Without a retirement plan and lacking financial independence meant that he and the other old professors would stay on as long as Purdue allowed them to draw their salary—in essence, they would work for their pensions.

When Professor Latta arrived at Purdue University, classes had only been held for eight years, the entire faculty could be listed on a single page, and the enrollment was about 150 for the whole campus. He would watch the university grow to more than 500 faculty and staff, and more than 5,000 students.

In one sense, his dedicated efforts in attracting more students and working to get additional faculty members led to his own diminishing importance. Time overcame Professor Latta. In the 1880s and 1890s, students were taught by professors who were by necessity generalists. The land-grant schools could not afford to hire many faculty members, and the ones they brought on board had to teach multiple classes addressing diverse disciplines. Textbooks were quite limited, and research was almost nonexistent for agriculture. This is why many of the first hires at Purdue University and other land-grant schools were themselves at one time farmers or managers of university farms. At the time, the university needed educated men who had experience tending fields and livestock. Professor Latta fit the bill nicely for practicality and for his broad knowledge of agriculture.

As these early educational pioneers began their research programs, the amount of scientific and agricultural information began to accumulate. Over time, the generalists were replaced by the specialists. Faculty members such as Professor Latta, educated in all areas of agriculture and farming, became dinosaurs, relegated to the sidelines and supplanted by younger men celebrated for their specialized study. This specialization was noted in the 1907–08 course catalog, which indicated that a student could select a specialized program of study in his or her area of interest—"General Agriculture for those expecting to operate and manage farms; Agronomy for those who desire to fit themselves for special work in soils and crops; Agricultural Chemistry for those who desire to become agricultural chemists; Animal Husbandry, In Dairying, In Horticulture."[76]

But while the generalists lost some prestige at the university as professors, their breadth of knowledge and practical skills would continue to be sought after by the agricultural community through their field work as Extension specialists.

Professor Latta spent his life selling an agricultural degree and Purdue University to the men and women of the farms. Every chance he had, he would advocate the use of education and science as a means of advancing agriculture and talk about the benefits enjoyed by students who enrolled in agricultural courses. Throughout his career, Professor Latta would continue to tell the farming community that Purdue was the place for them. Then he would mobilize these same people into a formidable political force that would support Purdue's requests to the state legislators for additional appropriations for the School of Agriculture.

While Latta's teaching duties ended in 1911, he remained an imposing figure at the university for another quarter century, his considerable energies focused on enhancing the quality of rural life. He would be remembered for his work as a teacher:

> The introduction and development of courses were chiefly the work of one of the early giants—Prof. William Carroll Latta, a White appointee whose contribution to Purdue agriculture was comparable to that made by W. F. M. Goss to Purdue engineering.[77]

Latta's teaching career spanned a period of tremendous change in agricultural education. His pride in having helped guide the university's School of Agriculture into the modern age is apparent in his remarks about Purdue in *Outline History of Indiana Agriculture:*

> In view of the good record made by its former students, may we not regard the product of the Purdue School of Agriculture as the crowning work of the University in behalf of agriculture? In view also of its growing material equipment and the increasing number and efficiency of its teaching staff, may we not rightfully expect that Purdue's School of Agriculture will continue to turn out an unbroken succession of scientific farmers and public-spirited agricultural leaders who will help to put and keep Indiana among the foremost agricultural states of the Union?[78]

The Field Researcher:
Using Science to Answer Agricultural Questions
(1882–1901)

CHAPTER  FOUR

With test-tube, micro-telescope,
Explore new realms, doors wider open:
Thus seeking truth, more surely find
The tracing of the maker's mind.

—William Carroll Latta
from "A New Year Meditation," 1929

INDIANA'S FARMING PIONEERS OF THE 1800s were tough, self-sufficient agriculturists who worked hard to scratch out a living and raise their families on the state's prairies and woodlands. Often miles from the nearest neighbors, they worked long hours only to face the worst that nature could throw at them: droughts, floods, and disease. Life on the frontier was harsh, and it tested the fortitude and perseverance of even the hardiest settlers.

Those pioneers survived by their wits, with a conservative approach to life and a no-nonsense view to whatever challenges they faced. Young men and women learned about raising a family, serving the church, growing a crop, and caring for livestock by watching and learning from their parents. In turn, they broke with tradition by experimenting—through trial and error—to find solutions to life's problems that were better than what previous generations had relied on.

As transportation improved, farmers gained wider contact with experts outside of the community who brought new ideas to the marketplace. Departures from past practices allowed farmers to do things quicker, better, safer, and cheaper.

The late nineteenth and early twentieth centuries were noteworthy for agricultural innovations resulting in improved livestock breeds, better crop selections, increased mechanization, and new pest control practices. For instance, tile draining was not introduced until 1872, crop rotations in 1874, fertilizing in 1894, silos in 1897, alfalfa in 1899, balanced rations in 1901, livestock vaccinations in 1908, and soybeans in 1910. (A more detailed list is found in Appendix 2.)

Each introduction soon led to an avalanche of new products. Ideas came fast and furious in those days as everything from plows to planters were being built and marketed to the farming community. However, unscrupulous peddlers intent only on separating the farmer from his money promoted new practices and products, too. Farmers generally did not have independent means of knowing whether a new technology that they had just bought would actually work or result in a ruined crop or, worse, harm to health.

What farmers lacked at that time was a source of information, independent of the marketplace, that could provide research-based answers to their questions on the variety of products and services that they were being offered. Would they see measurable increases in corn yield to warrant the increased purchase price for commercial fertilizers? What was the best long-term solution for building up the soil: commercial fertilizers or manures? Which insecticides really worked?

Questions such as these encouraged a discussion in agricultural circles on the value of research targeting practical problems in farming. The result was the passage of the Hatch Act in 1887. The Hatch Act—named after Missouri Congressmen William Hatch—provided money to create agricultural experiment stations at land-grant schools. Two important aspects of the Hatch Act were that research, in addition to education, was recognized as an important mission of the land-grant schools, and it was the first time that the federal government would directly appropriate funds to the land-grant universities.

The Hatch Act of 1887 helped land-grant schools expand their research capabilities by hiring more specialized professionals to focus on the variety of challenges that farmers faced. The research component of the state agriculture schools began to prosper and become more effective in impacting farmers' daily lives. Farmers could see that the research being done was practical, effecting savings of time and money.

The Hatch Act was a watershed event for agricultural research at the land-grant schools. Purdue President Smart would remark in 1888 that

> [t]he most important addition to the facilities of Purdue University is the establishment of an experiment station by the United States, with an income of fifteen thousand dollars per annum. The university has been

struggling along for several years, taking money that it could ill afford to spare from the annual appropriations for experimental purposes. It is a remarkable thing that up to the present time the university has been able to do so much experimentation with so little means. This new endowment is the most notable occurrence in the history of the university so far as its relation to agricultural pursuits is concerned.[1]

The new funds provided by the Hatch Act gave President Smart a golden opportunity to fund the farm and its expenses. He outlined his ideas on how the farm would pay for itself and yet provide the kinds of experiments necessary to advance agricultural science in Indiana:

That the Purdue Experiment farm, farm buildings, implements, stock, and all property connected with the old Purdue Experimental Station be and are to the new Experiment Station, provided—

1. That in compensation to the University for the use of whatever farm products beyond what may be needed for the use of the Station and for the proper finding of its stock shall belong to the University, and provided
2. That the farm horses and wagons may be used, when needed, to haul University supplies from the city of Lafayette to the University.

The following rules and regulations for the Experiment Station were after careful consideration adopted:

1. The Purdue Experiment Station is hereby declared to be a Department of Purdue University and is like other Departments under the general control of the President of the University.
2. The Professor of Agriculture of Purdue University is made *ex officio* the Director of the Purdue Experimental Station.
3. The Director and Chiefs of Divisions and Assistants connected with the Station are subject to the same rules as those which cover the members of the Faculty of the University; unless otherwise provided. While they will devote their time to special work in the Station and not to Academic work in the University, they will be expected at all times to assist in every practical way to build up the University as a whole.
4. Heads of Divisions, assistants, and all employees of the Station will be under the immediate supervision of the Director in so far as their Station work is concerned.
5. The moneys, accounts and records of the Station shall be kept separate and distinct from those of the University from and after January 1st, 1888, and the same rules and regulations which now govern the ordering and

purchase of supplies and the auditing, recording and payment of bills
chargeable to the University shall be in full force in regard to the Station.[2]

Purdue research would fill a void and provide answers to farmers' questions, which in turn helped Purdue's recruitment efforts in attracting students to the agricultural program. In later years, it was practical research and acknowledged campus expertise that helped the Extension agent reach out to the farm family. Extension outreach, using university research, played an instrumental role in changing attitudes about Purdue University and helped create a strong, vocal constituency that would aid Purdue administrators in their political battles.

❦ ❦ ❦

While it is tempting to think of the Hatch Act of 1887 as the beginning of agricultural research at the land-grant schools, there were many events preceding its passage that led farmers, agricultural associations, and politicians to rely on Purdue University as their main source of reliable agricultural information. William Latta wrote that those working at Purdue University were nearly a decade ahead of the federal legislation that led to the development of agricultural experiment stations:

> Gradually, by means of the contemporary agricultural and scientific literature, and through comparison and discussion of results obtained by leaders in agricultural production, the need and value of experiment and research in agriculture came to be recognized. Thus step by step the way was paved for systematic field and laboratory investigation in agriculture which was inaugurated at Purdue University eight years prior to the passage by Congress, in 1887, of the so-called Hatch Act which made provision for government Experiment Stations in cooperation with the several states.[3]

Professor Latta wrote about the events he believed triggered others to want a public-supported agricultural college to investigate farm-specific problems. His thoughts on the initiation, development, and progression of agricultural research at Purdue are documented in two unpublished manuscripts. One is a twenty-page, unedited and handwritten manuscript titled "Calendar of Events Preceding and During the Evolution and Growth of the Indiana Agricultural Experiment Station." The other is a forty-two-page, typed document titled "Indiana State Board of Agriculture: A Historical Sketch."

First, Latta argued, the time had to be right for the agricultural community to recognize the need for a college to conduct research on its behalf. Latta concluded that the 1830s and 1840s were too early for such an interest to develop because the farming community "was not then fully awake to the importance of agriculture, and that the actual farmers of Indiana were still too actively occupied in clearing away the forest and equipping their farms to engage in formal organization of the general advancement and improvement of agriculture."[4] Farmers didn't have time to listen to or participate in matters of this sort as they were too busy just trying to eke out a meager living from their farms.

Professor Latta thought the point where agricultural research went from being a nonissue to one of significant importance to farmers had its roots in the onset of county and state fair competitions:

> There was, however, early and repeated legislative provisions in Indiana for the encouragement of agriculture through the competitive production of agriculture and home products, and these contests must have focused the thought of alert and enquiring minds on the problems of improvements through selection of adapted soils, better varieties of crops, better breeds and strains of livestock and better methods of farm and house production.
>
> The holding of an annual fair and thus giving opportunity for the yearly display of agricultural, domestic and mechanical products; the showing of the classes and breeds of improved livestock reflecting the intelligence and skill of successful breeders and feeders; the display of many hundreds of useful and beautiful products of art and applied sciences; all of these varied productions of intelligent human activity presented to the eye in myriad attractive forms, afforded not only pleasing entertainment, but also convincing evidence of progress which proved both inspiration and material incentive to improvement. Doubtless in no other way could have been presented so well the many evidences of advancement in such pleasing and effective form for the enlightenment of the thousands of visitors to the State Fairs.[5]

Latta thought the awards for essays and exhibits helped to encourage more innovations on the farm:

> At this fair [1852] premiums of $25.00 each were awarded respectively on best plan for reclaiming and improving swamp land; for best plan of farm buildings, and for best method of rendering useful the hilly lands of the state. Premiums were also awarded early for best managed farms, for

best crops of corn, wheat, timothy, hay, and potatoes and for garden and orchard products.[6]

But those that excelled at the county or state fair did far more than bring home accolades, blue ribbons, and cash prizes. They also advanced the notion that research at a basic level was important for improving farm life. With the results on display for all to see, competition brought forward new ideas in the best of what was grown in the field, raised on the pasture, or made in the home.

Information shared at the fair was extended from farm to farm as others in the farming community adapted these new ideas to meet their own needs and purposes. This would become the model that Purdue University would use—develop the technique, test it on the farm, train others on how to use it, and then let the farmer apply his own ingenuity to change a good idea into a better one. While issues and technology have changed, today's approach to applied agricultural research and Extension outreach is essentially the same as that used in the early days of Purdue University.

Latta also credited agricultural societies in the 1880s as another important factor in the development of agricultural research at institutions such as Purdue. Local agricultural organizations provided respected farmers, business leaders, and elected officials the opportunity to speak out about the need for agricultural research conducted by an agricultural school for the agricultural community. They challenged farmers with simple messages: manage the farm, avail yourself of the best scientific facts to base decisions on, and make use of farming practices that improve production.

It was inevitable that the question would be raised as to why Indiana needed an agricultural college geared to developing scientific principles about all aspects of farm life. Latta asserted that honest talk and open discussion helped galvanize the farming community around a school and a research mission that did not exist at that time. In his writings, Latta quoted B. F. Morris speaking before the Agricultural Society of Ohio and Switzerland Counties in 1852:

> And that we should have a class of scientific farmers there is an indispensable need for the institution of agricultural school.... We have a soil that ought not be exhausted by unskillful quackery in its tillage; hence, the duty of creating and fostering schools of agriculture where our young men would be qualified to be scientific farmers.[7]

Samuel R. Perkins, who addressed the Marion County Agricultural Society in 1854, was quoted by Professor Latta as saying:

Do you wish to know whether drilling in wheat or sowing it broadcast will be attended by the better crop? Try the experiment.... Do you desire to be certain whether it is better, more profitable, to cultivate less land well or more land slovenly? Try the experiment.[8]

Finally, Latta acknowledged the formation of the Indiana State Board of Agriculture in 1851 by the General Assembly as the defining moment in the evolution of Indiana agricultural research. The board was well organized, held an annual convention, and published an influential annual report. Professor Latta paid tribute to the Indiana State Board of Agriculture as an organization ". . . whose annual meetings for many years were the headquarters for the presentation and exchange of the progressive agricultural thought of the state."[9]

This board brought together politically astute individuals, progressive farmers, and agricultural leaders to discuss the current state of agriculture in Indiana. Speakers would read their written reports, which were recorded, compiled, and published yearly beginning in 1851 and ending in 1907. Each volume contained agricultural information dealing with the changing trends of agriculture, new production techniques, scientific papers, policy recommendations, and legislative proposals.

With a farming public expressing interest in applied agricultural research through participation in county fairs and agricultural associations and the need for agricultural science articulated by the Indiana State Board of Agriculture, the stage was set to establish an agricultural research program at Purdue. And Latta would be there almost from the outset to guide that program to national prominence.

⸙ ⸙ ⸙

To better understand what Latta faced when he arrived at Purdue in August 1882 requires a discussion of the Purdue farm and its management. The farm was located just west and south of the intersection of present-day Russell and State Streets. Professors Latta and Plumb provided a wonderfully detailed description of the Purdue farm in 1893:

There are five buildings on the farm proper. (1) A barn accommodating about 40 head of cattle and suitable for experimental feeding. This is well arranged, and is equipped with the modern tools necessary in a stock barn, such as cutters, grinders, grain bins, engine, scales, a variety of cattle fasteners, stalls, etc. A silo is connected with it and there is ample room for hay and rough fodder. (2) A tool building, especially constructed for the purpose, contains a large assortment of modern agricultural implements, such as plows, harrows, cultivators, mowers, rakes, hay loaders, grain drills, reapers, etc. A room containing a large assortment of small hand tools is also in this building. All tools are arranged in groups in this room, and their use is recorded by a model check system. (3) A large storage barn is arranged for hay and grain above and horses and cattle below. The space for livestock is divided up into box stalls for bulls or calving cows, with a row of horse stalls across one end of the barn. (4) The sheep and pigs are sheltered in a small but conveniently arranged building, which has storage room above, and numerous pens on the first floor. (5) The dairy building is described below.

The FARM consists of about 160 acres, and is divided into two unequal parts by the main highway. It is laid off into a large number of experimental, systematic, rotative plats and fields, in which different methods of cultivation, tillage, fertilization, etc., are in constant trial. Thirty acres are set aside for pasturage. One large block of land is devoted to permanent plat experiments, laid out by survey with iron pipe corners, but the general work of the farm always involves practical experimentation.

The HORTICULTURAL GROUNDS occupy an area of 10 acres devoted to fruits and vegetables.... A large collection of varieties of apples, peaches, apricots, pears, plums, cherries, grapes, currants, gooseberries, black-berries, raspberries, strawberries and other fruits, as well as many kinds of vegetables, come under the observation of the student.

The DAIRY is specially constructed for its purpose, and is a model building of its kind. It contains four rooms, viz: (1) general worker room, (2) milk setting room, (3) cheese room and (4) ice house. This building is fitted with a complete set of dairy utensils, such as DeLaval separator; Polar, Cooley and Mosely & Pritchard creamers; churns, cheese vat and press; butter workers and presses; Babcock and Short fat testers; Boyd cream ripeners, etc.[10]

But the picture-perfect, well-equipped farm described in 1893 was a vast improvement over conditions in the 1880s. In those days the Purdue farm lacked important buildings, good animals, and leadership. For many years, the university trustees vacillated in their position about the role of the Purdue farm in relation to the university. The ebb and flow of opinion on farm management reflected changing concerns about whether it should be operated as a model farm or used for agricultural research and teaching only. Also at issue was,

Who should be responsible for its operation: the Purdue president, the board of trustees, a superintendent, or the professor of agriculture?

In 1874, prior to having a professor of agriculture on campus, a Superintendent Luke A. Burke managed the farm and reported to the board of trustees. Much of what we know today about those first years of the Purdue farm is written in his reports to the trustees. It was obvious that the board of trustees and the president were interested in showing a profit from the farm.

The board members were ecstatic when the farm covered its operational expenses. For instance, the farm superintendent wrote in October 1874 that he had spent $659.77 for labor, harvesting, feed, blacksmithing, threshing, etc. He reported revenue of $1,419.60, resulting in a profit of $759.83:

Source of Revenue	Amount
474 bushels of oats at 40 cents [each]	$182.60
30 bushels of tomatoes at 50 cents [each]	15.00
7 bushels sweet potatoes at $1.00 [each]	7.00
110 bushels potatoes at 90 cents [each]	99.00
500 heads of cabbage at 5 cents [each]	25.00
50 tons of hay, $12.00 [each]	600.00
800 bushels corn, 50 cents[each]	400.00
Pasturage [rent]	91.00 [11]

In 1874, the trustees replaced Superintendent Burke with "a practical farmer" named John W. Haynes of Daviess County. They thought the change would reduce labor and supervision costs, and it seemed to be successful at first. With this new arrangement, the farm turned a profit of $1,000, but with the cyclical nature of farming, profits one year turn to debts in following years. Revenues are dependent on weather conditions and commodity prices. Building repairs, equipment replacement, etc., also determine expenses in any given year. Purdue University tried to offset some of those expenses by relying on gifts and donations. Those who gave were well recognized for their charitable giving and were listed by name in the annual reports.

In 1877, President Emerson White questioned whether the farm should continue to be managed as a model farm with profit as the measure of success or whether it should instead be conducted as an outdoor laboratory for agricultural students. He recognized the changing need to use the Purdue farm as a place to teach students and to conduct research:

As soon as the School of Agriculture is fully organized there will necessarily be a demand on the farm for experiments and illustrations, if not
for practice, under the direction of the Faculty. . . . Hitherto we have been
governed by a desire to make good crops, such as are ordinarily depended
upon in this section of the State. Two motives have led us to follow this
course. The first is, that most farmers must at present confine themselves
to staple crops, and if any advance flows from our management of these
crops to the surrounding country and to the State, its effect will be more
immediately and more widely felt. The second motive is, that experimenting on special and unusual crops is always expensive, and must often be
unsatisfactory. While such experimenting, if properly conducted, would
be expensive to the University, it must be profitable to the State.[12]

Overall, the farm would continue to spend more money the following year
than it earned. The board of trustees decided that something had to change.

The present plan of managing the farm dispenses with a superintendent,
and it was adopted to bring the running expenses of the farm within its
receipts. It is earnestly hoped that the efforts of the Board in this direction
may be successful. For five years past the farm has been a tax upon the
limited income of the University, the deficit being from $1,700 to $1,000
a year. A farm of one hundred and sixty acres of good land, all improved
and under cultivation, ought to pay its running expenses.[13]

The year 1881 was difficult as the corn faced a severe drought and a harsh
winter killed the wheat. The farm was running deep in the red, so "with the
view of securing a wiser management of the farm and a needed improvement
in its condition,"[14] the trustees transferred the management of the farm to the
professor of agriculture.

Professor Ingersoll took over the Purdue farm on March 1, 1882, and found
upon his inspection a neglected and run-down operation. He briefed President
White on his findings, who then informed the board of trustees that the
appearance and management of the farm was unacceptable.

Under Ingersoll's direction, the farm began to show improvement. He was
assisted by Ransom H. McDowell, another former Michigan Agricultural
College employee, who was hired as foreman on March 1, 1882. McDowell,
whose short time at Purdue University overlapped Ingersoll and Latta, would
stay through October of that year before returning to Michigan.

Professor Latta took charge of the farm later that year on August 21, 1882. He described what he had to do on the farm prior to the coming of winter:

> When I assumed control of the farm, August 21, 1882, the work of the season remaining to be done embraced the putting in of fifty acres of wheat (with less than ten acres plowed), the threshing of fifty acres of wheat and oats of previous crop, the harvesting and marketing of about nine acres of heavy sorghum, the cutting of twenty-four and the husking of thirty-four acres of corn. The work as outlined was done in due season, but this involved the employing of a large amount of extra help to assist the regular farm force of only two men.[15]

In December 1882, Latta hired William O. Fritz, also from the Michigan Agricultural College, to replace McDowell as foreman. Latta then reviewed the day-to-day operations of the farm; took an inventory of stock, equipment, and buildings; and described the types of research projects being performed. Managing the farm was a pressure-packed position that required Latta to keep the farm in the black while reporting his efforts to numerous parties with differing interests.

After assessing the status of the farm, Latta compiled his findings. In a report called the "Supplementary Report of the Agricultural Department," he expressed the need to continue the experiments started by Ingersoll:

> The experimental work of the department has been carried forward in accordance with the plans projected by Prof. Ingersoll. It will be the aim of the department to continue every experiment begun, until satisfactory results can be reached. And, as far as means and facilities will permit, the department is desirous to conduct such other field and feeding experiments as will further the interest of Agriculture in the State.[16]

He judged the land to be in "fair, but not high condition"[17] overall and reported that the buildings were deteriorating and in need of great repair or replacement. He summarized the immediate needs of the farm as: one good horse, suitable for general farm work; an increase in the stock; a mowing machine; two heavy harrows; a power feed-cutter; and fence repairs. He also recommended increasing the number of cattle, purchasing a pair of registered Poland-China pigs, and moving the piggery. He wanted to build cattle stalls and a small silo, and he recommended a six-course rotation when it came to planting crops.

A year later, in 1883, Latta had become the professor of agriculture in addition to the farm superintendent. The trustees had given him full control and responsibility for managing the farm. He wrote an update to his initial report on the status of the farm. After a year at Purdue, he had a better handle on the farm's needs.

The Purdue farm now consisted of:

- 82 acres of wheat yielding 11 bushels per acre
- 22 acres of oats yielding 46 bushels per acre
- 27 acres of corn yielding 40 bushels per acre
- 20 acres of meadows yielding 2$^1/_3$ tons of hay per acre, and
- 20 acres of pasture, which supported 10 head of cattle.

The farm was earning $1.08 to $1.15 per bushel for wheat, 75 cents per bushel for seed corn, and 42 cents per bushel for corn.[18]

An important contribution that Professor Latta made in his second report was establishing a vision for the farm's success. As the farm superintendent, Latta brought structure and organization, and set goals for the farm:

> The farm needs to be stocked to its fullest capacity with improved cattle and swine, at least. The livestock now upon the farm is not sufficient to consume all the rough feed produced. As a result, a large amount of coarse feed must be sold at prices hardly sufficient to pay the cost of handling. In this way the farm is annually being stripped of its fertility, much of which might be retained by keeping more livestock.
>
> The farm will hereafter be devoted more to the growing of pure and improved grains for the benefit of the farming classes. It will also be used to a considerable extent as a means of illustrating and enforcing the classroom instruction of the agricultural students. The farm will also be used to conduct such field experiments as require more space than the experimental field affords. Such feeding experiments, also, as our limited facilities will permit, will be conducted on the farm during the winter months.[19]

By 1884 Professor Latta was already trying to convince President Smart to operate the Purdue farm for field experimentation and classroom instruction rather than manage it as a profit center. President Smart's written remarks on the subject are so detailed as to suggest that Professor Latta helped with its composition:

I am in the opinion that the experimental work [of the farm] should be largely increased; indeed the chief value of a college farm will be realized only when the larger part of it is used for experimental purposes. It is not the business of the State to manage a farm as a money-making scheme; such a purpose is entirely foreign to the end for which Purdue University was established. If the Purdue farm can not be used for other purposes, it should be sold or rented. A farm attached to an agricultural college can be made to justify its maintenance in two ways:

First, it may be used for purely educational purposes and for the benefit of the students of agriculture within the Institution. If this purpose is realized, it must have its model granaries, store houses, stock barn, piggery, and its model implement house. These should be provided with facilities for conducting a great variety of experiments, and with appliances for illustrating the instruction given in the class-room. For the purpose of illustration and comparison, a greater variety of the different breeds of stock must be kept than would be found in the herd of a farmer whose chief purpose is to make money. So, also a greater variety of farm implements is necessary than would be used by an ordinary farmer; indeed, the implement house should be a museum of farm implements and machinery. A college farm managed upon a purely financial basis will not afford the best facilities for the instruction of students. It is therefore useless to expect that a college farm managed chiefly for the purpose of educating students will yield large financial results.

Secondly, another very important use for a college farm is in experimental work, done not for the students chiefly, but for the benefit of the large body of people in the State who are engaged in agricultural pursuits.

We must experiment with seeds and try to find out the best methods of seeding. We must experiment in regard to the adaptability of soils to the various crops and in regard to crop rotation, the use of fertilizers and the gathering, curing and preservation of farm products. We must experiment upon the best methods of feeding and taking care of stock. We must also make very careful investigations for the purpose of including the best means of preventing the enormous destruction of crops by insects and fungi.

Now a farmer can hardly afford to experiment on a very extensive scale. Experiment implies failure; it often involves nine failures to one success. It also implies a microscope and a laboratory, hence also a considerable outlay of money.

While we shall manage the Experiment Farm with as much economy as possible, we shall manage it first for educational purposes, and secondly for the purpose of making valuable experiments. In accordance with the direction of the Board, the distinction between the farm and the Experiment Station will be abolished after July 1, 1884, and the two will be called the Experimental Farm. A much larger part of the farm will hereafter be used for experimental purposes, and the part not so used, will be kept in good condition and made as profitable as possible.[20]

President Smart's comments to the board of trustees were clear. The farm would be managed for education, research, and then profits, in that order—a different tactic than had previously been taken by Purdue administrators.

President Smart used the word "experiment" frequently in his text. The concept of creating an experimental station became fashionable early in Purdue's history. At the September 5, 1879, meeting of the trustees, they directed the president of the board of trustees, the president of the institution, and the professor of agriculture and horticulture to make the experimental field a reality:

An experimental field of ten acres has been surveyed, platted, and a portion put under experimental cultivation. It is proposed to make this field an "agricultural laboratory," where accurate and valuable experiments can be made on a scale that will not overburden our resources. The experiment begun two years ago on the farm, to determine the proper amount of seed wheat to the acre, was not, it is feared, conducted with sufficient care to make the result very reliable. It was repeated last year in the same field, but owing to a change in the management of the farm, the information necessary to determine the result was not obtained. I must reaffirm the conviction, deepened by wider observation and experience, that experiments in agriculture must be made under the supervision of a scientific man, who knows the conditions and limits of an experiment and the value of the results reached.[21]

Today a commemorative plaque at the site of the first Purdue experimental plots is attached to a boulder on the southwest side of Stewart Center on the West Lafayette campus. The original research plots occupied the ground where Stewart Center and the Memorial Union stand today. Professor Latta described the original experimental plots as a

ten acre plat for field experiments laid out on the north side of State Street where Fowler Hall, the library, and the Memorial Union Building now stand. As this series was later abandoned since its continued use could not be assumed and as the conditions of the experiments therein started were not very uniform further mention is unnecessary.[22]

Professor Ingersoll moved the experimental plots from the north side of the street to a location near the current Agricultural Administration Building.

> In the early part of 1880 a second series of plats was laid out on the south side of State Street just west of what is now Marsteller Street. The diagram of this plat appears on page 39 of Prof. Ingersoll's report for 1880 which also gives an account of the experiments started on the plats.[23]

With the construction of Agricultural Hall in 1881, Professor Ingersoll would once again relocate the plots, but they remained in the same general area. The Agricultural Hall occupied the site directly in front of the current Agricultural Administration Building. In 1888, Professor Latta also had to move the long-term experimental plots—he referred to them as plats—to section 5, which was in the vicinity of today's Pfendler Hall and Smith Hall. The Purdue farm was due west of the experimental plots.

Professor Latta offered a detailed description of his plots in the 1888 annual report for the Experiment Station:

> Early in September, 1888, about twelve acres were laid out in plats in field No. 5, which lies just west of the present experiment field. The plats are laid out with interspaces and surrounding borders so that each one is isolated from the others. Each plat is $14^2/3$ feet wide by 297 feet long, and contains exactly one-tenth acre. The interspaces are just half the width, and hence, half the area of the plats. To secure permanence of location a piece of galvanized iron pipe, four feet long, was driven almost its entire length into the ground at each corner of every plat. The plats were staked off in sets of five or seven—with one exception to be mentioned—and each set is surrounded by a border $7^1/3$ feet wide along the ends, and $14^2/3$ feet wide along the sides of the set. Outside the border is a driveway extending entirely around each set of plats. The design is to devote to crops, not only the plats, but the interspaces and surrounding borders as well, so that no plat will have any outside exposure. The driveways will give access to, and permit work upon, any set of plats without disturbing any other set. Owing to the small size of the sets, it will be possible to perform the operation of planting or cultivating, or harvesting or weighting, etc., on all the plats of a set in a single day, which will largely eliminate variations in results due to difference in time of treating the plats. The

purpose is to devote eight sets, comprising fifty-two plats, to tests of various systems of cropping with and without manures, in order to demonstrate and illustrate the effects of good and bad methods of farming on soil, and on quality and yield of crops. From one set of plats, soil samples for analysis were taken to the depth of over four feet in September, 1888.[24]

Those studying agriculture at Purdue University would hear about Latta's long-term plots into the late 1930s, even though they were no longer in existence by then.

Professor Latta's work in setting up these early research plots was highlighted in the board of trustees records of the late 1930s, where he was recognized for his "foresight and wisdom" for advocating the need to conduct long-term agricultural research at the university. He was given further due during the seventy-fifth anniversary of Purdue, when he was acknowledged as the first to use experimental plots at the university. [25]

Professor Latta was provided an office on the northwest side of Agricultural Hall. The 1881 Purdue *Annual Register* gives more details about the first building that was dedicated to the agricultural faculty:

> The "Agricultural Hall" is a new building, designed for use in connection with the experimental work of the University, and is an important addition to its working appliances in agriculture. The main part is 44 by 32 feet, and contains on the lower floor a seed room, a tool room, a convenient office, where are kept the indoor meteorological instruments, and a room for a museum of agricultural, horticultural, and forestry products. The second floor contains a finely lighted and conveniently arranged class room for the use of the Agricultural class, a room for work in Comparative Anatomy, and one for the person in charge of the building and the instruments. In the rear is a large store room, 56 by 24 feet, with drive-way, in which is located a pair of scales for the accurate weighting of the products of experimental plats. The remainder is divided into compartments for the storage of these products until threshed, and weighed again as grain, etc. The whole is plainly but substantially built, and is surmounted by deck and balustrade, which reached by a stairway, makes a good place for mounting the instruments exposed to wind and rain.[26]

In addition to the museum, Agricultural Hall also contained a library that consisted of approximately 1,000 books and 75 periodicals. The 1899 Purdue *Debris* said, "Here one may find almost everything discussed . . . [27] These resources were important research tools for the students and faculty.

Eventually, the original Agricultural Hall became too crowded to function well, so it was remodeled in 1888. But despite the renovations, Agricultural Hall began to develop serious structural problems. A new building was needed, and Professor Latta, embarrassed by the lack of facilities, pushed for additional space:

> The arrangement of the buildings here is perhaps unfortunate in that it tends to give a wrong impression as to the relative equipment in the several courses. The buildings on the south side of the road are wholly devoted to agriculture. All the general subjects—including mathematics, English, history, etc.—in all the courses are taught on the north side of the road and the buildings and appliances for this purpose are of course located there. It happens, too, that the appliances and buildings for the Science and Engineering Courses—of which there are four—are also located on the north side of the road. Massing these all together as against the buildings devoted to agriculture makes them seem large and appear to over-shadow the buildings devoted to agriculture.[28]

He worked with President Stone in helping to design a new building that would become the second Agricultural Hall in 1902—renamed in later years as Entomology Hall and more recently as Pfendler Hall. Latta made the claim that it was the ultramodern and spacious second Agricultural Hall that marked the real beginning of the growth of the School of Agriculture. The building itself would become a landmark at the center of the agricultural campus that set the School of Agriculture apart from the other disciplines.

🌾🌾🌾

Latta kept a field notebook where he would write down his research observations. He addressed questions that agronomists still ask today: Which varieties are best, how deep and how far apart should seeds be planted, what are the optimum seeding rates per acre, when is the best time to plant and harvest, and how much fertilizer does the crop actually need? While in later years he focused more on corn and wheat, in the first few years his research interests were quite varied. In 1882, for example, he wrote in the annual report:

The Black Mexican sweet corn was tried and was found to be excellent. Some seed of Egyptian early sweet corn, sent from Washington, D.C., was tried, and produced very fine samples of early garden corn. It was sweet and very tender. The Durra, or Egyptian rice corn, was tried a second time, as a forage plant, and showed that it had remarkable qualities to withstand drought. It remained green when all else was dried up. The seeds are excellent for poultry.[29]

For a few years, he kept his promise to the board of trustees to conduct feeding trials during the winter months. One feeding study in 1883 involved feeding cane-seed meal to dairy cows and pigs. He fed different rations and slowly changed the percentage of cane-seed in the mixture. Latta measured milk output and weight gain. He concluded that cane seed had a food value.

But the hallmark of Latta's research would be his wheat studies. In 1888, the director of the Experiment Station wrote of Latta's successful wheat experiments in the university's annual report, noting that he had improved cultivation, provided better crop protection, and determined interactions between wheat and other crops.

The Experiment Station's annual report for 1889 included the following complimentary letter from the assistant secretary of the U.S. Department of Agriculture:

> In our investigations relating to wheat, its culture, etc., there are no more satisfactory experiments than those of the Indiana Station. I am much pleased with your work. Have you any suggestions to make with reference to varieties that we should purchase for general distribution? Are any of the varieties, tested by you, in your judgment worthy of such purchase? If so, will you please indicate which ones and from whom we may be able to purchase the seed?[30]

A further evidence of the confidence in Latta's early experimental work with wheat was later shown when the U.S. Department of Agriculture purchased the station's supply of Velvet Chaff. In 1894, Professor Latta was even asked by Rand, McNally & Company to write a textbook on the production of wheat, but he declined due to his workload at that time.

Professor Latta's experiments covered the gamut of applied agronomic research, including farm economics. The research topics that he found most interesting included:

Wheat Experiments
  Comparison of wheat varieties
  Seeding rates per acre
  Early and late seeding
  Broadcast versus drill seeding
  Rolling after seeding
  Wheat cultivation
  Mulching wheat for winter protection
  Harrowing wheat
  Agronomic characteristics of varieties
  Large seed versus small seed
  Commercial fertilizers and stable manure
  Evaluating grain testers used by millers in grading wheat
  Treatment of seed to prevent loose smut
  Effect of change of soil on yield
  Mowing in spring to prevent too rank growth
  Early and late harvesting
  Continuous wheat growing with and without fertilizers
  Depth of plowing

Corn Experiments
  Variety trials
  Types and rates of fertilizers, including manure
  Marketability
  Planting rate
  Harrowing versus ordinary cultivation
  Germination of early gathered seed corn
  Deep and shallow plowing
  Effects of previous manuring on yields
  Early and late planting
  Differences between corn cultivators
  Thick and thin planting
  Evaluation of corn cultivators
  Maturity studies based on early and late-planted corn
  Hill and drill planting

Oat Experiments
  Rates of seeding
  Broadcast and drill seeding
  Variety trials
  Rates and timing of fertilizer applications
  Effects of previous manuring on yields
  Early and late planting

Barley Experiments
  Commercial fertilizers and manure applications

Crop Rotation Experiments
  Continuous grain growing versus rotation cropping
  Intercropping studies[31]

Field studies such as those conducted by Professor Latta require tremendous time to plan, implement, and analyze. Most of all, they require constant attention, which would have meant that Latta must have been pressed for time to teach his college classes and conduct his field research program. In an 1892 Experiment Station bulletin, he credited the farm foreman, W. F. Cash, for his assistance, but in April 1892, he again mentioned having insufficient time to fulfill all of his obligations. He was, by then, also engrossed with the demands of the Farmers' Institutes:

> Owing to pressure of other duties, the experiments with common field corn at this Station have not been reported in bulletin form since the spring of 1889. It seems proper, therefore, to give at this time a brief resume of the more important experiments in this line to date. Only a brief statement of facts will be given, as the writer is still too busily engaged with other duties to attempt a discussion of the results obtained.[32]

From this point forward, Purdue University would hire agricultural assistants to help Professor Latta conduct his research. Many of his assistants were Purdue graduates themselves who were familiar with field experiments. His assistants included George R. Ives; Samuel P. Caruthers; William B. Anderson; John H. Skinner, who would later become Purdue's dean of agriculture; Alfred T. Wiancko; and Martin L. Fisher. They undoubtedly did much of the legwork in maintaining the plots and collecting data while Latta taught classes and, in later years, conducted Extension workshops. In a few instances, the assistants would share authorship with Professor Latta on the bulletins. Many would become well known as scientists, professors, Extension specialists, and university administrators in their own right.

From the very beginning of his career at Purdue, Professor Latta worked to disseminate his research findings by speaking to farmers and writing articles for the agricultural press:

> In addition to my regular work as instructor, I prepared a paper for the annual meeting of the State Horticultural Society, and delivered an address before the State Board of Agriculture. I have also written for the *Indiana Farmer* several papers embodying the results of field experiments at the University. This labor, though undertaken under pressure of other duties, was most cheerfully performed with the design of more fully acquainting the farmers and horticulturists of the State with the work being done at the Agricultural College for their special benefit.[33]

He also published twenty articles in technical and scientific journals and magazines.

For all intents and purposes, success of research conducted by the School of Agriculture was measured by the demand for Experiment Station bulletins. The bulletins were mailed to thousands of Indiana farmers who requested them.

> These bulletins have been issued from time to time, and the demand for them has been much greater than the supply. Nine hundred copies of one of them have been called for by the people of one county alone. This demand could not be met, because the edition was limited to 3,000 copies. The question is sometimes asked, "What is Purdue doing in the interest of agriculture and horticulture?" If these bulletins could be spread broadcast throughout the State, that question would receive its satisfactory answer. If our experimental work could be enlarged and adequate means provided for the thorough distribution of the results, I believe that Purdue would be worth ten times its cost to the State.[34]

Bulletin information throughout the 1880s and into the early 1900s would have been cutting-edge science. There were a total of eighty-eight Experiment Station bulletins published by the time Professor Latta wrote his last research summary for the May 1901 issue. Overall, he contributed his name and research findings to twenty-five of them. (See Appendix 3 for a list of these publications.)

The research results in Professor Latta's bulletins provide unique opportunities to see what was taking place during that era. Quoted here are interesting tidbits from the bulletins he authored, which allow us a better understanding of agriculture just before and immediately after 1900:

> The corn for germination for this experiment was gathered from the field crop in two ways: (1) picked and hung up to dry, and (2) cut and shocked in the field. The picked lots were each hung by the fire for one week, after which they were hung in an open loft. To prevent excessive molding of the shock corn, two days were allowed to elapse between the cutting of the central and outer portions of each shock. I venture the assertion that good seed can be obtained every year from the late varieties by gathering the corn early and curing it thoroughly. (Bulletin 6, 1886)

> These fertilizers cost from $25 to $35 per ton, and 200 to 300 pounds is required to the acre. This means an outlay of $2.50 to $5.00 per acre, without counting the cost of applying the fertilizer. It is easy to see, therefore, that when wheat sells at seventy to eighty cents, an increase of two to six bushels per acre will not pay expenses. It may be urged that commercial fertilizer also improves the quality of the crop. This is doubtless true in many cases, but there has been no observable difference as to quality of grain in the experiments on the college farm. (Bulletin 12, 1887)

> Rotation of crops is the most feasible and most effective preventive of insect ravages. There have been no serious insect depredations on the crops of the college farm since the writer took charge of it in 1882. A judicious crop rotation equalizes the demands on the land, prevents mixing of crops, increases the yields, provides a variety of feeds for live stock, and is thus a means of maintaining the fertility of the soil. (Bulletin 14, 1888)

> Our various experiments with commercial fertilizer have not given results favorable to their use in central and northern Indiana. Fertilizers have, however, given satisfaction in the south part of the State, and their use on all thin and worn soils, when home-made manures are not available, is to be commended. (Bulletin 16, 1888)

> Stable manure has had a more marked effect than commercial fertilizers on the yield of crops at the Experiment Station. Being a complete manure, it will benefit all classes of soils that need to be enriched. It

should never be wasted, and whenever it can be cheaply obtained in towns or cities its use will prove profitable. (Bulletin 23, 1889)

— —

Select a hardy, prolific wheat, adapted to your soil, and *stick to it* [Latta's emphasis]. Give it good treatment and it will *not* "run out" [Latta's emphasis]. Sow not less than six pecks of sound seed to the acre. (Bulletin 27, 1889)

— —

Adopt a rotation of crops suited to your soil and needs. It will (1) increase the yield and improve the quality of your crops; (2) enable you to take better care of your live stock; (3) prevent serious insect depredations and fungus diseases; (4) improve your soil and make it more lasting, and (5) put money in your pocket. (Bulletin 27, 1889)

— —

The destruction of the smut spores is easily effected, and every farmer who has smutted wheat, should at least treat two or three bushels to insure an abundance of pure seed next year. The copper sulphate or "blue stone" process and the "hot water" method . . . were both tried on oat seed last spring with entirely satisfactory results in destroying the smut. The latter method is preferred as it does not retard germination. (Bulletin 32, 1890)

— —

Sow [wheat] neither very early nor very late, but at a medium date—about September 20th in central Indiana, one or two weeks earlier in the north part of the state, and as much later in the southern portion. (Bulletin 36, 1891)

— —

The implements that have been under trial as corn cultivators are
1. Albion cultivator, a two-horse implement, with five spring teeth in each gang.
2. Gopher, a two-horse implement, with two wide shovels, or blades, in each gang to set as to merely shave the surface of the ground, and scrape the soil alternately to and from the rows.
3. Harrow, a one-horse adjustable tool with numerous vertical spike teeth.
4. Planet, Jr., a one-horse adjustable garden tool, with numerous small shovels and an attachment for leveling the soil.
5. Corn plow, the earlier form of two-horse corn cultivator, with two pointed shovels in each gang.

6. Rock Island disk cultivator, with three disks in each gang, set to throw the soil to the rows. (Bulletin 39, 1892)

———

The best yields of corn have been produced from the earliest planting—May 1st. As a rule the yield of corn has been proportionate to the thickness of stand, but size of the ear has been reduced by thick planting. It is advisable, therefore, to plant thickly for silage, while a medium stand will prove more satisfactory if the crop is to be husked. Better yields of corn have been obtained from plowing eight inches deep than from any less depth. Considerably better yields of corn have been produced by growing this crop in rotation with other crops than by growing corn every year on the same land. The average increases in yield of corn from rotative cropping is over sixteen per cent. The good effects of fertilization [to corn] are curtailed in both dry and wet seasons because, in the first case, the added fertility does not readily become available, and in the second case it is either partly washed out of the soil, or it produces a too rank—and consequently—unprofitable growth. (Bulletin 50, 1894)

———

Experiments have shown that a dozen years of constant cropping will not fully exhaust a liberal application of horse manure. (Bulletin 64, 1897)

In Bulletin 2, *Experiments with Nitrogenous, Phosphates and Other Fertilizers*, Latta indicated that the research was "conducted at the Indiana Agricultural College." It would be Bulletin 13 before the "Indiana Agricultural College" designation was removed and the cover page would read "Purdue University Bulletin of the Agricultural Experiment Station of Indiana."

In *Experiments with Nitrogenous, Phosphates and Other Fertilizers*, Professor Latta described the results of experiments that Professor Ingersoll had initiated and that Latta had continued. Latta's recommendations offer a rare glimpse of his research philosophy. His conclusions reveal a man not afraid of taking a stand:

The following conclusions will apply more strictly to those portions of the State having soil and climatic conditions similar to those of the college Experiment Farm:

1. In most cases the immediate effect of commercial fertilizers on soils like that of the Experiment Farm will not repay the cost of using the fertilizer.

2. On such soils, the profits from using commercial fertilizers will depend largely upon their effect on subsequent crops.

3. At the present prices of commercial fertilizers and farm products, an increase in the yield per acre of ten bushels of corn, oats or potatoes, or of five bushels of wheat, will not repay the cost of using 200 pounds or more per acre of such fertilizer.

4. At present prices, it is doubtful, at least, whether commercial fertilizers can be used at a profit on half-worn soils similar to that of the College farm.

5. The fertility of farms that will produce grass and clover can doubtless be maintained and improved more profitably by a judicious system of farming and stock raising than by the intensive use of commercial fertilizers.[35]

By the time he published Bulletin 4 in 1885, he was not only testing forty-one wheat varieties on small plots that measured 55 feet by 1.8 feet, but he had also learned the need to test the varieties on larger plots:

> In order to determine more accurately the relative merits of the more promising wheats, those which gave the best results on the college farm in 1884 were sown in large quantities last fall on plats of one-half to three-fourths acre each. These plats extend entirely across the field, side by side.[36]

He would revisit the issue of plot size time and time again in other bulletins that followed as he tried to obtain results that farmers would be able to replicate. He must have been sensitive to farmers' criticisms:

> I desire to remind the farmers of the State that the facts of this bulletin have been developed under farm conditions. *Farm* and not *garden* methods [Latta's emphasis] have been employed. With the exception of the harrowing and mulching before referred to, every operation has been performed with the ordinary farm implements. The aim has been, not to produce phenomenal yields, but rather to show what good farming can accomplish on average soils throughout the State.[37]

On one hand, Professor Latta did his best to promote his research results as relevant to farmers, stating:

> I do not claim that the results obtained here can be duplicated exactly elsewhere, as the endless variations of soil and climate render this simply impossible. But I do claim, however, that, with the best management, a large proportion of Indiana farmers could easily accomplish more than has been done here. In other words, the results of agricultural experiments

conducted on the college farm, indicate—not the certainties, but—the reasonable probabilities in agriculture, under similar conditions, elsewhere in the State.[38]

But Latta believed that definitive conclusions from any research project would only emerge after many years of work, so he also expressed concern that farmers would too quickly change how they operated based on Purdue research:

> The common experience and most successful practice of the past should be our guide for the present; but let us encourage on every hand, *careful, exact, repeated* experiments [Latta's emphasis], in order that we may attain a more definite knowledge to guide us in all our farming operations.[39]

He used the bulletins to share his research results, all the while cautioning farmers to use his information with discretion. He advised farmers to set up their own small-scale experiments to see how ideas would work on their farms. In fact, he remarked, "The chief value of this bulletin, I think lies (1) in the hints it gives as to methods of conducting reliable field experiments, and (2) in the evidence it affords of the great influence of surrounding conditions on crop production."[40]

At first, Professor Latta was uncomfortable telling the farmer how his results at Purdue would apply to farms in other regions of the state. His concern in the early years seemed to stem from his failure to achieve significant increases in production. In 1885, he informed his readers that "to get marked results from the use of commercial fertilizers on the College Experiment Farm, it was decided last fall to test a single fertilizer on wheat in various parts of the state."[41] It would mark the beginning of on-farm field trials to test various hypotheses around the state.

After that, he instituted a number of research projects throughout Indiana to see how crops responded to local growing conditions, farming practices, and soil conditions. And he began to recruit farmers throughout the state to conduct experiments on their own farms on behalf of Purdue. One of his cooperators was his brother, James Latta, who farmed in Noble County in northeastern Indiana. James volunteered to test ammoniated phosphate on corn, and he would remain a cooperator for a number of years.

Professor Latta singled out two of his cooperators in 1885, touting W. J. Quick, who helped Latta form the American Shropshire Registry Association, and W. S. Ratliff as Purdue graduates. This was an astute move by Professor Latta. By highlighting these men among his cooperators, he used name recognition as a means of selling agricultural research and Purdue University. He was telling the readers of his bulletins that prominent alumni were interested in participating in research and using the results.

James Latta and the other growers volunteered their time, but they were told "that the fruit-trees, shrubs and plants of various kinds, sent out for trial, shall become the property of the experimenter, upon his complying with the conditions necessary to the success of experimental work."[42] They would have to sign contracts that outlined the conditions of the work, the handling of plants, and the reporting of results.

The early Purdue researchers went to great lengths to ensure that each farmer who agreed to help test their ideas was doing everything according to a written plan. Each farmer was given a detailed plot map with specific instructions on how to put the experiments in the field, the procedures for managing the crop, and the types of records to keep, because consistency among the field cooperators was an extremely important research element. Instructions for a series of fertilizer experiments conducted in 1905 read:

Series A-Corn
1. Apply manure to manured plots as shown on blue print shortly before plowing in spring.
2. Plow ground and prepare seed-bed as ordinarily for a good crop.
3. Record dates of plowing and planting.
4. Use good seed of a standard variety and plant at the rate of 3 to 4 kernels per hill in hills 3' 6" x 3' 6", putting 4 rows on each plot and 1 row on the space between plots.
5. Thin to 2 stalks per hill when corn is about 5 to 6 inches high.
6. Cultivate and tend the growing crop according to approved methods and be sure to treat all plots in the series alike.
7. Make a record of the stand of plants per hill before cutting the corn and calculate and record the per cent of a full stand for each plot.
8. Cut and shock the corn as soon as ripe. Record date.
9. At husking time weigh the shocks or total produce on each plot, husk and weigh the ear corn and record for each plot as indicated in the record book, including date.
10. Estimate and record the per cent of good marketable corn at the time of husking.[43]

Each farmer who participated in this research project would write detailed notes about his farm, its history, and what he did to the experimental plots.

One such cooperator was Almon Mace, a 1901 Purdue graduate and Scottsburg farmer who would work with Purdue researchers for more than thirty years. Mace kept a ledger book called "Data Concerning Experiments in Crop Rotation and Soil Fertilization. Farms of C. L. Mace and Son. Lexington, Scott Co. Ind." It provides valuable clues about what it meant to be a cooperator with Purdue researchers. In it Mace recorded his experiences with the 1905 fertilizer experiments, writing:

> In the summer of 1905 an experiment in soil improvement by means of fertilization and crop rotation was begun on the farm of C. L. Mace and Son about 2 miles northeast of Lexington, Scott Co. Indiana . . . with the object of determining the best methods of soil fertilization and crop rotation to be employed in the permanent improvement of the fertility of the more or less run down soil of Southern Indiana.
>
> The experimental field consists of about six acres and is located on the west side of the northeast quarter of Section 29 in Lexington Township.
>
> The soil is described by the Bureau of Soils of the U.S. Department of Agriculture as Scottsburg Silt Loam and at the time the experiments were begun it was in an unprofitable state of fertility.
>
> The land was originally well timbered with beech, poplar, ash, walnut and some oak. It has been cleared and under cultivation for seventy years or longer. It was tile drained about twenty years ago.
>
> The crops produced have been corn, wheat, and clover, with grass for pasture occasionally and a few crops of buckwheat and one of cowpeas. At different times hogs were fed on the clover. For the last 20 years more or less commercial fertilizers have been used on the wheat crops. The land was subsoil plowed about 1890 or a few years later.
>
> The plots were laid out during the summer of 1905 and the boundaries of the various series marked by iron stakes driven down flush with the surface of the ground.
>
> A plat of the ground and blueprint copies bearing also an outline of the treatments and crop rotations, were made for record.[44]

The data that Purdue researchers generated on working farms bore a direct connection to the work of Hoosier farmers. These early farm trials were key in establishing the relevancy of Purdue's agricultural research program.

On September 1, 1900, Latta's activities with the Experiment Station came to an end as he focused his attention on the ever expanding responsibilities of the Farmers' Institutes. His views on research and the connection to agricultural economics are well framed within his comments on the larger context of farm life. He wrote persuasively about how farm life requires intellectual ability and about how it influences culture, taste, and refinement:

Is farm-life favorable to the cultivation of the intellectual faculties? Yes, in three ways: First, in the head-work actually required in the successful management of the farm; secondly, in the facilities afforded for observation and experiment; and lastly, in the opportunities presented for independent study and reading. Farm economy requires head-work in keeping up the fertility of the soil, by a judicious rotation and by the timely application of proper manures; in managing crops with references to the kind and amount of labor, the character of soil, the market and its distance, and the kind and amount of stock. A farmer may place a rotation adapted to his soil, market and stock, and be unable to get the labor which such a rotation would require; and so he must try again and again. There is a call for head-work in making improvements as to secure utility and cheapness without sacrificing appearance and durability.

Again, headwork of the sharpest kind is required in keeping an accurate account of the expenditures and receipts of the farm as a whole, the separate fields, and the individual crops. Not one farmer in ten can give the exact expense in labor, tools and seed, of any given crop; and although he may know the yield exactly, he has no means of telling the amount of gain or loss, or even whether the crop "paid" or not. For the same reason he can't tell just where he has gained or lost; and hence it will be impossible for him to transform this year's losses into next year's gains. The facts already adduced, were there no others, are sufficient to show that the successful management of a farm not only requires brains, but also calls into active exercise the powers of a well disciplined mind. Besides this, there is no better field than agriculture for the exercise of our powers of observation, reason and judgment, in the way of experimenting.

But farm-life gives opportunity for a broader intellectual culture than pertains to work exclusively agricultural. The long winter evenings, rainy days and spare hours in the intervals of busy work, may be devoted to general reading or special study, without detriment to the farm and without fear of interruption from others. It is not so with the lawyer, preacher, doctor, merchant and others, who must hold themselves ever ready to go at the bid of an exacting and oft-times capricious public.

Finally, agriculture is suited to develop taste—a perception of, and regard for the beautiful. The farmer is every day brought into contact with nature's own models of beauty. No cloud of smoke and dust obscures the sunlight. No forbidding walls of contiguous dwellings shut out the glory of sunset. In the country, hill and dale, forest and fields, sunshine and shade, landscape and sky, all conspire to give a thousand pleasing effects. Enliven this scene with the horses, cattle, sheep, swine and poultry of the farm, and you have a picture which daily greets the eye of the farmer. But the agriculturalists can do more than simply admire the beauty and order around him. His broad acres and extended views give him full scope for the exercise of taste in the arrangement of his fields, the grouping of his buildings, and the planning and ornamentation of his grounds.

But the so-called practical man, who sees nothing but facts and can't interpret even those, (or them), will say "If these arguments are true, why do we find so little evidence of culture among the farmers?" Several reasons might be offered, two of which I will give. The farmers in the newer portions of the country are yet engaged in clearing up and paying for their farms. Home embellishments will come when the farm is once secured. Again, most of the farmers of to-day are deficient in education—the very foundation of all liberal culture; and for the fundamentals of an education we must ever look to the schools.

But there are, even now, many intelligent, refined farmers; and as our agricultural colleges are yearly adding to this class, the time is not far distant when there will be no need of argument to show that agriculture is favorable to culture, for the two will exist together.[45]

Professor Latta and his colleagues would set the stage for researchers that followed them by showing farmers the value of agricultural research. It would take some time, but farmers came to have confidence in the research, accepting advice given by the school's professors.

Latta saw the need early on for long-term experiments on the Purdue farm, and he was one of the first to experiment on family farms. He understood that getting good results would require multiple years of testing in various areas around the state. In 1896, Experiment Station Director Plumb recognized Latta's contributions, stating that ". . . certain field experiments have been continued now for fifteen successive years by the agriculturist, W. C. Latta—a record that probably has not been made by any other Station in America."[46]

Professor Latta and his research colleagues at Purdue University opened the doors of agricultural research to the farmers of Indiana. Their success also created the need for a state Extension outreach program to deliver the research information to the farming community. While Latta himself, in later years, became better known for his work with the Cooperative Extension Service, his efforts toward finding science-based solutions to the practical problems of farmers cannot be underestimated.

The Extension Specialist:
Taking the University to the People
(1889–1923)

CHAPTER  FIVE

O day of work, of eager strife,
When earnest men invest their life
In open field, in city mart,
In learning's hall or mine so dark,
Upon the sea or in the air,
In quest of truth, men everywhere
Strive for gain, for fame, for power.
Some win, some lose; one vict'ry sure
A man's estate all may secure.
O day of strife, O day and hour
Of manhood's prime and manhood's power.

—William Carroll Latta
"Today" from "Yesterday, Today, Tomorrow," 1925

THE PURDUE FACULTY OF THE EARLY 1880s recognized that they needed to secure the support of Indiana's farmers to increase enrollment and the impact of their research. To that end, Professor Latta made many overtures to farm groups to introduce new faculty to them. He was a prolific letter writer, frequently suggesting to associations that they include Purdue staff on their educational programs. Faculty members made farm visits, acted as competition judges, and wrote letters to answer questions about the latest research. Latta himself lectured in front of many associations and is credited with 400 presentations.[1]

Professor Latta realized that the more he and his colleagues shook hands with growers, the more they could encourage farmers to send their children to Purdue to study the science and practice of farming. And Latta pushed hard to get farmers to attend the agricultural Winter Short Course. Latta felt that if he could get the latest research in front of the short course students, Purdue could rely on them to support the university's mission. The dissemination of research information could foster undergraduate enrollment, too. Communication between the farmer and the Purdue faculty would prove to be an essential element in the future successes that Purdue University would eventually enjoy.

But what more could Purdue do to communicate better with farmers across the state? This must have been the subject of long discussions on campus. How could agricultural research be disseminated to the farming community with just a handful of production-oriented professors and only scarce funds to carry out such a program?

The need to extend information and communicate with their clientele was based on the philosophy that Purdue staff were employed to solve the problems that Indiana agriculture faced. In 1889, the director of the Experiment Station made it clear that Purdue University and its employees wanted to engage the agricultural community:

> In order to carry out the purposes of the Station in the spirit in which it was established and to make its results directly available to its patrons, those connected with its work desire to place themselves in intimate relation with the farmers and horticulturists of the State, and thereby learn what problems are of immediate practical importance to them, and also secure co-operation in making trials and observations.[2]

With this "we can help" attitude, the next logical step was to get research working on the farm. From the earliest days of the Agricultural Experiment Station, Latta and his colleagues began writing results from their field experiments in the form of Experiment Station bulletins. These bulletins quickly became the vehicle by which researchers could communicate with farmers on how to improve crop yields, fruit production, and animal performance.

And to make applied research work for more than just a few farmers, the Experiment Station put up scarce funds to mail the bulletins free of charge to Indiana farmers who requested them. The concept of communicating with farmers and sharing results through bulletins was a source of pride for Experiment Station Director Charles Plumb, who noted the growth of the mailing list from 7,650 names in 1893 to 16,512 names in 1899.[3]

The bulletins were extremely important to the development of Purdue's Cooperative Extension Service. They were one of the first connections that would strongly link Purdue to farmers. And these early bulletins were essentially the first Extension-type publications written for farmers.

But while the bulletins were very successful, many farmers remained oblivious to what Purdue was doing on their behalf. The question then became, How could the university get information out to even more farmers? In December 1888, Horace E. Stockbridge, director of the Agricultural Experiment Station, had a novel idea when he suggested that Purdue researchers could revise their articles to focus on essential information. The summaries would then be sent to the state's newspapers as press releases. By 1894, the Experiment Station listed these press releases as accomplishments worth noting in its annual reports.

There would be hundreds of articles sent to the press, and Professor Latta would write his fair share of them. His press releases would deal with oat, wheat, and sweet corn varieties, alfalfa without irrigation, and growing crimson clover, winter oats, cowpeas, awnless bromegrass, and soybeans in Indiana. He also wrote other articles for the popular press that dealt with the location of buildings on the farm and modern farm buildings.

It is important to remember that the Agricultural Experiment Station, whose main function was agricultural research, conducted this outreach effort. The detailed Experiment Station bulletins and corresponding press releases would, in a short few years, become the foundation by which the Farmers' Institutes would link Purdue science to an audience wanting to hear the latest scientific breakthroughs. And as their research became widely disseminated, the request for personal appearances and presentations by faculty members began to increase. Men such as Professor Latta began to make important connections with leading agriculturists and powerful politicians, who would later be called on to help Purdue University and the School of Agriculture in times of financial need.

Carving out the Purdue University Cooperative Extension Service from the Experiment Station was a slow process occurring over a quarter of a century. Farmers' Institutes often are recognized as first in the sequence of events that led to the formation of the Cooperative Extension Service. The pamphlet "25 Years of Extension Work in Indiana" published in 1939 listed the important milestones:

> Observance of this noteworthy silver anniversary of Federal-State cooperative extension provides the occasion to look backward into earlier

Indiana history which also contains some notable extension birthdays. Of special significance is the fact that the

- first extension activity in Indiana was authorized by state legislation in the Farmers' Institute Act of 1889—51 years ago;
- first provision for organized extension work in Indiana was made by Purdue University in 1906—34 years ago;
- Department of Agricultural Extension at Purdue University was organized in 1911—29 years ago;
- first county agent was employed in Indiana, October 1, 1912—28 years ago; and
- 27 county agents were already on the job in Indiana at the beginning of federal extension work in 1914 (Smith-Lever Act).[4]

Not mentioned in the list but of significant importance was the Smith Act of 1905. This legislation appropriated state funds to support the dissemination of research information from the Experiment Station.

The Farmers' Institutes, held annually in each county, laid the foundation for future Extension programs, including 4-H, home economics, and community leadership and development. It was one of the most successful university outreach programs ever developed in Indiana and helped Purdue University establish firm ties to the state's rural communities.

Professor Latta wrote in the 1930s that the Farmers' Institutes were first in many aspects of Extension outreach and education of rural farm families:

> The farmers' institutes in Indiana, as well as elsewhere, are the earlier forms of wide-spread, systematized, extension activity in which the farmers have had an active share in the organization and conduct of the work.
>
> In its socializing influences through its appeal to the farm family, the Grange alone, preceded the farmers' institutes in the State; but that appeal was nowhere community wide, as has been and is the case with the Farmers' Institute work. In its active enlistment of the farm family, including the children above the age of ten years, the Farmers' Institute was truly the leader in Indiana in point of time, in its outreach to the remotest rural districts and in the regularity of its annually-recurring service to the entire rural community.[5]

Professor Latta linked the first developments of the Farmers' Institutes and the creation of the Cooperative Extension Service to the agricultural societies of the mid-nineteenth century. Legislatures from Maryland, Massachusetts, Michigan, New York, and Ohio early on funded farm associations to put on educational programs centered around chemistry, plant and animal physiology, and botany. The agricultural societies provided speakers who would give lectures on modern farming practices. These lecturers were often accompanied by an education fair where farm products were exhibited.

By the 1860s, agricultural lectures given in agricultural associations or by state-funded programs were common. In 1860, a Yale organic chemistry professor, John A. Porter, held a four-week course on agricultural chemistry, pomology, agriculture, and domestic animals. A total of 500 farmers attended.

Toward the end of the 1860s, the notion of conducting Farmers' Institutes began to emerge and take root among agriculturists. At this time, land-grant schools were little more than words on paper—a few professors, students, and buildings, and little funding. Evidence suggests that in 1868 Kansas was the first to hold a program with the name Farmers' Institute but that Edward Hitchcock, president of Amherst College, might have been the first to coin the term in an address to the Massachusetts State Board of Agriculture.[6]

The notion of Farmers' Institutes became so popular that soon most states began holding them. In 1869, Illinois Industrial University held a four-day course in the state. The Iowa State College in 1870 included the restriction that its institute meetings would be limited to fifty farmers, with "the understanding that the expenses would be met by those for whom the meetings were held." New Jersey added a unique twist when, in 1872, its State Board of Agriculture established County Boards of Agriculture.[7]

For all practical purposes, it was the Michigan program that was the blueprint for Professor Latta's management of the Farmers' Institutes in Indiana. Latta approved of the shared responsibilities between local organizers and university officials that the Michigan program offered. He adopted the same approach for the Indiana program, establishing a cooperative method that would become his trademark.

During the 1880s, Farmers' Institutes grew rapidly in twenty-six states. Who organized them and managed their affairs differed across the country. In many places, it was a state board of agriculture working in conjunction with the state agricultural college. In others, the land-grant college was sole manager of the Farmers' Institutes. In five of the states, independent organizations handled the affairs of the Farmers' Institutes. The Indiana program was first arranged by the Indiana State Board of Agriculture in 1882 and later managed by Purdue University until the early 1960s, when the program ended.

❦ ❦ ❦

The Indiana State Board of Agriculture first recognized the opportunity to develop institutes for their members in 1882. At their annual meeting in January, the members of the board met and proposed that

1. four farmers' institutes be held as an experiment—two early and two late in 1882.
2. the secretary of the State Board receive proposals for places of meetings.
3. the places of meetings pledge to meet the expenses incurred.
4. Purdue University be requested to furnish at least two of its faculty for each meeting.
5. each institute be held two days with four or five sessions.
6. the secretary of the board in conference with the local committees prepare the programs.
7. the legislature be asked to appropriate $500 for the holding of farmers' institutes [these funds never materialized].[8]

However, only the spring institutes were held that year, with one in Columbus on March 8 and 9, and the other at Crawfordsville on March 22 and 23. Indiana Governor Albert Gallatin Porter was the keynote speaker at the inaugural program in Columbus. His presence there showed that the institutes were a likely place for politicians to gain visibility and to deliver their messages to farmers.

Professor Latta selectively incorporated the governor's speech into his history of the Indiana Farmers' Institutes:

It has been thought by the Board and by the college that they [Farmers' Institutes] could do a good service to farmers . . . by immediate communication with the people; by imparting and receiving in return from farmers the valuable knowledge derived from observation on their part in their fields, from their thoughts at the fire side. . . . It is in pursuance of this belief that this institute is held here today. It is to be a free conference. . . . Every question is to be laid bare for debate. . . . I have never for one moment since I have been Governor of the State, felt so satisfied with my position as I do today in the presence of this vast assemblage of citizens met to consider the interests of agriculture.[9]

Those attending the Columbus and Crawfordsville meetings heard presentations on a wide variety of agricultural topics primarily relating to production: industrial education, commercial fertilizers, source and value of statistics, sanitary measures, mutual dependence of all branches of industry, farm drainage, breeding and feeding, and the true dignity of the American farmer.

The discussion about continuing to invest in the Farmers' Institutes was resumed the next year on January 4, 1883. Professor Latta was in attendance when the following resolution was read:

> WHEREAS, The experiment of holding a series of Farmers' Institutes, inaugurated by this Board at its annual session, January, 1882, as a means of imparting scientific and practical information, and awakening an increased interest in education and better and more successful modes and methods of practical agriculture, have proved eminently successful, and, in the opinions of this Board, should be continued as a permanent educational measure, tending to a higher appreciation of the practical value of a more general knowledge of the sciences in the successful prosecution of agriculture; therefore, be it
>
> Resolved, That this Board use its influence and memorialize the Legislature for an annual appropriation of $1,000 [these funds never materialized], to be used in the defraying of the expenses of these Institutes. Ours being an agricultural State, the highest interest of the commonwealth, will be promoted by stimulating and fostering a more perfect and complete development of our agricultural resources in this manner.[10]

The resolution passed as proposed, but it had already become a political issue. There always seemed to be disagreement among the board members over the need to ask the legislature for additional funding. This was because some of the members thought that money given to the board for institute work would compete for additional funding that the Indiana State Board of Agriculture needed in order to manage the work already assigned to it by the General Assembly.

It appears that members of the Indiana State Board of Agriculture lost interest in the Farmers' Institutes for a few years until they met on February 1886, where the subject was once again broached. Embarrassment over not hosting more Farmers' Institutes also surfaced the following year at the Indiana State Board of Agriculture meeting in January 1887. Board President W. B. Seward from Bloomington said, "Farmers' institutes are now held in many of our sister states, and have been tried to some extent in this state, but results have not been altogether satisfactory with us, owing to the fact that we have had no money provided us as is the case in other states."[11] From his speech, the board once again offered up the only thing it seemed capable of doing by passing yet another resolution. This time a request was put before the board to formulate a set of rules to organize institutes at the county and township level. It had come down to the fact that if the members wanted Farmers' Institutes, they would have to organize the efforts in the districts they represented and find local funding to pay the expenses for hosting an institute.

At the January 1888 meeting of the board, more plans and ideas were discussed. When the talking came to an end, one more resolution was passed, giving direction to the future of the Farmers' Institutes: "Resolved that the State board be instructed to provide for a series of farmers' institutes to be held during the coming year and such meeting to be held in each member's district."[12]

In his January 1889 address to the board, the board's president provided evidence that Farmers' Institutes were actually held across the state:

> At our last Delegate meeting [January 1888] it was resolved that the State Board be instructed to provide for a series of farmers institutes to be held during the year in each agricultural district. In compliance with the order, thirteen were held in different parts of the state. The work was accomplished by members and delegates naming a date in localities where such meetings were desired, the entertainment and expenses being provided by friends of the enterprise.[13]

Institutes were held in 1888 at Anderson, Franklin, LaPorte, Peru, Plainfield, Princeton, and Rockville. The types of subjects discussed there were similar to the presentations offered in Columbus and Crawfordsville six years earlier.

Farmers' Institutes continued to occupy the attention of the Indiana State Board of Agriculture, but little did its members know that during 1889 Purdue would assume responsibility for managing the affairs of the Farmers' Institutes. While Professor Latta was pleased with the efforts of the Indiana State Board of Agriculture, he felt that it had failed the Farmers' Institutes in some respects. He thought that the board should have been more vocal in requesting state funding, believing that it would have been successful. He also felt that board members had expended considerable time and money to accomplish what they had. But in the end, he recognized their competing interests in holding annual state fairs in addition to the Farmers' Institutes, and he gave them deserved credit for keeping the institutes going from 1882 until Purdue assumed responsibility for them in 1889.

On March 9, 1889, the Indiana General Assembly passed the Farmers' Institute Act, a landmark piece of state legislation for Purdue University that gave the university full responsibility for managing the Farmers' Institutes. It also marked the beginning of formalized Extension in Indiana.

A representative from Miami County, William W. Robbins, introduced the Farmers' Institute Act at the request of his constituents. He stipulated that the Farmers' Institutes receive an annual appropriation of $5,000 to support the program, which was also accepted.

At Purdue the responsibility devolved to the General Management Committee. This group, working under the auspices of the Purdue Board of Trustees, would provide general oversight and direct management of the institutes. The General Management Committee consisted of the president of Purdue University, the director of the Experiment Station, and the professor of agriculture; thus, the first committee members included, respectively, James Smart, Horace Stockbridge, and Latta.

The board of trustees approved Latta to head up the program on June 4, 1889, as the superintendent of the Farmers' Institutes. He assumed total control of the state-administered, locally driven educational program for farmers until 1923. The Farmers' Institutes would, in most counties, continue to be held until the late 1950s, with a few counties continuing to convene meetings until the mid-1960s.

Did Purdue University have anything to do with maneuvering control of the institutes away from the Indiana State Board of Agriculture? Indications are, from Professor Latta and others at Purdue, that they did not have anything to do with what took place in the General Assembly:

> You may be under the impression that the Institute act was passed at the suggestion of the University authorities. This is not true and I can bring you the proof of it. The authorities were in no way concerned with the passage of the act. Indeed, we were very much discomforted at the amount of work which the act piled upon us without our having been in any way consulted.[14]

While it may well never be known why Purdue, rather than the Indiana State Board of Agriculture, was granted authority over the institutes, a motivating factor was certainly concerned legislators, who worried about the use of the Farmers' Institutes as a political tool by members of the Indiana State Board of Agriculture. What if the institutes were to become political and endorse one party or politician over another? Latta's own words suggest this possibility:

> Like other beginnings the farmers' institute work in Indiana has had its share of vicissitude and obstacles to overcome. Some were but uninformed, politically-minded persons [who] wondered whether the farmers' institutes were starting or promoting a new political party.[15]

With the Farmers' Institutes securely controlled by Purdue, however, they would be removed from unnecessary political influences and free to focus on educating farmers about the latest research developments.

🌾🌾🌾

Professor Latta was a good choice as superintendent for the Indiana Farmers' Institutes. He had a strong desire to help improve farmers' lives, and he knew that education was the key:

> I enclose herewith some circulars which will give you an idea of what we are undertaking in the way of education of farmer's sons and, to some extent, the result. It seems to me that the subject might take up two lines with profits: First, the value of education; second, the best kind of education for those who expect to farm. The world is moved today largely by men who have been educated either in schools or by their efforts. Knowledge is power, especially if it is the kind of knowledge that may be applied in the every-day calling of men. Knowledge, and the ability to use it, is the one thing that lifts men from the common level and increases their usefulness and influence for good. An education greatly increases a man's capacity to enjoy life as it unlocks the secrets of nature and opens up many avenues of pleasures that would otherwise be largely sealed in the man without education. The farmer, included as he is of necessity, is in greater need of a general education than other men who, by their contact with their elbows, get an education as they go along through life. Any true education will tend to give the power of application, stability of purpose and persistence in offers to its possessor and this will add immensely to

the chances of success to men who, in addition to natural powers, are thoroughly drilled by an education to systematic effort.

Now as to an education for the farm. Agriculture is a business which is subject to a greater range and variety of conditions than any other. One who engages in farming has occasions to make use of a knowledge of chemistry, botany, geology, physics, meteorology, entomology and other sciences. A knowledge of these sciences will enable the farmer to understand more fully the processes which are constantly going on in field and stall, and he will be better able to hold in check the processes which tend to waste and to reinforce those which tend to increase the productiveness of the soil, etc. An agricultural education, such as Purdue and other agricultural colleges afford, will not only impart a knowledge of these sciences that relate to agriculture, but will, at the same time, tend to exalt agriculture in the minds of the pupils by giving them a higher conception of this noble calling and its possibilities. The agricultural colleges are seeking to do three things: 1. Train the pupils to be larger and better men; 2. Give them a practical knowledge of the sciences that relate to agriculture so they can pursue the calling with greater success; 3. Instill a higher regard and liking for agriculture, which will lead them to take up this calling from choice and devote themselves earnestly and patriotically to the interest of the farming classes.[16]

Latta also was acquainted with the mindset of the Hoosier farmer. He understood that growers would stick with practices they knew worked, leaving experimentation with new approaches and technologies to their more inquisitive neighbors. The "what-if-this-fails?" mentality was a major deterrent for Indiana farmers to try out new ideas on the farm.

He had specific goals in mind when it came to the organization of the Farmers' Institutes and that of his overall outreach program. He would write:

From 1889 to 1895 the immediate objective was the organization of the Farmers' Institute in every county in Indiana. The larger objectives were:

1. To raise the general intelligence and success of the farmers of the state by bringing to the rank and file the teachings of the School of Agriculture and the results of the experimental and research work of the Experiment Station.

2. To encourage and inspire them to practice the methods of the most successful farmers.

3. To improve the rural home and enrich rural community life.

4. To make clear the real unity of interest of all members of the community and banish clannishness and class antagonisms.
5. To cultivate a more sympathetic fellowship and better cooperation among the religious denominations.
6. To develop a higher appreciation of the value of education, especially agricultural and home building.[17]

Latta used the most successful farmers to teach other farmers about what could be done to improve various aspects of farming. He relied heavily on successful farm families to make educational inroads in the state, knowing farmers were more apt to change when they heard the message from one of their own. Latta made this point clear in a letter to a county chairman who had mistakenly titled farmers who spoke at institutes as "professors":

> I have just received the poster announcing your meeting. You have made a mistake in dubbing all these workers "Professors." Every one is a practical farmer and you will find you have done the work harm by the way you have introduced these men to the public. The aim is to make the work eminently practical by sending everyday farmers, and to destroy this effort by dubbing the farmers "Professors" is in my judgment very unwise.[18]

Professor Latta also drew from the experiences of the Indiana State Board of Agriculture volunteers. He knew that any success that the institutes achieved would require that he put in place a well-coordinated program and, some argued, state controlled. While it would be managed by Purdue, it was primarily a volunteer program. As superintendent, he would have to focus his attentions on managing the daily affairs of the program, suggesting how it would run on a statewide basis, securing local volunteers to do their best work, and offering opinions, compliments, and criticisms when necessary. In effect, Latta became the focal point—the face—of the program.

From 1889 to 1891, Farmers' Institutes were held in 91 of Indiana's 92 counties. Latta teamed up with whomever would help to organize the Farmers' Institutes in each county, including the Indiana State Board of Agriculture, county fair associations, county agricultural and horticultural societies, the Grange, and farmers' clubs. The first Farmers' Institute of 1889 was held in the Corydon Courthouse. The last of the fifty meetings that took place that same season coincidentally occurred in the assembly room of the Indiana State Board of Agriculture in Indianapolis.

The topics at early institutes covered a broad spectrum. Typical programs included: increasing farm profits; sheep husbandry; growing pigs for the market; dairying; the ideal horse for the farmer; the value of ensilage and other fodder; injurious insects and how to destroy them; small fruits and how to grow them; food and its preparation; fish culture and protection; cooperative efforts for the farmer; the improvement of public highways; the agricultural press; how to bear the intellectual and social conditions of farmers' families; and the privileges and possibilities of farm life.

Just two years after assuming control of the institutes, Latta was already seeking to improve and strengthen them. In his first annual report, he wrote:

> At the end of two years the district plan was abandoned for the more direct method of appointing a local head in each county, which placed the responsibility for the success or failure of each institute directly where it properly belongs, namely, *within the county* [Latta's emphasis].[19]

Latta had decided to require each county to take a more active and organized role in the programming of the institutes. He wanted local farmers to design a program agenda that would include the topics they wanted to learn about, the speakers they desired, and a location that would attract the most farmers and their families. Those responsible for the local implementation would be required to advertise the program, keep track of their expenses, and submit reports back to the superintendent.

Latta controlled the $5,000 that the General Assembly awarded the institutes annually. He set guidelines on how much each county would get to deal with local expenses, including room rentals and advertising fees. However, Latta retained responsibility for identifying the best speakers in the state that the local committees could select from, and he would pay those speakers a small fee for the week (e.g., $15 to $35) and pick up their expenses (e.g., hotel rates were approximately $2 an evening, regular meals cost 25 cents, and the business lunch was 15 cents).

Many of the institute speakers donated their services during the first years. Indeed, early success can be credited to speakers who donated their time, such as James A. Mount, who would become the governor of Indiana. One notable volunteer, Virginia C. Meredith of Cambridge City, was the first woman institute worker in Indiana. She began her work in 1889 and worked for free for two years "as evidence of her real interest and faith in the Agricultural Extension work."[20] Virginia Meredith was more than just another Farmers' Institute speaker. She was in her own right a very successful farmer and livestock producer, and operated a state-of-the-art livestock farm. Meredith would later become a prominent member of the Purdue University Board of Trustees, and her adopted daughter, Mary Matthews, would become the first head of the Home Economics Department at Purdue University.

Professor Latta provided other descriptions of institute management:

> The counties are thrown into groups of three each and two-day meetings consisting usually of five sessions are the rule. As far as practicable the counties are grouped with reference to the speakers desired so that the same speakers—two to each series—attend the Institutes in the several counties of a group, the first meeting being held on Monday and Tuesday, the second on Wednesday and Thursday and the third on Friday and Saturday.
>
> ... The special feature of the Indiana plan is that it enlists actively the cooperation of the people in every county of the State. The meetings are not always so well presided over and the programs are frequently not so well arranged as might be under a more central supervision. It is believed, however, that a substantial compensation is secured in enlisting the people throughout the State actively in the work. In a large degree the people have come to feel that the success of the work devolves upon them and a very commendable rivalry has sprung up among the more enterprising counties as to which shall hold the best Institute....
>
> To an outside observer many Indiana Farmers' Institutes would lack the snap and impressiveness of a convention conducted by men specially appointed to do the work. Many a local worker who is placed on the program presents a sorry appearance the first time, but his assignment to duty has been a means of arousing him to new effort and achievement and it has also awakened a new interest in the work on the part of his neighbors. In this way a permanent interest is maintained in the locality where the Institute is held, and the good effects of the work are silently diffused throughout the neighborhood.
>
> Each Institute is required to send a report to the Superintendent on a blank furnished for the purpose. These reports show clearly that the Farmers' Institute work is steadily gaining ground in the State as shown by the more general interest of the people, the more intelligent participation in the work of the Institutes and in the attendance. In not a few instances during the last two years the halls—the largest that can be had—had proved insufficient to accommodate those desirous of attending the Institutes.[21]

Every county had a permanent association by 1894. Normally, members met on a quarterly basis to conduct their business, plan out programs, and review expenses. Most associations had a county chairman, secretary, treasurer, and vice president. They would elect a chairman for their county and forward his name to Professor Latta at Purdue. Latta would make the choice official by providing the chairman with a certificate of appointment. The chairman's term was a one-year appointment ending on March 31, with the option of being reelected the following year.

Latta could have hand-picked each chairman but instead left it up to the locals to decide. The county chair was an important position because correspondence normally ran between the central office and the chairmen. Professor Latta depended heavily on the county chairmen to make sure everything went off without a hitch:

> It is essential for the highest success of the work that the superintendent and chairmen should be thoroughly in touch and mutually helpful to each other in this work. While I do not ask you to accept my views of the thing, I do request your co-operation that the plan may be in the highest possible degree a success.[22]

Consequently, chairmen took credit when things went well and criticism when complaints were lodged. The necessity that county chairmen were successful farmers was mentioned often in Latta's correspondence:

> An Institute can not be successfully run by men who have retired from the active business of farming. That is the experience all along the line. We are working for the younger men—these will have something to learn and who will not dwell on the retrospective too much. Forward is the word.[23]

For many years, Professor Latta convened an annual conference for the institute workers and the officers of each Farmers' Institute. This annual conference was normally held six weeks before the Farmers' Institutes season started in November. With the first state conference at Purdue in 1898, he developed the annual meeting around themes that enhanced the institute workers' base of knowledge, improved their professional delivery, and bettered their management skills in running the programs. In an ongoing effort to promote the university, he shrewdly used some of the speakers to support programs that he was proposing to the General Assembly.

The program for the 1899 conference addressed topics such as beef cattle, industrial education for women, building a relationship between Purdue and

farmers, and improving rural schools and public highways. The 1901 conference for institute workers reflected more of the specialization that was going to
be taught in the state that year, including such subjects as improving soil
fertility, the farm home, better management of livestock, and agricultural
specialization, cooperation, and education.

🌾🌾🌾

While the first key to the success of Indiana's Farmers' Institutes was holding
county chairmen responsible for local organization and implementation, the
second key was making institutes available to everyone with an interest in
farming. In some counties, this meant holding the meetings centrally, such as
in the county seat. In other counties, this meant moving the location around in
an effort to reach farmers who might have been unable to attend at other
locations.

Courtrooms were popular places to hold institute meetings. In some cases,
judges would find another room in the courthouse to do their work. In the
more rural areas, churches were commonly used, and still later, institute meetings took place in the larger rooms of the consolidated schools in townships
and in public halls that could be rented.

The third key to success was that the programs were open to the public.
While an admittance fee was charged in limited cases, such as to support the
cost of special music, Latta frowned upon this practice and encouraged chairmen to keep the meetings free of charge.

The fourth key to success was Professor Latta's development beginning in
1894 of a list of paid speakers who he knew could deliver practical information
in an understandable and pleasant manner. This allowed him to better control
the quality of the speakers that the local farmers would hear. Latta paid
each speaker a salary based on experience and demand by the counties. The
best speakers received $25 to $35 a week, plus expenses for meals, hotels, and
passenger train tickets.

At any time, Latta had approximately 100 speakers around the state that he
could call upon to attend the institutes, with 30 or so speakers routinely sent
out on the lecture circuit. Latta was particular on what it took to get on his
speaker's list:

> I am compelled to look more and more sharply for men who are thor
> oughly successful farmers and men of unimpeachable character. It is

desirable, of course, that they should also be able to give in a clear, forcible manner the results of their experience, study and observation. You must see, however, that no amount of training of tongue or pen can take the place of a successful experience in the growing of crops and live stock.[24]

His speakers were, for the most part, farmers and farm wives who understood science, could express themselves well, and could entertain the audience. However, what he wanted most in a speaker was one who was well experienced in their subject area and who could explain to others what they could accomplish on their farms and in their communities.

Professor Latta worried considerably about the need to hire qualified and experienced farmers. He knew that the meager salary didn't go far when one considered their time away from families, homes, farms, and businesses. He wrote openly to Virginia Meredith about his concerns over the low pay he offered institute speakers:

> I confess to some solicitude for the future of the Institute work on the score of workers who shall maintain the interest already aroused and continue to enlarge the work. The thing that most discourages me is the feeling on the part of some of our best workers, including yourself, that they do not care or can not afford to continue in the work. I regret that it is impossible under our current plan to offer the best workers what their services are really worth.[25]

To keep costs down, Latta depended on the free services offered by local volunteers to fill in the remaining agenda at the institutes. Latta's paid speakers would teach about half of the two-day program, while the local volunteers would teach the other half. The local workers were not paid if they taught in their own counties. If a local worker spoke at a program outside of the county, the local chairman could pay approximately five dollars out of his own funds. Professor Latta would not pay for local speakers otherwise, because that would quickly run the program into the red.

Latta was singularly hesitant about selecting young, inexperienced speakers. He wanted them to make themselves available free of charge at their own local county institutes. If they were received well locally, then he would find out about them in the reports that were sent to him from the county chairmen:

> I will be pleased to enroll your name with subjects on our list of institute workers for the coming season. I will be unable to make any assignments

for a year, however. It is our uniform rule to assign as regular workers only
those who have had considerable experience and concerning whom favorable recommendations are received at this office, from county officers....
In placing your name on the list I do so with the understanding that you
will respond whenever practicable to invitations coming direct from
county chairmen to attend their meetings. This would give you the opportunity, which I suppose you desire, for demonstrating your fitness for general institute work. [26]

On the other hand, Latta knew that he had to bring in new and young talent to keep the programs fresh and moving forward. He would time and again
ask his former students to try their hand in speaking at Farmers' Institutes and
would selectively see to it that they were put on programs where they could succeed. At the same time, he encouraged them to speak to the audience about how
they benefited from their education at Purdue University:

I am especially desirous to enlist all the graduates in the agricultural
department in Institute work the coming winter so far as it is practicable.
...I trust, however, that you will be willing to take a place on the list of
workers, and that you will prepare four or five subjects suitable for presentation at Institutes if there should be a call for same. I desire that one
of these subjects, at least, should set forth what Purdue is doing for the
farmers in such a way as to interest the people in agricultural education.
...It will be a means of advertising Purdue and it will do you good to do
some work in this line.[27]

Professor Latta would send out a letter to each county chairman in early
summer requesting from him the month and place of his next institute program
and which state-supported speakers he preferred. Each county chairman could
choose who he wanted from the speaker list, with certain limitations and stipu-
lations. But Latta made every effort to accommodate the preferences of each
chairman, as indicated by this correspondence:

We enclose herewith certificate of your appointment as chairman, list of
institute workers for the season of 1900–1901, and list of questions to be
answered by yourself, after consulting others interested. We write you
early that you may give the matter attention before the rush of spring
work begins. If you prefer to let me select the assigned speakers, please so
state in answer to question 4. Please answer carefully as we shall use your
reply in making up the next schedule of meetings. Bear in mind that we

must, as heretofore, assign the same two speakers to the three meetings in a series in order to save expenses. If practicable, please consult at least three or four of your best farmers before answering the questions. If at all possible, let me have your answer within ten days.

1. What are the subjects of most interest and importance to the farmers of your county?
2. Do you prefer two men or one man and one woman as assigned speakers?
3. If a woman is assigned, can you arrange for one or two separate sessions for women?
4. What assigned speakers would, in your judgment, be most practically helpful to you? Name half a dozen.
5. In what month between Nov. 1 and Mar. 31 do you wish to hold your next annual institute? In answering, please bear in mind that December has been overcrowded heretofore, and that farmers are generally too busy in November to attend institutes.
6. At what point do you expect to hold the institute?
7. Will it be satisfactory to group your county with the same counties as last season?
8. Do you expect to hold a midsummer institute or any local meetings during the winter season?[28]

Despite Latta's best efforts and intentions, institutes were not guaranteed their speaker of choice. The final assignment of speakers depended on availability and practicality. Wherever possible, Latta designated speakers to more than one institute in an area in an effort to save time and money:

In blocking out the schedule of Institutes for next season I have found it most convenient to throw Carroll, Cass and Wabash counties together in the order named and assign them the second week in December. As no request for speakers has been made as yet I would respectfully submit the following names of persons who I think would be available that week if desired. If the several chairmen can agree upon some two of them I will endeavor to have them assigned.[29]

Experiment Station staff members were also available to speak, but they had to be invited. If they accepted, the county had to pay for their travel and lodging expenses. Purdue would pay their salary. Professor Latta thought it would be good for the professors at Purdue to attend a few of the institutes and assigned them to Farmers' Institutes as their class work and research permitted their absence from Purdue:

It seems to me that the professors of the college, especially those whose work has to do with matters of interest to farmers, should attend Institutes whenever desired, if it is at all practicable to do so. I think that good comes to the college and to the professor from association with the farmers at Institutes.[30]

But in a letter to Virginia Meredith, he also acknowledged the limitations associated with this practice:

I wish it were possible to have a thoroughly well-informed, all-around scientist at each meeting who could help to correct the misstatements that are made and the false inferences that are drawn. It seems almost out of the question to have such a worker, partly because they are exceedingly scarce and partly because the workers here can not be away for any considerable length of time.[31]

The list of speakers caused Latta trouble over the years. He had little money to pay the speakers, some of whom knew they were underpaid. He also had to renegotiate each speaker's availability, subjects, and fees annually—all the while trying to meet the demands of the local chairmen:

I find upon the return cards that your name is quite frequently mentioned and this is evidence of quite a general and earnest desire to have you actively engaged in the Institute work next year. I therefore write you thus early in the hope of securing your services for say about a fortnight at a time at intervals through the season. I am sorry to say that we are not able to hold out strong financial inducements to you to enter this work. I am compelled, therefore, to appeal largely to your patriotism, pride in Hoosierdom and interest in the farming community generally to induce you to again engage actively in this work.[32]

Superintendent Latta found himself resolving numerous petty squabbles concerning speakers, including complaints about a lack of assignments for some and dissatisfaction with the quality of others. There were many instances where Professor Latta had to make speaker substitutions contrary to the wishes of the local committees. In his usual way, he would highlight the strengths and virtues of speakers and try to soothe the ruffled egos of the chairmen:

A word as to the speakers assigned you may be of interest. Mr. W. B. Stevens—a Washington County farmer—has done very acceptable Institute work in a number of counties in previous years. He is well informed on live stock and feeding topics; has used a silo for a number of

years, and can give information as to the building of silos and merits of
silage for different classes of live stock. Mr. Cal Husselman is a Dekalb
County farmer who has had much experience in general farming, farm
drainage, swine breeding and farm dairying. He is an all-around popular
institute worker of much experience. I feel sure that your people will be
greatly interested with what these speakers have to say, and I trust that a
large audience may come out to hear them and join in discussing the
questions that may come before your people.[33]

In later years, Professor Latta changed the manner by which he assigned
speakers. He began asking his county chairmen to list the topics that they
wanted and leave the selection of the speakers to him:

> It may be well to explain to you, as you have opportunity to pass it along,
> that we found years ago that it would be impossible to grant the requests
> of most of the chairmen for particular speakers for the reason that the
> more popular workers would be wanted at several places at the same time.
> After encouraging them to express their preferences for workers, I found
> it very difficult to explain why they were not sent. It has seemed better in
> every way, in recent years, to request the chairmen to indicate the subjects
> they would like to have presented. When I know this, I do the best I can to
> assign speakers who will fill the bill.[34]

Professor Latta himself also delivered many speeches at Farmers'
Institutes. But it proved difficult for him to meet the great demand from the
counties wanting him to appear on their programs. First he had to teach classes
to the regular agricultural students, and in the winter he was heavily involved
with the Winter Short Course, which lasted for three months. He often would have
to refuse any invitations until after mid-March, when those classes would be
nearing an end.

Latta apparently enjoyed giving presentations at local institutes. He
seemed especially pleased to give an evening talk that dealt with getting an
agricultural education at Purdue. At that time, he was giving the presentation
using lantern slides:

> I find that the institute program announces that I am to give a lecture on
> Agricultural Education at the evening session next Friday. Will you kindly
> announce that this lecture will be illustrated with about 80 stereopticon
> views and that it will be interesting to old and young alike? By so doing
> you will confer a favor upon the undersigned, and help to draw out a good
> audience for that session.[35]

In some years, another favorite talk of his dealt with preventing damage by the Hessian fly. Interestingly enough, he even gave some talks in German in communities where English was the second language.

But even Professor Latta was not immune from complaints about some of his own speeches at the institutes. In his usual manner, he dealt with them head-on. At one program the audience apparently did not comprehend what he was trying to teach them. While he apologized for what had happened and wanted a chance to redeem himself, he offered an opinion about the audience, too:

> I accept with best of good nature the criticism of your friends. I would like to meet them face to face and talk this matter over with them. It would doubtless do both them and me good. I am sorry I shot so far over their heads. I am sure it is not beyond what they might do, but may be far beyond what many of them are doing. . . . I hope you may have a good meeting and that the work may be leveled to the understanding at least of the majority of your farmers. It ought, however, to be above the average because the average is far lower than it ought to be. The institutes will be worth little if we only tell what the average farmer can do under average conditions. It should be the purpose to set forth what the earnest, industrious, economical, intelligent farmer can do, if he will, under existing conditions.[36]

Professor Latta's duties as superintendent of the Farmers' Institutes extended to include budgetary concerns. He had to economize as much as possible to administer a statewide program on meager funds. The counties were responsible for all expenses except for those dealing with the speakers assigned to them by Professor Latta. Expenses in excess of the twenty-five dollar maximum were not reimbursed. Through careful planning, he proved to be an efficient administrator:

> The holding of institutes in every county in the short period of five months, with the meager appropriation therefore, necessitated careful plans to economize the time and traveling expenses of speakers. Accordingly, the counties have been arranged in groups of three each, placing those near each other in the same group so that the foreign speakers [usually two] could attend consecutively all three meetings the same week, with a minimum amount of travel. Simultaneously, two or more groups of counties have held institutes the same week with independent

sets of workers. This plan has enabled the Committee to grant approximately the date desired for each meeting, and, also, to furnish at least two experienced workers for almost every institute at very moderate expense.[37]

He paid the speakers for working a series of three institute programs, which meant they would be teaching Monday through Saturday and traveling on Sunday. Most were assigned for two weeks at a time, but the more popular and most requested speakers worked for four weeks or more.

Transportation costs consumed much of the institutes' budget. Latta handled the arduous task of scheduling the train routes so that the speakers would reach their destinations in as efficient a manner as possible. His speakers typically arrived at their first assignments by passenger train, then they would be transported by horse and carriage to the other assignments in the area.

Professor Latta was a shrewd businessman in many respects. For decades, he successfully negotiated with approximately a dozen passenger train companies to cut their rates in half for Farmers' Institutes speakers traveling on their lines. Once established, he used his friendship with the railroads for reduced rates for all of his educational programs, from his annual Farmers' Institutes conference to his more focused specialty programs that he held across the state:

> If your association [Central Traffic Association in Chicago, Illinois] could grant half-fare rates to these speakers, within the limits of our State, while attending said Institutes, we could send two speakers instead of one to each meeting. Two speakers at half-price rates would bring to the railroads the same revenue as one full fare, and the increased attraction of having two good speakers would swell the attendance at the Institutes, thus making a clear gain to the railroads on account of increased travel.[38]

In a letter to one of the railroad associations requesting half-fares for institute workers, Latta wrote in the margin the costs of traveling on a passenger train:

- Sunman to Lawrenceburg, 60 cents at half rate;
- Aurora to Greensburg, 90 cents at half rate;
- Greensburg to Hope, 30 cents at half rate; and
- Hope to Columbus, 20 cents at half rate[39]

Professor Latta would also ask that the half-rates be extended to his passage as he crisscrossed Indiana on behalf of Farmers' Institutes and Purdue University. He was careful to point out the advantage of this discount to the railroads:

I expect to do considerable traveling during the summer vacation in the interest of Farmers' Institutes and in canvassing for students for the university. I would like to visit a number of points on your lines within this State and will appreciate it if you can grant me a permit for half-rates over your lines from June 10 to August 31 inclusive on account of Farmers' Institutes. The work which I did in this line last summer resulted in an increased attendance both at the university and at farmers' institutes, which of course means increased passenger traffic for the railway companies.[40]

Passenger trains were a dependable method of transportation during much of Latta's time at Purdue. However, it would often take some time to get speakers to their destinations. For instance, traveling from Petersburg to Indianapolis was a seven-hour trip; Peoria, Illinois, to West Lafayette took six hours; Fort Wayne to Lafayette was a three-hour trip; and the train from Indianapolis to Terre Haute took nearly two hours. Occasionally, Latta had to ask for additional favors to get where he was going in time:

I am to lecture at Henryville tomorrow (Tuesday) evening and desire to take train #18 to that place. I notice in the guide that it is marked "G" and that trains so marked stop Sunday on signal only. I cannot reach Indianapolis so as to take the morning train and cannot go to Louisville as the returning train will not reach Henryville in time. Train #30 will of course get there too late. Will you therefore grant as a special favor, that train #18 be stopped at Henryville Tuesday evening Aug. 8?[41]

Once Professor Latta had made the arrangements with the railroads, he then corresponded with each speaker regarding the location of their assigned institutes and the routes they would take to reach those sites. They would be sent documents—certificates or letters—that the institute speaker would show to the train station agent to get the special half-rates that Latta had worked out with the passenger train officials.

The time spent writing to the speakers about which lines to travel on and other expense-related issues consumed much of Latta's time. But through it all, he remained attentive to even the smallest details on behalf of his workers, always striving to provide for them as they carried out this important work:

I am willing to pay for the conveyance of your assigned speakers to the place of your meeting and also from there on to the Switzerland County meeting. I wish you would arrange, however, to get a good conveyance—

comfortable, covered rig with plenty of wraps—and a good team to take them from the leading hotel in Aurora to the place of meeting. Please secure a conveyance at as reasonable a figure as possible. You may also arrange for a rig to convey them across to Vevay at the close of your meeting. I desire that they shall have a comfortable, covered rig with plenty of wraps so they will not take cold. We can not afford to have these workers get sick from exposure when out doing this work. [42]

As a general rule, I desire you to go to the best hotels in order that you may be comfortably housed and fed. Please take such precautions while traveling as will make you comfortable and reduce, as far as possible, the risk of sickness. While I desire you to exercise a prudent economy in expenditures, economies that involve risk of exposure to health are unwise. I wish you to be at your best before each audience. To this end if you can avoid a late night run by leaving a meeting a little before its close, try to get the consent of the chairmen to release you. [43]

Each chairman was required to submit a proposed agenda for their annual institute meeting to Professor Latta for his review. He offered positive remarks and, when appropriate, constructive criticisms:

Your program has just come to hand; it is entirely too full for the evening session and also for the second day's sessions, I fear. Permit me to suggest that you have Mrs. Meredith and Mr. Husselman each on but one of the subjects announced for the evening session. This will make the session of a suitable length, I am sure, and be better for the audience in every way. If you want to put in one or two recitations or a little music, that will make a spicy, pleasant evening program. As it is it will be too lengthy.[44]

In late fall Latta would send out a complete schedule of Farmers' Institutes that listed times and locations, the chairmen in charge, and the assigned speakers. He would send these to farm magazines, local papers, and to each chairman. The chairmen advertised their programs in local papers and placed posters throughout the county at schools, businesses, and churches.

Professor Latta sometimes helped a chairman write a press release to send to local county papers. An example appeared in the newspapers in Paoli and Orleans about the county's upcoming Farmers' Institute in December of 1894:

ATTEND THE FARMERS' INSTITUTE
At Orleans, Dec. 17–18
A Good Program and Efficient Speakers Secured.

The farmers of Orange County should not fail to attend, enjoy and profit
by the annual Farmers' Institute to be held at Orleans on Monday and
Tuesday, Dec. 17th & 18th. These Farmers' Institutes are recognized by the
leading farmers of this and other States as a most potent means of
progress in agriculture. In some counties in this State the farmers have
attended their annual Institutes in the number of one thousand or more
and in these counties the institute work is voted a great success.

An interesting and profitable program has been arranged by the local
authorities and the questions which will come up for discussion will be of
every-day practical moment to all engaged in agricultural pursuits. The
young farmers especially will find the Institute very helpful to them and
the interchange of ideas and experiences by the older men can not fail to
give them many pointers which will enable them to attain a greater success and avoid the mistakes of their seniors.

Mr. D. B. Johnson, one of the assigned speakers, has been chairman of
the Morgan County Farmers' Institute for years. He is a successful practical farmer with much experience in the preparation and feeding of silage.
His talks upon this and other subjects will be interesting and profitable.
Mr. James Riley, of Boone County, is a highly successful general farmer
and stockman. His specialties are the growing of farm seeds and pure
bred swine. He is thoroughly conversant with the various topics assigned
him and will discuss them in an eminently practical and interesting manner. Prof. H. A. Huston, State Chemist and also chemist of the Indiana
Experiment Station at La Fayette, will also be present to discuss topics
concerning the chemistry of soils and fodders and the commercial and
agricultural values of fertilizers and manures. There is no higher authority
in the State on these questions than Prof. Huston and he will present his
subjects in a manner intelligible to all. The local workers who have been
assigned places on the program will discuss matters of special interest to
the people of the county.

Farmers should not fail to make their arrangements to attend this
Institute which comes but once a year and they should also take their
wives and grown-up sons and daughters, if possible. The Institute is for
the entire family and will prove alike entertaining and profitable to all.[45]

At the meeting, each speaker—paid or volunteer—would normally read a
previously prepared paper to the audience. Generally, speakers had twenty

minutes to make their points, with the remaining forty minutes of their time spent addressing questions. A good presentation sometimes meant being assigned to Latta's list of speakers:

> I have just received copy of the marked *Journal* for Jan. 19, 1899, which contains a paper read by Mrs. Oliver Kline at your last institute. It has occurred to me that perhaps she should make a valuable institute worker. What do you know of her standing, intelligence and ability in this line of work? I could not, of course, use her this year, except as a possible substitute, but might sometime in the future.[46]

Presenters would include charts showing dairy and beef types, classes of horses, hogs, or other pertinent information. At other programs they would use large muslin sheets to show the illustrations:

> Please have these charts and diagrams, tables, etc., prepared on good muslin of sufficient size to be seen over a large room. They should not be less than one or one and a half yards square, in my judgment. . . . Please allow for a sufficient margin at the top on your charts that they may be attached to a cord or in some way mounted so that they may be properly displayed before the audience.[47]

In the early years, the subjects at Farmers' Institutes mainly consisted of basic agronomic and livestock production lectures, but gradually those subjects began to be augmented by topics dealing more directly with the work of farm women and young people. It was clear over time that the Farmers' Institutes had evolved to address the interests of the farm family as a whole. And it continued to evolve to encompass subjects dealing with the entire community. Economic and cultural subjects, improvement to highways, marketing of agricultural products, the country church and school, rural beautification, and community betterment all came to be normal and expected presentations that drew local businessmen and community leaders to the program.

Latta noted the effects of one such presentation that was delivered at the Tippecanoe County Farmers' Institute:

> One year ago tomorrow Mr. J. L. Caldwell read a paper before this institute on the subject of "Free mail delivery in the rural districts." As a direct result of that paper three rural routes have been established in this county. I take the figures given on the last one as an average; 31 square miles are accommodated by rural delivery on route 3 on which the carrier will start

Dec. 4; or in round numbers 19,000 acres. Asst. Postmaster General says that rural delivery of mail increases the value of land $5 per acre. The land on route No. 3 is increased in value $95,000. It being taken as an average, the land on the three routes has increased in value $285,000 during the past year, all through the reading of one paper by Mr. Caldwell at the Tippecanoe County Farmers' Institute.[48]

Professor Latta did not have funds to publish the entire proceedings of what was being taught annually in the county institutes, but he did pursue publication of selected presentations. He made arrangements with the Indiana State Board of Agriculture to publish a representative collection of these papers, each limited to a thousand words. He thought publication would serve two purposes: (1) it would provide a measure of compensation to local workers, who would see their names in print; and (2) information discussed in the counties and contained in these papers would benefit the agricultural community across the state.

Latta requested that local workers submit papers for inclusion in the annual reports of the Indiana State Board of Agriculture. He also asked the paid speakers to let him know about any local presentation that might be worth publishing. Latta was the final judge as to which papers were appropriate for inclusion in the annual report. Over many years, this report would contain hundreds of pages dealing with papers read by institute workers. Cleverly, it appears that Latta did not select papers based solely on quality and subject but also to represent as many counties as possible.

The diversity of the presentations at the Farmers' Institutes is reflected in their titles as they appeared in these annual reports. Topics pertained to the field, family, and farm community. A partial list follows, with additional examples found in Appendix 4:

Care of cream and churning. *Mrs. Jennie Hill, Union County*
The Hessian Fly. *Bert Hart, Warrick County*
Farm accounts. *F. J. Heacock, Washington County*
What is the basis of an equitable land rent? *J. C. Goodwine, Warren County*
Our daughters—what shall we teach them? *Mrs. S. J. Gunkle, Clinton County*
Fruit growing and spraying. *Eli Hemmer, Dubois County*
Is the production of winter eggs profitable? *T. Blair, Hamilton County*
The value of a higher education for the farmer. *B. Volga, Jefferson County*
One hundred acres and how to manage it. *J. Young, Hamilton County*

Needs and improvements of our rural schools. *Mrs. L. Dyer,*
    Tippecanoe County
Can farmers of Kosciusko County afford to grow wheat at present prices?
    E. F. Diehl, Kosciusko County
A canning factory on the farm. *E. Tufts, Ripley County*
Forestry—past, present, and future. *J. Parks, Marshall County*
Sanitation of the farmer's home. *Miss F. Noe, LaPorte County*
How to select food. *Miss F. Little, Cass County*
Soil fertility. *W. Artman, Marion County*
Silos and silage. *A. Hoadley, Hendricks County*
The farmer's contribution to society. *Mrs. A. Trusler, Fayette County*
The relation of parent to child and child to parent. *Mrs. A. Hootman,*
    Lake County[49]

The last scheduled Farmers' Institute of the season was a special occasion. Professor Latta attended these programs and often provided additional funds to close out the institute year:

> If, however, you desire to hold the closing meeting which will be in the lat-
> ter part of February, I will of course be with you with two other workers.
> . . . It is our rule to send three speakers including the Superintendent to
> each closing meeting, all expenses paid from the state fund.[50]

What would Professor Latta have considered a successful program? One that he especially enjoyed was a Farmers' Institute that he attended in Putnam County in 1895. It apparently had everything that Latta wanted to see in a program: good turnout, excellent speakers, and many young farmers and families interspersed throughout the audience:

> The Putnam County Farmers' Institute was held at Bainbridge on the 13th
> and 14th of Dec. and the reputation of Bainbridge for excellent Institutes
> was fully maintained. . . . By actual count over five hundred were found to
> be present at the afternoon session the first day. . . . [F]amilies attended the
> meeting from over fifteen miles away. The features of the Institute that
> especially pleased the writer were: the evident intelligence of the audi-
> ence; the large percentage of young men; the presence of ladies in very
> considerable numbers; the hearty participation in the informal discus-
> sions on the part of the audience; the friendly, social spirit and harmony
> of the proceedings; the pointed, practical papers by some workers; and
> the spirit of progress which characterized the meeting.[51]

He seemed to be very sensitive when someone asked him about what the impacts of the Farmers' Institutes had been:

> I do not know where you can find bulletins bearing upon the value of Farmers' Institutes to the farmer. "The proof of the pudding is in the eating," and the value of the institutes has been demonstrated over and over again by the meetings themselves, and by the testimony of farmers who have attended. No one has thought it worthwhile to prepare a bulletin to demonstrate a self-evident proposition to those who are acquainted with the Institute work.[52]

The number of farmers and their families who attended the programs also measured success to him. While the number of programs started at 50 meetings in 1889–90 season, it increased to 354 in 1909–10 and to 528 in 1919–20, the highest number of institutes in any single season. During Latta's management, the Farmers' Institutes provided education to more than 5 million individuals.

Attendance at the Farmers' Institutes across the years was astounding, reaching a peak of well over a quarter million people in the years just before World War I. (See Appendix 5 for yearly attendance.) In some years, attendance would be down due to outbreaks of disease, such as influenza. Other factors also conspired to increase or decrease attendance at institutes over the years:

> Owing to variations in weather, conditions of roads, amount of advertising, health, hall accommodations, geographical location, transportation facilities and community spirit, attendance at the farmers institutes has varied widely. In the earlier years when inclement weather conspired with almost impassable roads the attendance sometimes dropped below 50 and, in some cases, owing to a combination of unfavorable conditions, meetings were even abandoned. In recent years, with improved highways, good weather and the automobile as a common farm possession, the attendance at a single institute often exceeds 1,000, and sometimes runs over 3,000. The aggregate attendance for the state was 276,013 for the season of 1915–16, which remains the busiest year to date in total attendance. However, the average attendance per institute—which is a better measure of the general interest in the work—steadily increased until it reached 393 in 1924–25 and was only three less in 1927–28.[53]

Reports from the counties confirmed the popularity of the programs. The chairman for LaGrange County wrote, "At the second session 300 people were turned away, for all the standing room was taken." St. Joseph County reported,

"Great interest was taken in the institute from start to finish. All that we lacked was room. We could have an average of 2,000 if we had a hall large enough to seat them. We managed to get about 500 farmers and their wives to attend the first sessions." And a report from Union County stated, ". . . 1,300 persons attended one or more sessions of the institute. One-half or more were ladies. The exhibit was a great success."[54]

Latta worked tirelessly to maintain the quality and, thus, the success of the institutes. Once a meeting was concluded, he required each chairman to complete a detailed report on the outcome. He had specific instructions for each chairman to follow, requiring itemized expenses, estimated attendance figures, and an accounting of the strengths and weaknesses of the speakers. Much of his correspondence with the chairmen dealt with incomplete reports. If a chairman didn't fill out the form according to Latta's wishes, it was sent back. This meant that the chairman would have to resubmit the information, which could seriously slow down the process by which a county was reimbursed for its expenses:

> Your bill and the reports accompanying letter duly received. I trust you will not think me unduly exacting when I say that your reports are not very satisfactory. In the report of the Greene Co. meeting you say under the head of comments on preparation "Not time enough to give notice to far-away townships." . . . Under the head of attendance you say "Did not count" although this was specially mentioned in my letter of instructions to you. In your comments on home speakers you say "Quite good, but I am at a loss to know whether any would be fit for assigned speakers or not." . . . If you will stop to think a moment you will recognize the fact that these reports give me very little insight into the actual condition of things, and therefore can be of very little assistance to lay any future plans for the betterment of the work. I write you thus frankly, believing that you want to do a thoroughly good work when the need of it is pointed out.[55]

Latta could also be very blunt when he felt programs were not advertised adequately enough to attract the crowds that he thought they should have had at the institute. He disliked it when organizers neglected to advertise thoroughly and instead spent the money on special music or expensive meeting places. He believed it was more important to get the word out so that people could make plans to attend:

I deem it fair to say that there seems to be some little dissatisfaction with your management of the last Institute. I have on my table a clipping from the Chronicle stating that the newspapers were not furnished any program of the meeting beforehand so as to publish it. I have a report from another to the effect that the meeting was evidently not properly advertised among the townspeople and that the management appeared to be such as to estrange this class from the work. I do not, of course, know what foundation there is for these statements, but deem it proper that you should know what is said.[56]

One particular chairman drew the wrath of Professor Latta when his Farmers' Institute program had a paid advertisement for a firm selling liquor:

Some one has sent me a copy of the program of your Greenwood meeting held last Saturday. I find on one side the marked ad. of J. T. Powers and Son, of Indianapolis. I take it that the firm in question sells some form of intoxicant. Need I remind you that the advertisement of such firms is not in good taste on an Institute program? Many farmers will resent it every time.... I trust that you will bear this in mind and not permit anything of the kind in the future.[57]

Professor Latta's letters reflect his style of dealing with problems of politics, personal grievances, and petty arguments that seemed to be a constant source of annoyance for him:

I believed at first that you would be glad to have information and get the facts as they are. I really can detect no such desire in your last letter, as it appears to indicate that you are generally dissatisfied with what is.... I always take pleasure in replying to men who desire information, but have not time to reply to those whose opinions are at variance with my own. ...While I have nothing to say to your denunciation of the general condition of things, I shall always give reasonable attention to the queries of men who desire information.[58]

He handled problems directly, sometimes bluntly, and often requested specific information about a given problem so he could address it. More than once he would later have to apologize for his lack of tact or when what he wrote was misunderstood by or offensive to the reader.

The General Assembly in 1901 approved an increase of funds from $5,000 to $10,000 a year for the Farmers' Institutes and funded a new building for the School of Agriculture. With the increased funding, President Winthrop Stone addressed the Purdue Board of Trustees about how the money should be allocated to the Farmers' Institutes.

He, along with Latta and Charles Plumb, wanted to build on the existing program, extending and strengthening the institutes by adding more meetings, district conferences, and by improving the quality of the speakers. And since Latta devoted half of his time to institute business, a portion of the money was earmarked to pay half of Latta's university salary. Finally, Latta also received funding to hire a much-needed clerk to assist him in executing his work on behalf of the Farmers' Institutes.

In 1901, Latta was relieved of his duties in the Experiment Station to devote more time to the management of the Farmers' Institutes and to teaching his college classes. His assistant, John Skinner, also left that same year to take a position at the University of Illinois. Consequently, Latta turned his attention to hiring an assistant professor of agriculture and an assistant instructor to help in the day-to-day teaching duties in the classroom. As Latta searched about for an assistant professor, he outlined what he wanted in the skills and personality of someone who would be working closely with him:

> I wish to secure a competent instructor in Agriculture to assist me in my work at Purdue, in order that I may give my own attention more fully to the large affairs of the Agricultural department. I want some one who can intelligently instruct in Soils and Crops, Farm Equipment, Farm Drainage, Soil Physics, etc. I desire for this work some one who has grown up on a farm in the middle west, an earnest Christian man of good address who has done some Post Graduate work away from his Alma Mater and who has had some experience in teaching. I want one who can do acceptable work at Farmers' Institutes, who has the caliber and elements of growth in him that would fit him eventually for a very responsible position, and who would be an agreeable and loyal subordinate and co-worker.[59]

Latta's teaching and research career was coming to an end. With someone to take his place in the classroom and manage the fieldwork, he could continue to manage the School of Agriculture and focus his attention on running the Farmers' Institutes.

With the 1901 appropriation, Professor Latta continued to provide twenty-five dollars to each county for expenses toward hosting an institute, and he still paid for salaries and expenses for two speakers. However, if any monies were left over, the county could put remaining funds toward hosting a second institute that same year. The change resulted in what became known as supplemental Farmers' Institutes that were used to augment the annual meeting:

> We now propose to hold fifty or more supplemental Institutes at points intermediate between the places of annual meetings, with a view of reaching a new class of farmers, and hope in this way, within a period of two years, to so place the Institutes as to make them accessible to every farmer in the State.[60]

The chairmen could ask for these supplemental programs for their remote sites, but they would have to assume much more in the way of paying for local expenses:

> To each 1-day [supplementary] Institute we send an experienced speaker, some good practical farmer, fruit grower or dairyman, as may be preferred, to assist the people of the locality in holding a morning and afternoon session. The expenses of such a speaker are met from the general Institute fund. [Speakers were paid five to six dollars for a one-day program.] The people of the locality would provide a hall, church or school room for place of meeting, secure local workers to assist in making up a program and meet all the local expense, which however, would be very slight, indeed.[61]

The number of institutes continued to grow with the regular two-day program, extra programs when the county had leftover funds from their annual meeting, and the one-day supplemental programs. It soon became a difficult project keeping up with everyone's requests. Professor Latta instituted his own rule on how many institutes of all kinds that the county was allowed based on the total acreage in the county:

> Those having less than 200 sq. miles are to have two days of institute work each; those having from 200 to 350 square miles are to have 3 days each; those having over 350 and 500 sq. miles 4 days each; those having over 500 sq. miles 5 days each.[62]

Soon thereafter, Professor Latta began pushing the counties to adopt a membership fee and county constitution for the Farmers' Institutes. He presented his arguments in favor of this in many letters to the various chairmen:

You can assure any audience, however, that the proposition is solely for the benefit of the locality interested, and that what would be raised by membership dues would be used in the county, not a cent would ever go outside. There are two purposes in having a paid membership: (1) to provide the chairmen with some fund for meeting expense as he may find it necessary to incur them in advancing the work throughout the county, until he can be reimbursed from the State fund. (2) To provide for an extension of the work in the County.[63]

The Tippecanoe Farmers' Institute was one such example, adopting its constitution by January 1904. It claimed between 60 and 75 paid members with membership fees assessed at 25 cents per person.

But with the growing number of meetings during each institute season, the counties were finding it increasingly difficult to take care of their expenses. A state appropriation was therefore urged to secure additional funds for the institutes. The appropriation, passed in 1907, authorized an allowance of $100 to each county institute chairman on presentation of a bill of expenses incurred in holding an institute meeting. This timely aid to the counties permitted Latta to withdraw the previous apportionment of the state appropriation and use it in the further advancement of the institute work.

After several years of hosting county-based institutes, Professor Latta knew it was time to offer something new to spice up the curriculum of the standard program. He began to see a need for more advanced training for farmers in what would become very specialized and detailed instruction on a single subject:

There is an increasing demand for specialized instruction concerning modern phases of agricultural practice, as well as for discussion of the social and economic aspects of rural life. It is noticeable in contrast with the earlier institutes, that now only high grade speakers and instructors are acceptable. The "all-around" speaker is not wanted but rather the one who can bring the latest information on a special subject. Needless to say, that it is far from easy to supply such instructors. The present need of the work is not so much funds or new legislation as thoroughly posted speakers and instructors.[64]

The first specialized Farmers' Institutes were held in 1901. The first one offered a program that dealt with dairy at Plymouth, followed by two programs

on horticulture at Orleans and South Bend, and a fourth on livestock at
Huntington. In later years, Latta would add horticulture and melon growing
at Princeton, a butchers' stock at Anderson, and horticulture and good roads at
New Albany to the list of specialized Farmers' Institutes. An outline from the
District Dairy Farmers' Institute shows the depth of coverage:

Dairying promotion of agricultural prosperity
American dairying
The place of the dairy in Indiana agriculture
Selection of dairy stock
Rearing the dairy herd
Care of cows during pregnancy and parturition
Causes of variation in the per cent. of butter fat in milk
Relation of form and function in the dairy cow
Why farmer's wives like the creamery
Mutual interest of business men and farmers
The cow barn
The silo
Care and delivery of milk
Dairy feeding rations
Summer feeding
Producing a balanced ration on the farm
Silage: its value, production and preservation[65]

Professor Latta remarked that the

. . . purpose of these meetings was not only to instruct those engaged in
the special lines of work in question, but also to awaken a more general
interest in the lines of agriculture under consideration. As was expected,
the attendance was not large, ranging from 150 to about 300. The interest
in all these meetings was excellent, however, and it is believed that much
good was accomplished in the way of emphasizing the importance and
profitableness of specialization in agriculture.[66]

Latta thought that these types of programs would offer an even bigger
draw if he brought in speakers from other states. To that end, he contacted
superintendents of Farmers' Institutes in other states about who they would
recommend to cover various subjects. Latta also began putting in place institute programs that would attract both the farm family and the city family. He
understood that both had to prosper for the larger community to be successful:

I think, however, there is a growing appreciation of the fact that we need to enlist both town and country in this work and that in so doing we will not only popularize the work itself, but tend to bring into pleasant social and business relations the people of town and country. To this end there should be a broad gauge effort on the part of the local management in each county to enlist the leading businessmen, including merchants, manufacturers and professional men in the Institute work.[67]

*   *   *

Professor Latta was an early proponent for broadening the programming of the Farmers' Institutes to appeal not just to farmers but to their families as well. Indeed, from the very beginning of his tenure as superintendent, he included female speakers on the program in an effort to draw more women attendees. Latta felt so strongly about this that he even wrote to a county chairman in 1895 to express his views:

> I like your program although it is pretty nearly snowed under with the advertisements. Sorry not to see any ladies on the program. I think this is a mistake as the Institute is for the farmer and his family, and the presence of ladies is the best means of drawing out the attendance of the wives of the farmers and businessmen.[68]

A 1901 letter to a friend illustrates why Latta thought it was so important to create programs for rural families at the Farmers' Institutes:

> I frequently turn from well kept fine live-stock to the Farmer and his wife with a feeling of great regret. It not infrequently happens that the Farmer and his wife and children are apparently the last to receive attention. In many cases it has been necessary for the husband and wife, and perhaps for the children as well, to lend their energy towards improving the farm and making it profitable.... It frequently finds the farmer's wife broken in health and spirit and the children with a settled dislike for the farm and everything that pertains to it. It will be well to point out that the ideal home can really be found only in the country. Only here do we find the real conditions under which such a home can exist. The country also affords opportunity to those, who know how to take advantage of it, for culture of higher and finer qualities, as well as those sterling qualities which make strong men and women.[69]

Latta knew that special sessions offered at the Tippecanoe County institute in 1898 had met with great success, and twenty additional counties had offered similar programs the following year. This would have allowed men and women to share some sessions, while women could also receive topics relating to their special interests.

Latta contacted county institute chairmen, asking them if they would like to have a female speaker assigned to their programs. What he had in mind was to bring a speaker of high caliber to teach a domestic science topic and offer cooking demonstrations for women attendees in a separate session. In the summer of 1900, his plans began to take shape:

> Some time since, I wrote to the several December chairmen who had expressed a desire for women workers and a willingness to undertake a separate session, asking if they would like a demonstration lecturer in domestic science. The replies were very largely in the affirmative and I have therefore arranged to have such a lecturer for some four weeks at the opening of the season. . . . We are to have a Miss McDermott of Allegheny, Pa. to give the demonstration lectures.[70]

Unfortunately, McDermott contracted typhoid fever and could not make the meetings. After seeking the appropriate references, Latta instead ended up hiring Mary Lamson Clarke, who was in charge of the Milwaukee Cooking School, to address women's interests. By late October of 1900, he sent to all of the newspapers in the state an announcement of a new program being held in many of the Farmers' Institutes:

> The new feature of the work will be the introduction of Domestic Science at a number of the December meetings. This work has been arranged by conference with the chairmen interested. Miss Mary Lamson Clarke, who is in charge of the Milwaukee Cooking School has been engaged to do this work. She will speak on Foods and their Relation to Health at the general sessions and give demonstration lectures in cooking at separate sessions for women, if desired. Miss Clarke did work of this kind at the Wisconsin Farmers' Institutes some years since and comes to Indiana well recommended by Supt. McKorrow of Wisconsin.[71]

In the ensuing years, Latta continued his campaign to expand women's programming:

> Further special provisions for women were made in the summer of 1905, by holding a series of 31 institutes for farmers' wives and children. These

meetings proved so valuable that when the necessary state funds became sufficient a second series of 41 summer institutes for farmers' families was conducted in 1907.[72]

Latta had an unwavering belief that Purdue should offer women an opportunity to better themselves by getting an education. Including topics of importance to women and utilizing women speakers at Farmers' Institutes helped Latta create a demand for educational opportunities for women. This was a crucial step in Latta's simultaneous effort to set up the Department of Household Economics at Purdue University, which was eventually created in 1905. (The next chapter, "The Purdue Politician," includes a discussion of Latta's efforts to create educational opportunities for women at Purdue.)

The Farmers' Institutes played an important role in this process because they gave a voice to women at a time when there were not many intellectual outlets for them in American society while helping break down many commonly held stereotypes of farm wives.

Virginia C. Meredith, a long-time friend and confidante of Professor Latta, gave a strong testimonial about her views on the role that Farmers' Institutes played in educating farm women:

> The earnest and unmistakable response of farmers to work in agricultural extension carried on by Purdue University was in an eminent degree due to a factor sometimes overlooked. I refer to the attendance of women at the very first farmers' institutes which were held in the state. Among early institute speakers it was a subject of frequent comment that many women should with interest and patience sit through programs devoted to grain and livestock. Naturally, this attendance and interest meant discussion, later, at home of both subject and speaker. Most speakers were shrewd enough to make an appeal to these alert farm women. The dairy and poultry formerly were almost exclusively the concern of farm women and, of course any instruction pertaining to these two subjects was understood and used. Very probably in no other two lines has the influence of the Purdue guidance been more marked.[73]

Latta's efforts to expand programming at the Farmers' Institutes didn't stop with women's interests. Indeed, he strongly believed it was necessary to consider the needs of the entire family, even the children. Professor Latta was proud that the children from the rural areas found the Farmers' Institutes a popular place to meet. More importantly, they came with projects—things they made and grew—and competed against each other for prizes and awards. This activity of the farm boys and girls grew until it evolved into the 4-H program. Farmers' Institutes organized by Latta were given credit for "furnish[ing] the early leadership in the boys' and girls' 4-H club work in Indiana."[74]

Evening sessions were offered for children at the Farmers' Institutes. It was as much a social gathering as it was an educational program. The children played music and games, delivered recitations, and acted as ushers. Oftentimes the boys and girls were divided into competing teams, which added an element of challenge and fun. These evening sessions became an important aspect of the Farmers' Institutes.

Professor Latta gave credit to the officials who managed the Tippecanoe County institutes for being the first to have the young boys and girls at the Farmers' Institutes:

> Very early in the development of the institute work in the state, the boys and girls of Tippecanoe county were encouraged to make exhibits of farm and home products for which awards were made. At the start the boys showed corn of their own selection from the corn crib. The girls exhibited bread, cake and sometimes butter-products or products of their own skill. These exhibits soon spread to other counties and have now become a well-nigh universal feature of the farmers' institute meetings. Soon the need of improving the quality and increasing the uniformity for the exhibits became important. For this purpose, score cards for guidance in making and judging the exhibits were prepared and distributed from the central office. Both boys and girls were required to grow or make the products shown by them. As time passed, the entries came to have, in many cases, such uniform excellence as to make the placing of the awards a perplexing problem for the judges. School clubs under the direction of the county Superintendent of Schools and coached by the public school teachers were formed in the more progressive counties.
>
> With the coming of the county agents this work for and by the farm boys and girls received a marked impetus. The enthusiasm of the young folks became contagious and spread to the adults, many of whom joined in making exhibits in a separate class for the grown-ups. Interest in these exhibits in many cases became so strong as to divert the attention of many from the institute programs. This made necessary the placing of the articles on exhibition in a separate room and the closing of same during the hours of the institute sessions.[75]

All indications are that the children were an important component of the Farmers' Institutes by the 1890s. The Adams County annual report for 1896 noted, "The young people were more numerous than at any previous meeting." The Jennings County 1896 report stated, "The half day given to the young people was well improved and was quite a success. We never had so many young people at our institute before."[76]

Latta promoted the use of premiums for the children who competed in the contests. This simple paragraph, written in December 1895 to a county chairman, fairly summed up his intentions for reaching the entire farm family through these efforts:

> If the business men of Francesville are willing to offer free special prizes in the way of goods that they may have for sale, for exhibits of grains, fruits or butter, this would be a desirable auxiliary to your Inst[itute] work. The butter exhibit with two or three classes that would tend to interest the girls and women would doubtless be a means of drawing out their attendance. I hope you may be able to secure one or two ladies in addition to the ones assigned you so that there may be a full attendance of ladies at your meeting. Try to arrange so as to enlist the entire family in this work.[77]

The first annual report of Purdue's Department of Agricultural Extension also emphasized the education of young men and women at the Farmers' Institutes:

> In connection with the farmers' institutes and the county superintendents of schools in many counties of the state, contests for young people, in the growing of corn, baking of bread, making of butter, sewing, etc., have been carried on. These contests have not only turned the attention of the boys and girls to the work of the farm and home, but they have also done much to give inspiration to the boys and girls for school work.[78]

Professor Latta offered advice to the various Farmers' Institutes chairmen on how to encourage youth to participate in the programs:

> I suggest that you confer with your County Sup't. of Schools with reference to topics for the prize essays. I would suggest further, that you write to Prof. L. H. Bailey and get such publications [a nature series] as he can send you. I think the children might appropriately write on farm topics. This might stimulate them to make some experiments the coming Summer, and would certainly arouse an interest in many operations of the farm. No doubt some of the children have had experience in rearing poultry and in caring for pigs and calves, as well as in the larger farm operations. Essays giving their experience and their conclusion would be, to my thinking, in

place. We should, I think, take care that the children have some subject in which they have a working experience, or of which they know something by actual personal observation. If any school gardens have been kept in the county, that would be a very suitable subject for some of the children to write upon. Perhaps "The Home Vegetable Garden" would be a suitable subject for some. This will, I think, suggest enough in the way of subjects.

In this county [Tippecanoe] we have in mind the growing of crops, or live stock by the young folks; the products to be exhibited at the County Fair, and an essay describing the work to be given at the next Institute. It is a very important thing to interest the children, and I am glad to know that you are thinking along this line. In a good degree we shall have to "blaze" the way as the track is not a beaten one. [79]

Professor Latta himself was working hard in Tippecanoe County to make children a regular feature of his Farmers' Institutes. In 1904, Professor Latta proudly wrote that the county fair association was giving awards totaling forty-nine dollars for various activities that the children were doing. First-place winners were given three dollars for the best half bushel of yellow corn, white corn, white oats, mixed oats, and Irish potatoes, and for the best loaf of bread and the best butter. Children placing second in these and other categories were given two dollars, with one dollar going to the third-place finishers.

Latta began a letter-writing campaign to let others know about the work with children and how premiums could be used to have the children participate in the Farmers' Institutes. He also wrote a column for the agricultural press about the competition at the Farmers' Institutes supported by the fair association. In addition, he wrote about the youth competition and sent articles to the *Agricultural Epitomist, American-Grange Bulletin, Breeders' Gazette, Farmer's Guide, Farmer's Review, Farmer's Voice, Indiana Farmer, Jersey Bulletin, National Stockman, Ohio Farmer, Orange-Judd Farmer, Prairie Farmer,* and *Up-to-Date Farming.*

The Farmers' Institutes participants also worked to improve education for children in the public schools. In 1907, attendees at the tenth annual conference of Farmers' Institutes workers at Purdue University passed a resolution on the need to improve the quality of education in the rural schools that stated:

Whereas the great majority of the boys and girls of the farm do not acquire an education beyond that given in the home schools and,

Whereas these schools do not effectively prepare their students for the life and work of the farm,

Therefore Resolved, that this State Conference of Farmers' Institute Workers commends the action of the State Board of Education in recognizing this need by the preparation of a more appropriate course of study for use in the rural schools.

Resolved further that we urge upon the school officials the adoption and use of this course of study.

Resolved further that we urge that provision to be made for the better preparation of teachers to give instruction in nature study, elementary agriculture, manual training, and household science.

Resolved further that we favor the provision by which professional preparation in the above lines may be recognized among the qualifications of teachers employed in the rural schools.

Resolved further that we urge upon Farmers' Institute speakers the importance of calling attention to the new course of study and its practical value in preparing the boys and girls of the farm for their life work.[80]

Professor Latta became one of many players in a Purdue University initiative to create publications for teaching agriculture to school-age children. Twenty-four leaflets were developed by the Purdue staff that "introduced children to science through the exploration of topics related to agriculture and the rural environment."[81] Professor Latta wrote two publications in the series: *Experimental Farm for Young People* (No. 22) and *Points for the Young Farmers' Club* (No. 23). Purdue University ultimately shipped more than 100,000 copies of the nature leaflets. By 1900, the demand for the nature leaflets had outstripped the supply, and new printings were stopped because funds were lacking.

During the early 1910s, there was a concerted movement to introduce agriculture, domestic science, and manual training into the rural schools. Purdue instructors were sent to the county teachers' institutes to give demonstrations and techniques that could be used to teach rural school children about agriculture. Latta was listed in 1911 as being the Purdue instructor at Rockport (August 17–18), Rensselaer (August 29–30), and Winchester (August 31). Latta would speak to nearly 500 teachers at these three programs.

The teaching of domestic science and agriculture to public school students opened up a whole new clientele for the Purdue professors.

The teaching of agriculture and domestic science in public schools gives to these subjects a permanent place on the programs of many teachers' institutes, and causes many requests for instructors from Purdue. During the year such instructors rendered 116 days service at 35 county institutes attended by over 6,000 teachers. In addition, the University instructors attended 76 township teachers' institutes, having an attendance of over 5,000 teachers.[82]

※ ※ ※

It is important to recognize the Farmers' Institutes as the precursor to the Extension programs that exist today—agriculture and natural resources, home economics, youth development, and community development and leadership. The Farmers' Institutes were the first formal program designed to deliver the research of the agricultural universities to the farmers. What began as an effort to introduce farmers to better management practices for their farms evolved into a county-based outreach effort that strived to improve the lives of entire farm families and their rural communities. The university's annual report for 1910 made note of the progress:

> The Institutes have been characterized in recent years by the development of new features not originally anticipated, this including consideration of the farmer's home as well as his fields; of sessions devoted to young people and calculated to stimulate their interest in rural affairs; of cooperation with the public schools, in connecting school life with home and farm life; in the organization of boys' and girls' clubs and promoting contests in rural industries. The latest development is the proposal to interest the pastors of country churches in the mapping for rural improvement.[83]

Purdue University evolved as well when, in 1906, it organized this outreach effort as "Extension Work" within the Agricultural Experiment Station. Responsibility for its management was assigned to Professor George I. Christie, who was highly regarded for his work in this area. In the pamphlet titled "25 Years of Extension Work in Indiana," he and Professor Latta are pictured before a brief, printed summary describing the work of both men in developing outreach programs for the rural agricultural community.

The year 1911 was an important one for Extension in Indiana. The state passed the Clore Act, which created the Department of Agricultural Extension at Purdue. It also provided $30,000 a year to fund all Extension activities. This allowed the Extension department to become a distinct program within the Experiment Station.

However, the Clore Act also brought to an end the autonomy of the Farmers' Institutes.

> On February 28, 1911, an act of the Legislature, approved February 27th, replacing the Acts of March 9, 1889, and subsequent acts and amendments, went into effect, thus closing the record of twenty-two years activity of the Farmers' Institutes as a separate branch of the University. The new law, more broad in its scope, provided for the continuation of farmers' institutes as one of the important branches of the work of agricultural extension. The change, therefore, is one of organization and it is believed will not detract from the efficiency or influence of this important agency for agricultural betterment. Professor W. C. Latta, who from the beginning has been the superintendent of institutes and to whose faithful and wise direction the efficiency and successful development of the work is due, continues in charge of this phase of the great movement for the improvement of agriculture and rural conditions.[84]

A noticeable change occurred in the lengthy and detailed reports that Latta issued on the Farmers' Institutes. After 1906 they were reduced to mere paragraphs in the Extension Department's annual reports. The institutes had become one of many Purdue outreach efforts.

What did Professor Latta think about placement of the Farmers' Institutes as a unit within the Extension Department? He addressed this issue in "The Story of Farmers' Institutes," a manuscript he probably wrote in the early 1930s:

> From 1889 to 1911 the farmers institute work was carried on as a distinct—not organically related—activity of Purdue University. But under the provisions of the so called Clore Law of 1911 the institute work was made a division of the Agricultural Extension Department of Purdue University in which relations it has since remained. This has in no way interfered with the freedom and efficiency of the Institute management. This closer union with other related lines of work has made possible a better coordination of the several field activities of the Extension Department. Conflicts in dates of meetings and duplication of effort are more fully avoided and, through mutual understanding of the distinctive phases and fields of extension work, more intelligent and more effective cooperation is secured. The Clore Law also authorized a county appropriation of 25 [dollars] per square mile of land in each county for defraying the local expense of the institute meetings.[85]

With its 1911 creation, Purdue's Department of Agricultural Extension preceded the May 8, 1914, federal law known as the Smith-Lever Cooperative Extension Act. The Smith-Lever Act allocated federal funds to launch a national system for the teaching of agricultural science and home economics education at the land-grant schools. The Smith-Lever Act also provided a mechanism by which the U.S. Department of Agriculture—with its employees, resources, and expertise—could partner with the states in working directly with the farm population. The act further stipulated that Extension funds could not be used to support teaching in college classes, thus "insuring that the media of non-formal education would remain intact."[86]

It was the final major piece of federal legislation that would help define the core principles of the land-grant universities: the linking of teaching, research, and Extension. The Smith-Lever Act connected the national land-grant schools, which had been established by the Morrill Land Grant Act of 1862, and the national agricultural experiment stations, established by the Hatch Act of 1887, to a nationwide federal and state partnership whose primary responsibilities were to teach agriculture and home economics to the adult farming community.

Superintendent Christie organized the Department of Agricultural Extension into broad program areas: the Farmers' Institutes, Short Courses and Exhibits, Boys and Girls Clubs, and in later years, Agricultural County Agents and Home Economics. Christie would assign a person to take charge of each of these departments while he retained control of the special projects, including the education trains, rural school agriculture, instruction at county teachers' institutes, corn shows, farm management studies, demonstrations through county agricultural agents, newspaper articles, and publications.

꙼ ꙼ ꙼

On April 25, 1923, the Purdue trustees relieved the seventy-three-year-old Latta of his responsibilities to the Farmers' Institutes, at the same time reassigning Walter Q. Fitch to replace him as superintendent:

Relating to: Change in Title and Duties of Professor W. C. Latta
That, on the recommendation of the President, and the Director of Agricultural Extension, Professor W. C. Latta, who has served the University for forty-one years, be relieved of the strenuous work that his position as Farmers' Institute Specialist demands, and be appointed

Consulting Specialist in the Department of Agricultural Extension at his present salary ($1,600), and at the same time that he retain his present position and salary in the School of Agriculture ($400).[87]

But even after he retired, Latta continued to work "with such a zest that a young associate was led to remark that, for all practical purposes, Latta did not know about his retirement."[88]

Indeed, Professor Latta would continue to work for twelve more years at Purdue, serving as an editor for the Department of Agricultural Extension and writing the histories of Indiana agriculture, the Agricultural Experiment Station, and the Department of Agricultural Extension. In this new position, Latta now enjoyed sufficient time to reflect and write about the impact of the Farmers' Institutes on Indiana's agricultural community:

> Briefly summarized, Farmers' Institutes have done much to allay the feeling of antagonism between town and country, which was so prevalent at first; to foster friendly relations among the agricultural classes themselves; to increase the general intelligence of the farming classes; to foster a desire for the more thorough education of farmers' sons and daughters as a means to higher success and greater happiness on the farm; to point out the causes of failure and the conditions of success and thereby improve the methods of agriculture; to awaken a new interest and pride in agricultural pursuits; to lift the agricultural classes up to a higher plane of living and to a clearer recognition of the duties, responsibilities and privileges of the farmer as a business man, neighbor and citizen.[89]

Professor Latta observed with quite some pleasure the expanded appeal of the institutes during his tenure as superintendent. He noted that in the early days the Farmers' Institutes drew mostly retired farmers, but over time the meetings attracted active farmers, farm women, and eventually the farm youth and people from the towns. He took pride in what the institutes had accomplished on behalf of both rural and nonrural citizens.

Under Latta's direction, the Farmers' Institutes were responsible in large measure for changing the attitudes that the state's farmers and others held toward Purdue. Latta worked tirelessly to bring together his teaching, research, and outreach efforts in a manner that allowed Purdue to demonstrate its worth to all citizens of Indiana. As Indiana residents began to look upon the university as a resource to be tapped, they began to recognize its worth and increasingly came to support Purdue with their time, money, and votes.

Through his example, Latta demonstrated time and again that the out-reach efforts led by Purdue could be enormously successful when the university responded to what its clientele wanted in terms of education. As he shaped the Farmers' Institutes, Latta steadfastly held to his guiding principles of locally determined programming, communication of university-generated research, and reliance on a network of institute proponents to bring Purdue programs to the people. As a result, the Farmers' Institutes that Latta directed became so popular that they created a need for even more Purdue-led programming.

The Farmers' Institutes of Latta's day became the foundation on which the Purdue University Cooperative Extension Service was eventually built. Latta's colleagues paid tribute to his contributions in 1939:

> From those pioneering lines of work in agricultural instruction and research at Purdue, successively developed the first agricultural extension work through Farmers' Institutes beginning in 1889, and later the estab-lishment of the present Agricultural Extension Department in 1911. This early inauguration of the extension idea, and its continuous development through more than half a century of years, reflects the farsighted vision of Professor Latta, the founder of teaching, research and extension phases of agricultural education in Indiana.[90]

Shortly before his death, Professor Latta left behind his own thoughts on Purdue's Extension efforts:

> The results of over 45 years of extension work are seen in:
> 1. The readiness and eagerness of farmers to utilize the results of scien-tific investigation in their farm operations.
> 2. The greater prosperity of the leading farmers.
> 3. The rapidly increasing number of modern farm homes.
> 4. The friendly cooperative relations of town and country folk, especially in promoting 4H Club work.
> 5. The waning of religious sectarianism and the springing up of commu-nity churches.
> 6. The growing self respect of farmers as seen in their better garb when off the farm and their ability to mingle with people of other callings on terms of equality and mutual appreciation.[91]

The institutional mission and characteristics of the Farmers' Institutes are clearly recognizable in today's Cooperative Extension Service. Locally determined programming, the hallmark of Latta's institutes, continues to be a guiding principle for modern-day Extension work. Just like the institutes, today's Extension programs are still the avenues by which university-generated research is communicated to Indiana citizens. And, significantly, the network of institute outreach efforts aimed toward farmers, their families, rural communities, and youth provided the structure for current Extension programming such as Agriculture and Natural Resources, Consumer and Family Science, Leadership and Community Development, and 4-H and Youth Development. More than any other person, William Carroll Latta was responsible for establishing the roots of this vital, progressive Purdue University Cooperative Extension Service that continues to develop ways to provide for Indiana's future more than a century after its inception.

The Purdue Politician:
An Unwavering Belief in the University

CHAPTER  SIX

God grant that pulpit, platform, press,
Men so inspire, both near and far,
That high resolve, our souls possess,
To 'stablish Peace, abolish War.

From making instruments of war,
The hand and brain of man release:
Let Art and Science, evermore,
Promote the industries of peace.

Locarno, League, World Court express
The Nations' need, the Nations' quest
For a world-wide abiding peace,
Which, ages long, will make man blest.

E'en now, let Nations all unite
To War outlaw, just Peace enthrone:
And men, of ev'ry hue, delight
To chant, for aye, the Angels' song.

—William Carroll Latta
from "Peace," 1926

EARLY IN HIS CAREER, William Latta became a key political operative for Purdue University. He was the individual to whom Purdue presidents and trustees turned for help to convey their interests to the Indiana General Assembly. Information describing Professor Latta's involvement with politicians and the political process is contained in his surviving correspondence dating from 1894 to 1904.

Professor Latta was adamant that political subjects, campaign speeches, and political innuendos were out of bounds at Farmers' Institutes. The programs were to remain nonpartisan, and those that neared or crossed that line were called to task:

> In this connection permit me to say that I fear you made a mistake in Randolph Co. by following up your Institute work there with alleged political speeches. Some dissatisfaction over it has been expressed to me and I fear it will do you no good. It is the aim of the General Management just as far as practicable to secure Institute workers who are, first, thorough successes on their own farms; second, men who are able to set forth the results of their work in a forcible and attractive manner at the Institutes; third, men who do not dabble with politics, especially during the time of their Institute work. Now do not understand that political speeches are a harm or that the men who make them are all scoundrels or anything of that sort. Some of our best Institute workers have been active political workers as well, but I think you will agree with me that their political work has in no way strengthened their Institute work, but on the other hand it has been a source of weakness to them.[1]

In 1901, Purdue President Winthrop Stone reaffirmed the rule that politics were not welcomed at the institutes, nor would politicians be permitted to use the institutes to make a pitch for farm votes:

> It is becoming evident, also, that as the institutes occupy more and more the public attention, there will be a tendency to make use of their organization to further many interests foreign to their purpose. It should be kept clearly in view that the Farmers' Institute act is specifically, as well as by intent, educational in purpose and that it intentionally makes no provision for any other interest of commercial or political character of however much importance they may be to the farmer.... Any consideration of matters leading to controversies; any diversion of the meetings for political or private ends is a perversion of the proper function of the institutes and will certainly diminish their efficiency and value.[2]

While Professor Latta enforced political neutrality in the content and delivery of the Farmers' Institutes, he himself was remarkably adept at making things happen through political connections. Latta's positions as professor of agriculture and superintendent of the Farmers' Institutes put him in a unique position to befriend influential people—farmers, doctors, judges, and elected officials. He turned to them time and again to ask them to use their influence to advance state legislation beneficial to Purdue:

Am glad to know that you [a Farmers' Institute chairman] are to be a member of the general assembly next winter. You have an intelligent understanding of the needs of the Institute work and can be a power in securing such provision for the work as its inherent merits demand. We shall spare no efforts to maintain the efficiency of the service and, if possible, improve it with the limited funds at our command. You will agree with me, however, that it is an up-hill work to compete with near-by States which have much money for this work.[3]

His friendship with State Senator James Mount, who later became governor of Indiana, was a particularly important personal, professional, and political relationship for Professor Latta. That alliance grew, as the then Senator Mount, a farmer by profession, became a popular lecturer on the Farmers' Institutes speaking circuit. Latta wrote that Mount was a tireless proponent of the agricultural interests of the state:

[Senator James Mount] has doubtless done more to encourage young men who are about to engage in farming than any other man in the state. He is entirely loyal to agriculture; is now actively engaged in it and expects to make farming his business throughout life. . . . It seems only fitting that farmers everywhere who desire to honor their calling and see it honored should, without regard to political affiliations, be pleased to cast their vote for Mr. Mount.[4]

Professor Latta and the Purdue administration knew that the $5,000 the General Assembly allotted to the Farmers' Institutes in 1889 was insufficient to get the job done. Latta used every opportunity in his capacity as professor of agriculture and superintendent of Farmers' Institutes to make the case that Purdue could do more for farm family education if more resources were provided by the state legislature. Specifically, Latta wanted the institute funding doubled to $10,000. He expressed his argument in an annual report that he sent to the state legislature. In the report, Latta pointed out that much of the early work of the institutes had been accomplished not only with state funding, but also with the donated time and money from volunteers, including speakers and local businessmen. In fact, Latta asserted that such donations were equal in value to state appropriations in the first two years. But he maintained that greater state funding was an essential component for maintaining and improving the initial success of the institutes:

[T]he successful inauguration of the work throughout the State must be largely attributed to this spirit of generosity, everywhere so helpfully manifested by the people. It could not be expected, however, that such generous support of the work would continue, as Farmers' Institutes are no longer a novelty in the State. The services of men who are well qualified for institute work are truly valuable. Such men can not be expected to neglect their own farms and herds from year to year to do gratuitous work at institutes outside of their respective counties.... That the work should be *not only maintained, but improved* [Latta's emphasis], will be conceded by every true friend of progress who desires that agriculture shall keep pace with the other rapidly growing interests of our State.

If the institute work is to continue it is the deliberate opinion of the writer that the annual appropriation therefore should be greatly increased in order to secure the best institute workers available and command the services of an active Superintendent throughout the year. The law should also be so amended as to enable its authorized executors to require prompt and active co-operation in every county as a condition of bestowing upon the same State aid for institute work.[5]

However, Professor Latta's written requests went unheeded by the legislature. Toward the end of 1894, he began waging a campaign to increase institute funding by having his friends across the state work directly with their state legislators. Latta was politically savvy and had the tenacity to pursue a cause for years on behalf of Purdue and the agricultural community.

In the final days of 1894, he called upon the county chairmen of the Farmers' Institutes, asking them to have their farmers adopt a funding resolution that he could present to the General Assembly. Sixty-eight counties passed this funding resolution. This support allowed Latta the opportunity to summarize in his Farmers' Institutes annual report just what the farmers of the state desired. This, of course, was shared with the governor and other elected officials in an attempt to gain their support for increased funding.

In December 1894, Professor Latta contacted State Representative S. Jett Williams to request that he introduce an appropriations bill that would increase the funding level for Farmers' Institutes. Latta offered to write the bill if Williams would support it. Latta believed it was important for others to lead the lobbying effort on behalf of the university, fearing that any direct lobbying effort by the university faculty members could be misconstrued. In the letter, Latta noted that, despite early misgivings, Purdue had undertaken the management of the Farmers' Institutes and made them successful. He even went so far as to suggest that the program could be moved out of Purdue's hands in order to ensure continued success of the institutes, but he would later recant this portion of the letter:

> I have noted carefully what you [Representative S. Jett Williams] say and am glad not only to find that your views so nearly coincide with mine, but that you feel willing to use your influence to ensure a larger appropriation for this work.
>
> The University authorities sustain such a relation to the Institute work that they can hardly do much aggressive work directly for an increased appropriation without their motives being misunderstood....
>
> We all believe that the work is a great one, that its efficiency can be greatly increased, and it is the opinion of the undersigned that it should remain under the direction of this institution as the Institute work is a kind of university extension of agricultural education among the farmers and naturally links the University and the farmers together in closer ties. Every friend of agricultural education realizes the importance of knitting more closely the bond between the agricultural college and the farmers. While I believe that the Institute work should continue to be carried on by Purdue University, I am not anxious to continue the work unless there can be such an appropriation as will enable us to greatly increase its efficiency and I believe this represents the view of the University authorities. There doubtless are those in the State who think the work should be conducted under some other auspices, but I believe a great majority of the friends of the work believe that the management is in the proper hands at present. Although the University authorities are willing to carry on the work to the best of their ability, they very properly feel, I think, that if it could possibly be more successful under any other auspices a change of management should be made, as nothing should stand in the way of the greatest possible success of this work.[6]

Williams was receptive to Latta's proposal, so in the last weeks of December, Latta wrote and delivered a new Farmers' Institute Act to Williams. Latta didn't include a dollar figure in the proposed legislation, leaving that to Williams. However, he did suggest that $10,000 would be appropriate, but he noted that improvements could still be accomplished with $7,500 if necessary.

To garner support for passing the new act, Professor Latta pulled out all of the stops in the form of resolutions, letters, and personal contacts. He was able to persuade Purdue President James Smart to support the request for more funding in his annual report to the Purdue Board of Trustees and to Governor Claude Mathews:

> I wish to say that the Committee in charge of Farmers' Institutes, with the exception of the Superintendent, have done their part of the work without compensation. Many members of the Purdue faculty have also given more or less of their time to Institute work and without compensation except for traveling expenses.
>
> The Superintendent has devoted himself to this work with great energy and with a zeal and devotion that cannot be measured by the small compensation which he has received from the Institute fund.
>
> I think it is apparent, to all those familiar with the Institute work that has been done, that the amount of money appropriated for Institutes is inadequate and that the results obtained have been accomplished largely through the self-sacrifice of the Superintendent and of the large corps assisting him.[7]

It would be one of the few times that Purdue administrators in the mid-1890s would publicly ask for more money for the Farmers' Institutes, preferring, more typically, to leave that job to Professor Latta and his legions of institute workers and farmers.

And Latta continued to write, sometimes chastising the General Assembly for not providing the funds he thought so important in improving the lives of farm families:

> An appropriation of less than one-half cent per capita of our population would more than double the allowance of State funds for Institute work and make it possible to place the work on a footing to compare favorably with the same in other States. The way has been well opened up for a great work in behalf of agriculture in the State and it is earnestly hoped that the General Assembly will make ample provision for carrying on this work in the future on a scale commensurate with the magnitude of our agricultural interests and the dignity and importance of the State.[8]

Still, the 1894 campaign pushed by Professor Latta failed in its efforts to double the level of appropriations. He lost the battle but did not give up his relentless pursuit for more money for the Farmers' Institutes. In 1896 he continued to publicize the value of the institutes, which he said provided the impetus for better jobs and "higher and truer living in the country."[9]

A rumor in the fall of 1899 led many to think that the Farmers' Institutes were the recipient of an additional $2,500 from the General Assembly. Professor Latta asked Governor Mount what he knew about the extra money, but it was, in fact, a baseless rumor. But it prompted Latta to organize a concerted effort by Purdue to once again make the case for the Farmers' Institutes in the fall of 1899. This would be a well managed and highly choreographed political campaign involving Professor Latta, President Stone, and the Purdue University Board of Trustees. And in addition to seeking further appropriations for the institutes, Purdue University officials also decided to ask the General Assembly for a substantial sum of money for a new agricultural building, new equipment, and hiring more professors. As the head of the School of Agriculture, Latta was also responsible for seeking additional funding to keep the school competitive with the land-grant schools in the surrounding states.

He clearly expressed these views in a letter on October 16, 1899:

> I think we should have a much larger appropriation for farmers' institutes for a number of reasons among which may be mentioned, (1) the importance of getting the very best workers to be had anywhere in the land; (2) the need for holding special institutes in different parts of the State for the purpose of encouraging or developing new industries, such as dairy institutes, fruit-growers' institutes, good-roads' institutes, sugar-beet meetings, etc. etc. to the end of the list; (3) the great advantage of publishing proceedings of the annual conferences and institute papers by prominent workers for distribution among all interested; (4) the need for an active superintendent of institutes who should give his entire time to this work. . . . We need a great addition to the teaching force in the school of agriculture. This school of agriculture should be so well equipped and so thoroughly manned as to be the pride of the farmers of the State. We need such an equipment, (1) to arrest the attention of the farmers themselves and impress all who see the equipment with the importance of agricultural education; (2) to attract students to the school of agriculture. It is high time that measures were taken to attract the brightest young people of the country to the school of agriculture in order that they may make the preparation necessary to be in the highest possible degree successful on the farm and promote the great agricultural interests of the State; (3) because other States are adding largely to their equipment and teaching force. It will not do to have the farmers' sons look elsewhere for their education. Indiana can and should afford the best there is to be had. I believe you see the force of these remarks and if so, you can make the

points in your own way. In my own judgment we should have at least $10,000 per annum for institute work. We should have a $100,000 building properly equipped for the school of agriculture, and a considerable enlargement of the teaching force of this school.[10]

Professor Latta understood that to get funding for the building or Farmers' Institutes would require that the farming community speak up loudly and often. He put on a brilliant display of political maneuvering using every conceivable way of getting Purdue University the money for buildings and programs while remaining in the background. He would bring to bear on the political process all of the resources and skills he had accumulated over his nearly twenty years at Purdue University.

Latta was smart enough, however, to realize that successfully prodding legislators required more than just having farmers write letters. Real political clout would come from dedicated Purdue University alumni and expanded enrollment in the School of Agriculture. At the turn of the century, enrollment had been slowly increasing, but not to a level that would impress anyone. Latta clearly understood that he had to get more students into the School of Agriculture, writing, "Our people are just beginning to realize the need of granting a liberal support to the College, but they do not yet fully recognize that patronage is just as essential."[11]

Latta had been unable to attract large numbers of agricultural students to the regular two- and four-year agricultural courses, so he shifted his focus to a student recruiting drive for the ten-week Winter Short Course. If he could boost numbers in the short course, then he could make the claim that the farming community valued the educational opportunities offered by Purdue University. He believed this would go a long way toward persuading the General Assembly to increase Purdue's funding.

Latta encouraged Farmers' Institutes speakers who were traveling all over the state to promote the opportunities that the Winter Short Course offered to farmers. His letters revealed that his campaign to recruit students was having the desired effect:

> You will be pleased to know that we shall doubtless have 75 or more young people in the winter course. Twenty-five of last year's students wire that they will return, which is the best possible endorsement, we think, that the course could have. Whenever you hear any criticism of Purdue do not fail to set forth clearly all that the authorities are doing, especially in behalf of the course in agriculture. That course is growing more rapidly than the

other courses here, and the fact that we have outgrown our equipment is the best possible indication of the need of further provision for the agricultural department, and of a healthy condition of things.[12]

His efforts proved immensely successful so that by October of 1900, a record-setting attendance of 200 students seemed possible in the short course. While he was pleased with the initial results, he continued to push for more students by promoting the program to his contacts throughout the state.

Without referring to the still rather low numbers of students in the regular programs, Latta focused his written remarks on the tremendous demand placed on the School of Agriculture from increased enrollment. His intent was to suggest that burgeoning enrollments were putting a strain on the educational system. He instinctively knew that generating a consistent, positive message would likely have an influential effect on politicians and the general public:

> Judging from the correspondence, the Winter Course at Purdue University will be larger than in any previous year. As the number that can be accommodated is not large, applications are being registered in order in which they are received. As it is "First come, first served," those who are intending to take this course should promptly apply for admission to the same by addressing W. C. Latta, Lafayette, Ind.[13]

The annual conference of the institute workers in 1900 saw Professor Latta working behind the scenes, corresponding with some to bring up resolutions that supported Purdue's requests for funding while asking others to publicly support the resolutions when they were presented to the full conference. Professor Latta made sure that the men and women who attended the conference would be bombarded with pro-Purdue resolutions and that the passage of the resolutions would be supported by those working the crowd from the inside. It was political posturing that only Professor Latta and a few others knew was taking place:

> I shall probably suggest your name, subject to the approval of the presiding officer, as a member of the Committee on resolutions, to be presented at the coming Conference. I would be glad to have you turn over in your mind the matters that you think should come up for consideration. Permit me to suggest, that, as the Conference will be a sentiment-molding body, the resolutions should be of such character as to rightly inform and influence the general public. As I see it, the time has come for a dignified, but earnest stand in favor of better provision for Agricultural Education, including both the School of Agriculture and the Institute work. The only

proper basis for a plea for additional State aid to these causes, is the good that has already been accomplished under the existing conditions. Therefore any expression of approval of the work done and of confidence in those having the work in charge, will best pave the way for such a plea.[14]

Latta stacked his Committee on Resolutions with some of the more influential Farmers' Institutes speakers, chairmen, and supporters. These included H. F. McMahan of Fairfield, Naomi De Vilbiss of Ft. Wayne, G. M. Naber of Treaty, J. J. W. Billingsley of Indianapolis, and Milton Trusler of Connersville. With everything in place, Professor Latta got exactly what he had worked out with them in private. That year's resolution read:

> We the Workers, Officers and Friends of the Farmers' Institutes of the State of Indiana assembled at Purdue University in Conference:–
>
> *Resolve:—*
> (1) That we thank the President and Faculty of Purdue University for their hospitality on this occasion, and for their untiring efforts in behalf of education for the farmers and their families of the State of Indiana.
> (2) Where-as we appreciate the value of the Institute work already being done, acknowledge its success considering, the limited appropriation, and, feeling the need of largely extending the work. Therefore we pledged ourselves as a body and as individuals to do all we can to arouse public sentiment in favor of a largely increased appropriation, and that we will instruct our State Representatives to this end.
> (3) That a Committee of three (3) be appointed by the general Committee on Institutes, whose duty shall be to assist in securing an increased appropriation for Farmers' Institutes.
> (4) That we commend the excellent work of the Agricultural College at Purdue; That we appreciate the urgent need for buildings and equipment to accommodate the rapidly increasing class of Agricultural Students and to keep pace with the growing importance of Agriculture; and that we will send our boys and girls to Purdue University for an excellent training in Agriculture.[15]

Latta continued working behind the scenes even after the conference. In an attempt to gauge support for the increased funding, Latta used his network of associates throughout the state to assess and, as necessary, cultivate the needed support:

You will be pleased to learn that the Trustees of Purdue University expect to ask the Legislature for an appropriation for a suitable Assembly room and for a commodious, well arranged and imposing Agricultural Building. We desire to find at least one influential man in each County who is friendly to Purdue from whom we may get information and assistance as we may need it. We wish to learn how each member elect of the coming General Assembly stands, with reference to these desired improvements. ...With the timely judicious assistance of our friends, I feel confident that we shall be able to secure for Purdue and the Institute work, the assistance of which both stand so much in need. ... P.S. Please say nothing of having received this letter. Please make no public statement of what the Trustees expect to do as I fear it would jeopardize our interests. You may certainly count on them to carry out their intentions, but to announce it publicly would almost surely harm the cause we want to help.[16]

With numbers in the Winter Short Course reaching record highs, positive resolutions issued at the annual conference, and support from top administrators at Purdue, Professor Latta asked his speakers to energize local farmers to support Purdue's request for a new agricultural building and funding for institutes work. Professor Latta warned speakers to be discreet in how they asked for local support. He did not want the slightest appearance of impropriety to jeopardize his agenda. Latta's message was consistent: Get others that are supportive to do the talking.

Permit me to suggest that you do not introduce, or strongly urge the passage of, a resolution favoring an increased appropriation for farmers' insts. People might conclude that you, as an assigned speaker, were paid to do this. It is better that this matter be pushed, if at all, by the *local* [Latta's emphasis] officers and workers. You will accomplish most by doing so thoroughly the work assigned you that every one will be led to recognize the practical value of the inst. work and be ready to favor its extension in the future.[17]

Professor Latta's network wasn't limited to county chairmen. He also had many friends as editors of agricultural and daily newspapers. He had cultivated their friendship for nearly twenty years, making certain that each institute reported to its local media. In many cases, the media were present at the programs to record firsthand what was taking place. Latta actively encouraged newspapers to report what Purdue agriculture was doing for farmers:

> I am much interested in your closing paragraph expressing your desire to be helpful in interesting the people generally in Purdue. I would be very glad indeed to furnish some articles along the line of agricultural education but my hands seem so full that I hardly dare promise. It is perhaps a little too early as yet to began an active campaign for a better building. I think the thing to do is to bring the subject of agriculture education before the farmers and make the plea for the necessity and importance of such training if young people are to realize the most there is for them on the farm. . . . The thing I am interested in now is to get as many students to enter the School of Agriculture next Sept. as possible. Next we want to make the winter course as full as may be. Then join in a vigorous effort to get the needed equipment. Numerous letters on my desk which I will be pleased to show you, indicate the very deep interest in the building up of the School of Agriculture.[18]

This helped promote the idea that Purdue University was an important institution worthy of taxpayer support.

Two bills—one dealing with Farmers' Institutes and another on an Agricultural Building—were introduced in the General Assembly in 1901. These bills required President Stone and Professor Latta to spend considerable time discussing them with the members of the General Assembly. Professor Latta coordinated Purdue's response to both bills by continuing to encourage his friends and professional associates to work toward successful passage of the bills:

> I hope you may have an opportunity to get in a word with your member elect of the General Assembly before he leaves for Indianapolis. I hope you can interest him in a larger appropriation for Farmers' Institutes and also in a liberal appropriation for Purdue. . . . If you can approach him, I would be glad to have you do so, if not, induce some other friend who has influence with him to accomplish something for Purdue.[19]

He also followed through on the resolution passed at the Farmers' Institute workers conference by forming a committee to lobby the General Assembly on behalf of the institutes. In addition to Latta, the committee included G. Naber of Wabash, J. J. W. Billingsley of Indianapolis, and C. Hobbs of Bridgeport. They set up a meeting with State Senator Fremont Goodwine in February 1901:

At the suggestion of President Stone, I write to ask whether it would be convenient for you to confer about the Farmers' Institute work some time next Monday afternoon or evening. If it is convenient, I will be pleased to meet you and a special committee on Farmers' Institutes some time that afternoon or evening. . . . I judge from yesterday's *Indianapolis Journal* that Senator Parks has introduced a bill looking to an increased appropriation for Farmers' Institutes.[20]

State Senator John Parks and Latta corresponded often during that session of the General Assembly, planning out their next moves. The bill eventually sailed through the Senate side, passing by a vote of 36 to 6.

On the House side, Parks's bill stalled. State Representative Zachariah Scifers had introduced House Bill 429, an unrelated bill that included language making the Farmers' Institutes responsible for electing the delegates to the Indiana State Board of Agriculture. Members supporting House Bill 429 wanted this bill to pass first before they would vote for Parks's bill.

Purdue University officials were opposed to House Bill 429. They clearly understood that if it passed, the Farmers' Institutes would be transformed from a purely educational program to one where partisan bickering and political posturing would ensue. By late February, Professor Latta had voiced his opinions on why House Bill 429 would be detrimental to the institutes:

First:— It would introduce Politics into every Institute in the State, because the several persons desiring to be sent to Indianapolis as delegates would canvass the members of the Institute to secure their votes.

Second:— Such canvassing would distract the minds of those in attendance and largely destroy the spirit and success of the Institute work.

Third:— The Institute work as set forth in the act of 1889 is entirely different from that of the State Board of Agriculture. The success of the Institute work thus far, has been largely due to keeping it carefully in the line prescribed by the law.

Fourth:— It would give the Institutes no real control over the management of the State Fair or public acts of the State Board of Agriculture, although they (the Institutes) would be held responsible for any mistake that might be made.

Fifth:— It proposed no new method of electing the members of the State Board proper which has been regarded as a great farce by many. The Bill in question merely proposes that a new body of men shall elect the State

Board without seeking in any way to eliminate the bargaining and swapping alleged by many to be notorious features of the election of said Board.

Sixth:— It would doubtless fail to prove at all beneficial for the State Board of Agriculture as the delegates uninformed and inexpert in Fair management would certainly be incompetent to elect an efficient Board of Managers.[21]

Latta's correspondence with Senator Parks suggests that a motivating force behind House Bill 429 was constituent pressure on Representative Scifers to prevent additional funding for the institutes:

I enclose herewith, a brief statement of reasons why House Bill No. 429 introduced by Mr. Scifers should not be concurred on by the Senate if passed by the House. I am doing what I can in a quiet way to prevent the measure from passing the House. It is possible that the author of the Bill has some special object in having it passed through the House and that he will not care to push it farther. I have private information to this effect, but I do not feel assured on this point.... From the best information that I can get, the measure is brought forward to gratify the personal peak and ambition of one man and not from any great love for either the Institute work or the State Board of Agriculture. . . . If the measure in question should come to the Senate, watch it carefully and keep me advised. I will run over to Indianapolis on short notice any time.[22]

The institute funding issue changed for the better when Professor Latta went before the House Committee on Agriculture to testify on behalf of the Farmers' Institutes bill and found a positive response by the members of that committee. Representative Scifers consequently decided that there was no additional political benefits from continuing his support of House Bill 429:

Mr. Scifers has assured me that he does not care to push his bill through the House and I have promised him that I would not oppose it further in that branch of the Legislature. We must watch it however, if it comes up in the Senate and prevent it making head-way in that body. I now feel reasonably sure that it cannot become a law.[23]

Professor Latta then began a letter-writing campaign to dozens of his contacts asking them to get their representatives to vote for the Farmers' Institutes appropriation bill in the House. Finally, following an effort expended over many years, the General Assembly passed the bill that doubled funding for the Farmers'

Institutes. The $10,000 would be used to expand the Farmers' Institutes into every corner of the state.

In gratitude, Professor Latta asked Senator Parks's constituents to do something special for the senator. Latta hoped to have the efforts of Senator Parks acknowledged, appropriately enough, at an institute program in his county.

The legislative battle over additional funds for the university itself had its ups and downs, too. Purdue would not know until the end of 1901 whether the General Assembly would provide the requested funding. The Purdue Board of Trustees had asked the General Assembly to appropriate $150,000 for an agricultural building and an assembly hall. Purdue's Chapel in the University Hall, the oldest building still on campus today, could seat only 600 students, and Purdue University had an enrollment of 1,000 students. The new assembly hall was necessary to accommodate larger gatherings, such as those at commencement exercises. The trustees also needed money for a new agricultural building because the original Agricultural Experiment Station had so deteriorated that it was nearly condemned as unsafe by the university. He would write the following to Cal Husselman, a popular institute speaker, on January 30, 1901:

> Prof. Biting tells me that he understands there will be opposition on the part of the minority in the General Assembly to liberal appropriations. I do not understand that this applies to Purdue in particular but in general there will be a tendency to secure reduction in the appropriations if possible. I have no doubt that this will be a commendable thing in some cases, but I shall greatly regret it, if Purdue does not get all that has been asked for. I think President Stone has been very reasonable in what he asked for, indeed I wanted him to ask for more. . . . I understand that there is a somewhat prevalent belief that we will get an appropriation for an Agricultural Building but not for an Assembly room. . . . Should it develop that we cannot get the Assembly Room, I should certainly favor a round $100,000 for an Agricultural Building.[24]

It did not take long for bad news to reach Purdue. The Senate and House committees that were assigned the bills were unwilling to provide funding for the assembly hall. Consequently, Professor Latta and President Stone reduced their request to $100,000 for the agricultural building only. The General Assembly, through its committees, thought the idea worthy of state funds, but only to the sum of $60,000. Still, Professor Latta was not about to give up on fully funding the building in the amount of $100,000. In a letter to Mrs. W. L. Berryman, Latta was very clear about the needs:

> Please accept my thanks for the interest you are taking in securing an increased appropriation for Farmers' Institutes. I trust that we may count on you for like assistance in securing the appropriation desired for Purdue. The Committee has recommended only about one half of what we asked for and we are very desirous that every cent that we have asked for shall be granted for the development of the School of Agriculture.[25]

Latta also urged his colleagues at the other land-grant schools in Illinois, Iowa, Ohio, and Wisconsin to write letters dealing with the need for full funding, which he forwarded to Indiana Senator Freemont Goodwine. His friends all said the same thing: increased state appropriations lead to increases in student numbers. Professor Latta had obviously offered some coaching with respect to letter content. In the end, however, Professor Latta and President Stone had to settle for $60,000 for the building and $10,000 per year for new equipment.

⚜ ⚜ ⚜

It seems that both Stone and Latta were busy working on building plans even before the funds were secured from the General Assembly. There appeared to be competition for a contract between a company in Chicago and one in Indianapolis, and they were both making prospective drawings for the new agricultural building. The architectural firm that was eventually selected for the building project was R. P. Daggett & Company, and the general contractor was William P. Jungclaus (today known as Jungclaus-Campbell).

Professor Latta worked with Stone in developing what would be needed in the building. They had hoped to include a veterinary wing on the new building but had to forego that portion given the limited funds that were eventually supplied for the project. This 1901 letter written to the architect shows the extent of Latta's involvement in planning the building's construction:

> Replying to yours [R. P. Daggett & Company] of the 5th, we will of course cheerfully wait for the drawings until you have had time to complete them. I failed to indicate the names of the rooms on the drawing that President Stone submitted to me. I think the simple word "Office" will answer for the several offices.

Beginning with the basement there will be under the rear wing a "Farm Machinery room," then at the east end, north east corner, in front "Cheese Room"; next to this toward the center, "Home Dairy" room; next, "Milk Testing" room. At the end of the passage at the east end "Weigh Room"; in the south east corner, "Separate Room"; next to this, "Cream Room" then "Churn Room"; the "Cheese curing rooms" are directly under the entrance. The other insulated rooms may be called "Cold or Horticultural storage rooms." The room under the vault "Dairy Store" with refrigerator in the end fronting on the Hall. Between the Farm Machinery room and the hall will be a motor and fan. In the east end of the basement there will be on the front, north west corner, a room for the "Horticultural Laboratory." Adjoining the Soil Physics Laboratory and between it and the motor room there is a room for "Soil Storage" and south of this, a small soil preparation room. The room adjoining the Horticultural laboratory is for lockers, lavatory, baths and toilet as the plan indicates. Beginning at the east end, the rooms of the First Floor are in front, north east, corner, "Class Room"; next to it, "offices," next to this "Reading Room." On the back, "The livestock and Dairy class room" will be sufficient; next to this, "Office." In the east end, in front, north west corner, "Class room"; next to this an office; then "Horticultural, Herbarium, and Entomological laboratory." On the back side, "Class room or laboratory"; next to this, "Office."

Passing up to the second floor and beginning again at the north east corner, there is first, a "Laboratory of Comparative Pathology with adjoining Bacteria and cold and temperature rooms" which need not be named, I think. Beyond this, and in the center, the "Anatomical Room," so named in the first blueprints sent. On the back side in the southeast corner, a "Class room" which extends west to the shoulder in the wall on the south side; next to this, "Agricultural Society and Grange Hall" which adjoins the Assembly Hall on the east. Adjoining the Assembly Hall to the west, "class room"; then "Ladies Parlor with baths and toilet adjoining"; then "Class or Y.W.C.A. room." On the front side, north east corner, an "Agricultural Museum" which occupies this whole side up to the center.[26]

By July 1901, construction of the new agricultural building was in progress and scheduled for completion the following summer. The additional funds had also allowed for the expansion of the faculty, including the hiring of Frederick Johnston as associate professor of agriculture and Albert Hume as part-time assistant in agriculture, the promotion of Hubert Van Norman to instructor in dairying, and the addition of a new assistant for Professor Plumb to replace Van Norman.

Professor Latta lost no time in using these new developments as recruiting tools for the School of Agriculture. He quickly sent a letter about the changes to sixty-five of his former students in the Winter Short Course asking them to suggest students for the fall term, including women for the agricultural courses that had been modified to include domestic science:

> You will be pleased to learn that work on the new Agricultural building has begun. The excavation is now about completed, and the work of construction will go forward without delay. The building will be erected and enclosed this Fall. It will be finished in the early Summer of 1902. The contract was awarded to a strong Indianapolis firm, and we feel assured of a thoroughly good building. . . .
>
> We are perfecting plans which we trust will insure the continued earnest effective cooperation of the farmers in all measures for the promotion of the Agricultural interests of the State. I feel sure that hereafter we can secure what we need from the General Assembly as the need becomes apparent, provided the increase in the attendance of students will justify. . . . To be successful in the work of securing new students we must have the co-operation of present and former students of the Agricultural Department.
>
> On the strength of the good you received at Purdue, can not you assure your young friends that the course will be a good thing for them? Will you kindly turn your attention especially to young men and women who think of entering school in September? Pick out the strong ones and make your appeal to them. Kindly send me the names and addresses of those who you think would make good Agricultural students.
>
> I have already learned of two young women who desire to enter the school of Agriculture in September. I wish there might be a class of five or six. We would so adapt the course as to make it suit their needs. Provision will be made for continuing the work in Domestic Science as heretofore.[27]

The new building was completed in 1902 at a cost of $58,208. It was called Agricultural Hall, but even the name created a small controversy of sorts. Professor Latta's friendship with Governor Mount, who had died in 1901, made for an awkward situation when his widow asked Professor Latta to name the building Mount Hall:

> I beg to say, that I highly appreciate your kind offer to present a picture of Gov. Mount to be placed in the new Agricultural Building. I cannot of course, speak in anticipation of the action of the Trustees with reference

to designating the Building as "Mount Hall." President Stone received the suggestion with favor and I doubt not that the suggestion will be approved by the Board of Trustees.[28]

However, the trustees had another opinion about naming the new building, one quite different from that held by Professor Latta and President Stone, as revealed in this letter written by Latta:

> President Stone was at first disposed to consider favorably my suggestion [about naming the new Agricultural Building]. The matter was referred to the Board, I understand, and they questioned the advisability of naming the building after any one who had been an active politician, as they feared it might tend to injure our chances with the opposite party in the State Legislature. After conferring together, President Stone and I both came to the same conclusion. While we greatly appreciate the work that the late Governor Mount did for agriculture and for Purdue, we think it would be wise, everything considered, not to name the new building after a man who had been prominent in political circles.
>
> It has occurred to me recently that we could with great propriety, either in our general assembly room in the new building, or in the Farmers' Club Room, ornament with portraits of our former governors. We should be very glad indeed to have a portrait of the late Governor Mount for this purpose.[29]

Mrs. Mount's wishes were met, but not by Purdue. A Mount Memorial Hall was built in 1902 at Winona Lake and held many tenants over the years. At the turn of the twentieth century, Mount Memorial Hall was used as an agricultural high school. The school was a boarding school in which the students worked half a day in the classroom and the other half in the fields. In 1999, the building underwent a major restoration and was rededicated as Mount Memorial Hall. Today it is leased and managed by Grace College.

The next political battle was not with the General Assembly but an internal fight between Professor Latta, who wanted the School of Agriculture to have a domestic science program, and Purdue administrators, who seemed reluctant to implement such a program.

Professor Latta was a proponent of women speakers on various subjects of home, farm, and education at the Farmers' Institutes. He had been successful in getting women to attend these county programs, and over time they made up a significant portion of the audience. A district meeting he had organized for women in the summer of 1900 had drawn 800 attendees, mostly comprised of farmers' wives and daughters. Resolutions passed there favored agricultural education for women, including a state appropriation to establish a women's course at Purdue. Latta was clearly gearing up for another fight by trying to make this an issue of importance to women.

Professor Latta was eager to develop a separate course of study for the women at Purdue University. He faced some opposition from President Stone, who observed that women were really not very interested in coming to Purdue to study home economics. President Stone thought that Latta should concentrate his efforts on training women at the Farmers' Institutes.

Professor Latta felt that if he could interest more young women to enroll at Purdue for the Winter Short Course, it would help persuade President Stone to his point of view. President Stone seemed to bend a little in that he allowed Professor Latta to hire various women instructors over the years to teach domestic science courses at the Winter Short Course. At the time, the enrollment of women at the short course could be counted on one hand.

In all probability, President Stone gave Latta the opportunity to get women to support the teaching of domestic science at Purdue, and Professor Latta took up the challenge. Classes dealing with home economics were placed on the short course curriculum. Latta also began using out-of-state speakers to do demonstration work at Farmers' Institutes to help generate interest by women in home economics.

He brought to the Winter Short Course one of the leading teachers of home economics, Nellie Kedzie Jones (1858–1956). She was a much sought-after speaker on issues dealing with women and the home. Kedzie Jones was a graduate of Kansas Agricultural College, where she had organized a domestic science department. She would do the same at Bradley Institute in Peoria, Illinois, and would serve a fifteen-year career in Extension as the state leader for home economics at the University of Wisconsin. Kedzie Jones also traveled across the Midwest speaking at Farmers' Institutes.

Professor Latta thought if he could showcase Kedzie Jones's skills in improving home life that a demand would develop for Purdue University to implement a program for young women. He began writing to various women of the state to get out and see what could be done in the way of educating farm women and their daughters:

> I am counting much on your association [Tippecanoe Homemakers] to encourage the growth of the sentiment in favor of a liberal education for the girls which shall include a training for the "Home" and "Home-Making" as an important part of the Education of women. Our purpose in securing Mrs. Kedzie of Illinois to lecture at Purdue on Saturday during the present Winter [term] was to interest the women generally in this very project. It seems that the women of Indiana are coming slowly to recognize the importance of such education. Just why this is, I am unable to say. It is perhaps because it is as yet something new in our State. Surely an education for women which omits training for the home is sadly defective. Most women will find their highest and truest sphere as home makers. The well being of society and the Nation depends in a large measure on the character of the home. Is it not time that the light of Science should be turned upon the problems of the home maker and the house-keeper as they are upon those of the farmer, stockman and manufacturer? The schools are ready to give such training when there is a real demand for it. One great work of your association will be to encourage the growth of the sentiment in favor of liberal education on women and their adequate training for that most important of all positions for women "The Home Maker."[30]

Latta was especially interested in Kedzie Jones's views on the subject, as this letter from March 1901 indicates:

> I would like to have a talk with you about Domestic Science work at Purdue. In order that the subject may be a little more fully in your mind, I will now state some things that I need light upon.

> *First:* Is it wise to have a course designated Domestic Science as it is in Ohio?

> *Second:* Is it wise to have a woman's course closely affiliated with any one of the other courses in the Institution as is the case in Ohio?

> *Third:* Is it better to have a Woman's course in connection with an Industrial College like Purdue, specially adapted to the needs of farmers' daughters or should it be adapted to the needs of all girls?

> *Fourth:* Should Domestic Science (cooking, sewing, household management etc.) constitute so large a part of the course as to designate it or

should those subjects with Music, Literature, History, Mathematics, General Science constitute a thorough general and technical course?

Fifth: Is it feasible with the subjects we already have in our Science and Agricultural courses to construct a really good, general and technical course for young women by the addition of work in Domestic Science, by which I mean to include all that has a direct bearing on the home and its relations?

Sixth: Does not the fact that we have nothing and have done nothing here-to-fore in the line of Domestic Science make it possible for Purdue to develop an ideal course for women and escape in a large degree the mistakes that have been made elsewhere?

Seventh: How does the situation here impress you with reference to the possibilities of a Women's course, including of course, Domestic Science as a prominent feature? . . .

My thought now is, to start this work in a small way next year and devote much of the time of an instructor to Institute work, in order to arouse sentiment, educate the people and prepare the way to secure in the near future, additional state provision in the way of buildings etc. for a Woman's course. I believe there is an opportunity here for someone to begin with the *stump* [Latta's emphasis] and develop a really good thing in the line of work for women. In my own opinion, and I am not at all alone in this, you are the person who could do this best. My fear is, that the field may not seem as inviting to you as it does hopeful to me, and that we may not be able to offer you what some other school can. This letter is entirely unofficial, indeed, I am thinking out loud as it were, because I feel that I want to talk frankly with you.[31]

By the spring of 1901, Professor Latta's prospect of having the women's program in place by the end of 1902 looked rather dim. But he continued to hold out hope that he could persuade Kedzie Jones to start a program at Purdue:

Whatever may come out of it, I shall recommend that you be invited to "cast your lot" with us at Purdue. If such an invitation should come to you, don't turn us down ruthlessly. I had been wondering whether or not an arrangement may not be made for a year or two that would give you considerable leisure during the summer months and permit you to do a good deal of Institute work during the first winter or two. I presume this will make you take a long breath, when you think of it. I presume that other Institutions may be able to offer you stronger financial inducements than

Purdue, but would question whether there is a better field to be developed any where than right here in Indiana at the present time.

> . . . Since you were here, I have been thinking a great deal of the work ahead. I have also conferred at some length with President Stone. He is very much pleased with your work and would be glad indeed to have you as a member of the faculty here. He is however, unable (much as he would like to see one established) to see as bright an out-look for the future for a women's course as I can, and he is therefore, very cautious about proceeding. I presume there are local conditions which color his view and make him hesitate. I know he agrees with me as to the desirability of the thing I have in contemplation. We both recognize the fact that you can have any position you desire and are very glad for you that this is so. I would consider that we were fortunate indeed if we could secure you for a permanent position here at once. [32]

With little likelihood of a course on domestic science in sight, Professor Latta applied tougher political tactics. He was used to getting his way, and this was proving more difficult than he had originally estimated. Quietly working around the Purdue president, Latta risked overstepping his bounds. He planted the idea with a number of women across the state to unite the homemakers associations as an auxiliary to the county Farmers' Institutes. He believed that an association for homemakers could help enhance the political power of Indiana's farm women and make the Farmers' Institutes an even stronger voice for Purdue. His long-time friend, Virginia Meredith, was one of those he contacted:

> We are, also, planning to have a conference of twenty, or more, women, who are interested in the Farmers' Institute work. . . . The suggestion of a conference, which is my own, grows out of a desire to interest the Farmers' wives and daughters, largely, and cultivate a sentiment which will insure patronage of the work in Domestic Economy at Purdue, as well as to look after the interests of the women of the farm at Farmers' Institutes.[33]

Latta began to mail information about a similar Illinois organization to select women in the state. He wrote letters to the presidents of the homemaker associations, knowing that these were many of the more progressive women of the state. He thought that by linking women together in a larger association, it would increase the bargaining power of his Farmers' Institutes and push the issue of an educational program for women at Purdue. To jumpstart the new organization, Latta invited two dozen women to attend a conference at Purdue on August 16, 1901. He even offered to pay expenses for those who attended. Ironically, once Stone learned about the conference, he agreed to let Latta use Purdue funds for this purpose.

In another letter to Meredith, Latta clearly outlined what he hoped the conference would achieve in the long-term:

> There are several things that I want to accomplish, but I am not yet clear as to the method of procedure. I want, *1st.*— To have the women who come, realize the importance of organization in their interest. *2nd.*— To effect both a State and County Organization that shall have for their purpose the betterment of the condition of the women of the country. *3rd.*— To carry home and fix the truth that the farmers' daughters need a liberal education which shall include a thorough training for home-making and house-keeping. *4th.*— To show those who come that the Agricultural college is the place where this training should be secured. *5th.*— To have them realize that the Agricultural College must have both financial support and patronage in order to do the kinds of work for which it was established.[34]

Latta knew that he was bucking the system in trying to get a home economics course of study at Purdue University. He confided in Meredith, asking her not to repeat anything that he put in his next letter to her. He clearly indicates to her that his views are not in perfect agreement with those of President Stone:

> Since first writing you, I have advised with President Stone with reference to what we should undertake at the [Women's] Conference. While he and I do not view the work for women from exactly the same standpoint, yet we are agreed on the main essentials. In his letter he says he thinks we ought to emphasize what can be done for women at the Farmers' Institutes. He feels just as I do that there is a restlessness and irrational expectancy as to what the Agricultural College should do for the farmers. I presume you have felt it. We have most painfully. Too many farmers are ready to complain and too few are ready to lend support, and only now and then one is ready to give his son, or daughter, the education which the Agricultural College is established to impart. Doctor Stone would empha-size what we are now doing and what we can do for the farmers, rather than lay stress upon other things that we might do. Eager as I am to have additional provision for farmers' daughters at Purdue, I believe Dr. Stone is substantially right. By substituting a few subjects that may be grouped under "Home Economics" for certain technical subjects of the Agricultural

Course, I believe our course here would be well suited to the needs of farmers' daughters. For some years, in our Winter Course circulars, we have advertised instruction in Domestic Economy (cooking), House-hold Chemistry, House Sanitation, Horticulture, Floriculture, Botany, Dairying, English and Art. The response thus far has been very meager. The result is depressing to Dr. Stone, and it would be discouraging to me if I were disposed to be discouraged. I have, however, made up my mind not to be discouraged, but "Fight it out on this line." So far as the Agricultural College will come under discussion at the conference, I desire to emphasize and have emphasized by others, the fact that we have made and are now making provision for Agricultural education beyond the demand for it. As I see it the thing is to emphasize the value of such an education as the Agricultural College can afford for the practical farmer and home-maker. If we are right in this view and can convince the people of Indiana, they will seek such an education and secure the facilities necessary to make it most effective. It is my desire to keep in the line President Stone advises,

1st.— Because I believe he is essentially right,

2nd.— Because we must pull together to accomplish the great work that lies before us.

In writing you thus I am speaking in confidence and trust you will so regard it.[35]

Clearly, the poor response to Purdue's efforts to attract women to the school was the reason why President Stone was not interested in a Home Economics course. Why should he support a new department when women would not support the cause? Latta knew this but never seemed to be able to garner the necessary support from the farm women.

Still, Latta would not quit. The meeting to discuss the Farmers' Institutes and the future of women's education at Purdue went on as planned in August 1901. The conference agenda was as follows:

SUBJECTS FOR CONSIDERATION BY THE CONFERENCE
10 A.M.
Needs of Farmers' Wives and Daughters

2 P.M.
What can be done for the women of the county?
(a) By farmers' institutes.
(b) By the Agricultural College.

Women's Auxiliaries:
(a) What they may accomplish.
(b) Their relation to farmers' institutes.
(c) How they may be organized.

8 P.M.
Address: The Education of the Home-maker,
by Mrs Virginia Meredith, Cambridge City, Ind.,
Prof. Home Econ., Univ. Minn.
Discussion.
Adjournment.[36]

Twenty-six women attended the special conference at Latta's request. The women agreed with Professor Latta's views that they should organize as auxiliaries of the Farmers' Institutes using the constitution drafted by Latta as a guide. But the conference attendees skirted the issue of whether a domestic science course should be offered at Purdue. Instead, Professor Latta was given support in hiring a woman speaker for the upcoming Farmers' Institutes to teach subjects dealing with "home-making, household management, domestic economy, and a more thorough education of women along economic and cultural lines."[37]

Latta naïvely believed that women would gladly support what he wanted for them once they were made aware of the benefits. Latta also knew that if women failed to attend the Winter Short Course and demand their due from the president and the trustees regarding a domestic science program, then his efforts would be futile. So he used the same strategy—a targeted letter-writing campaign—that had worked to increase enrollment of men in the winter programs. He wrote letters to influential women throughout the state, encouraging them to get their daughters and friends enrolled in the Winter Short Course. His letters indicate that he still believed that a regular program for women could be in place by the September 1902 term.

With President Stone's approval, Latta hired Laura G. Day, a former student of Nellie Kedzie Jones to begin instruction that fall. He wrote often to Day, making sure that she understood what he wanted her to do and warning her about the uphill battle she might face in Indiana:

> I beg to state that the Domestic Economy work is in a formative stage here. Mrs. Kedzie came over each Saturday during the last Winter term. She gave a series of popular lectures of a general introductory character. These were given before the general public. I suppose in all two hundred different ladies attended her lectures.

The girls who came for the Winter Course were only nine in number. In addition to these I suppose fifteen or twenty of the girls, taking the regular course, attended quite regularly, although they were not required to do so. It is my thought to have the subjects of "Cooking" and the "Care of the Home" taken up again this Winter in a more or less general way.

We expect to so plan the work as to use a Domestic Science lecturer here at Purdue, during the Winter term [1901], two or perhaps three, days a week. On the other days I would want one in charge of this work to attend Farmers' Institutes. The reason for this last wish is to get a constituency and pave the way for future and more systematic work in the matter of Domestic Science.... We must do foundation work yet for a year or two, but I firmly believe that if we can find the right person to take hold of this work at this state that both the work and the worker will grow together into something desirable and permanent in this Institution in the line of Domestic Science.[38]

He then began working with the speakers for the annual Farmers' Institutes conference at Purdue University, arranging for them to discuss why women needed an education in the regular course. He wrote dozens of letters to various women, personally asking them to attend the annual conference to hear lectures on the benefits of a Purdue University domestic science program.

Success eluded Professor Latta through 1901 and early into 1902. He still desired to make a Purdue University education more available to women. However, his efforts were frustrated not just by Purdue but also by the failure of women to take advantage of the opportunity to enroll at the university. He uncharacteristically seemed to realize that his plan for a domestic science program was not going to happen:

Permit me to caution you not to lose sight of our great purpose, that of securing a large increase in the number of young men attending our Winter course. If we could get one hundred and fifty young men here, I am sure the work for the women will be taken care of. If we expend our fire in trying to get women, the result will be meager at best, as the women are very, very slow to respond.... I am with you, heart and soul, for the education of farmers' daughters as well as their sons, but a given amount of effort will bring a half dozen men to one girl, and we must have results in numbers to justify the expenditures that are being made in behalf of the School of Agriculture. Domestic Science will receive at least double the attention this year that it did last year and I feel that we have a very competent instructor [Miss Day], so all who wish to take up that work will be well cared for.[39]

He began advising prospective women attendees to take the science course at Purdue and add a few courses on domestic science to "make it an ideal woman's course."[40] His enthusiasm for creating a course of study in domestic science was faltering, but he still put pressure on the Farmers' Institutes to have Laura Day on their programs. Latta even offered the counties an inducement: Purdue would pick up all expenses for Day if they could find a way of putting her on their programs. He must have hoped that Day could energize women to attend the Winter Short Course in large numbers. It never happened.

In August of 1902, Latta was still pursuing political channels to see whether he could get a state representative to support a proposal to fund the domestic science program. President Stone would not likely have approved such a move, since the number of women attending the Winter Short Course was insignificant. Latta wrote State Representative Christian Holler inquiring about his interest in advancing the proposal. In his letter, he asked Holler two key questions:

> ... Do you think the subject of Domestic Science of sufficient importance to justify giving it a permanent place in a college course for women?
>
> ... Would you be willing to use your influence, if it should be desired by the authorities of Purdue University, to secure ample state provision for instruction in Domestic Science in this institution?[41]

It seems that his letters to Holler and others did not prove fruitful. By the start of the 1902 winter term, Latta's confidence was shaken, and he reluctantly agreed with President Stone that domestic science would not be an option at the Winter Short Course. At the time, it also seemed unlikely that it would eventually become a major at the university:

> [I]t has been decided not to undertake any work in the line of Domestic Economy, the coming winter. I have reluctantly given my consent to the dropping of this work in view of circumstances that I can more fully explain verbally. Suffice it to say the Winter Course is undergoing a thorough over-hauling. We shall project, for the Winter course students, four prominent lines of work, Agriculture, Horticulture, Live Stock Husbandry and Dairying. In view of the large numbers here, and those yet to come, and our meager funds for instruction, equipment, supplies, etc., there is excellent reason for curtailing in all lines where there does not seem to be an active demand.[42]

President Stone, however, continued to allow Latta to pursue that line of instruction at the Farmers' Institutes, as Latta shared in this letter to J. J. W. Billingsley, a Farmers' Institute speaker, in October of 1902:

> You will, doubtless, be pleased to learn that instruction in Domestic Science will be continued at Farmers' Institutes. The President has given his approval to this. We have been fortunate in being able to secure the services of Mrs. Kedzie Jones to devote five weeks to the Institute work at the opening of the Institute season. Mrs. Helen Armstrong, of Chicago, who has for several years successfully carried on similar work in Wisconsin, will also devote some time to this work in our State in December. The "ball will be kept rolling," you see, and the right sentiment will grow and manifest itself later.[43]

Letters from 1903 and 1904 indicate that Professor Latta retained hope for an eventual program but was no longer actively pursuing coursework in domestic science:

> With reference to the matter of domestic economy, I am unable to make any definite promises. You will recall that I wrote you about this last spring, and agreed to recommend it if ten or more young women desire it. I was not able to get half that number. As I said in my last letter, if ten or more should appear here and desire this work, I believe that some provision can yet be made for it.[44]

In 1905, President Stone did finally create a Department of Household Economics within the science curriculum, but it was not in the School of Agriculture. President Stone was quoted as saying, "Purdue should offer to women opportunity comparable in scientific and technical value with those enjoyed by men."[45] However, it was not until 1926 that a separate School of Home Economics was created.

Ultimately, history would judge that the Farmers' Institutes helped spark interest in home economics by women in the state. Latta was ahead of his time when it came to the education of young women. He was partially successful in their education by increasing the number of subjects offered at the Farmers' Institutes that addressed the needs of rural women. While the Farmers' Institutes held in each county greatly advanced the education of women, it would be many years before a full-blown domestic science program was instituted at Purdue University.

Professor Charles Ingersoll served as the first professor of agriculture at Purdue University from 1878 to 1882. He left Purdue to become president of Colorado Agricultural College. ©2005 CSU/Photography and Digital Imaging.

A commemorative plaque marks the spot of the original agricultural experiment plots planted by Professor Charles Ingersoll. The plaque is located on a large boulder on the southwest side of Stewart Center. Courtesy of Frederick Whitford.

This view of the campus, circa 1890, shows research plots (right) that were planted to corn. These original agricultural experimental plots were located on the ground where Stewart Center and the Purdue Memorial Union stand today. Courtesy of the Tippecanoe County Historical Association.

A view of Purdue University in 1893 showing a trolley running down State Street. Purdue buildings are shown in the background, and the property that belonged to the Marsteller family is in the forefront. Courtesy of Tippecanoe County Historical Association.

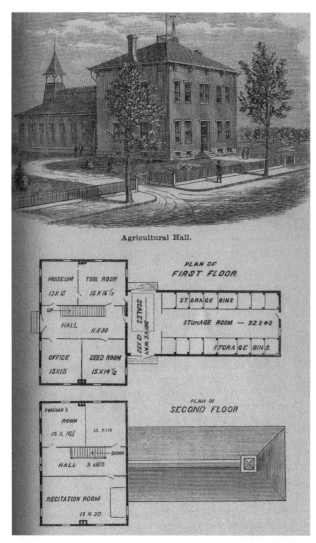

Agricultural Hall.

PLAN OF
FIRST FLOOR

MUSEUM	TOOL ROOM			
13 X 15	15 X 16½		ST ORA GE	BINS
UP		SCALES	STORAGE ROOM — 22 X 43	
HALL	11 X 30	DRIVE WAY		
		12 X22	S TORA GE	BIN S.
OFFICE	SEED ROOM			
15X15	15 X 14½			

PLAN OF
SECOND FLOOR

FOREMAN'S
ROOM
15 X. 16½   13 X 15
DOWN
HALL 9 X 80

RECITATION ROOM
17 X 30

Illustration and floor plan of the original Agricultural Hall, which was built in 1881, remodeled in 1888, and demolished when the new Agricultural Experiment Station was built in 1908. This building was on the property located between State Street and the current Agricultural Administration Building. Courtesy of Purdue University Libraries Special Collections.

Agricultural Hall in 1896. Courtesy of Purdue University Libraries Special Collections.

The second Agricultural Hall, completed in 1902. Known for many years as Entomology Hall, it was remodeled and renamed Pfendler Hall in 2004. Courtesy of the Tippecanoe County Historical Association.

The Agricultural Experiment Station as depicted on a postcard in 1908. Courtesy of the Tippecanoe County Historical Association.

Professor Latta lived in the superintendant's farm house during his first years at Purdue University. It stood in front of today's Poultry Building, just south of State Street in West Lafayette. Courtesy of Purdue University Agricultural Communication, J. C. Allen Collection.

An aerial view shows State Street near the top of this photograph. The farm house that Professor Latta lived in is due south of State Street (near upper right-hand corner), with the university farm buildings, plots, and fields south of the farm house. Additional farm acreage extended north of State Street (upper left-hand corner). Courtesy of Purdue University.

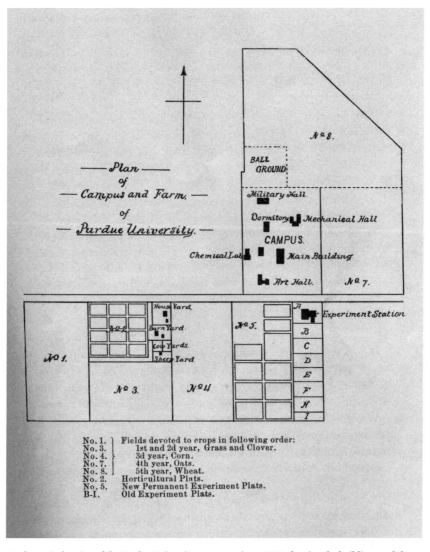

A schematic drawing of the Purdue University campus prior to 1900 showing the buildings and the School of Agriculture's farm and experimental research fields. Courtesy of Purdue University Libraries Special Collections.

Professor Latta teaching students the practical side of farm drainage in 1893 in the original Agricultural Hall. Professor Latta is seated by the door (second from right). Courtesy of Purdue University Libraries Special Collections.

A group of agriculture students and their families pose outside the Experiment Station on June 3, 1899. Professor Latta's office was located in this building. Across the street (in the background) the white fence borders what is believed to be the Marsteller home, located where today's St. Thomas Aquinas Center now stands. Courtesy of James Turley.

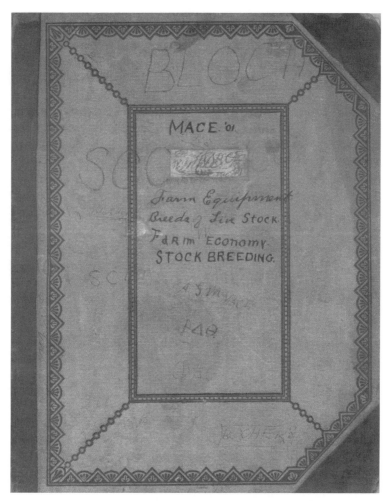

The handwritten class notes taken by Almon Mace, a graduate from the Purdue University School of Agriculture in 1901. The cover of the ledger indicates that the notes are for "Farm Equipment, Breeds of Live Stock, Farm Economy, Stock Breeding." Courtesy of James Turley.

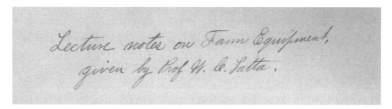

Mace wrote on the inside cover of his notebook that the class on Farm Equipment was taught by Professor W. C. Latta. Courtesy of James Turley.

Almon Mace (far left), a 1901 Purdue graduate, participated in regional agricultural experiments with Purdue University on the farm owned by him and his father, Cyrus Mace (second from left). Other family members pictured include (left to right): Caroline Mace, Carrie Mace, and Laura Mace. Courtesy of James Turley.

Above: The home of Cyrus L. Mace in Scott County, Indiana, as viewed from a cornfield. Courtesy of James Turley.

Right: Almon Mace photographed with corn taken from the joint research plots with Purdue University. Mace reported the findings to researchers at the Purdue Agricultural Experiment Station. Courtesy of James Turley.

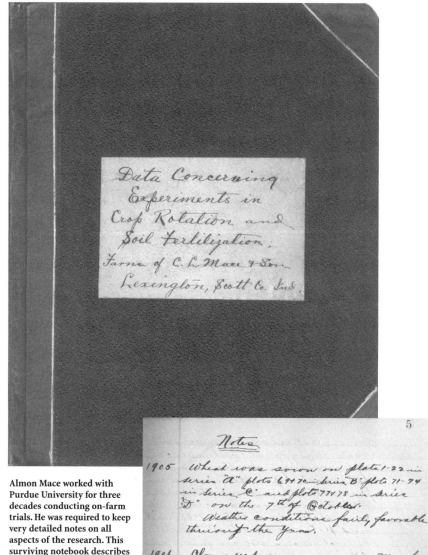

Almon Mace worked with Purdue University for three decades conducting on-farm trials. He was required to keep very detailed notes on all aspects of the research. This surviving notebook describes his work on crop rotation and soil fertilization experiments.
Courtesy of James Turley.

A poster promoting the 1909 Redkey Farmers' Institute program. Courtesy of Mark Thornburg.

TWELFTH
ANNUAL

Farmers Institute

LAGRANGE COUNTY

JANUARY 23 and 24, 1899
Ruick's Opera House
LaGrange, Indiana

**The front cover of the program for LaGrange County's twelfth annual Farmers'
Institute in 1899.** Courtesy of Purdue University Libraries Special Collections.

Monday Morning, January 23

10.00.   Call to Order by President Mills.

Invocation by Rev. E. E. Neal.

Opening Remarks by the President.

10.30.   "Fruit Culture,".............J. C. GROSSMAN

Discussion...................B. B. BOLLINGER

11.00.   "Free Mail Delivery for Farmers,"..GEO. SMITH

Discussion....................H. F. McMAHAN

11.30.   "Dairy,".........................NATE REED

Discussion..................CAL HUSSELMAN

Afternoon

1.00.   Music by Brighton Quartet.

1.10.   "What is Good Tillage?".....CAL HUSSELMAN

1.40.   "Domestic Economy,".......MRS. CHAS. SEARS

Discussion...............MRS. J. N. BABCOCK

Music.

Appointing Committees.

2.20.   "How to Secure a Stand of Clover and Keep It Through the Summer,".......H. F. McMAHAN

Query Box.

Evening

Music.

7.00.   "Should the Elementary Principles of Agriculture be Taught in Our Public Schools?"........
.........................MRS. J. W. MILLS

Discussion.....E. G. MACHAN, H. F. McMAHAN

7.30.   Lecture, "Habit,".............CAL HUSSELMAN

Music.

Exercises by Each of the Literary Societies of the County. Subjects must Pertain to Farm Life.

Original Recitation.........DEAMOR R. DRAKE

Music.

The LaGrange County Farmers' Institute of 1899 is representative of programs held across Indiana. Production practices, community issues, and the farm family were all part of the discussion. The state-sponsored speaker, Cal Husselman, was a very popular and much sought-after speaker at the time. Courtesy of Purdue University Libraries Special Collections.

Tuesday Morning, January 24.

9.30.   Institute Called to Order.

Music.

10.00. "Feeding Hogs for Profit,"....... JOSEPH CRAIG
Discussion.................... H. F. MCMAHAN

10.30. "Forage and Grain for Farm Animals,"....
.... CAL HUSSELMAN

Music.

11.00. "Breeding and Feeding Cattle for Profit,"....
.... S. E. CRAMPTON
Discussion....... WARREN DAVIS, JAMES KLINE

Query Box.

Afternoon

1.00.   Music.

Report of Committees.

Election of Officers.

1.30. "Breeding and Feeding Sheep, "WEIBLE FOSTER
Discussion......... A. H. PRICE, DANIEL KELLY

2.00. "How to Use Cement,"............. L. E. DEAL
Discussion.................... WILL HUDSON

Music.

2.30. "A Talk to Young Farmers and Their Wives,"
.... H. F. MCMAHAN

Query Box.

OFFICERS

President—J. W. MILLS.   Vice-President—L. E. DEAL.
Secretary—H. M. PRICE.   Treasurer—L·F. SHOWALTER.

Township Vice-Presidents

JOHN KIMMEL, Lima.   G. E. CRAMPTON, VanBuren.
WM. WILER, Newbury.   SAMUEL OLMSTEAD, Clay.
ANDREW DECKER, Bloomfield.   EMORY ROGERS, Springfield.
FRANK NEWMAN, Milford.   FRANK CLUGSTON, Johnson.
A. H. PRICE, Clearspring.   A. R. ZOOK, Eden.

Professor Latta and Virginia C. Meredith were pictured on the cover of the Farmers' Institutes schedule for 1924–25.
Courtesy of Purdue University Libraries Special Collections.

Professor Latta's Purdue University identification card with his signature on the back.
Courtesy of Purdue University Libraries Special Collections.

John Harrison Skinner served as the first dean of the Purdue University School of Agriculture from 1909 to 1939. Courtesy of Purdue University Agricultural Communication, J. C. Allen Collection.

Attendees at the 1923 Farm Home Conference pictured in front of Agricultural Hall at Purdue University in West Lafayette. Professor Latta is in the front row, eighth from the left, holding a hat. Courtesy of Purdue University Agricultural Communication, J. C. Allen Collection.

PROGRAM

OF THE

Fifth Annual Conference

OF

FARMERS' INSTITUTE
OFFICERS and WORKERS

Tuesday and Wednesday,
October 14th and 15th, 1902.

PURDUE UNIVERSITY, LaFayette, Indiana.

For ALL who are interested in the Prosperity and Progress of Agriculture, and ESPECIALLY for those who seek to make
the Farmers' Institutes more promotive
of Agricultural Advancement.

PRESERVE THIS PROGRAM, SHOW IT TO YOUR FRIENDS,
AND BRING IT WITH YOU TO THE CONFERENCE.

☞ For Special Railroad and Hotel Rates see last page.

Each year Professor Latta would bring the state-sponsored speakers and the executive
officers from each county to Purdue's West Lafayette campus to discuss the current status
of the Farmers' Institutes. This 1902 program announcement indicated that the attendees
could travel by street car from Lafayette to the Agricultural Building, purchase meals for
25 to 50 cents, and stay at the Lahr Hotel for $2 per night. Courtesy of Purdue University
Libraries Special Collections.

PURPOSE OF THE CONFERENCE.

It is the desire of the Institute Management that this Conference of Institute Workers shall exceed all previous ones in interest and helpfulness to those who attend, and in practical value to the Agricultural, Horticultural, Live Stock and Dairy Interests of the State.

To realize the end in view it is *essential* that EVERY COUNTY be represented at the Conference, by at least one delegate, preferably the County Institute Chairman. If he cannot attend he should deputize the Secretary or some other suitable person to represent the county and promptly notify the Superintendent of Institutes.

PURDUE UNIVERSITY

Is located in West LaFayette, one mile west of the court house of the City of LaFayette. The Conference will be held in the Assembly Room, second floor, of the new Agricultural Building.

STREET CARS.

There is a direct street car line between the city of LaFayette and West LaFayette. Street cars run each way every fifteen minutes and pass directly in front of the principal hotels. Delegates can take street car at Wabash, Big Four and L. E. & W. depots, and by asking for transfers can be carried to the University for a single fare each. The Monon depot, (corner Fifth and North Sts.,) is only two squares from the street car line. Delegates will leave cars directly in front of the Agricultural Building.

HOTELS AND RESTAURANTS.

LaFayette is well supplied with good hotels and restaurants, centrally located on or near the street car lines. The hotels announce special rates per day, as follows:

Lahr, hotel headquarters, $2,00. Capacity 100 or more.

St. Nicholas. European. Rooms 50 cts. Meals 50 cts. Capacity 75. Gribling, $1.00 and $1.25.

Bramble, rooms 25 and 50 cts. Meals 25 and 35 cts. Capacity 30.

Kramer, rooms 50 and 25 cts. Meals 25 cts. Capacity 15.

Numerous restaurants in the city and in West LaFayette furnish meals at 25 cts. and business lunch at 15 cts. A limited number of private lodgings can be secured in West LaFayette if requested before the time of the Conference.

N. B.—A Certificate that will entitle the holder and family to Round Trip tickets at ONE FARE, will be sent on application to W. C. Latta, LaFayette, Ind.

FACULTY AND ASSISTANTS. No. 1.

An 1890 publication listing Professor Latta (fourth row, far right) as a faculty member at Purdue's fifteenth anniversary. Courtesy Purdue University Libraries Special Collections.

The 1903 Purdue University agricultural faculty as featured in a 1928 newspaper article. Pictured are (left to right) Charles Plumb, Hubert Van Norman, James Troop, Robert Craig, William Latta, John Skinner, and Henry Huston. Courtesy of Purdue University Libraries Special Collections.

These Purdue University faculty members were honored for providing at least forty years of service at the institution, circa 1930. In addition to William Latta (second from right), the School of Agriculture was represented by Joseph C. Arthur (far left), George Spitzer (third from left), and James Troop (fourth from left). Also pictured are Stanley Coulter (second from left), of the School of Science, and William Turner (far right), of the School of Mechanics and Engineering. Courtesy of Purdue University Libraries Special Collections.

Moral Obligations and Civic Responsibilities:
A Life of Service

CHAPTER  SEVEN

To work from morn till night
In fields for harvest white
To help men choose the right
May this be my delight.

—William Carroll Latta
from "My Easter Prayer," date unknown

WILLIAM CARROLL LATTA was well into his sixties when he directed his attentions to persuading government agencies, civic organizations, churches, and Purdue University to broaden their efforts in the area of humanitarian relief. He wanted the invisible members of society—the poor, the young, the battered, the troubled and downtrodden—made visible to the public. Latta hoped to convince various public and private institutions that they had the power to make the world a better place for those in need. He realized that achieving such major reform in the time remaining to him clearly necessitated his assuming a more outspoken role. Latta began to articulate a philosophy that blended personal responsibility with social activism to meet the needs of the community.

In actuality, such advocacy on behalf of the underprivileged probably came as no surprise to those who knew Latta personally. For thirty years, Professor Latta had used his position at Purdue University not only to improve the productivity of farmers but to include activities to engender personal improvement for women and children through the Farmers' Institutes. But the rural communities that he loved were more than just farmers and their families. Once he began to focus on rural America, Latta saw problems that demanded the cooperation of a larger body of leaders and institutions committed to a rewarding life for all members of the community.

And so began a new journey for Latta as he tried to organize community resources to come to the aid of those less fortunate. Latta believed strongly that local issues were best dealt with by local people; securing the support of religious leaders to help him implement his ideas would be his starting point. Latta looked toward the churches of the community, with their armies of volunteers and access to funds through donations, because he truly believed that they could make a difference if the various denominations would work together for the common good of the community.

Latta was not alone in thinking that religious institutions could help solve problems facing rural America. In the late 1800s and early 1900s, churches in the United States were increasingly viewed as having become isolated from the working class. In response to this concern, a development known as the Social Gospel Movement swept across America.

The movement was led by religious speakers, writers, and practicing clergy, such as Washington Gladden and Walter Rauschenbusch, who began to portray the church as uncaring, self-serving, and heedless of the plight of those living in poverty. They made the general case that churchgoers were content to attend church services and meet their obligations to society by giving money to worthwhile charities. No more active participation was necessary. These proponents of church responsibility for social welfare argued further that while people prayed indoors in fine churches, the homeless found shelter wherever they could. While the church came together with generous meals to celebrate special occasions, the poor in nearby neighborhoods were going to bed hungry each evening. And while the church promoted children's education, young boys and girls of the poor were working everyday in sweatshops instead of going to school.

The social gospelers held that it was a disgrace for the church to sit back and witness injustice without trying to remedy it, and they blamed many of the problems of the day on the business barons, who amassed enormous wealth by using men, women, and children as if they were disposable commodities.

The Social Gospel Movement was given voice by Charles M. Sheldon, who made the call for social action more personal in his popular book, *In His Steps*.[1] The book centered on a fictitious account of a pastor who refused, at first, to see the plight of the poor. One day an uninvited tramp unexpectedly addressed the congregation, asking what it meant to follow Jesus. The pastor turned that around to ask if Jesus were here today, would he simply pray for change, or would he roll up his sleeves to lead a charge to improve people's lives?

Religious leaders heard the message of the movement clearly. *In His Steps* brought to many the realization that compassion should extend beyond the stained-glass windows of the church. The book has since been regarded as initiating a drive toward pushing churches into social activism not unlike the effect that *Silent Spring*, a book about widespread pesticide use, had in sparking an environmental revolution.

Those who attended church also brought pressure to bear on elected officials and powerful business people. They demanded that child labor be abolished, working conditions for women and men be improved, and workers be given a living wage. Their message turned political when the issues identified by the movement resonated throughout America. Soon politicians began to take up the cause of the working poor, and their solutions turned into legislation under President Franklin D. Roosevelt's New Deal.

Newly formed unions took many of the issues expounded by the religious leaders and made them key elements in helping to better organize labor into unions. The successes of the labor unions slowly led to the decline of the Social Gospel Movement as a force to be reckoned with in the national political arena. However, the Social Gospel Movement of the early twentieth century had a lasting impact at the local level. Social activism and federal legislation at the national level gave birth to a movement of volunteer work within communities. Churches, at first unaccustomed to working with other denominations, soon learned that if they combined their resources with churches of different faiths, they could effect positive changes in their communities.

Churches also began to collaborate with businesses and civic organizations to perform good works in the community. Church leaders and their followers expended considerable time and effort working together, helping others in the community on projects that would be recognized today as food pantries, family nights, preschools, soup kitchens, shelters for battered women and the homeless, senior centers, and a variety of lifestyle classes teaching adults about making a budget, raising a garden, and preparing food.

The Social Gospel Movement in the early 1900s spurred the church to assume a broader role in society. While prayer and church attendance were still an important part of a spiritual life, helping others to reach their full potential became a vitally important aspect of how one's own life on earth would be judged.

William Latta could easily recall the influence that his local church had had on his youth. Not only was the church central to his life, but he also remembered well the church and its pastors representing the heart and soul of the community. His country church and all of the churches that served isolated communities not only shared a vision of a better world, but under the guidance of church leaders, churches became deeply involved in social activities, education, and welfare programs within the community. When the community members needed help, such as disaster relief after a tornado, food for a hungry family, clothing and shelter after a house fire, or help with harvesting when a farmer was sick, the church offered its full support.

In the early years of settlements, rural people turned to the church for guidance, assistance, and social contact. Marriages, baptisms, funerals, religious-themed plays and concerts, and carry-in dinners often formed the core of rural social life. Religious leaders enjoyed a prominent role in the community and were often asked to make decisions for the larger group. The rural church, for all practical purposes, brought people together. Without the rural church, people would have lived their entire lives virtually devoid of contact with the world beyond their farm.

And for much of Latta's life, the rural church provided structure for the community. It was the place to which people gravitated, knowing they would find a friendly smile, sage advice, or just a temporary reprieve from days of demanding labor. The church, according to Latta, was "a life purifier, a conserver of the sterling virtues, a wholesome leaven and restraint in social relations, an inspirer of strict honesty in business, and had a virile membership."[2]

As Latta traveled throughout the state, he began to see a slow decay in the rural church. He recalled how the church had provided him friends, taught him right from wrong, and was a meeting place for happy and sad occasions. How could this have happened in his lifetime?

The more questions he raised about what he saw as the decline of the rural church, the greater his belief that if rural churches did not take action, they would soon become irrelevant within their communities. If church elders did not adapt to changing circumstances, membership in rural churches would continue to dwindle. This cascading effect meant that the church would not have enough volunteers or enough money to plan, promote, or participate in meaningful community projects. Latta felt that the downward spiral of the rural church would leave these once prominent institutions sitting on the side-lines watching the local people look for assistance from the more civic-minded organizations, consolidated public schools, urban churches, and local governmental agencies.

Latta claimed that the expanded free rural mail delivery, improved rural roads, daily newspapers, central township schools, electricity, telephone, and radio had loosened the ties that had once bound people to their local church. Communities once isolated were now more strongly connected to each other, the state, the nation, and the world.

While advances in technology and the building of infrastructure within communities had changed the rural environment, Latta thought that many of the problems facing rural churches were self-inflicted:

- Church leaders were not forward-thinking and rural-minded.
- There were fewer activist religious leaders than in the past.
- The methods used by the church to deal with today's social problems were based on outdated techniques from the past.
- The rural church no longer seemed to have definite community goals in mind.
- The growth of many neighborhood churches had ceased and, in some cases, was declining.
- The rural church had little influence on youth.
- Churches lacked the cooperative spirit of their predecessors.[3]

Latta believed that the churches were working for their own benefit rather than toward meeting community needs. They had become self-centered rather than community focused. Latta suggested that as membership continued to decline, these neighborhood churches would come to "recognize the futility of maintaining church activities with reduced membership, decreased financial support, nonresident ministers and infrequent services."[4]

As Latta expressed his concerns about the rural church, he came to two conclusions that must have pained him deeply. He wrote that the church was, by the 1920s, no longer the preeminent institution in the community, but it instead "has only a secondary influence in the community life," and is "no longer highly esteemed by outsiders."[5]

The one thing that Latta demonstrated time and time again was that he was not a quitter on people or organizations. With every critical remark, he would also offer a solution. Nearing seventy years old, he saw possibilities for helping rural churches to regain their prominence in the local community. He offered two suggestions: that rural churches consolidate into larger, same denomination or nondenominational community churches and that churches focus on collaboration instead of competition.

His arguments for such a consolidated church were based on biblical references:

> You recall that on another occasion Jesus said: "If I be lifted up I will draw *all* men unto me." Please note that he said *all* [Latta's emphasis]. Christ evidently intended his church to become an all-inclusive, all-conquering institution. . . .[6]

On June 22, 1934, Latta addressed a joint session of ministers and laymen in Battle Ground, Indiana, on the subject of merging rural churches. He defined rural as "villages and towns with 2,500 population or less."[7] Latta confidently addressed the group saying that the rural churches as separate units were not meeting the needs of the people of the communities in which they served. He also indicated that many of the churches were "weak, struggling, or decadent."[8]

He went on to say in his address that the rural churches were operating as competitors when it came to community affairs and recruitment of new members. He argued that just the opposite was occurring with businesses and civic organizations as they were becoming more cooperative in dealing with and solving local problems.

He also laid the groundwork for his argument that all churches needed to address the moral education of the younger generation. The young, he said, were leaving rural churches because what the elders had used in the past to help youth learn to cope with problems was no longer meeting the needs of young people. He explained that "a widening and regrettable breach is forming between the old and the new, between the passing and the rising generation."[9] And while the church and its leadership were once the centers of the community, today's citizens were turning to "the consolidated school, the community hall, and the business and social organizations of the farmers and young people"[10] for their inspiration, education, training, and advice. Latta would go on to say that "this is indeed a somber picture but many extension workers affirm that it is sadly true of numerous rural communities in the state."[11] It must have been very quiet in the audience as church leaders from different faiths listened to Latta, a prominent figure in his own right, talk so negatively about the church.

His proposal that rural churches merge to enhance their service to the community was controversial. He wrote:

> . . . thoughtful rural church laymen require that it is both unwise and unchristian to maintain weak, competing, denominational churches, that must be bolstered up with outside support, when the religious forces should unite in solid phalanx to render, unaided, community and world service.[12]

He was actually promoting the consolidation of smaller rural churches—including those of different denominations—into larger churches, which would require church leaders and their congregations to elevate religious outreach efforts on behalf of community development above differences of faith.

Latta's vision for rehabilitating rural churches consisted of the following:

- A clearer perception and a keener appreciation of the opportunities growing out of the changing conditions in the rural field;
- Merging into larger units for greater efficiency, now possible because of automobiles, better roads, and the increasing tendency to cooperate;
- Full-time, well-trained, rural-minded, resident spiritual leaders;
- Long-term rounded, attractive programs for old and young; and
- Better provision for the social life, religious education, and moral training of the rural youth.[13]

Clearly, he was using what he had learned in his early Extension work with the Farmers' Institutes. Latta wanted the small churches to merge, creating more volunteers and more muscle to get the job done. He understood that the current pattern of using part-time pastors and priests, and moving them from location to location was not conducive to having a leadership that understood the needs of the community. Essentially, he wanted a commitment that spiritual leaders would be full-time servants and would reside in an area for an extended period of time in order to better understand the needs of the community.

Latta believed the combined interests of the churches should be in "promoting material prosperity, helping the weak and backward, fostering education, promoting civic interest and virtue, promoting cultural interests and activities, and promoting wholesome recreation for old and young, and securing community protection from various hazards."[14]

He offered throughout his writings the following suggestions to meet these lofty goals:

- a. Choice of definitive, *immediate* [Latta's emphasis], worthwhile community goals—material, economic, social, recreational, civic, cultural, spiritual.
- b. Community-wide appeal for cooperation and support in achieving these several objectives.
- c. Enrollment of old and young, church and nonchurch folks on committees for the study and promotion of all worthy phases of the local community life.

    d. Making the example and simple but sublime teaching of Christ the sufficient guide for individual and social living.

    e. Emphasizing only the fundamental of true living and omitting creedal distinctions and denominational promotion.

    f. World betterment as the *ultimate* objective [Latta's emphasis].[15]

Latta chose his words with considerable care. He himself was a devout member of Trinity Methodist Church, and his own life was built around Methodism.

    Latta even wrote about worthwhile projects that the churches could undertake with other civic organizations and government agencies to have the kind of impact for which he saw a need. He suggested the following:

1. A telephone installed in every home with a local exchange operating day and night and with phone connections to other centers. This would afford some protection and reduce the losses from fire, theft, and accidents.

2. A local police with power to arrest in order to afford further protection and promote a sense of security.

3. Annual competent inspection of dwellings to reduce fire hazards and arrangement for township fire protection.

4. An emergency committee to prepare for natural and manmade disasters.

5. Enlistment of young people in various group activities for their own entertainment and development and for increasing wholesome community attractions, such as musical, literary, and forensic organizations, plays and pageants, and 4-H and other clubs.

6. Two or more strong committees of the most successful businessmen, farmers, and homemakers to promote the best methods of production, distribution, sale, purchase, and use of products and commodities.

7. Group insurance for disabling illness, accident, or disaster.

8. A civic association to consider taxation, law enactment, enforcement, or annulment.

9. A goodwill or home missionary committee to care for the sick, help the unfortunate, and restore the erring.[16]

Latta saw an opportunity to use Purdue's Extension organization in helping rural churches reorganize to reach out to the community, to build leadership skills among church leaders, to help promote cooperation among churches, and to identify the needs of the communities they served. He wrote, "The present situation in many rural districts affords an opportunity to the Department of

Agricultural Extension to render an important community service by encouraging cooperative or united religious effort on the part of the religious forces." [17]

The role of Extension would expand to help churches promote public
good. Latta thought combining the skills and leadership of the people working
in agricultural Extension with the various churches could produce more impressive results in improving the lives of people in rural communities than
either could accomplish on its own.

He reasoned that Extension and religious organizations shared similar
objectives. He argued that Extension should attempt:

1. to improve the methods and increase the returns of agriculture.
2. to enrich rural life and make it more potent in local, state, national and
   world affairs.
3. to secure for agriculture just recognition, encouragement, and protection.[18]

Latta then went on to formulate the following argument that went well beyond
concern with just the physical conditions that rural people found themselves
in. He would link being good, productive, and helpful to moral principles that
the university was also interested in promoting:

> In addition to this fundamental and essential work, to lift up agriculture
> to its proper level by inspiring the farmer to so live and work that he will
> be a positive and vital factor in building a better community, a better state
> and nation, and a better world; to convince the rural youth that, whatever
> the useful calling, the highest success and happiness are attainable only
> through intelligent effective unselfish service, is a still finer and better
> work for the agricultural college, whose function is to develop the finest
> and best in rural life.[19]

He believed that working with rural churches was a vital means of helping
Extension reach its goals for rural communities:

> The efficiently functioning, character-forming, rural church, because of
> the universality of its appeal to the highest motives of men of all classes
> and races, and of all ages and conditions, is essential to the highest attain-
> ment of these objectives of agricultural extension.[20]

Latta wrote that "the development of the rural church *as a factor in agricultural and rural community betterment* [Latta's emphasis] is, therefore, a
legitimate project of agricultural extension."[21] By highlighting these nine
words, Latta was emphasizing his belief that rural churches could be useful
partners in helping Purdue's Extension meet its obligations to the people.

Support from university officials was not immediately forthcoming, so Latta wrote a letter to Extension Director George Christie on April 19, 1928, to clarify his motives for university involvement:

> I judge from your note that you have not quite understood my objective. It is mainly to reduce the number of church buildings by uniting church societies where feasible in order to represent a solid front and make a winning appeal to right thinking men and women, to enlist for community advancement, under some simple confession of faith, as faith in the teachings of Christ, but who do not care to become Baptists or Disciples or Methodists or Presbyterians. Several members of the faculty, including Baptist, Disciple, Methodist and Presbyterian faiths, have already given their permission to mention their names in approval of the statement.[22]

Christie gave his support, saying, "[T]his has my approval and I am willing to be quoted."[23] And based on a few surviving papers, it appears that Purdue President Edward C. Elliott also agreed. President Elliott's secretary wrote to Professor Latta on April 20, 1928, to tell him that "President Elliott sees no objection to this."[24]

🌾 🌾 🌾

On November 12, 1934—just one year before Latta's death—he wrote to Clyde W. Warburton, who was at that time the director of Extension Work at the U.S. Department of Agriculture (USDA). Latta was requesting USDA support for a state program leader to direct the land-grant school's work with churches. Warburton replied:

> It would seem that the first step in this direction is to employ spiritually-minded men and women in Extension, who, in their everyday work live their beliefs. Their help in building up strong, serving rural churches will depend somewhat on the knowledge of the church and how to work with it. It would help greatly if agricultural colleges had such church surroundings and connections that agricultural students who were so minded could get proper orientation on how to go about helping develop better rural churches while they are still in college.
>
> Then, if we could have a spiritually-minded Extension sociologist on each State Extension staff, to work with county agents and to help and stimulate them in their educational and spiritual work, we might make rapid progress in helping build up the spiritual side of rural life. We get a little of the spiritual in the vesper services of our 4-H club and women's

camps. It is further inculcated in the attitude of Extension forces toward what is true and right in their everyday work with rural youth and adults.[25]

In further discussions with the USDA, Professor Latta had proposed that "[i]f necessary, [Extension] can hold occasional conferences and provide informational and inspirational addresses to enlighten the community on the need and value of concerted religious work in forming right ideals and promoting community interests."[26] On April 26, 1935, Latta brought together ministers, lay persons, and Purdue University staff in the Faculty Lounge of the Memorial Union. The Purdue-sponsored Conference of Community Church Pastors was billed as a first of its kind in Indiana, implying that other states were also instituting cooperative work with churches.

Professor Latta wrote that the conference was made "possible by the invitation which Purdue President Edward C. Elliott extended to the pastors of independent rural community churches, to spend a day at Purdue University in considering what they and the institution might accomplish in joint efforts to promote advancement in agriculture and the enrichment of rural life in its social, moral, and religious aspects."[27]

There were five visiting pastors, accompanied by four laymen, representing nine independent rural community churches located in Clark, Johnson, Lake, Ripley, St. Joseph, Steuben, and White Counties. The participating churches had been identified through a survey conducted by Latta the previous year.

President Elliott greeted the attendees. The morning session included Professor O. F. Hall from the Purdue Department of Education speaking on opportunities of the community church. He "stressed the challenge of the new situation and on the shake-up of thought and religious beliefs." [28]

Latta addressed the group on the subject of building the rural community. He "emphasized the importance of building the material features of the rural community, as basic in developing the cultural and spiritual phases of the community life."[29]

In the afternoon, presentations focused on improving the rural home and on the importance of home life. The sessions included ways in which the agricultural agent could participate in the process. By late afternoon, Purdue staff members gave a scrics of talks outlining methods that could be used to enlist youth in community improvement, including 4-H Clubs, drama and pageantry, musical activities, art, and recreational games. President Elliott concluded the conference and offered to publish accounts from the pastors about their communities' experiences in a report.

Latta would follow up with these independent churches to encourage them to provide write-ups about their mergers with other churches. He provided a suggested outline to each conference attendee that would include a historical sketch and a summary of approximately three to five lines. While letters responding to his requests still survive, it doesn't appear that the materials were ever assembled into a single report.

Latta died the following December, and the plan for continuing these conferences died with him. In all likelihood, the drive to hire a program leader to connect the university with rural churches was never acted upon by the USDA, nor does it seem that anyone else was interested in advancing the cause. Extension would never work as closely with the churches as Latta had hoped.

Latta was active also in Tippecanoe County in most of the major civic organizations dedicated to improving the lives of local citizens. The January 1936 issue of the *Purdue Alumnus* recognized Latta's social activism:

> He founded and fathered two or three miscellaneous social movements, each designed to break down prejudices and small group conflicts. Of these the Tippecanoe County Layman's Association, more recently known as the Tippecanoe County Civic Improvement Association, received a greater portion of his spare time. The original and the most persistent purpose of this organization is the uniting of all church leaders into a single functional group to combat evil influences and to promote that which all recognized as socially desirable.[30]

The Tippecanoe County Laymen's Council started in the 1920s with the objective of breaking down the religious prejudice and barriers that prevented the various denominations of churches from working together. Its membership included lay representatives from Catholic, Jewish, and Protestant churches, including African-American churches, from around the area. The plan and mission of the council became a leading force in the community.

The Laymen's Council eventually became incorporated into the Tippecanoe County Civic Improvement Association, which Latta had founded and developed into an influential force "for good-will, moral and social uplift"[31] across Indiana. The Civic Improvement Association tackled such issues as improving the "standard of motion pictures and newsstand literature and a better health standard for school children."[32]

The full scope of the Tippecanoe County Civic Improvement Association is discerned from its charter:

> The purpose shall be to promote and secure, through acquiring and disseminating trustworthy information, the following objects:
> 1. A better understanding of the moral and political issues of the community, state, and nation.
> 2. An intelligent, aggressive, public moral sentiment in the community.
> 3. A regard for law and order that will secure willing observance and faithful enforcement of the duly enacted laws of the state and nation.
> 4. True temperance as a personal virtue for the health and efficiency of the individual, and for the protection of the community.
> 5. Knowledge of the qualifications, attitude and record of all candidates for public office.
> 6. Support and backing of public officers in the faithful discharge of their official duties.
> 7. The election of honest, efficient persons to public office.
> 8. Continuous education of the school children and youth on the viles of intemperance, including the harmful effects of tobacco as used by children; on the destructive nature of alcohol, in all of its forms as a beverage, on the body, mind, and efficiency of the drinker; and on the devastating effects of the traffic in alcoholic beverages on business, politics, and the social order.
> 9. Suppression of the social, political and commercialized evils that may be found to exist in the community, including gambling places, houses of prostitution, suggestive and immoral literature and moving picture shows, and bribery and graft in public officials.[33]

As chairman of the Committee on Policy and Program, Latta asked members to lead by example, encouragement, and action rather than condemnation of wrongdoing. He urged members to join other associations, such as the American Business Men's Prohibition Foundation of Chicago, the Federal Council of Motion Pictures in America, and the International Reform Federation, by which its members could report back current issues of concern. It also "seems equally important to seek to inform and secure the cooperation of the luncheon clubs, parent-teacher associations, school officials and teachers, altrusa, chamber of commerce, YMCA and YWCA for outreach."[34] He also encouraged the membership to work with the press whenever possible to further the association's goals.

Latta was particularly concerned with the effects of alcoholism on the community. Albert Ferris, an elected official to the Indiana General Assembly, provided an insightful observation about the value of Latta's temperance principles. On March 10, 1935, he wrote the following note to Latta:

> Your wisdom and moral fiber have been most inspirational to me. One of the very distressing features of my work here in the Senate has been the experience of working with so many who, tho adequate in brains, are deficient in high ideals. Thirty hours work as a member of the erroneously named Public Morals Committee, considering the liquor bill, has convinced me the younger generation needs more men of your type.[35]

Latta's work in the associations occupied much of the eighty-year-old man's time. At the time of his death, his close friends in the associations provided a number of tributes to their untiring friend. Dr. Thomas Williams, the minister at Trinity Methodist Church in Lafayette, said that Latta "was 50 years ahead of his time in his plans for the future of American youth. His scholarship, mentality and unselfish community service were also emphasized."[36] Williams noted that to Latta "[b]rotherhood . . . meant love and kindness among all creeds and races."[37] A Rabbi Simon said Latta "strove to advance the health and moral standards of the community."[38]

The Lafayette Young Men's Christian Association (YMCA) was founded in 1889. Affectionately known as the "Y," its basic organizational philosophy was "to put Christian principles into practice through programs that build healthy spirit, mind, and body for all."[39] Lafayette was one of Indiana's first communities to have an organized YMCA.

Latta, whose name appears on the organization's original charter, was elected to the board of directors of the YMCA in 1889 and remained an active member of the board until his death in 1935. He was vice president of the board from 1889 to 1913. Latta never held any other office, but he was assigned to numerous committees during his more than forty years on the board: Auditing, Budget, Educational Work, Hiring, Member Conduct, Nomination, and Summer Religious Work. Latta faithfully attended the monthly board meetings, except for an extended, unexplained absence from February 1922 to April 1923.

Latta's work as chairman of the Religious Work Committee appealed to him most. He could see the YMCA's impact on young men with increasing program enrollment. Still, Professor Latta's tenure on the board must have been very stressful and often discouraging. He was always faced with the reality that doing good for others bore a cost. He learned early on that without obtaining contributions from outside sources, the programs that the YMCA offered would be curtailed or eliminated.

Members not paying their annual dues constantly plagued the YMCA. In addition, membership numbers fluctuated widely from year to year, with lean years sometimes triggering a financial crisis. Board minutes invariably mentioned some new campaign to raise money from outside contributors, to attract new members, or to encourage payment from those whose dues were delinquent.

In fact, the YMCA was often forced to borrow money just to pay bills so it could keep the doors open. To the credit of the board of directors, the YMCA never closed its doors or curtailed activities. It somehow persisted through a series of tough financial times.

Professor Latta was an effective fund-raiser on behalf of the YMCA. He worked all of the angles that he could to help the organization attract new members. He used his long-standing working relationship with the railroads to ask them for a trip to be given out as a prize during a membership drive:

> The Y.M.C.A. of La Fayette is endeavoring to increase its usefulness and enlarge its membership by offering a number of prizes to those who will secure the largest number of members within the next five or six weeks. Several valuable prizes have already been offered by the business men of our city. The committee having this movement in charge—of which the undersigned is a member—would like to offer a trip to Washington, D.C. sometime in the first half of 1900 as one of the prizes.
>
> I write to ask if you would not like to lend a hand by favoring our association with a complimentary ticket to Washington and return (or at least one at a very low rate) as one of the prizes?
>
> You, of course, know of the good work of the Y.M.C.A. through its railroad branches. We have no such branch at La Fayette, but a number of the railroad employees are members of the association.[40]

As chairman of the committee on endowments, he grew the YMCA endowment fund from a modest gift in 1928 to a sum of $29,280 at the time of his death in 1935. Latta would often write letters on Purdue University stationery asking those who he thought had the means to donate to what he considered a worthy cause:

The urgent needs of the Lafayette "Y" have led the Directors to seek additional aid in the way of endowment, through bequests, or other gifts. . . . There surely is no better work than helping the boys and girls of the community to grow up into strong, pure, true men and women and become law-abiding, useful and loyal citizens.

Does not this worthy and needy cause appeal to your heart and conscience to lend a helping hand in such manner as your circumstances will permit?[41]

Latta remained active in fund-raising throughout his life, as shown by this campaign for 1935 that was directed at the Purdue staff:

Through the courtesy of President Elliott we are permitted to appeal to you through the Campus Mail on behalf of the Community Fund for the support of the Boy Scouts, the Salvation Army, and the Y.M.C.A. in 1935.

Each of these organizations must depend very largely upon public support for its maintenance, and their needs are the more urgent in this time of unemployment. . . . In responding to this joint appeal for 1935, will you kindly contribute and pledge enough to cover what you have given in the aggregate in previous years to these worthy causes. . . .[42]

Professor Latta's work to raise funds from outside sources did not escape notice. The recognition from the YMCA attested to Latta's untiring efforts:

Professor Latta has worked harder than any other man in raising money for the Lafayette Young Men's Christian Association. He has walked more miles, donated more time, and made more friends for the Association than any other individual. [43]

In addition to giving freely of his time, Latta was also generous in his own right. In 1902 he pledged $100 to be paid in two installments within two years to help support a new YMCA building. His contribution was part of a building drive that year that would eventually collect $25,050 for construction of a new facility on Columbia Street [the building has since been razed].

❦ ❦ ❦

During his tenure at the YMCA, Latta was involved in a major transition faced by the organization: the question of whether or not to admit young girls and women to the all-male organization. At its December 11, 1917, meeting, the board of directors heard a petition from women in the community who wished to use the YMCA's swimming pool. Their request was denied for an unknown reason.

Eight years later, the women would once again ask for admission to the YMCA or to rent the facilities. The women had offered a multipage proposal about their opportunities to join the YMCA. In a handwritten note on the women's written proposal from E. R. Brown, general secretary of the Central YMCA of Lafayette, Professor Latta was asked to "[l]ook these over and make whatever suggestions you have."[44]

Latta sent a questionnaire to other YMCAs that had already admitted women to their programs, asking them for information and their views on granting women membership to the YMCA. In a November 9, 1925, letter from Professor Latta to the secretary of a YMCA in New Castle, Indiana, he noted:

> There is a growing interest here in some kind of work for girls and women in connection with our Lafayette Y.M.C.A. . . . Some of the more important questions concerning which we desire information are:
>
> 1. In what privileges do the girls and women participate?
> 2. On what days of the week and what hours are the gymnasium and swimming pool given up to the young women and girls?
> 3. On what terms are the women admitted to privileges in your "Y"? Is the "Y" compensated by renting the privileges to women or by membership dues as for men and boys?
> 4. Have you a Y.W.C.A. [Young Women's Christian Association] organization or do you have merely a committee of women to supervise the women's work?
> 5. Have you paid women officers, if so, what officers?
> 6. Are the women and girls largely participating in the privileges which the "Y" has offered?
> 7. What is the effect of the combined work in the general tone of your Y.M.C.A.?
> 8. Has the introduction of women's work made the financial problem easier or more difficult?
> 9. Kindly give briefly the several steps taken by the women in inaugurating the work for women in connection with the "Y."
> 10. We should be glad to learn your views concerning the combined work whether favorable or unfavorable to it.
>
> I have been a director of the Lafayette "Y" for many years and therefore have an official as well as a personal interest in the questions raised.[45]

On April 6, 1926, the Lafayette YMCA board of directors reversed its earlier position and admitted the women. The board's decision to open membership to women was made, doubtless, in part, to relieve the organization's chronic financial troubles. Allowing women into the YMCA had the potential to bring in many new members and, thus, much needed revenue.

Professor Latta had also worked out a deal prior to the board meeting whereby the women were admitted. Women would be allowed membership privileges only if they could attract 400 new paying members:

> Professor W. C. Latta of Purdue University led a movement to make this possible. A meeting was called of representatives from clubs and churches. The proposition was made that if the women secured four hundred members, the Y.M.C.A. would lend its building to their use. Mrs. Kern was chairman of the drive for members. Marked interest was shown at once in the drive which continued until the members had reached four hundred and forty-five. Tuesdays and Thursdays were designated as days when the entire physical department of the building should be given over to girls and women. Thus in June, 1926, was organized the Woman's Division of the Y.M.C.A. Mrs. Kern was made president of this group.[46]

A June 9, 1932, letter from Flora W. Kern to the board of directors described an embarrassing situation that occurred when the women owed back payments. Kern indicated, "We appreciate the YMCA and we want your good will. We regret our inability to pay rent just now—This implies a stipulated sum which we cannot guarantee. Our financial struggle is more difficult than it possibly looks to others."[47] The women's membership agreed to dismiss the office secretary and to apply the savings from her salary to the overdue rent. The women would ultimately form an independent group called the Young Women's Christian Association, or the YWCA, and move into their own facilities.

Latta was very interested in providing opportunities for all children, even those who could not afford the yearly membership dues of the YMCA. While the annual dues for the children were only a dollar between 1898 and 1901, it was still a difficult amount for some children to raise. In fact, it probably bothered him greatly that these children of lesser means could not afford to join the YMCA, so he worked to overcome the problem:

In recent years [Latta] has been especially interested in providing Y.M.C.A. memberships for worthy or underprivileged boys. With the financial assistance of his many friends he has been able to aid in part or all together approximately one hundred boys in securing the privileges of the Y.M.C.A. A host of boys in the community owe their larger outlook on life, their strong physical bodies, their broader circle of friends and their change to make better and more useful citizens to Prof. Latta.[48]

On April 29, 1930, the eighty-year-old Latta was given a special tribute at the monthly meeting of the YMCA board of directors. The notes from the minutes indicate:

This meeting was held as a recognition event for Prof. W. C. Latta who is serving his thirty-third year as a Director of the Young Men's Christian Association. The wives of most Directors were present and also several former Directors and friends who had served the Association in former years.

Following the supper, brief statements of appreciation were spoken by Rev. D. L. Monahan and Rev. T. F. Williams. A response was made by Prof. Latta. Music was furnished by an orchestra supplied by S. P. Templeton.[49]

Reverend Williams recounted that Latta's "great friendship for underprivileged boys and his successful efforts to have the 'Y' privileges extend[ed] to many of them"[50] were important contributions. Williams also said that "women and girls of the community have Prof. Latta to thank more than any other person for the fact that they are now privileged to use the 'Y' building and facilities several days each week."[51]

In an interesting footnote, E. R. Brown, a former secretary to the YMCA, was asked to send a picture of himself to Lena Baer, who worked on a history book of the YMCA in 1941. His reply letter dated February 24, 1941, said, "I am sending under separate cover a picture that you requested some days ago. I think your plan of securing the pictures of the past presidents and others is a fine one. I would suggest that a picture of Prof. Latta be included in this group with some of the record of his service. I would feel highly honored to be in a group containing the picture of such a great man."[52]

When William Latta perceived a need, he was often at the forefront in providing a solution. In 1914, Latta and three of his university colleagues agreed at a meeting of the Northwest Indiana Methodist Conference that a Methodist church was needed on the campus to tend to the religious essentials—training, development, and education—of Purdue University's Methodist students.

All four professors were affiliated with the School of Agriculture. Latta's colleagues included Dr. George L. Roberts, head of the Department of Education, who taught courses dealing with hog cholera and contagious abortion diseases; Professor Martin L. Fischer, dean of the men and director of student loans, who taught agricultural courses on soybeans, corn, and wheat; and Professor Zora M. Smith, who later became known as the "Father of Indiana 4-H Clubs." Together, they became the lay founders of the Wesley Foundation at Purdue.

Three years after their initial discussions, the constitution and by-laws of the Wesley Foundation were completed on May 10, 1917. The purpose of the foundation was "the intellectual, social, moral and religious care and instruction of the students in Purdue University, especially those who are adherents of the Methodist Episcopal Church."[53]

Fremont E. Fribley was one of the original student pastors. He offered a philosophical basis for why the Wesley Foundation was an important part of the training of Purdue University students, saying, "[T]echnical training, unsupplemented by a training in studies which develop a sane appreciation of the fundamental, moral, and spiritual principles which underlie an enduring civilization will defeat itself."[54]

The Wesley Foundation was built on the campus of Purdue University despite the fact that Trinity Methodist Church was located in Lafayette and the First Methodist Church already served West Lafayette. But the pastor who led the Wesley congregation had a clearly defined role. Specifically, he was to be a personal friend and spiritual advisor to Purdue students and train them for Christian leadership.[55] The church was open to students of all faiths.

Near the end of 1920, a struggle began between the founders of the Wesley Foundation and the Methodist hierarchy. Word had gotten out that the Methodist Church planned to annex the Wesley Foundation and make it part of the First Methodist Church; the pastor would be reduced in rank to an assistant pastor working under the leadership of the pastor at the other church.

Foundation supporters gathered up a petition to prevent annexation. Signatories included Latta and his daughter Mary. The opening paragraph reaffirmed the need for religious education of Purdue University students:

> In seeking the establishment of the Wesley Foundation at Purdue University, its projectors in the Faculty had in mind an institution equipped and manned to render a large service, not only to Methodist

students but also to any other students who might care to enjoy its privileges and share its benefits.

. . . The Foundation, as at present organized, shall continue to grow and develop and that the church authorities shall continue the present liberal policy of keeping here a strong leader and a wise counselor of youth—a broadly trained, cultured, liberal-minded man, intellectually, spiritually, morally, and socially, richly endowed.[56]

The petition concluded with a clear statement regarding the negative aspects of annexation:

We have recently understood that there is, in contemplation, a change of policy that would make the Foundation the annex of a single church and the student pastor the assistant pastor of the same church; and we hereby respectfully enter objection to the proposed change for the following reasons:

1. It would, in effect, destroy the Foundation, as such, by taking away both its authority and its purpose.
2. It would greatly narrow the field and opportunity for service of the student pastor.
3. It would make different, if not impossible, a truly Catholic-spirited appeal to the student body.
4. It would prejudice, against the student pastor, many students who are not responsive to sectarian or denominational appeal and thus defeat, in large measure, the fundamental purpose of the foundation.[57]

The petition fell on deaf ears among the leaders of the Methodist Church in Indiana. On April 30, 1921, Latta and three others signed their names to a terse, four-page letter to the Reverend William McKenzie of South Bend, Indiana, who was supporting the consolidation and subordination of the Purdue campus church:

The most charitable view of your unauthorized statement is that there had been a slip of the pen and that unconsciously your wish had given expression to your thought.

The course you have taken logically leads to the conclusion that you have been pursuing a fixed purpose to superimpose upon the University community, a policy relative to the student pastor in opposition to the known and expressed desire of the Methodist members of the University Staff, and that in your desire to carry this purpose into execution you have employed methods that appear to the undersigned to be unwarranted, irregular, illegal and ethically indefensible.

We are sending you this review of the proceedings which has been carefully and prayerfully prepared to refresh your memory of the record, as set forth in the minutes of the secretary, in the hope that your changes of view, due possibly to a lapse of memory and to the multiplicity of your official duties, may be made clear to you. [58]

This pressure resulted in the Wesley Foundation being allowed to remain as a separate entity. It continues today as an independent church with the purpose of providing spiritual teaching to the students of Purdue University.

🌾 🌾 🌾

Latta lived his religion from the time of his youth to the last days of his life. Faith was fundamental to him, exemplified by the way in which he lived his life. But religion was more than personal manifestation. Latta's religious practice extended far beyond reading the Bible, attending weekly services, and tithing to the church.

Professor Latta avowed that people who sustained religious ideals and principles were obliged to provide leadership in improving the lives of those in need, regardless of their religious affiliations or personal views. He believed that the church could realize a positive influence on the lives of the poor, disadvantaged, and helpless—uninhibited by their individual beliefs and practices—and firmly maintained that the church had the opportunity to lead by example in helping communities to develop wholly and charitably.

Latta wrote later in life that

[as] individual Christians we must be truly successful on the farm, in the shop, store, school room and in office both private and public. As a church our projects must be so sensible, so feasible, so worthwhile, so evidently desirable and necessary for community advancements, prosperity and rural betterment, as to secure the co-operation of the fair-minded, though non-church, men and women whose recognized leadership will secure community-wide following. [59]

His goal in integrating Purdue University's Extension activities with the religious principles of its staff was "[to] make clear that real unity of interest of all members of the community and banish clannishness and class antagonisms and to cultivate a more sympathetic fellowship and better cooperation among the religious denominations."[60]

And he believed that Extension's collaborative efforts with the rural churches of Indiana over forty-five years could be "seen in the waning of religious sectarianism and the springing up of community churches."[61]

At the time of his death at the end of 1935, many articles appeared that seemed to focus on his work with the church. The *Christian Community* paper on March 21, 1936, offered the following commentary on Latta:

> The community church movement has had no better friend in America than Professor W. C. Latta connected with Purdue University in Indiana. He was an active church worker of the Methodist denomination, but visited conferences of his denomination to speak upon the need of the consolidation of churches in small rural communities. One of his last acts prior to his final illness was the writing of a bulletin on The Rural Independent Community Church which was made ready for printing, but which is not yet available for distribution.[62]

Latta's efforts during the last fifteen years of his life surely fulfilled one of his missions in life. Today's churches quite clearly reflect the values that members of the Social Gospel Movement had worked so hard for during their time. And while Purdue University did not pursue Latta's dreams in regard to establishing a formal connection with rural churches, his words from that time reflect what Extension does today:

> Look forward, shake off traditions and old methods, recognize changed conditions, visualize new opportunities, widen the door to membership, get or develop strong rural-minded leaders.[63]

No religious organization was beyond the scope of Latta's vision of "church" as synonymous with compassion, humanity, and the enrichment of society, in rural Indiana in particular and mankind in general. Latta's advocacy was free of sectarian bias, as evident in the diversity of religious causes to which he offered his encouragement and influence. Repeatedly, he expressed his dedication by writing letters, serving on executive committees, and providing guidance to new associations. Professor Latta was a vital constituent of the civic and religious organizations he supported. In some he would lead crusades; in others he exercised his effectiveness as an enthusiastic follower. And always, he lent his considerable powers to manage people and resources in the pursuit of ideals.

The Private Life of
William Latta:
A Time Away from Campus

CHAPTER EIGHT

Words spoken, written, printed,
Goodwill express unstinted.
Thanks, friends for words of greeting
They cheer the hours fast fleeting.

—William Carroll Latta
from "Remembered," 1935

WILLIAM AND ALTA LATTA moved to Chauncey, later renamed West Lafayette, in the fall of 1882. Their first move from Michigan as husband and wife, the West Lafayette campus would be home for the rest of their lives. They would raise four children in the community, and husband and wife would be laid to rest in a local cemetery.

On August 1, 1883, the Purdue University board of trustees unanimously approved William Latta's promotion to the professorship of agriculture and horticulture at an annual salary of $1,600, to begin the next month. The following resolution was also offered and unanimously approved at the same meeting:

> Resolved that the following standing rule be adopted, to wit: The Professor of Agriculture and Horticulture shall be required to assume the general supervision of the Farm and the Farm Hands and to reside in the Farm House at a rent of $100 a year.[1]

The Latta family lived in the university's farm house until they moved to 140 South Grant Street in 1886. This house would have been on the very eastern edge of campus, where the Grant Street Parking Garage stands today. Then in 1899, they moved to a home at 1016 First Street:

> The summer has been an unusually busy one. We have moved into the addition west of the college campus and hope to make our friends more comfortable when they come to see us than when in our former house.[2]

Indeed, one of those friends was Mrs. Mount, wife of Indiana Governor James Mount, to whom Latta would write, "You can come by street car within one minute's walk of our home, which is near the corner of First and Waldron Streets in University Park (West Side).[3]

The house on First Street was designed in the Dutch Colonial style by a local architect, Will Mann, and built by Milton Smalley. The Latta home was one of eight houses found in the area popularly known then as University Park on the western edge of the campus. (This area today includes residential housing mixed with student apartments, fraternity and sorority housing, and university buildings.)

In any given year, one could find the Lattas taking on boarders. Most of them were students majoring in agriculture, but the Lattas were also known to welcome children of their relatives. These relatives and students who boarded with the Lattas were required to work for their keep, a very common practice in those days.

The locations of the homes on both Grant Street and First Street were ideal for Latta, as he could walk from each home to campus in just minutes. His walk would become a daily routine, and the slender, bearded old gentleman striding to his office was a familiar sight to Purdue students as late as the 1930s:

> Professor Latta was a thorough, kindly, patient man of unusual personal distinction. Everyone knew him because it was his custom, in a gesture of individualism, to wear a skull cap around the campus and at faculty meetings. In his old age he was the finished gentleman and scholar, courtly in dress and manner, cheerful, friendly, and alert. A youngster on the staff, back in 1929, met him on the street just in passing and was greeted with a bow, a smile, and a "Good morning" that stuck in his mind ever after. There, said the youngster to himself, is a man who has done something in this world.[4]

William and Alta became parents at an age somewhat older than most couples of their era. Their first child, Bertha (1884–1960), was born when William was 34 years old and Alta was 30. Two years later Robert was born (1886–1970), followed by Pauline (1890–1955) and Mary (1894–1973). Their three daughters and one son were all born, raised, and schooled in West Lafayette, and all would eventually graduate from Purdue University.

Bertha taught home economics before becoming a supervisor of domestic sciences for the state of Indiana.

Robert would become head of the Dairy Department of New Mexico State University. Later, he served as manager of the Rio Grande Valley Dairy.

Pauline graduated from Purdue University in 1913 and for three years held the position of instructor in home economics at West Lafayette High School. Four years later, through her work as the church secretary for the First Presbyterian Church in El Paso, Texas, she met the Reverend Henry J. Reemtsma, pastor of the Presbyterian Church at Alpine and Sanderson, Texas. A graduate of Dubuque Seminary and Theological College, Henry began his ministry work in Illinois before transferring to Alpine. Romance ensued and, soon thereafter, a marriage in 1921. Pauline's youngest sister, Mary, served as her bridesmaid. William gave the bride away.

After marrying, Pauline and Henry took up residence at the manor of the First Presbyterian Church in Las Cruces, New Mexico, to accommodate Henry's candidacy at First Presbyterian and the opportunity to work in cooperation with the New Mexico Agricultural and Mechanical School. The Reemtsmas served congregations in various parts of the United States before answering, in 1938, their final call to missionary work among the Navajo at Fort Defiance, Arizona.

Pauline and Henry had two children: Carol, born in 1923 at El Paso, Texas, and Henry Keith (called "Keith" by family members), born in 1925 at Madera, California. Pauline was the only one of William and Alta's children to marry and raise a family.

Mary, the youngest of the Lattas' children, grew up to teach home economics in various high schools in Indiana as well as in El Paso, Texas. Mary and Bertha would later own a gift, framing, and antique shop in Lafayette.

William Latta served the Trinity Methodist Church in Lafayette for most of his adult life. Not only did it afford him the opportunity to guide the youth of the congregation and to participate in various church committees, it allowed him to grow spiritually and intensify his own devotion.

The historical records from Trinity Methodist Church indicate that Latta and his four children were very involved in church affairs of the day. While there is no record showing when William joined the church, it is assumed that it would have been close to February 11, 1883, when his wife joined.

William must have enjoyed Sunday school, as he was recorded in the directories of the church as being "a teacher in the Intermediate and Senior Department."[5] He would have taught students who were old enough to attend middle school or high school.

The church also listed William Latta as a steward in most of their official records. A steward was a lay officer with official responsibility for managing church work. In the late 1880s, the stewards were appointed by the pastor of the church. It was an important position as it allowed the leaders of the local church to run the day-to-day operations. In turn, the stewards would answer to the trustees of the board. Latta was not only listed as a steward, but he was involved in many committees: Benevolences, Complaint, Districting and Apportioning, Finance, Foreign Mission, Program, Reception, and Temperance. And lastly, he was a founder of a group of men called the Trinity Brotherhood and served as vice president of the group.

Professor Latta's son, Robert, served the church as an usher, while daughter Pauline was a recording secretary for the Queen Aster Circle and was a Sunday school teacher for the younger children. Mary Latta served as secretary for the primary department of Sunday school, and Bertha was listed in church records as being a vice president of the Epworth League.

Though the records indicate that Alta Latta joined Trinity Methodist Church in 1883, her name does not appear again until 1914. Official records, undated, show that Alta suspended her membership in the church in the late 1880s, when the records simply indicate "withdrawn."

The Lattas took time off in the summer to visit their vacation home at Eveline Orchards, located between the towns of Charlevoix and East Jordan, Michigan.[6] Eveline Orchards was a project conceived by Levi R. Taft, a horticulture professor and head of the Horticulture Department at Michigan Agricultural College. Taft's idea was to develop and sell land along the Lake Charlevoix shoreline as a resort area. In turn, the proceeds from the sale of the land along the shore would provide funds to develop a commercial orchard.

Eveline Orchards consisted of 300 acres of prime farmland, which was planted to 8,500 fruit trees, including 4,850 apple, 1,700 cherry, and 850 plum trees. A professional manager was responsible for daily operations. The orchard was known for the quality of its products, with items being shipped all around the country and also available for purchase at the farm. Professors Taft and Latta used the orchard to run many experiments on growing and taking care of fruit trees.

Latta, one of the first buyers, purchased lot number fifteen for fifty dollars in 1910.[7] The following year he built his summer cottage. Latta named his cottage "BEROPAMA," which was derived from the first two letters of each of his children's names. BEROPAMA became his home away from home. The Latta family would head for the cottage in the spring, after Purdue had completed its graduation ceremonies, and stay until the end of August.

The *Purdue Exponent* reported on September 15, 1925, about an eight-week trip that Professor Latta, then seventy-five, and his family took that eventually ended at their summer home. Professor Latta described the trip for the newspaper:

> Our trip took us over the Santa Fe Trail to Flagstaff, Arizona. We then detoured, first to Colorado Springs and later to Phoenix, Arizona, from which point we took a more southern highway to San Diego and other southern California localities. We motored up the San Joaquin Highway into Madera County, located in the foothills of the Sierra Nevadas. Later, we went on to San Francisco, from which point we began our return trip over the Victory and Liberty Highways, passing through Sacramento to Salt Lake and then going north to Yellowstone National Park. From there we came on through the Black Hills, northern Nebraska, Minnesota, northern Wisconsin and Michigan to St. Ignace. After crossing the straits, we resumed our trip southward, stopping enroute at Eveline Orchards. There we found Professors Gunn and Rubenkoening and their families. From there we wandered home through southern Michigan and northern Indiana.[8]

Dr. Henry Reemtsma, the son-in-law of William Latta, wrote in his memoirs that "Dad Latta" would go to his cottage in Michigan, because his hay fever never bothered him there as it did in Indiana. He also indicated that his father-in-law would get up at six o'clock each morning and swim the two miles back and forth across the lake—an amazing feat considering he began this practice when he was in his sixties:

> Usually Mary or one of the others was in the canoe in case of cramps and they could bring him back to shore. He was an expert swimmer and I cannot remember that he ever had to be brought in by canoe. Most of us were satisfied to wait until late afternoon before we had a swim. The water in the morning was very cold, but it did warm up by afternoon.[9]

His "youthful" exploits at age seventy-five were also chronicled by the *Purdue Exponent* on September 26, 1925:

> How many persons 75 years of age will take a daily plunge in a lake when it gets as cool as it does in the summertime in northern Michigan? This is what Prof. W. C. Latta of the agricultural extension department did. Prof. Latta who came to Purdue in 1882 and for years taught agriculture and then directed the farmers institutes, came back recently from Charlevoix, Mich., with Mrs. Latta and other members of their family. Despite his 75 years, Prof. Latta walked or ran 70 yards from his cottage to the lake and dived from the spring-board for a short swim and walked or ran back to the house, scorning the use of a bathrobe over his bathing suit to keep off the chilly breezes.[10]

Invariably, they would drop in to visit Alta's family at Mason, Michigan, on the way to their vacation home and again on the return trip to West Lafayette. The Lattas were also fond of entertaining visitors while staying at BEROPAMA. Young Paul Cheney, William's nephew, wrote:

> From July 17 to August 1, 1914, my mother took my brother and myself up to northern Michigan at Eveline Orchard, East Jordan, Michigan. We went by the way of the Michigan Central R.R. through Bay City, and came back by the way of the Pere Marquette R.R. through Grand Rapids. . . . While we were there we stayed at my Uncle Will Latta's cottage. He was spending his vacation there and he sure gave me some fine times.[11]

Photographs, pictures, and portraits taken during the late nineteenth and early twentieth centuries portray their subjects as stern and serious people. That Professor Latta wrote serious agricultural essays, addressed professional men and women, conducted scientific experiments, published his research results, and traveled Indiana talking about improving agricultural production and promoting community growth gave Indiana citizens a view of only one side of the scholarly man.

Professor Latta had a fun and creative side to him of which few individuals beyond his family and close friends were aware. Latta's obituary revealed his alter ego as a poet, stating that, "He has also written many beautiful philosophical poems although, modestly, he would never consent to their publication."[12]

While Latta is best known for his fifty-three-year career as a faculty member in Purdue's School of Agriculture, he also had a lively interest in writing poetry. Latta penned most of his poetry in the final two decades of his life. (See Appendix 6 for an anthology of Latta's poems.) He was aware of his limitations as a poet; in an untitled poem to his grandchildren, Carol and Keith Reemtsma, dated January 14, 1933, he wrote, "Grandpa is too busy to smooth up this rhyme, / Maybe he can do better when he tries next time." He marked many occasions with verses. Latta's poetry, in fact, can best be characterized as "occasional verses," since most were written for or inspired by specific occasions or events. His poems reveal his devotion to his grandchildren, his wishes for the future for them and for others, his patriotism, his faith, and his support of temperance.

Most of Latta's existing poems are written to his grandchildren, Carol and Keith. Latta's poems to them, like many of his other poems, are positive and happy and often humorous. For instance, in "To Four-Year-Old Carol," he stretches his rhymes with "Californy" and "not stormy," as well as with "Injiany" and "piany." But these poems also suggest his earnest wishes for his grandchildren's moral development. In "Henry Keith at Three," he projects his image of the children competing to be able "to lead in table thanks" and describes them taking turns at alternate meals: "To keep the peace twixt sister, brother / Keith prays one meal, Carol another." In the next stanza, this sibling competition becomes the source of their projected moral living: "May each one with the other vie / Life's wholesome lessons to apply; / In kindly acts strive to excel, / Thus striving on, each will do well."

In "To Four-Year-Old Carol," he characterizes his granddaughter as an obedient child who "[w]hen rest time comes she makes no noise / Because she loves her mother," and who is already being introduced to church attendance by her father, following which "[s]he helps to get the dinner." On Carol's fifth birthday, he expresses his hopes for her quite explicitly, ending the poem with this verse: "Her grandpa hopes that this sweet child / Will ever choose the true and good / And thus grow up pure, undefiled, / The gracious noble womanhood."

These poems, meant for family, are full of private references, obscure to outsiders but probably meaningful to family members. In "That Lad of Four," Latta writes about a Reemtsma family trip to New York and includes the references to various means of transportation—subway, commuter's train, the "L" and "Tube," and the ferry boat. In "Carolings," the lines " 'I'd rather Mary's "Cupie" be / Than Grandpa's "Bossie Calf," ' said she" appear to refer to the nicknames bestowed upon Carol by her Aunt Mary and Grandpa, respectively. This poem and "A Little Maid of Seven" also demonstrate Latta's interest in Carol's language development. In fact, "Carolings" is likely a play on his granddaughter's name as well as a way of identifying "Carol's words so sage and queer" that he will "jot some down right here." In "A Little Maid of Seven," he notes that his "little maid of Mountain View / Ofttimes says things that are brand new."

But Carol and Keith are not the only recipients of birthday poems. In one poem written to his son, Robert, on his forty-first birthday, William reminds Robert that although he is an adult, he is always welcome at home. William also wrote a more somber, though still hopeful, poem to note his own eighty-fourth birthday, titled "Four Times Twenty-One."

Latta wrote a series of poems marking the New Year, as well as poems marking the Fourth of July and Easter. When he began writing the New Year's poems is unclear, but surviving copies begin in 1921 and continue through the year of his death, 1935. In many of them, he personifies the New Year, as he does in "1921," when he refers to it as the "husky youngster" and to the year ending as "gray-beard twenty." Often, the poems both welcome the new year and bid farewell to the old.

Most New Year's poems are short, with traditional wishes for a good year ahead, but some are quite topical—and quite serious. He greets 1926 with a poem titled "Peace," in which he reflects on the end of World War I and expresses his prayers for peace, saying, "Let Art and Science, evermore, / Promote the industries of peace." He refers to the Treaty of Locarno, which was signed in Locarno, Switzerland, on October 16, 1925, in an effort to stabilize borders and secure peace in Europe. He also writes of the League of Nations and the World Court, established in 1919 and 1921, respectively (neither of which the United States participated in, having refused to ratify the Treaty of Versailles). The poem for 1934, "Keeping Step," also focuses on key events of the time. It includes references to the NRA (National Recovery Administration), the AAA (Agricultural Adjustment Administration), and the CWA (Civil Works Administration)—all programs in Franklin Roosevelt's New Deal efforts to pull the country out of the economic despair of the "Old Depression." Latta also mentions Hugh S. Johnson, who Roosevelt appointed to administer the NRA and who was *Time Magazine*'s 1933 Man of the Year.

Another political poem, though apparently not written to mark the New Year, is the untitled, undated poem that begins, "Their slogan is 'Prepare to fight.'" The poem seems to be a criticism of American militarists, those who rejected the League of Nations, Locarno Treaty, and World Court as naïve pacifisms. But in addition to criticizing these "Jingoes," Latta also cautions against an internal danger caused by the repeal of Prohibition in 1933.

One of Latta's more interesting New Year's poems, "A New Year Meditation" for 1929, again combines wishes for peace with wishes for advances in human knowledge. It bears a note that makes it clear that Latta had sent a copy to Purdue President Edward Elliott, who acknowledges it and says he has sent his "copy to the Editor of the *Purdue Alumnus* for publication in the next number of that journal."[13]

Latta is not above recycling his work. His 1933 New Year's poem contains the lines "May God inspire both you and me / To help U.S. keep sober, free, / In Nineteen Hundred Thirty-Three." The same lines close a longer poem, "Whither Bound," a poem on temperance that was apparently written around the same time. A note indicates that on December 27, 1932, Latta sent the poem to E. H. Cherrington, requesting that Cherrington publish it in the "next *American Issue* if it will come out in time to make it worthwhile."[14] (*American Issue* was a leading temperance newspaper; Cherrington was its editor.) The first three verses of one poem in this collection are identical to the New Year poem for 1925, but this last poem adds a fourth verse titled "Beyond" to the verses titled "Yesterday," "Today," and "Tomorrow." Since this last poem is undated, it seems likely that Latta revisited his 1925 poem at a later date to add the very clearly religious and hopeful final verse.

Latta's poetry, apparently all unpublished, provides us with insights into Indiana's "Father of Agriculture" that we would not otherwise have. In these lines, we are privileged to see the loving grandfather, the reflective citizen, the committed patriot, Christian, and advocate of temperance. We see his sense of humor, his recognition of his own mortality, and his imagination at play.

The poems take on a deeper and richer meaning when read along with the surviving letters from "Grandpa Latta" to his grandchildren. The letters were mainly written to his oldest grandchild, Carol. Latta reveals in these letters that he misses the presence of his grandchildren in his West Lafayette home. Latta wrote to then three-year-old Carol asking her, "Do you still remember your grandpa and grandma Latta? We both remember Carol and we want to see her ever so much."[15] On August 26, 1926, he again wrote to Carol: "Your grandma wants your grandpa to write you a letter. She doesn't seem to realize what a big job this really is. Part of the trouble is that grandpa can't remember any thing about Keith except what his father and others have written."[16] The professor plainly missed seeing his grandchildren and let it be known in his letters.

Latta would ask the children about things that mattered the most to them (e.g., friends and dolls), give instructions on how they should act and behave at home, and put forth questions about their schooling. He included advice to them on being good children and helping their parents out around the home. He wrote, "Grandpa is glad to know that Carol is teaching Rose [her doll] good manners. He hopes that Carol is as careful not to 'contradict' her mother as she is in instructing Rose."[17]

In one letter dated January 1, 1926, Latta asked Carol to teach her younger brother. He wrote:

> Little brother will give you a lot of things to do and you must be patient with him if he learns slowly. Remember that he can't talk back or strike back or even scowl back. He is just a wee little bunch of almost complete helplessness. About the only thing he can now do is to 'root' for his dinner and I guess he must be doing that well to gain 6 ounces in one week. Can you teach him not to suck his thumb and not to put his little fist into his mouth? Don't let him have a pencil or any kind of stick as he might get it into his eye. But I guess I better let your mother tell you how to care for little brother. Be sure to take good care of him so he will be nice when his grandpa Latta gets a chance to see him.[18]

However, most of all the letters were simple questions asked to the children with a request to have them answered. Carol was very good about responding, as Latta noted in his letter on January 1, 1926: "Your nice letter came yesterday. We all enjoyed it and have sent it to your Aunt Mary."[19] Another time he wrote:

I wonder whether Keith is wearing the shoes and dresses that you have outgrown. It will save your mother a lot of work if you will let Keith wear your old clothes. While he is so young he would not know this difference. When he gets older and finds out that he is a boy I am almost sure he wouldn't want to wear girl's clothes. Aren't you glad that you are your mother's first child and don't have to wear any old clothes of an older brother or sister?[20]

He again referred to Carol's doll:

Rose must be quite a young lady by this time. Does she want to have her hair bobbed like the other girls? Does she paint her cheeks as the other girls do or is she such a rosy-cheeked girl that she doesn't need to put on rouge. Only I am afraid I didn't spell that right.[21]

On September 26, 1926, he wrote Carol:

Your mother thinks Keith's hair is going to curl. I doubt it. Please write me the truth about it. You used to have blue eyes. Are they still blue? What is the color of Keith's eyes?

Do you still have that nice black board that your Aunt Mary gave you? If you do I hope you will soon learn to make pretty marks on it so that before long you can sign your name to your letters by your "own self." Are you going to a kindergarten school this winter? I hope you can as you are now just about the right age to begin. Grandpa and grandma enjoy those pictures of you and Keith ever so much, but I like that one best in which you are smiling. Bushels of love. Grandpa Latta[22]

Even religious teachings were part of Latta's letters to Carol. On April 11, 1927, Latta sent four-year-old Carol a letter in which he asks her to pray:

Here is a beautiful child's prayer that your grandpa wants you to paste in your book of remembrances. He wants you to learn it so you can pray it before you go to sleep.

> Dear Father:
> I thank thee for the night's rest
> I thank thee for the new day
> I thank thee for papa and mama and my little brother
> I thank thee for my playmates and my playthings
> Help me to be kind to everyone
> Help all my playmates to be good for Jesus' sake—Amen[23]

He also writes about his garden to Carol:

Your grandpa has lettuce and radishes up. He has also planted onion sets
and spinach and last evening heard your Aunt Bertha set 40 strawberry
plants. The grass is growing green and the bushes are pushing out their
pretty leaves. The plums are in blossom and I guess they got their noses (if
they have any) frost bitten Saturday and Sunday nights. Please dictate a
letter to your mother telling what all you and Keith are doing.[24]

And often Grandpa Latta would ask questions in hopes of getting more
information about his grandchildren:

Carol, how many names of birds and flowers do you know? How many
kinds of poultry does Mrs. Brooks have?

How much do you help your mother with the dishes and sweeping,
bed making, and wood cleaning? Please dictate a long letter to your mother
for grandpa and grandma.[25]

There is only one surviving letter to Carol from her Grandmother Alta Latta.
In it she calls Carol "Grandma's little birdie":

I am enclosing Grandpa's birthday message which he will take to the post
office when he gets up from his afternoon nap. We sent it to Aunt Mary
who typed it on her typewriter in Chicago. We hope the poem will be a joy
to you not only now but when you are older. Aunt Bertha helped Grandpa
to get the thoughts worded correctly and Aunt Mary O.K.d it.

Do you take care of Keith when mother teaches school? That mother
of yours is great. You will appreciate her more and more as you grow older.
We all are looking forward to your visit with mother and brother next
summer both here and at the orchards. We will canoe on Lake Charlevoix
and play in the sand on the lake shore.[26]

William Latta also tried his hand at writing short stories for his grandchildren.[27]
These are quite involved and cover topics for children that are often difficult to
talk about and even more difficult to write. These five prose pieces share qualities both with one another and with his verses. (See Appendix 7 for the full text
of Latta's short stories.) The narratives are written with children in mind and,
in one case, are clearly intended for his grandchildren. The story titled "An
Autobiography" is written by a puppy named Lindy, who, as we learn from the
poems, belongs to Latta's grandchildren.

As is also the case with the verses, several of the stories reflect Latta's faith. In these stories, each of which deals with the natural world in one way or another, Latta frequently emphasized God's hand and God's plan. For instance, in the first part of "Two Streams," Latta explained the natural phenomenon of the watercycle, describing how "a tiny tricking rivulet" joins with other streams on its flow to the ocean, then evaporates, becomes a cloud and then rain, and returns to the land. This cycle, he said, provides a "ministry of good to man." In the second part of "Two Streams," Latta used the stream analogy to write about "[a] separate tiny stream of life, love-engendered, heaven sent," which, like the literal stream, grows in strength. But while the "earth-born passive stream" may grow from benign to destructive, overflowing its banks wreaking havoc, Latta explained that "this human stream . . . has early in its course the power of choice" and can choose a good and moral life, thus "flow[ing] into the ocean of God's love."

Similarly, in "The Sunbeam, the Zephyr, the Cloud, and the Child: A Fairy Tale," Latta explained another natural phenomenon, the interaction of sun, wind, and cloud to bring about plant life, including the food that nourishes the child. But he also explained that the source of all of these wonders lies with the "King of the fairies," the "good king God, Jehovah," also called "our Heavenly Father because He so loved boys and girls, that, hundreds of years ago He sent His Son, Jesus Christ down to this world." Latta called this story a fairy tale, though it does not really conform to that genre—no "Once upon a time" beginning or "happily ever after" ending. Rather, the tale is more of a moral lesson, as are some of the poems, designed to teach the young reader or listener that the reward for being good in this world is that "they can all go to live with Jesus and His Father for ever and ever."

In "Cornucopia—An Autobiography," Latta presented a riddle, though until the last line—"What is my name?"—it's not clear that this is the case. In addition, as is true in some of the verses, Latta used wordplay. The riddle is not, after all, about a literal cornucopia, but instead the title reveals that the answer to the riddle is corn. Latta's agricultural expertise is evident in this riddle in details which far surpass those of any of his other literary writings, but while he described the phenomenon of a corn plant's growth in mostly homely language, he nevertheless included the science, explaining, for example, that "[the] lowly earthworm and tiniest bacteria helped to make food ready for me." Those with knowledge of Latta's dedication to the temperance movement will find more than meets the eye in the line "I am a great drinker but I drink nothing stronger than water." Toward its end, the piece introduces both religious imagery—"Then I realized that by giving up my life as a seed and being born again into a living, growing, plant"—and the working of God—"I was truly thankful that in accordance with the wise plans of Divine Providence I could indeed be a world benefactor and a blessing to all mankind."

"A Child's Soliloquy and Questions and a Mother's Answers" is perhaps the most unusual of Latta's narratives. The piece is spoken by a ten-year-old girl he calls Esther. It addressed a topic most parents find rather intimidating: the response to a child to the question of how she came to be born. Told through analogy and with a fair degree of detail, though also enough ambiguity to leave room for some of the more difficult questions to be asked, Latta had the character of the mother use a fertile egg to explain how the ovum and sperm unite to form an embryo. The mother takes advantage of her daughter's observation of the rooster covering the hen and explains that this was mating, not fighting as the young girl has assumed. The mother explains that kittens and lambs and calves and human babies are born through a similar process. And young Esther's mother is careful to explain that fertilization occurs through a process "which only our heavenly Father understands," that "the Lord who is so good and kind to everybody permitted your brother Eddie to come and grow just as you came and grew," and to remind her daughter "to thank Jesus who was also born as you were."

Only "An Autobiography" does not contain an obvious moral or religious message, but, like the other narratives, it presents an aspect of nature—or perhaps, more accurately, of natural science—in a way that might be understood by a child. As mentioned earlier, "An Autobiography" is told by Lindy, a puppy that belonged to Latta's grandchildren. Lindy's autobiography begins with his birth "a few months ago," when he was small and blind. It explains how the newborn puppy sensed things that it did not understand, such as the tongue that licked him, which he later learned belonged to a big dog that was his mother, or the hunger that led him to nurse, or the sensation of the "other little bodies that seemed to be much like my little self," which turned out to be his littermates. Lindy explains his being taken away by a big man and then introduced to the two children who became his playmates.

Latta's prose provides additional insight into the imagination of the "Father of Indiana Agriculture," showing his ability to present the world of nature to young children in ways that are both scientifically and morally informed.

🌾🌾🌾

After a long and distinguished career, William Carroll Latta died at the age of eighty-five in his home on December 22, 1935. He had caught a cold a week earlier and succumbed quickly.

Members of Epsilon Sigma Phi would pay their respects to one of their own. The Extension fraternity placed men at the head and foot of Professor Latta's casket at Trinity Methodist Church. Volunteers who sat with the casket included Keller E. Beeson, Parke T. Brown, Bill Gralsess, Claude Harper, Leroy E. Hoffman, Tom Johnston, Mervill O. Pence, Lynn Robertson, John Sahursh, and Fred Shanlin.[28]

The *Lafayette Journal and Courier* carried an impressive and thoughtful editorial on the death of William Carroll Latta. It read:

> Many will think of the late William Carroll Latta, passed on at 85, as one of the foremost constructive leaders of agriculture in his time; as an outstanding educator and builder in the realm of farmer training. Many believe Prof. Latta will be missed most by those with whom he worked so long and so ably as a teacher and organizer. It is true Prof. Latta performed prodigies of intellectual achievement; that his thought and effort demonstrated a statesman's grasp of the significance of agriculture as our basic industry, a business calling for special training of a high order.
>
> While Prof. Latta will be sorely missed in the field of agricultural education, he will be missed even more in civic life and in that realm of culture where neighbors are neighborly.
>
> Fame had marked Prof. Latta out, more than nationally, as the father of the farmers institute and of farm extension activities in connection with university education, long before he earned additional distinction as originator of a plan for inculcating tolerance, friendliness, co-operation and cordial, true community spirit in the community. The laymen's council to surmount inter-denominational barriers and to unite all creeds and races for wholesome community ends and mutual benefit—the general welfare and advancement, was a Latta conception, and it became national in its scope.
>
> Because he maintained a lively and helpful interest in all around him, and in the varied activities of many elements in society, Prof. Latta continued alert, active, helpful and happy until a few days before his passing.

The 54 years he served the people as a forceful factor in the development of the progressive usefulness of Purdue University were golden years for both Prof. Latta and the friends of the school. The memory of this stately, modest, serene, poised and potent Christian gentleman, for many years a familiar and courtly personality, will abide long, a benediction and a blessing upon the lives and works of all who knew him either as teacher, associate, leader or neighbor.[29]

Latta's obituary in the *Journal and Courier* provides a succinct picture of the man and his accomplishments. It was probably written, in part, by the professor's colleagues at Purdue University, and while it contains several factual errors about details of Latta's life, the obituary conveys the deep respect that the Purdue community held for him:

Prof. W. C. Latta, Pioneer in Agricultural Education, Expires at 85; Famous Farm Leader. Fifty-fourth Year at Purdue University Where He Founded Farmers' Institutes, Experimental Work, Extension Department— Patriarchal Civic Worker, Good-Will Advocate—Funeral at Trinity Church Tuesday.

Agriculture in America lost one of its oldest and foremost leaders Sunday morning at 1 o'clock when Prof. William Carroll Latta, 85, a prominent member of the faculty of Purdue University for nearly 54 years, and as such the founder of farmers' institutes and agricultural extension in Indiana, died at the family home, 1016 First Street, West Lafayette.

The patriarchal educator and civic leader had been ill for a week, the result of contracting a severe cold while engaged in the multiplicity of useful activities in which he had long been interested, his condition becoming critical Thursday. He died surrounded by the members of his family and the news of his death was received with deep sorrow, not only in his home community but throughout the state and nation, where he was widely known as the "Father of Purdue Agriculture."

His death removes from agricultural education one of its outstanding authorities, a pioneer who played a prominent part in introducing the new conception of agriculture that has made Indiana one of the leading states in progressive farm operation. And it also removes a citizen who made himself useful in many other fields of human helpfulness, notably his contribution to the cause of religious goodwill among the various sects and to the social and moral improvement of the community.

TO PURDUE IN 1882. Born in LaPorte County March 9, 1850, Professor Latta was a son of Robert S. and Mary (Tumbleson) Latta. He received a bachelor's degree from Michigan State College in 1877 and alternated in agriculture and teaching for three years thereafter. In the spring of 1882, he returned to Michigan State for a master's degree, and in August of that year he came to Purdue as instructor in agriculture, the only instructor in the department. He has been continuously in the service of the university since that time.

As instructor in agriculture in 1882 he taught every course offered. The next year he received the title of professor of agriculture which he carried until the time of his death, although he had done no active teaching since 1911. At that time he retained direction of farmers institute work which he organized in this state, and in 1923 he was made consultant in agricultural education and extension.

Purdue University was eight years old and had only 150 students when Professor Latta came here over 53 years ago. The campus occupied only 30 acres, and the first agricultural hall, a small building, stood in front of where the present experiment station building now stands. The venerable educator lived to see the university's enrollment increase to nearly 5,000, the instructional staff increasing from 12 to more than 500.

FARMERS' INSTITUTES. In 1889, Professor Latta introduced farmers' institute work, of which he was active director until 1923. The organization of the institutes in farming communities throughout the state was a colossal task, but wisely and patiently, he built a structure that is recognized as one of the foremost in the nation. In 1911 the farmers' institute work was adopted as part of agricultural extension, but Professor Latta remained in charge until 1923, when he turned it over to Walter Q. Fitch. Several hundred thousand persons attended the institutes each year.

Prof. Latta was virtually the founder of the agricultural experiment station at Purdue, for he took it over two years after the plan was conceived in 1880, and before any definite program had been arranged. It was he who introduced the experimental field crop plan to improve the quality of farm crops, and increase yield and the return to the grower. The experimental feats were a pioneer educational experiment and led to Purdue being granted an experiment station in 1887 under the Hatch Act.

MANY ACHIEVEMENTS. By following dual or triple interests through most of his work at Purdue over half a century's time, Prof. Latta had crowded into his years more achievements than two or three men usually are able to record. Since 1923, although still at his office daily, carrying on as consultant, he had been engaged in writing several important books which are still to be published. One is a history of Indiana agriculture, covering the past century and another is a history of the Indiana board of agriculture.

In addition to these writings, he was the author of a work dealing with rural community churches of Indiana and was a leader in the movement to make these churches more effective. His volume on the rural community church movement was suggested by Edward C. Elliott, president of Purdue, at the time Purdue honored Prof. Latta on the occasion of his eightieth birthday. The manuscripts are all complete, it is said. He has also written many beautiful philosophical poems although, modestly, he would never consent to their publication.

GOOD-WILL LEADER. The university and extension work, engrossing as it was, did not absorb all of Prof. Latta's time. He was the founder of the Laymen's Council of Tippecanoe county, organized some 10 years ago, to combat religious prejudice. The movement grew and was introduced in many other communities, Prof. Latta having been recognized as one of the pioneers in this movement, which spread over the nation. He brought representatives of the various faiths together in a good-will movement and lived to see the plan bear abundant fruit.

Out of the Laymen's Council grew the Tippecanoe County Civic Improvement Association, which is now flourishing because of Prof. Latta's zeal and executive skill. This organization strives for a better community life, seeking to improve the standard of motion pictures and newsstand literature as well as encouraging a better health standard for school children. Only last week Prof. Latta was busy mapping out its program and personally striving to increase interest in the undertaking.

He was also vitally interested in church and Y.M.C.A. work. He was the oldest living member of the official board of Trinity M. E. Church and was also interested in the welfare of all churches. He had been a member of the executive board of the Central Y.M.C.A. for 37 years, retaining this office at the time of his death. In the Methodist Brotherhood, recently, he served as district vice-president.

FUNERAL TUESDAY. Service, wise and unselfish, over a period of more than half a century was the thing for which the "grand old man" of Purdue University and Indiana agriculture was best known, and the work he has done is recognized as one of the most valuable contributions one man has ever made to the welfare of a state and local community. Much of his most valuable service was rendered at a time in life when most men have ceased their activities.

He leaves his wife, Mrs. Alta Elvira (Wood) Latta, to whom he was married July 10, 1879; three daughters: the Misses Bertha and Mary Latta, at the family home; and Mrs. Pauline Reemtsma, of Anadarko, Okla.; one son, Robert W. Latta, South Bend; and two sisters: Mrs. S. J. Evinger, of Phoenix, Ariz.; and Mrs. Frank LaGourgue, of Anaheim, Cal.

The body was removed to the Templeton funeral home where friends may call until 11:30 A.M. Tuesday. Funeral services will be held at Trinity M. E. Church Tuesday afternoon at 2 o'clock, the Rev. Dr. Thomas Frederick Williams officiating. Burial will be in Spring Vale cemetery. The remains will lie in state at the church from noon until 2 o'clock Tuesday afternoon.[30]

Purdue University raised funds to help the Latta family offset the funeral expenses. The special Memorial Fund collected $101.71 toward that end. There were forty-two names and departments that contributed to the fund. The departments came from across the school: the Agricultural Engineering, Agricultural Statistics, Animal Husbandry, Club, Dairy, Farm Management, and Home Economics Departments.[31]

In addition, the Epsilon Sigma Phi fraternity sent a note of condolence to the family. Mary Latta wrote back to say, "Your kind expression of sympathy has been a real help this difficult week. Mother will be glad to be remembered with calls."[32] The small card was signed by Alta, Bertha, Robert, Pauline, and Mary.

Alta continued to live in the house on First Street after the death of her husband in 1935 until her own death five years later. In 1955, Mary sold the house to the Purdue Research Foundation but continued to reside there with her sister, Bertha. After Bertha's death in 1960, Mary stayed until 1964, when she moved to Asheville, North Carolina, with her brother Robert, where they spent the remainder of their lives.

Mary would write a letter on January 12, 1965, to a friend that described the selling of the house and told about the last boarders:

> I sold the dear old house the following year to the Purdue Research Foundation on a contract which permitted me to live there as long as I wished. I continued to pay taxes, insurance and upkeep, and in return was allowed to continue my income from sharing my house with students, as we had done during most of the life of the house. When Bertha died we

had just begun taking students from Hong Kong. They stayed with me for four years. The last student who left the house a few days before I did told me that the original four students who came to the house in June–September of 1960 had each completed the advance work he had planned to do. He said theirs was the "best apartment" and "you were the best land-lady at Purdue." [33]

The Purdue Research Foundation, a not-for-profit property management organization, rented the home on First Street for many years. On May 10, 2002, the Purdue Research Foundation sold the property to the North American Islamic Trust, which built the Greater Lafayette Islamic Center on the site.

William Carroll Latta, circa 1895.
Courtesy of Michael Slabaugh.

Alta Wood Latta, circa 1895.
Courtesy of Michael Slabaugh.

Bertha Latta at her graduation from Purdue University in 1907. Courtesy of Kim Sharpe.

Robert W. Latta, the only son of William and Alta Latta, as an assistant professor of animal husbandry at New Mexico State University, circa 1917. Courtesy of Kim Sharpe.

Pauline Latta, circa 1908.
Courtesy of Kim Sharpe.

Mary Latta in 1908.
Courtesy of Kim Sharpe.

William and Alta Latta's house at 1016 First Street in West Lafayette, Indiana. This house was just a few blocks north of the Purdue University agriculture campus. Courtesy of Kim Sharpe.

A Thanksgiving reunion in 1928 at the Latta home. Seated are (from left to right) Bertha Latta, Robert Latta, and Mary Latta. Standing are (from left to right) Myra Wood Cheney, John Tanswell, Nettie Wood Tanswell, Paul Cheney, Alta Latta, and William Latta. Courtesy of Phyllis Webster.

A family reunion of the Wood, Latta, and Tanswell families, circa 1900. Standing are (left to right) Arlee and Arthur Mosher (New York relatives), Myra Wood, E. B. Wood, and Pauline Latta. Sitting are (left to right) John Tanswell, Eunice Wood, and Amos Wood, with Robert Latta kneeling at front right. Courtesy of Phyllis Webster.

Two of William Latta's children, Robert and Pauline, sit in a carriage pulled by "Kittie" at Amos Wood's Maple Ridge Farm, circa 1905. Courtesy of Phyllis Webster.

Professor William Carroll Latta (right) with an unidentified person in front of his father-in-law's home in Mason, Michigan. Courtesy of Phyllis Webster.

Professor William C. Latta in 1908 at the age of fifty-eight. Courtesy of Purdue University Libraries Special Collections.

Alta Latta in 1924 at the age of seventy. Courtesy of Kim Sharpe.

Carol Reemtsma, daughter of Pauline and granddaughter of William and Alta Latta, is shown here at age three (circa 1926) playing with dolls. William Latta often mentioned Carol's dolls in the letters that he wrote to her. Courtesy of Kim Sharpe.

Carol at eight years old sharing a bike with her five-year-old brother, Keith, and their dog, Lindy, circa 1931. Courtesy of Kim Sharpe.

Professor Latta in a graduation cap and gown with Carol and Keith in 1929 in front of Purdue University's Agricultural Hall, now called Pfendler Hall. Courtesy of Kim Sharpe.

A family reunion at BEROPAMA, the Lattas' cottage on Lake Charlevoix, near East Jordan, Michigan, circa 1927. Front row (left to right): Henry Reemtsma, Carol Reemtsma, Pauline Latta Reemtsma, Keith Reemtsma, William Latta, and Mary Latta. Back row (left to right): Alta Latta and Bertha Latta.

A view of the Lattas' cottage. Courtesy of Phyllis Webster.

A view of Lake Charlevoix. Courtesy of Phyllis Webster.

Keith Reemtsma (left) plays with Carol (far right) and two other children in Lake Charlevoix in front of the Lattas' lakeside cottage, circa 1928. Courtesy of Kim Sharpe.

Professor Latta (right) with Keith Reemtsma (center) and an unidentified girl, circa 1929. Courtesy of Kim Sharpe.

Eveline Orchards with Lake Charlevoix in the background. Courtesy of Phyllis Webster.

Bertha Latta (left) and Mary Latta at Eveline Orchards inside the "Tuck Away," a small cabin directly behind the larger cottage that William Latta owned on Lake Charlevoix, circa 1950. The women sold the cottage but were given use of the cabin for life. Courtesy of Phyllis Webster.

Lasting Tributes:
The Man Remembered

CHAPTER  NINE

O day of rest and retrospect,
Of backward and of forward look.
The memory of manly strife
Warms the heart and cheers the life.
The past secure, some victory won,
No unrest o'er westering sun,
Since Hope looks for a brighter day
And Faith sees shining from afar
The evening and the morning star.
The rapidly approaching night
Shall merge ere long in endless light.

—William Carroll Latta
"Tomorrow" from "Yesterday, Today, Tomorrow," 1925

PROFESSOR LATTA'S CAREER at Purdue University was remarkable for the depth of his commitment to the Purdue School of Agriculture as well as the length of his service. A short biography written in 1922 noted:

> He is the pioneer of the pioneers at Purdue and might be called the "dean" of the agricultural workers of this state. Forty years of faithful and continuous service for a University and a State is a record to be envied and few are they that equal it.[1]

William Carroll Latta was there at every important early development of the School of Agriculture. He was instrumental in providing the leadership to make things happen and commanded the energy and determination to see things through. Within his first decade at Purdue, he and others helped to change a struggling agricultural program into one that captured the attention of Indiana's agricultural community.

Latta's work on education, research, and Extension formed the foundation of what would become the prime directive of Purdue University agriculture programs. He was one of the first to:

- recognize that practical research was needed if farmers were to prosper like their urban counterparts;
- understand that field research would be validated only if repeated over many years;
- appreciate the need for researchers to develop bulletins to communicate results in an easy-to-understand format for farmers;
- recognize that students majoring in agriculture needed four years to complete their studies to allow them to leave Purdue University as better informed and trained agriculturists;
- realize that the university would be successful only if the latest information coming out of research was extended to farmers by having Purdue researchers go out and speak directly to them;
- introduce the concept that Purdue University had an obligation to educate women and children;
- promote and provide opportunities for women as legitimate and knowledgeable speakers at outreach programs;
- push for the introduction of agricultural courses in public schools;
- understand that Purdue University should be directly involved in community development by providing technical training on building infrastructure and developing leadership skills; and
- encourage Purdue University to strengthen ties and seek greater cooperation with churches and civic organizations to address the needs of rural communities.

Implementing such an ambitious list of firsts at Purdue University required an entire career and life dedicated to formulating such ideas and putting those ideas to work.

After thirty or forty years, most men of his age would have stepped away from work and looked to settle down into the quiet life of retirement. Not so for Professor Latta. As he got older, his pace quickened and his interests expanded to doing more work within the community.

An exchange of letters between James Noel and Professor Latta clearly showed he had little interest in retirement. Noel wrote Latta on April 11, 1922:

> It is hard to realize that you have served Purdue for forty years. I was much interested in the [Purdue] *Exponent* article received this morning, and

without delay I want to extend my congratulations to you upon such a long period of such notable service to the University and to the State of Indiana. The State will reap its greatest benefits from your work in the far off future. You have laid the foundation in a wonderful way, and I am sure that you have built it better than you knew. Please accept my best wishes for a long and contented life, with the hope that you will lighten your work and experience much happiness in the enjoyment of its rewards.[2]

Latta replied:

Your kind, congratulatory letter of yesterday received this morning. It is indeed quite a surprise, but none the less appreciated. It does one real good to get such words from old-time friends. Since being relieved of my administrative work in connection with the School of Agriculture I have been able to carry my load very comfortably indeed and the work is so distributed that I can get, each year, a good vacation in mid summer. I am hoping, therefore, to be of some service to the University for a few years more. With great appreciation of your kindness and sincere well wishes, I am cordially your friend.[3]

His mind was still sharp, and his age took a backseat to his desire to improve the lives of his fellow Hoosiers. His energies never waned as he continued his work in the community.

Though Latta had many demands on his time, he was repeatedly recognized in his later years for a lifetime of faithful service to seemingly every organization he embraced. And this was no different for an organization that had its humble beginnings in Latta's very own classroom. Latta's interest in livestock production led him to help form the American Shropshire Registry Association on February 5, 1884. But Professor Latta would do more than just help organize the association:

The professor was then elected to the original executive committee and attended nearly every meeting during the next twenty years. From 1887 until professional accountants were hired in 1900 he chaired the auditing committee, served on the pedigree and memorial resolutions committees and was 1st vice-president from 1901 through 1904; a reliable, devoted hard-working founder![4]

By his own account, Professor Latta even maintained his own flock of Shropshire sheep in southern Indiana:

> It is and has been my opinion that, barring fluctuations, the sheep to grow is the one that will produce both mutton and wool to advantage. If you have a good grade of Shropshire sheep, my judgment would be to continue, then improving as time passes. What is the character of the ram that you expect to dispose of? I have a small flock of sheep in Southern Indiana and will need to purchase a ram this fall. Has the ram in question any marked defects or is it simply unsuited to the ewes that you have? Is he of good breeding and approved form? What is his fleece as to weight and compactness? What is his age? Is he a sure breeder? At what price are you willing to sell him?[5]

He would attend some of the association's annual meetings, such as the one held in Toronto in 1899. Professor Latta was the guest of honor at the Shropshire meeting in 1924, which marked the association's fortieth anniversary. Latta reminisced about the first meeting, stating, "We met in an upper room of the old two-story building [the original agricultural building] with some six or eight rooms and a back wing for storage of grain. I fancy not one of the founders had any idea of what was to come from that small beginning. . . ."[6]

Ten years later, Professor Latta gave the keynote speech again at the fiftieth anniversary of the American Shropshire Registry Association in Chicago on December 5, 1934. Once more, Professor Latta drew those in attendance back to the early days of the association and noted the growth in the number of Shropshire sheep registered, making it the largest registry society in the world at that time.

Drawing from a lifetime of experience, the eighty-four-year-old professor also gave his views on livestock breeding:

> In closing, permit the reminder that, owing to the plasticity of the animal organism, the livestock breeder has almost divine creative power to stamp his ideal on the animals which Divine Providence has given him control. May the word FORWARD be our slogan for the coming years, and may every breeder of purebred livestock have the persistent aim to maintain, not only purity of blood but also prepotency in transmitting vigor, quality, utility, symmetry, and beauty to the animals under his molding hand.[7]

Julia M. Wade, secretary/treasurer of the Shropshire association, later wrote Professor Latta congratulating him on his speech:

You certainly have a gift of expressing yourself in exactly the right way for each occasion. Our Association is very proud, and justly so, to have had you not only present at our Anniversary celebration, but to furnish the principal paper or address of the evening. Letters coming to my desk express satisfaction at having had the opportunity to hear you.[8]

As a token of the association's gratitude and respect, a fine brown-and-white coverlet woven from wool from the flock of association member Claude Harper was presented to Professor Latta at that meeting.

Professor Latta had been in charge of what was considered one of the nation's best Farmers' Institutes. He was the only superintendent in all of that time and had, more often than not, offered his services as an instructor when the organizers of the county programs asked him to do so. Over the course of his career, Latta would speak in nearly every county in the state.

In the fall of 1910, the Farmers' Institutes workers honored Professor Latta with "a comfortable chair upholstered in brown leather"[9] and an accompanying statement of their respect:

Dear Prof Latta

The Farmers' Institute speakers of the State wish to express in this formal way by a gift the profound regard they have for you—a regard inspired by the just and kind spirit you have shown toward us throughout our association together. Our relations under the stress of conditions in the field and your inflexible devotion to duty in the office have demanded on your part a degree of forbearance almost more than human and a courage almost heroic—always we have felt the steadying power of your encouragement and your patience.

Also we wish to congratulate you upon the good work you have sought for our State during your unbroken connections, since its beginning, with the Farmers Institute Management. That our state has advanced in agricultural Extension until now it has a place of the first rank such we believe to be due to the way in which you initiated the work—the movement—due to your comprehension of the fundamentals—due to your justice in foreseeing a balance between the several interests—due to the sincerity of your belief in the value of the ends sought.

Those who have come into the work during late years can never know how strong were the early influences that sought to force a narrower activity than demanded by your own vision of the field. From the first you seemed to recognize that the life lived on the farm by the farm family is the ultimate consideration which inevitably must condition all agricultural advancement and your steadfast loyalty to your own higher view has been a distinct benefit to our state.

May you have in this chair hours of ease—hours of pleasant retrospection—hours of placid reverie—hours of clear vision of a country life in Indiana that shall be based upon the foundations laid by yourself in your ideals of the function of the Farmers Institutes.[10]

This is truly a remarkable letter in its description of Latta's devotion to his position at Purdue University and to his unwavering commitment to the farm family.

Perhaps the most impressive display of affection and respect for Professor Latta by his friends and colleagues was the presentation of his commissioned portrait to Purdue University. Arrangements for the Latta portrait are documented in the minutes from Epsilon Sigma Phi meetings. Epsilon Sigma Phi is a national honorary Extension fraternity with state chapters and a national office. Latta was a charter member of the Indiana Chapter, which was started in January 1929.

At the January 13, 1930, fraternity meeting, the members voted to commission an oil painting of Latta to be presented to the university in honor of his contributions there. Latta himself was present at this meeting.

Robert W. Grafton was commissioned to paint the portrait. Born in Chicago and trained at the Chicago Art Institute, he traveled widely and painted in Holland, England, and France. He later settled in Michigan City, Indiana. While he often painted landscapes, he was best known for his portraits of important professional and public officials, including three Indiana governors, Warren T. McCray, Edward L. Jackson, and Harry G. Leslie. Grafton was paid $436 in three installments for the Latta portrait.[11]

The announcement in the program for the portrait unveiling ceremony noted that the portrait was

presented to Purdue University by the Alpha Lambda Chapter of the Epsilon Sigma Phi in cooperation with associates, faculty members, former students, friends and members of rural organizations with whom Professor Latta has been intimately associated for many years.[12]

So on March 9, 1930, dignitaries, professional colleagues, and personal friends from near and far gathered for the unveiling of the painting. The *Purdue Alumnus* reported "more than 200 persons, including a number from over the state,"[13] attended the ceremonies. Thomas A. Coleman, assistant director of agricultural Extension, presented the portrait to Purdue University President Edward Elliott. Three presentations were delivered that day, which included "Professor Latta and Farmers' Institutes" by Mrs. Morton Fordice, "Professor Latta Our Colleague" by M. L. Fisher, and "In the Beginning" by Virginia C. Meredith, who described the difficulties faced by Latta and the Farmers' Institutes in the early years. To add to the occasion, music was played and tea was served.

Dean of Agriculture John H. Skinner is credited with penning the tribute for the professor. He wrote:

> Professor Latta is a native Hoosier. He was born in LaPorte County, March 9, 1850. His college training was obtained at Michigan Agricultural College where he was graduated in 1877 with a bachelor of science degree and a master's degree in 1882. In August, 1882, he came to Purdue as instructor in agriculture and superintendent of the University farm. He was the thirteenth member of the Purdue faculty. His service to agriculture, civic and religious activities has been unselfish and unremitting.
>
> A capable, sympathetic teacher, wise counselor and good friend of all his students, Professor Latta has been a trail blazer and pioneer in the field of improved agricultural and rural education. He organized the School of Agriculture and very wisely laid out the first administered four year course leading in turn to the bachelor's and the master's degree. He conspicuously directed the administration of the School until 1907.
>
> In 1883 Professor Latta began a number of soils and crops field plot experiments. Five years later he laid out the first permanent soil fertility field experiments, inaugurating a system of research which was considered one of the best in the country at that time. These original lines of experiments stand today as a monument to the foresight and vision of this man.
>
> Professor Latta pioneered in the field of agricultural extension in Indiana. He was placed in charge of Farmers' Institute work immediately after the passage of the Farmers' Institute Act of 1889. These Institutes aroused interest in agricultural education among the farm men and women of the state and led to legislative provision for the Agricultural Hall in 1901, the first state appropriation for agricultural research in 1905, and the appropriation in 1907 for the Experiment Station Building.

Later, the Institutes played no small part in securing the passage of the Clore Act establishing the Department of Agricultural Extension in 1911. For thirty-five consecutive years Professor Latta supervised the Farmers' Institute work which, through four decades, has exercised a potent influence in advancing agriculture, enriching rural life, and promoting community cooperation. The stable character of this work appears in the fact that after forty-one years 437 Farmers' Institutes were held in the state, the past season, reaching more than 150,000 people.

During the last few years, Professor Latta has devoted his time to preparation of the manuscript for a "History of Indiana Agriculture" soon to be published.

Professor Latta has truly left a great impress upon the local community, Purdue University and the agriculture of Indiana.[14]

Skinner had, in a short few paragraphs, captured the life and achievements of Professor Latta, who must have felt a sense of pride when he heard Skinner's words.

It was a time of great reflection on the past for the professor. He wrote in the program guide:

In presenting my portrait to Purdue University you have given expression to a measure of kindness as unexpected as it is thoughtful and heart warming. It is your interest in perpetuating my memory—not the portrait which is a fair likeness—that appeals to my heart. With sincere thanks for, and grateful appreciation of, your very kind remembrance, I am, as ever, Your Friend.[15]

Latta would also send out this thank-you card to those who attended the portrait program:

The undersigned desires to express his sincere appreciation of the many courtesies extended to him on his eightieth birthday. To all who helped to make possible the presentation of his portrait to the University; to all who had a share in the making and rendering of the program for the unveiling; to all who enriched the hour with gracious hospitality; to all who graced the occasion with their cheering presence, and to all who tendered congratulations, he feels deeply indebted.

In the remaining years which may be spared to him, he hopes so to live as to merit in some small degree the esteem and well wishes of his many friends.[16]

Professor Latta was a gracious man. He must have been honored to know that people would remember that he was at one time an important person in the development of Purdue University and that his contributions were significant enough to have his portrait done as a symbol of that devotion and dedication.

Latta had become an icon at Purdue University. On May 6, 1933, a Founder's Day Banquet was held at Purdue to celebrate the sixty-four years of the university's existence as well as to honor those members who were part of the Quarter Century Club. At eighty-three years old, Latta was the longest-serving professor at Purdue, having joined the faculty in 1882. Along with Latta, thirty-seven others were paid tribute, including some of Professor Latta's old friends: James Troop (1884), Joseph Arthur (1887), Stanley Coulter (1887), John Skinner (1899–1901; 1902), Martin Luther Fisher (1903), and Alfred Wiancko (1903).

Even as Professor Latta was being recognized by Purdue for his many contributions, he was working hard to complete still more projects for the university. At the age of seventy-four, Professor Latta became a consultant specialist in the School of Agriculture. He was asked by his supervisors to write a series of history books and publications on Indiana agriculture, Purdue University's School of Agriculture, the Purdue University Agricultural Experiment Station, rural churches, and the Indiana State Board of Agriculture. Professor Latta would no longer be asked to look forward in terms of what Purdue needed; instead he would focus his energies on describing what had been.

His administrators understood clearly that Latta was only one of a few men still in a position to write the history of agriculture at Purdue and in Indiana. Latta was the ideal candidate to author such histories because not only had he lived during much of the period, but he was also an active participant in what transpired during those years. He could and would write from memory how Purdue University grew from a few buildings and a handful of faculty in his early days to a university that was currently attracting more students, hiring more staff, conducting better research, bringing in more money, constructing more buildings, and drawing more state, national, and international recognition.

In all, Latta drafted eleven historical papers:

- "Calendar of Events Preceding and During the Evolution and Growth of the Indiana Agricultural Experiment Station"
- "A Century of Indiana Agriculture in 1932"
- "Contrasts in the Last 50 Years of Agricultural Progress in Indiana"
- "The Country Church—Its Weakness, Its Importance, Its Opportunity, and Its Rehabilitation"
- "Early Agricultural Faculty at Purdue"
- "Evolution and Development of Agricultural Investigation Prior to the Organization of the Experiment Station"
- "Fifty Years of Extension in Indiana"
- "Historical Sketch of Purdue University Experiment Station from 1887 to 1932"
- "The Indiana State Board of Agriculture: A Historical Sketch"
- *Outline History of Indiana Agriculture*
- "The Story of Farmers' Institutes"

The *Outline History of Indiana Agriculture* is the only one of Professor Latta's manuscripts that was published in book form and is found today in many land-grant institutions' libraries and private collections. This single volume comprising 372 pages took ten years for Latta to complete.

Until his death, Latta continued to cross-reference his facts. He supplemented them by interviewing farmers who could help him determine the approximate dates when improved livestock, crop, and farm practices were introduced in each of Indiana's ninety-two counties. Unfortunately, he did not live to see the book published.

By the time Latta had largely finished his manuscript on the history of Indiana agriculture, there were no funds to pay for its publication. Professor Latta died in 1935, and upon his death, the typed manuscript sat in the files of Dean of Agriculture John Skinner.

The Epsilon Sigma Phi meeting on January 13, 1937, began a long and sometimes arduous effort to move Professor Latta's book to publication:

> Chief Royce brought up the matter of the printing of the Latta History of Indiana Agriculture. Figures supplied though T. A. Coleman showed that the first 500 books would cost approximately $1,536, while the next 500 would cost only $320. The quotation, which had been supplied by the Buford Printing Company of Indianapolis, did not include the cost of cuts. Mr. Johnston estimated that the cuts could cost at least $500.[17]

The dollar value of the printing project led to a series of discussions on how to finance the publication of the book. According to the secretary, Walter Fitch, Epsilon Sigma Phi only had $613.51 in the bank as of January 13, 1937. Fraternity members considered various ways to proceed, including selling books by subscription until publication costs could be covered.

Instead, the group decided to appoint a committee to explore its options. The Latta History Committee was asked to begin its work at once and to report its findings to the full group. The group was reminded, however, that the manuscript was the property of Purdue University. Dean Skinner would not turn over the manuscript to Epsilon Sigma Phi until he was assured that the group had a financial plan to ensure its publication. The committee was asked also to develop a prospectus for the book to help in promoting it.

The details of getting the book published were ironed out, and the committee requested that printers submit bids on the job. Lafayette Printing, a local company, submitted the lowest bid, which was $1.39 each for 1,000 copies.

At the October 6, 1937, meeting, committee member LeRoy Hoffman reported that the prospectus was mailed to 5,000 individuals. The front cover read, "YOU WILL WANT PROF. LATTA'S HISTORY OF INDIANA AGRICULTURE. Order your copy now. Price $2.50 per copy."[18] Initially 266 orders were received, raising $665.

Those initial sales must have been disappointing to Epsilon Sigma Phi. There weren't even enough orders to cover the cost of the printing. Members of the fraternity discussed two additional options for financing the book: placing sales quotas on the county Extension agents or having the fraternity borrow the remainder of the money. Members opted for the first choice and began working with the county Extension agents association to have them promote the book in their communities.

By January 13, 1938, with little progress to show, the group decided to have 1,000 copies printed. The members also agreed to underwrite the amount of the deficit between advance orders collected and the amount required to move the bid forward. By then, they had received orders for 375 books, raising more than $900.

Lafayette Printing published 1,200 books at a cost of $1,578.89. Total costs, including printing and promotion, amounted to $1,805.[19] By publication time, advance orders had soared to 893 books, generating more than enough money to cover printing costs.

The 300 or so books that remained would be sold over the next couple of years, though it would take some effort. In 1938, Hoffman wrote to Indiana vocational agriculture teachers to see if they could help sell the books:

> The book came off the press last May. Most of the copies have been sold, many of them to school libraries. There are a hundred or more copies still available. These copies will soon be purchased by people for their private use. We believe that far more people would read and appreciate the books if they were in libraries rather than owned by individuals. We further believe that every high school library where agriculture is taught should have a copy. Why not suggest to your school official that they buy a copy for your school library? The price is $2.50.[20]

Latta's book was—and, for all practical purposes, still is—the only complete book of Indiana agriculture dealing with crops, soils, livestock, and farm practices.

※ ※ ※

Perhaps the most significant tribute to Latta occurred nearly a decade after his death, when the country was engaged in the Second World War. With the United States' formal declaration of war on December 8, 1941, thousands of ships were needed to transport equipment, supplies, and troops to their overseas destinations. The United States Maritime Commission embarked on a crusade to quickly build cargo ships. These ships—called Liberty ships—were designed for emergency (i.e., rapid) construction, which meant that whole shipyards were converted over to their production.

Published accounts indicate that Liberty ships could be built in 60 days from the time the keel was laid with 14 additional days required to outfit the ship with equipment. The mass production techniques utilized by the shipyards and their suppliers made this quick turnaround possible. In many ways, construction of the ships followed the principles used in the automobile market; parts manufactured across the country were delivered to the shipyards for assembly. Many of the surviving ships—nicknamed "ugly ducklings" by President Franklin Roosevelt—found service again during the Korean conflict in the 1950s.

The U.S. government turned to the public for help in supporting the war effort, challenging patriotic Americans to buy war bonds to help build the ships that would deliver supplies to troops around the globe. One incentive offered any person or organization selling $2 million worth of war bonds the privilege of naming a Liberty ship after a person of their choosing, so long as the person was deceased. The challenge was taken up nationwide with so much zeal that Americans supporting the war effort raised enough money to build thousands of Liberty ships between 1941 and 1945.

In Indiana, the 4-H youth decided to take up the challenge by convincing the citizens of the state to buy war bonds. In fact, "the boys and girls of Indiana sold more Liberty Bonds than any other group from another state, and they were given the privilege of designating the person for whom the ship would be named."[21] The name they offered up was none other than that of William Carroll Latta.

It is interesting to note that Professor Latta was still remembered as someone important within 4-H circles. It was also fitting because Latta had dedicated his book, *Outline History of Indiana Agriculture,* to the boys and girls of 4-H. And they had now returned the favor.

The SS *W. C. Latta* was the 111th ship built by the Delta Shipbuilding Company in New Orleans, Louisiana. In an unsigned document dated April 30, 1944, a description of this shipyard shows the magnitude of the government's emergency shipbuilding project:

> The Delta Shipyards are really eight yards rolled into one, as each of the eight is able to operate separately with its own ways and its own assembly lines. In addition to the eight ships being built on the eight ways, there were sixteen additional ships in various stages of construction, including several in outfitting wet docks. These shipyards employ 18,000 people.[22]

The *W. C. Latta* had an all-welded steel hull painted gray, measuring 423 feet long and 57 feet wide. The height from the bottom of the keel to the top of the mast was 102 feet. The gross weight of the ship was 7,176 tons. The *W. C. Latta,* like other Liberty ships, was designed to carry upwards of 10,500 tons of cargo in five compartments. Liberty ships were equipped with enough bunks to house 28 seamen. Twelve of the bunks were in the forward position and 16 in the aft position.[23]

Professor Latta's granddaughter, Carol E. Reemtsma, christened the ship by breaking against its hull a bottle of champagne tightly wrapped in thick, braided red, white, and blue satin ribbons. The ceremony took place on April 13, 1944. Latta's grandson, eighteen-year-old Keith Reemtsma, could not attend the launching. He was in the U.S. Navy college program studying premedicine at the University of Idaho. All four of Latta's children—Bertha, Robert, Pauline, and Mary—attended the launching.

Carol and her sponsoring party were escorted to the launching platform by R. B. Ackerman, vice president and general manager of the Delta Shipbuilding Company, and A. D. Clyburn, representative of the U.S. Maritime Commission.

At 10 A. M., the company band struck up "Back Home Again in Indiana," Miss Reemtsma crashed the be-ribboned, wicker-encased champagne bottle against the bow and said, "I christen thee the W. C. Latta." The vessel quivered and slid into the water with a mighty splash. The band broke into the national anthem. Civilian spectators [it was a public launching] bared their heads, military men snapped to attention and saluted. Thus the memory of one of Indiana's "greatest" was perpetuated on the seas as it has been on the land.[24]

The *Lafayette Journal and Courier* described the patriotic scene for its readers back home with the following:

To the strains of "Back Home Again in Indiana," with flags and pennants flying and sparkling champagne foaming down her bow, a great ship, the S.S. *W. C. Latta*, came alive and slid from her cradle into the launching canal at the Delta Shipbuilding Company, New Orleans, La.

While ship launchings are remote to the land-locked middle-west, this particular ceremony holds much significance for Lafayette and Indiana. For the late Prof. W. C. Latta was known as the "Father of Indiana Agriculture." And it was at the suggestion of the 4-H Club boys and girls of Hoosierland that the U.S. Maritime Commission honored the late pioneer in agriculture extension and education.[25]

Because the *W. C. Latta* was not quite ready for sea duty, the party was taken to another Liberty ship, the *Parker,* for a shipboard tour. As they examined the *Parker,* the *W. C. Latta* was towed away by two tugs to be outfitted and made seaworthy. It was not until May 30, 1944, that the ship's three-inch, .50-caliber forward gun and five-inch, .38-caliber aft gun were finally fired and tested. The reports from the Armed Guard Center indicated that all of the weapons were found to be in good condition, without misfire or damage.

The *W. C. Latta* was assigned to the War Shipping Administration and the U.S. Maritime Commission during its life. During this time, independent companies supplied the men to load, transport, and transfer the cargo, while U.S. Navy sailors manned the ship's defensive weapons. (The names of the military men who served on the *W. C. Latta* are provided in Appendix 8.)

The first entry in the *W. C. Latta*'s logbook is May 25, 1944. It says the ship left Pittsburgh and arrived at Key West, Florida, on May 28, 1944. During 1944, the *W. C. Latta* primarily traveled along the eastern coast of the United States carrying freight between ports. However, by November of that year, the ship's log also recorded voyages to Liverpool, England; Malta; and ports in Italy, including Augusta, Leghorn, and Naples.

Atlantic Ocean travel was in the company of convoys due to the presence of German submarines, which were causing significant damage by sinking hundreds of Liberty ships. The *W. C. Latta*'s voyage from Liverpool, England, to New York in 1944 was in a convoy of 59 ships. The convoy itself was protected by 11 escort vessels.

The year 1945 found the *W. C. Latta* sailing to foreign ports in Algeria, Belgium, Canada, Italy, and the United Kingdom. In the United States, the *W. C. Latta* traveled to New York and Philadelphia as well as Pearl Harbor and Honolulu, Hawaii. In 1946, its course of sail was primarily along the eastern seaboard, but there are a few longer trips to the port cities of Porta Delgado, Portugal, and St. Nazaire, France. The 1946 war records indicate more restricted movements, with the last entry stating that the *W. C. Latta* was in Philadelphia on August 25, 1946.

Three men who sailed aboard the SS *W. C. Latta* during the war agreed to recount their experiences. They were Albert A. Rosati, Lawrence J. Muscoreil, and William L. Kingsley.

Albert A. Rosati, not quite eighteen years old when he joined the U.S. Navy, had this to say:

> They used to take ammunition, supplies, and tanks to Europe. We were gunners. A five-inch, .38-caliber gun was on the rear end of the ship for anti-aircraft. On the front end, the *W. C. Latta* had a three-inch, .50-caliber gun, which was a smaller anti-aircraft gun. At midship they had two 20-mm guns on each side of the ship.
>
> I was a sight setter on the gun. That's the guy who sits on the side and has earphones on. The lieutenant in the middle of the ship would give us the load range of the plane, and I would set the gun. Others would load the gun.
>
> We always had a convoy. We were an ammunition ship. We were always on the edge of the convoy because if we ever got blown up, we wouldn't hurt other ships. There were tanks and trucks on top of the deck from end to end. They really loaded the ships down going to Europe. Our ship often carried the "block busters," which were 2,000-pound bombs dropped over Germany from Allied planes.
>
> When you left the United States for Europe, you worked eight hours on, then eight hours off. As you got closer to the war zone, where the subs

were operating in the Atlantic, you worked six hours on, then six hours off. Then it got down to working two hours on and taking two hours off when you knew the German submarines were known to occur.

I remember a time when a German plane off the Italian coast got the flares on us. We had left the Rock of Gibraltar and were alone at sea. At nighttime, the ship would turn off all lights. The German planes would drop flares to identify our ships. I don't remember if bombs were dropped that evening.

The mess hall was in the middle of the ship underneath the smokestacks. When you had to go eat, you would have to hold onto a cable when you went from either end of the ship—hold on because the ship goes from one side to another. Every time you went to one side, half of the ocean would come with you.

We had one burial at sea. I didn't know if it was a merchantman or seaman. Had him in a canvas seabag with a weight on the bottom. Got shoved out to sea, and this was the man's burial.

After I was discharged from the Navy Armed Guard, I worked for the Pennsylvania Railroad and Amtrak from 1950 to 1987.[26]

Lawrence J. Muscoreil, seventeen years old when he joined the U.S. Navy, traveled on the *W. C. Latta* to Europe:

> The memory is very clear about the *W. C. Latta* because it was like my grandmother's ship. It so happened that my grandmother's name on my father's side was Rose Latta. I think I made three trips across the Atlantic Ocean on the SS *W. C. Latta*. It would take 18 days from Brooklyn, New York, to Africa. We were dodging everything in a zigzag motion. We went with a convoy one time, and the convoy went right and we went left. We wound up in the North Atlantic without any other ships. At nighttime all of the lights were off. We couldn't see anything. We followed the stars instead of lights. Lights would draw the attention from the submarines.
>
> When we left the United States, there were something like 54 Liberty ships going across the Atlantic Ocean, and by the time we got there we were lucky that there were 18 of us. The Germans were pretty smart with their torpedoes. It only took one torpedo to knock the Liberty ship out of the water. It was nothing but a big hull loaded down with ammunition. Once we delivered clothes to British soldiers in Italy.
>
> She [the *W. C. Latta*] sat very low in the water. We had waves come over the top of the side. When she was loaded, she was loaded. When she was empty, she was like sixty feet out of the water. Coming back from Italy we were always empty. We never brought anything back from Italy. An empty ship bobbled around like a cork.

We were a cargo ship. We did transport troops from Africa to Italy. We were in the Straits of Messina between Sicily and Italy. The soldiers got off the side with rope ladders and rope netting. They got into a landing craft that would take them to shore. We don't know what happened to them because we weren't supposed to be in the war. We were there to protect the cargo, get it over there. We were not a warship. Our job was not to fight a war or create a war.

We took the forward part of the ship where the three-inch, .50-caliber gun was. I was a seaman gunner in the Armed Guard, and my job was to maintain the guns and to fire and use them to protect the ship. When I was assigned to the three-inch, .50-caliber gun on my second trip, I became the pointer.

We certainly saw plenty of submarines and planes. We had plenty of combat duty. I burned most of the combat memories out of my mind. That's something I don't think anybody wants to remember.

When I was discharged from the Navy, I worked as a machinist for Bell Aircraft. I retired in 1988 as a shop machinist for Allied Chemical.[27]

William L. Kingsley served aboard the *W. C. Latta* after the ship had been moved to the Pacific Theater:

I was a gunner's mate third class in the Navy. I was only on the ship for a short period of time, maybe three or four months. We left New York after we got loaded up with 500-pound bombs. We went through the Panama Canal [May 24, 1945]. We went out into the Pacific Ocean to the Eniwetok Atoll [June 23, 1945]. Originally, I think we were going to Guam. But on the way, we were held up at Eniwetok because they were going to drop the bomb on Japan. We then headed back to Honolulu, Hawaii [September 10, 1945]. After the bombs were unloaded, we were loaded up with sugar. We carried the sugar to the Domino Sugar docks in East River in Brooklyn.

We were served food in the mess hall by merchant marines. When you hit rough seas, they would put a wet tablecloth on the table so the dishes would not slide off. You would have to hold the dish in your hands when you were eating.

Once in a while, someone would get really sick, but they did not have a doctor on those ships. They would have to notify the Navy to have the sick person picked up.

After I was discharged, I worked for the Singer Sewing Machine Company in their time-study department setting rates on jobs. I then spent twenty-five years in the U.S. Post Office as a clerk until I retired in 1983.[28]

The SS *W. C. Latta* was disarmed on December 12, 1945, in New York and moth-balled two years later as part of the National Defense Reserve Fleet. Eventually, the ship was sold by the U.S. Maritime Commission to be salvaged and recy-cled, and in 1961, the *W. C. Latta* was scrapped in Wilmington, Delaware. Only the ship's nameplate was saved.

Arrangements were made to deliver the nameplate to Purdue University so that William Carroll Latta, Indiana 4-H children, and those that bought war bonds could be honored. Larry Sullivan, a grandnephew of Professor Latta, began the retrieval process:

> I was a reporter at the *Bluffton News-Banner*. We happened to have a little news item in the paper from the U.S. Maritime Commission. It said they were dismantling all of these mothballed Liberty ships that were in port somewhere in the east. They were trying to get in touch with the people who were involved with the namesakes of these things. They invited any-body who knew anything about anybody that had a Liberty ship named after them to get in touch with the Maritime Commission so they could get a memento from the ship back to the sponsoring body. So I just clipped it out and sent it to Purdue, probably to the information office. I said my great-uncle had been involved in the formation of the School of Agriculture at Purdue, and this ship had been named after him. Somebody at Purdue made the contact. A few months later I got a phone call from someone at Purdue who said they had made contact and they were indeed getting the plaque from the ship. It was going to be presented to Purdue officials at a service club luncheon of the Kiwanians in West Lafayette, and they asked to know if I would come and be a representative of the family. I readily accepted.[29]

On the evening of December 7, 1962, a ceremony was held at which the Kiwanians, Purdue University officials, and others paid tribute to William Carroll Latta. Howard S. Kennedy, representing the Maritime Memorial Commission, participated in the ceremony. Dr. Earl Butz, dean of the School of Agriculture, introduced Kennedy, who had been present at the ship's launching in 1944. Kennedy presented the nameplate to the university, remarking that

> 3,900 Liberty ships were used during World War II. They were sitting ducks for everything, but 1,300 of them lasted through the war. The GI's who rode them can tell you what a vital part they played in our supply system.[30]

Purdue University President Frederick L. Hovde accepted the nameplate, noting that it would be placed near Latta's portrait in the Agricultural

Experiment Station Building. Latta's two surviving children, Robert and Mary, were on hand for the ceremony. Also in attendance were some of Professor Latta's former colleagues, including Mark Busche, Leroy Hoffman, Mervill O. Pence, and David Thompson.

From 1985 to 1995, the Purdue Agricultural Alumni Association, in collaboration with Professor Tom Turpin of the Department of Entomology, sponsored the Latta Games, an agricultural quiz bowl tournament with the motto "Creating a Better Understanding of American Agriculture."[31] The intent of the Latta Games was to "encourage capable young people to think about a career in professional agriculture."[32]

Counties first held their own contests among two class divisions. The two classes of competitors were the junior division for grades 4–8 and the senior division for grades 9–12. Competitions were often held at local county fairs with the junior and senior division winners advancing to a state competition held at the Indiana State Fair.

Teams that participated in the Latta Games were required to hail from an organized youth group, such as the 4-H, Future Farmers of America, Boy and Girl Scout troops, and school science clubs. A minimum of three members was required for team eligibility to compete.

Competing teams were given a total of sixteen toss-up questions. The moderator would ask a single toss-up question, and a student from either team pushed a buzzer to gain the right to answer. If a team missed a toss-up question, the opposing team was allowed an opportunity to answer. Questions covered such topics as livestock production, crop production, economics and marketing, farm management, engineering, forestry, wildlife and ecology, horticulture, foods, family living, weather, and public policy. Each correctly answered question was worth ten points. A correct answer also resulted in the opportunity to answer bonus questions worth an additional ten points each. Bonus questions addressed agricultural history, current events, people, and trivia.

The Latta Games offered a fitting, modern-day tribute to the life of Professor Latta, Indiana's first scientific agriculturist and advocate for rural communities. The following quote is taken from promotional material on the Latta Games:

W. C. Latta was one of the first professors of agriculture at Purdue University and was the best known of our early innovators. His pioneer work in the teaching of improved agricultural practices, in the testing of new ideas, and in the disseminating of information makes it logical to call him the founder of the School of Agriculture, the Agricultural Experiment Station, and the Extension Service at Purdue University. It is appropriate that we name these games in his honor.[33]

Professor Latta and forty-two Purdue University benefactors, administrators, trustees, faculty members, coaches, and students were honored when Founders Park was dedicated on the Purdue University West Lafayette campus on April 23, 1994. The dedication of Founders Park celebrated Purdue University's 125th anniversary and recognized individuals who were instrumental in helping to lead a new state university through its formative and difficult years, when money, buildings, and personnel were in short supply.

The park, which is located on the north side of State Street between Matthews Hall and Stone Hall, is equipped with outdoor tables, benches, plantings, and a flowing fountain. On the south side of the park is a large commemorative plaque—70 inches long by 40 inches wide and weighing 300 pounds[34]— inscribed with an overview of the early days of Purdue University along with the names of the individuals so honored as being pioneers at the university:

> On July 2, 1862, President Abraham Lincoln signed the Morrill Land Grant Act, which provided public lands to any state that would use the proceeds to establish and maintain a college "where the leading object shall be, without excluding other scientific and classical studies, and including military tactics, to teach such branches of learning as are related to agriculture and the mechanic arts . . . in order to promote the liberal and practical education of the industrial classes in the several pursuits and professions in life."
>
> Under the provisions of this visionary law, Purdue University was established in 1869. Lafayette entrepreneur John Purdue provided the founding gift and gave his name to Indiana's land-grant institution. However, hundreds of men and women were crucial to the University's survival and the shaping of its character during the uncertain early years between the founding and the early 20th century. While it is not possible to identify or name every person who played an important part in Purdue's early history, the individuals listed below are representative of those pioneers.

Located at the heart of the original campus, Founders Park recognizes all the students, faculty members, administrators, trustees, and benefactors who made it possible for a great university to rise out of an Indiana meadow.[35]

Individuals represented on the plaque were associated with Purdue University between 1870 and 1935. William Carroll Latta, "professor of agriculture; pioneer in agricultural extension; director of agricultural experiment station,"[36] is one of fifteen faculty members listed. Formal recognition, sixty years after his death, by the institution to which Latta devoted so much of his life's work underscores his impact on the development of Purdue University.

In 2005, the Purdue University College of Agriculture recognized the life and work of Professor Latta with the inauguration of an honorary organization, the W. C. Latta Society. This society was established to recognize individuals who reach a distinctive level of lifetime giving to the College of Agriculture. The generosity of Latta Society members to the College of Agriculture reflects Professor Latta's lifelong effort to improve agriculture and Purdue. Charter members of the Latta Society have their names engraved on a plaque for permanent display in the David C. Pfendler Hall of Agriculture on the West Lafayette campus. Through their donations, members of the Latta Society have improved academic programs, updated buildings and facilities, and attracted outstanding faculty and staff, which in turn strengthens teaching, research, and Extension opportunities for undergraduate and graduate students in the College of Agriculture.

In addition to this new society, Professor Latta will also be honored well into the future by a scholarship that bears his name. The W. C. Latta Scholarship, given annually to an outstanding undergraduate agriculture student, recognizes academic achievement and community leadership. This scholarship, made possible through funds raised from the sale of this book and through donations from individuals, is a fitting tribute to Latta's unwavering commitment to improve higher education, the university, and the community in which he lived.

Latta had a choice of pictures for his book on Indiana agriculture. He selected the now famous and most recognized photograph (below) of him wearing the "hat." Courtesy of Donya Lester, Purdue Ag Alumni Association.

YOU WILL WANT PROF. LATTA'S

HISTORY
of
INDIANA AGRICULTURE

ORDER YOUR COPY NOW
Price $2.50 per Copy

The Author at eighty

A memorial edition will be published as
soon as sufficient orders are received

By

EPSILON SIGMA PHI

National Honorary Extension Fraternity
In cooperation with the
Indiana County Agents' Association
Purdue Agricultural Alumni Association

For further information write:
W. Q. Fitch, Sec.-Treas., Epsilon Sigma Phi
West Lafayette, Indiana

The advertising brochure for Professor Latta's book on the history of Indiana agriculture.
Courtesy of Epsilon Sigma Phi, Alpha Lambda Chapter.

My dear Director Skinner:

    I have returned to Mrs. Harlan
the retyped chapters of my History of Indiana Agriculture.
I have these papers in duplicate, the carbon being on
file in my office. The tables in the appendix have not
been duplicated.

    I am handing you herewith some
photographs of the Jamesway Barn and Silo made by the
James Manufacturing Company of Fort Atkinson, Wisconsin.
These should be included with the other illustrations
which your Son, John, tells me you have on file in your
office.

      Cordially yours,

       W. C. Latta
      Consulting Specialist

Director J. H. Skinner
Agricultural Experiment Station
Purdue University

In this June 1934 letter to John H. Skinner, Professor Latta noted that he had completed his book on the history of Indiana agriculture. Courtesy of Donya Lester, Purdue Ag Alumni Association.

Left: This portrait of William C. Latta was commissioned by the Extension fraternity Epsilon Sigma Phi and painted by Robert Grafton in 1930. Courtesy of Mike Slabaugh.

Top: The gravesite of William Carroll Latta is located in the Spring Vale Cemetery in Lafayette, Indiana. Courtesy of Frederick Whitford.

A commemorative picture showing the four lay founders of the Wesley Foundation on the Purdue University West Lafayette campus. Pictured are (from left to right) George Roberts, Martin Fisher, Latta, and Zora Smith. Courtesy of the Wesley Foundation.

A woven coverlet made from the wool of Shropshire sheep was presented to William Latta at the fiftieth anniversary of the American Shropshire Registry Association in 1934. Courtesy of Kim Sharpe.

The 1934 program announcement celebrating the fiftieth anniversary of the American Shropshire Registry Association. Latta gave the keynote speech at the gathering and was honored for his work on behalf of the organization. Courtesy of Purdue University Libraries Special Collections.

George Allen
Vice President

S. R. Quick
President

W. C. Latta
Executive Committee

Albert Henderson
Founder

John L. Thomson
Pedigree Committee

Mortimer Levering
Secretary-Treasurer

CHARTER MEMBERS

AMERICAN
SHROPSHIRE SHEEP
REGISTRY ASSOCIATION

W. J. Quick
Senior Purdue Univ.

I. J. Farquhar
Executive Committee

The charter members of the Shropshire association, including Professor Latta (upper right).
Courtesy of the American Shropshire Registry Association.

Members of William Latta's family (near top of stairs) attended the launching of the SS *W. C. Latta*. Guests were invited to the public ceremony in New Orleans on April 13, 1944. Courtesy of Kim Sharpe.

Professor Latta's granddaughter, Carol Reemtsma, christened the ship with champagne at the launching. Courtesy of Kim Sharpe.

The launching of the SS *W. C. Latta* in April 1944. The Liberty ship would carry cargo and ammunition, both in the European and Pacific Theaters, during World War II. Courtesy of Kim Sharpe.

The full Navy crew of the SS *W. C. Latta* posed for this 1944 photograph while the ship was in Naples, Italy. Navy sailors such as Albert A. Rosati (front row, far left) and Lawrence J. Muscoreil (second row, fourth from right) were assigned to defend the ship as it transported cargo during World War II. Courtesy of Albert A. Rosati.

Above: Rosati (center) with shipmates Lawrence J. Muscoreil (right) and Sam Putt in Brooklyn, New York, in 1944. Courtesy of Albert A. Rosati.

Top left: Rosati wearing headphones, looking for German submarines. Courtesy of Albert A. Rosati.

Bottom left: Albert A. Rosati in his U.S. Navy photograph, 1944. Courtesy of Albert A. Rosati.

The nameplate of the SS *W. C. Latta* was transferred to Purdue University at this 1962 ceremony. In attendance were (from left to right) Purdue President Frederick L. Hovde; two of Professor Latta's children, Robert Latta and Mary Latta; and Howard S. Kennedy from the Maritime Memorial Commission. Courtesy of Kim Sharpe.

The 1990 Latta Game champions. Courtesy of Charles and Velma Krininger.

In 1994, Purdue University dedicated Founders Park on the West Lafayette campus. A plaque in the park recognizes Latta and others as being instrumental in leading the university during its formative years. Courtesy of Frederick Whitford.

Epilogue:
A Legacy of Caring and Commitment

CHAPTER  TEN

No distance can ever
True friendship's tie sever,

And mem'ry, repeating
Events of past meeting,

Give fresh demonstration
By friend and relation

That true hearts still cherish
Kind thoughts that won't perish.

—William Carroll Latta
from "Fond Memories," 1933

THERE CAN BE LITTLE DOUBT that William Carroll Latta was what we today would call a workaholic. His extensive career with Purdue University, especially his work with the Farmers' Institutes, his lifelong dedication as an active member of the board of directors for the YMCA and Trinity Methodist Church, and his involvement in a variety of civic groups left precious little leisure time.

Professor Latta was driven to succeed, but he was not an innovator. Latta's talent was implementing the ideas of others, and he demonstrated a ferocious drive and stamina in his work at Purdue University and in the community.

Pushing projects to completion meant that he had to work around obstacles and obstructionists. Latta was a steadfast critic of obsolete systems. Without hesitation, he voiced his opinions, in person or in writing, to the principals about their plans and activities. He was sought after for his wise council, but he spoke bluntly and, no doubt, alienated people.

Professor Latta was a man who enjoyed accolades, whether from people in the agricultural community or politicians and community leaders. Latta was well connected politically. He had the ear of Purdue presidents, state legislators, and county officials, and he used that influence to promote his projects. He worked hard to cultivate friendships with elected officials and was a savvy political character himself. It is likely that Latta was so highly regarded in Indiana that his superiors at the university occasionally felt compelled to relax their authority over him in anticipation of becoming a target for the wrath of irate citizens or politicians. Professor Latta was bypassed for important administrative positions during his tenure doubtless because of the animosities his personality and work style engendered.

Latta was a mover and shaker who put all his energies into his work. At his death, "The official flag on the campus of Purdue University was lowered as an expression of institutional bereavement."[1] On February 15, 1936, K. E. Beeson, the secretary-treasurer of the Indiana Corn Growers' Association, wrote to Bertha and Mary Latta:

> We feel that each of us has lost a staunch friend and co-worker; but of transcending importance agriculture has lost a great and influential leader. Though we shall ever miss his cheery face, we take consolation in the fact that his achievements for the cause of agriculture will live on and continue to be a lasting benefit not only to us, but to those who may follow.[2]

Professor Latta was indeed a prominent figure in drawing the agricultural program at Purdue University out of its obscurity during the late 1800s and early 1900s. But why did Professor Latta achieve fame while the names and faces of others who also worked hard in their jobs faded from history?

While celebrating his first Christmas at Purdue University in 1882, Latta could not have possibly known that he was about to embark on a historic journey that would last for fifty-three years. During his tenure, Purdue University would call on him to take charge of the School of Agriculture at every major juncture and to lead each and every new initiative in teaching, research, and Extension. In the waning years of his career, he became the elder statesman, the link between the past and the present, the agricultural historian for Purdue University. He was the face of Indiana agriculture for his generation.

Latta never forgot what it was like to farm the old way. He well understood that unless Purdue University was able to introduce new methods and practices, farmers and their families would never prosper. He also knew that if he could impress upon farmers that science could improve their yields, save their soils, and increase their profits, then Purdue University would be seen in a more positive light. To recognize his foresight, one has only to look at his efforts in designing practical, long-term research that could be used by farmers and the manner in which the research results were packaged into Experiment Station bulletins written specifically for farmers. Once he saw the resistance by farmers to science-based agriculture begin to crumble, he directed all of his energies toward bringing the university to the people through the Farmers' Institutes.

He came from a golden age, when agricultural science was new and exciting. Each success reinforced Latta's status as the person to whom agricultural and university officials turned when they needed things done. Each new endeavor focused him more squarely in the sight of the people of rural Indiana. And for university administrators, Latta's work brought more money into Purdue's coffers from the Indiana General Assembly and the United States Congress.

While Latta had the vision, ambition, and technical skills to succeed, he still required the dedication of others to help him reach his personal and professional goals. His aspirations were well beyond what could be achieved by any one person. His success, in large part, was due to his ability to inspire others. Latta was also fortunate to be the right person at the right time in the right place. When he stepped into his office in Agricultural Hall for the first time, he faced an agricultural program faltering under the challenge of finding its mission. To make matters worse, Purdue University was thought of primarily as an engineering school. Purdue agriculture would, for many years, play second fiddle to engineering. But with dedicated efforts by Latta and his colleagues, the School of Agriculture came to stand alongside the Purdue School of Engineering as an equal.

Latta was more than science, agriculture, and Purdue University. Clearly it disturbed him to see failing farms, people living in poverty, children denied educational opportunities, discrimination against women and minorities, and churches more interested in buildings than the well-being of their communities. Latta possessed an unwavering optimism that education could help people better themselves. He was able to blend agricultural science and social work to advance his vision of improved rural life. More importantly, he convinced others to take up his vision.

Purdue University and the School of Agriculture needed Latta, and he needed Purdue University to realize his dream of a better life for rural Hoosiers. Latta came to Purdue with a mission of helping others based on his religious upbringing. Without the profile of his position at Purdue University, his ability to influence the lives of rural people would have been lessened.

It is clear that Latta was a prominent spokesperson for rural people, expressing their needs and understanding their problems. He never gave up his ideal that the university along with churches and civic organizations existed to serve the people and that education, research, and a caring heart could solve many problems. It was indeed a mutually rewarding relationship between the man and the school in which Purdue gained respect and recognition and Latta fulfilled his dreams.

Every working hour brought Latta the well-deserved recognition that he enjoyed during his life, and that has endured long after his death. Today, we follow the same models that Latta and his colleagues designed more than a century ago, fine-tuned to fit our needs in the twenty-first century. In keeping with Latta's vision of helping communities prosper, thrive, and remain vital, today's Purdue University College of Agriculture continues to unravel scientific mysteries through innovative research, demonstrating how science can improve agricultural production, showing people how families can be strengthened, providing leadership to youth to make them good citizens, and working with communities to build local infrastructure and leadership skills.

Latta is one of those rare people whose work transcends time. While he might still be remembered by some for his book, the Liberty ship named after him, or even the Latta Games, it is his love for people and his single-minded drive to improve people's lives that history records and we respect. May this biography introduce future generations of Hoosiers to the life and work of William Carroll Latta and encourage them to emulate his passion for making a difference in the world.

Appendix 1

Selected Text of "Agricultural Education: Its Practical Value" *

The agricultural colleges of this country are the most purely educational institutions that exist in the interest of agriculture; and yet, these colleges are today comparatively unknown and unappreciated by a large proportion of the farm population. While it is true that, in nearly every farm community, there is an enlightened element fully awake to the importance of this question, it is equally true that a majority of the farmers have yet to learn the value of a thorough agricultural education.

Indeed, I believe there is, among farmers, a wide-spread misapprehension of what constitutes such an education; and as men of these colleges of agriculture are still young, and their fruits hardly manifest, it seems proper at this time to dwell at some length on the character of these institutions, the work they do, the influence they exert, and the benefits of the education they impart....

But what are the benefits of agricultural education? They are two-fold, accruing both to the community and to the individual.

While our agricultural colleges are doing a good work for agriculture in their various lines of experiment, I believe they are doing a much grander work in gradually, but surely, building up an educated class of farmers who will, in turn, give dignity and rank to their calling. The future progress of agriculture in this country will be commensurate with the elevation of the agricultural classes. The agricultural colleges of the United States are yet too young to show marked results; but time will prove me correct in asserting that agricultural education is a prime factor in elevating the farming classes, and thus hastening the day when agriculture will not only be a highly honorable, but also a highly honored calling.

Let us next consider the benefits of an agricultural education to the individual. I will group them under four heads: Such an education makes farm life more congenial, promotes success in acquiring wealth, confers social standing, and enlarges one's sphere of usefulness.

We have today many discontented farmers who, seeing only the brown side of farm life, are engaged in farming simply because they think they can do nothing

* William Carroll Latta, "Agricultural Education: Its Practical Value." Speech delivered before the Annual Agricultural Convention, Jan. 1883. Thirty-Second Annual Report of the Indiana State Board of Agriculture, 1882, vol. 24, 178–82.

else. Many of our farmers' boys are dissatisfied with their lot, and some of them even seek an education as a means of emancipation from what they consider the hard, dull lot of the farmer....

But the agricultural graduate who returns to the farm does so not with the unhappy thought they can do nothing else, but because it is his choice. His education has kept alive and cultivated his sympathy with agriculture, and conserved his physical energies. He has become a student of nature, and he knows that in farming he will be brought hand to hand and face to face with the forces of nature. As he engages in the various labors of the farm he is constantly an interested, intelligent eye-witness of the workings of forces of which he before knew nothing. Whatever his observations as he goes about his work, he is constantly on the alert to find the real cause of the phenomena that came to his notice, and the relation of these causes to the fertility of his soil, the curing of his crops or the health of his stock....

An agricultural education will confer material benefit on its possessor. The man who thoroughly studies the principles of his calling will more quickly and surely find out and establish the conditions of success. Particularly is this true in agriculture, with the complex relations and many unsettled questions. Every question, whether concerning methods or appliances, soil or seed, breeding or feeding, is thoroughly studied by the educated farmer, whose disciplined mind clearly distinguishes between cause and coincidence, inference and fact, between similar and identical conditions, between processes and results, between real and apparent, or full and partial success or failure....

He is better able and more apt to avail himself of the experience of his fellow farmers, and thus profit alike by their successes and their failures. He knows better how to utilize the results brought out by our experiment stations, and he can also institute careful, though inexpensive, experiments for himself, by which he can determine the best means of keeping up the fertility of his soil, etc. He is able to classify, digest, and thus profit by the heterogeneous publications of the agricultural press; and this, indeed, is a great advantage. Many of the articles in the agricultural papers are beyond the comprehension of the average farmer. Conflicting statements and erroneous views also creep into the columns of these papers, and, although even the uneducated man knows that some view must be wrong, he is at a loss to choose the right, and hence he receives comparatively little material benefit.

An agricultural education will also aid the farmer in saving money in his farm operations. It is generally the ignorant farmer who is duped by sharpers; who is led into expensive blunders in buying and selling, and who, therefore, exclaims the most bitterly against the hard lot of the farmer. But the farmer who is educated for his business can quickly tell when it will be unwise for him to invest in new machinery or make new improvements. He understands the subject of absolute and relative values as applied to his farm products; in other words, the relation existing between the feeding, manurial, and market values, and he can therefore tell when it will be sound economy to feed his farm crops or exchange them for manufactured foods. Again, a thorough knowledge of the conditions that affect the practical value of a fertilizer will often be a means of saving the farmer's money. For example, it is not enough for you to know that a fertilizer which sells at forty dollars has a possible manurial value of forty-five dollars. You must know the practical value of that fertilizer *on your farm* [Latta's emphasis]. It does not by any means follow that, because the possible manurial value of a fertilizer is five dollars above the selling price, every farmer will make five dollars by using the article. One man may make five dollars and another lose five dollars, or even ten dollars, by the operation. The result, in every case, will depend on the nature and condition of the particular soil and crop; and these questions every farmer must determine for himself. Hence the value of an agricultural education, which will materially aid the farmer in the solution of these problems.

An agricultural education will confer on its possessor social standing. An education greatly develops the social qualities and widens the social circle. The farmer graduate who is socially inclined will find ready access to the society of intelligent, refined people in his own calling, and in other callings as well. He is a welcome guest in these circles because he is entertaining, instructive, helpful. True, he gives largely, but he is always the debtor, for in these refining associations he finds needed relaxation, wholesome diversion, and new incentives. Coming in contact with many different minds, his own becomes better balanced; and being subject to a wider range of elevating influences he attains a broader and more symmetrical manhood.

Lastly, such an education enlarges one's sphere of usefulness. While this is true of any education, it is especially true of an agricultural education, which prepares one to enter a field comparatively unoccupied.

The professions are already crowded with educated men, while agriculture stands in need of men of this class. Men of special education are needed on the farm, that they may devise better methods of farming; in the friendly gatherings of farmers, that they may help to elevate the social condition of the agricultural classes; in the various agricultural societies, that these organizations may promote the highest interests of agriculture; and in our legislative halls, that agriculture may receive her just dues at the hands of our law makers. It therefore necessarily follows that the agricultural graduate who will enthusiastically devote his energies and his education to agriculture can not fail of enlarged usefulness.

To recapitulate briefly, our agricultural colleges beget and foster a liking, and bestow a special training for, agricultural pursuits. They educate *toward* the farm, while the literary institutions, as a rule, educate *away* from the farm [Latta's emphasis]. An agricultural education elevates manual labor and conserves physical energy, while classical education is apt to ignore both. The agricultural graduate is at home on the farm, and has a real love for agricultural pursuits; while the literary graduate generally finds the office more congenial, and prefers a literary or professional occupation.

It therefore follows that if our farmers' boys are to share the benefits of college education and still remain on the farm, as most of them certainly should do, they should seek a farmer's education.

In conclusion, fellow farmers, I bespeak for these agricultural colleges your liberal patronage and support. Their success in the past may not have been equal to your expectations, for many of them have been, and some are still, laboring under great disadvantages. And the chief obstacle to their progress has been the indifference of the farmers themselves. Remember that they are *your* schools [Latta's emphasis], working in your interest; and remember, too, that your earnest co-operation will greatly increase their efficiency and widen their influence.

Appendix 2

Introductory Dates of Agricultural Practices and Innovations in Indiana*

Soil Treatment

Tile draining	1872
Fertilizing	1894
Liming	1910

Crops and Crop Management

Clover	1851
Rotation	1874
Alfalfa	1899
Cowpeas	1904
Late Seeding	1910
Soybeans	1910

Agricultural Implements

Hay loader	1875
Gang plow	1880
Twine binder	1881
Fertilizer drills	1885
Corn picker	1915
Ensilage harvester	1927
Four-row cultivator	1928
Four-row planter	1928
Rotary harrow	1928
Soil pulverizer	1928

Livestock Management

Silo	1897
Balanced Rations	1901
Vaccination	1908

Breeds of Livestock

Beef Cattle	
Shorthorns	1862
Herefords	1888
Angus	1891
Polled Shorthorns	1892
Dairy Cattle	
Jersey	1881
Holstein	1891
Ayrshire	1905
Guernsey	1908
Brown Swiss	1910
Horses	
Percheron	1879
Clydesdale	1884
Sheep	
Merino	1863
Cotswold	1872
Southdown	1876
Shropshire	1886
Hampshire	1898
Oxford	1899
Rambouillet	1906
Swine	
Chester White	1873
Poland China	1873
Berkshire	1875
Duroc	1887
Hampshire	1903
Spotted Poland China	1908

* *William Carroll Latta,* Outline History of Indiana Agriculture *(West Lafayette, Ind.: Epsilon Sigma Phi [Alpha Lambda Chapter], Purdue University, and Indiana County Agricultural Agents Association, 1938), 371.*

Appendix 3

Purdue University Agricultural Experiment Station Bulletins Written by William Carroll Latta

Bulletin No. 2. 1885. *Experiments with Nitrogenous, Phosphates and Other Fertilizers.*

Bulletin No. 4. 1885. *Experiments with Wheat.*

Bulletin No. 6. 1886. *Experiments with Oats and Corn.*

Bulletin No. 8. 1886. *Experiments with Wheat.*

Bulletin No. 12. 1887. *Experiments with Wheat.*

Bulletin No. 14. 1888. *Experiments with Oats and Corn.*

Bulletin No. 16. 1888. *Experiments with Wheat: Crop Rotations.*

Bulletin No. 23. 1889. *Experiments with Corn.*

Bulletin No. 27. 1889. *Field Experiments with Wheat.*

Bulletin No. 32. Volume II. July 1890. *Field Experiments with Wheat.*

Bulletin No. 34. Volume II. February 1891. *Field Experiments with Commercial Fertilizers and Manure on Barley and Oats.*

Bulletin No. 36. Volume II. August 1891. *Field Experiments with Wheat.*

Bulletin No. 39. Volume III. April 1892. *Field Experiments with Corn.*

Bulletin No. 41. Volume III. August 1892. *Field Experiments with Wheat.*

Bulletin No. 43. Volume IV. March 1893. *Field Experiments with Corn.*

Bulletin No. 45. Volume IV. August 1893. *Field Experiments with Wheat.*

Bulletin No. 50. Volume V. April 1894. *Field Experiments with Corn and Oats.*

Bulletin No. 51. Volume V. August 1894. *Field Experiments with Wheat* (coauthored with George Ives).

Bulletin No. 55. Volume VI. March 1895. *Experiments with Corn and Oats.*

Bulletin No. 56. Volume VI. August 1895. *Field Experiments with Wheat* (coauthored with S. P. Caruthers).

Bulletin No. 61. Volume VII. August 1896. *Field Experiments with Wheat* (coauthored with W. B. Anderson).

Bulletin No. 64. Volume VIII. April 1897. *Field Experiments with Corn, Oats and Forage Plants* (coauthored with W. B. Anderson).

Bulletin No. 72. Volume IX. August 1898. *Field Experiments with Wheat* (coauthored with W. B. Anderson).

Bulletin No. 77. Volume X. March 1899. *Field Experiments with Corn* (coauthored with W. B. Anderson).

Bulletin No. 88. Volume XI. May 1901. *Systems of Cropping with and without Fertilization* (coauthored with J. H. Skinner).

Appendix 4

Selected Titles of Presentations Delivered at Farmers' Institutes in Indiana from 1888 to 1907*

Cattle for the farm. *Maurice Douglas, Shelby County.*

Poultry raising. *Mrs. C. M. Thomas, Crawford County.*

An ideal farmer's garden. *B. F. Crane, Fountain County.*

Care of cream and churning. *Mrs. Jennie Hill, Union County.*

The Hessian fly. *Bert Hart, Warrick County.*

How to avoid competition. *Miss Orpha Campbell, Brown County.*

Business methods of farming. *George Hartle, Wells County.*

What a women can do on a farm. *Miss Nellie Murray, Fayette County.*

Farm accounts. *F. J. Heacock, Washington County.*

The purchase and care of farm tools. *J. M. T. Welborn, Marion County.*

The farmer's workshop. *Otto Kamp, Vanderburgh County.*

What the farmer should know and do in order to succeed. *W. F. Edmondson, Newton County.*

The educated farmer. *Miss Laura Newlin, Parke County.*

What is winning true success on the farm? *L. E. Glazebrook, Jasper County.*

Why should not farmers have seats at the first table? *Ernest Hixon, Lake County.*

What is the basis of an equitable land rent? *J. C. Goodwine, Warren County.*

Views of farming from the tenant's standpoint. *Mrs. Belle Harding, DeKalb County.*

A few common birds and their relation to agriculture. *R. M. Heavilon, Clinton County.*

Unappreciated advantages of farm life. *Miss Alma Whaley, Monroe County.*

Our homes. *Mrs. Michael Yarling, Shelby County.*

Hereford cattle. *C. E. Amsden, Shelby County.*

Mothers on the farm. *Mrs. J. J. Wheeler, Perry County.*

Our boys and girls. *Mrs. Carrie Jones, Vigo County.*

The unexpected guest. *Mrs. C. E. Black, Lake County.*

Our daughters—what shall we teach them? *Mrs. S. J. Gunkle, Clinton County.*

Home sanitation. *Dr. J. L. Hendricks, Boone County.*

Trusts. *G. L. Furness, Porter County.*

Cow peas. *A. E. Kruse, Spencer County.*

Cow peas as a forage plant and fertilizer. *U. Coulson, Sullivan County.*

The tomato. *Isaac Whitely, Wayne County.*

What to plant and how to plant it. *C. B. Moore, White County.*

* *Indiana State Board of Agriculture Annual Reports, 1888–1907.*

Fruit growing and spraying. *Eli Hemmer, Dubois County.*
Small fruit culture. *D. A. McDowell, Miami County.*
Horticulture. *W. W. Palmer, Ohio County.*
Pastures. *E. A. Swope, Vanderburgh County.*
The Hessian fly. *J. McMahan, Union County.*
Is the production of winter eggs profitable? *T. Blair, Hamilton County.*
Caring for and feeding stock. *J. Ditman, Johnson County.*
One hundred acres and how to manage it. *J. Young, Hamilton County.*
Value of the lead pencil. *P. R. Lostutter, Switzerland County.*
Is it prudent for a farmer to sell his farm and move to town to educate
    his children? *Mrs. Eugenia Chappell, Pike and Gibson Counties.*
The farmer's home as it is and as it should be. *W. F. Robbins, Jennings County.*
Home on the farm. *F. Henderson, Tipton County.*
Relation of sanitation to health. *Dr. E. Shirts, Greene County.*
Reading and thinking farmers. *E. Tufts, Dearborn County.*
The farmer's son. *Miss M. Conger, Shelby County.*
The value of a higher education for the farmer. *B. Volga, Jefferson County.*
Needs and improvements of our rural schools. *Mrs. L. Dyer, Tippecanoe County.*
The farmer as an apologist. *Mrs. C. S. McCord, Parke County.*
How to live. *Wm. Noonan, Blackford County.*
How shall women accomplish the most good? *Mrs. J. McDermott, Johnson County.*
How I grow big crops of corn. *W. E. Lame, Pike County.*
Sorghum as a forage crop. *C. Dawson, Spencer County.*
Can farmers of Kosciusko County afford to grow wheat at present prices?
    E. F. Diehl, Kosciusko County.
A canning factory on the farm. *E. Tufts, Ripley County.*
Forestry—past, present, and future. *J. Parks, Marshall County.*
The farmer's poultry and its care. *C. Milhous, Owen County.*
Poultry. *Mrs. G. Ray, Johnson County.*
Sanitary conditions of the farm home. *Mrs. J. Chillas, St. Joseph County.*
Sanitation of the farmer's home. *Miss F. Noe, LaPorte County.*
Training of the homemaker. *Mrs. J. Saunders, Madison County.*
Making farm homes attractive. *J. Garr, Howard County.*
The ideal home. *Miss S. Barnett, Pike County.*
Opportunities of farm life. *Miss R. Curtis, Dearborn County.*
Can a college graduate utilize his education on the farm? *A. Rush, Whitley County.*
Nature study in the common schools. *Miss J. Meeker, Lake County.*
Why have a Farmers' Institute? *S. De Motte, Pike County.*
Farm dairying. *Mrs. B. Comer, Jasper County.*
Farm poultry. *J. Bunnell, Wayne County.*

Nation and state aid to public roads. *T. Day, Ripley County.*

The poetry of farming. *J. Roseberry, Scott County.*

Making the most of farm life. *Mrs. M. Brown, Fountain County.*

An ideal farm. *F. Dillon, Fulton County.*

Influence of home surroundings. *Miss G. Vaught, Shelby County.*

Some conveniences in and about the house. *Mrs. W. Beckett, Dearborn County.*

How to beautify the farm house. *Miss M. Cato, Dubois County.*

An ideal home. *Miss Nellie Davis, Grant County.*

Corn growing. *J. Boone, Sullivan County.*

Poultry. *Mrs. J. Ray, Spencer County.*

Money in poultry. *Mrs. C. Davis, Parke County.*

Home and farm sanitation. *Miss C. Whipps, Sullivan County.*

Saving strength. *Mrs. J. Moore, White County Summer Institute.*

Social side of farm life. *Mrs. C. Bridges, Spencer County.*

How to select food. *Miss F. Little, Cass County.*

Soil fertility. *W. Artman, Marion County.*

Silos and silage. *A. Hoadley, Hendricks County.*

How to grow the apple. *R. Barr, Daviess County.*

The appearance of the farm. *H. Pitts, Rush County.*

The farmer's contribution to society. *Mrs. A. Trusler, Fayette County.*

Country life and agriculture. *Miss E. Scott, Kosciusko County.*

The country girl versus the city girl. *Miss R. Jenkins, Orange County.*

How to keep the boys and girls on the farm. *E. Hughes, Ripley County.*

An evening in the farm home. *Miss H. Cottingham, Dearborn County.*

Home building. *Mrs. Wm. Standerford, Tipton County.*

Home life on the farm. *Mrs. P. Freshly, Spencer County.*

Why educate the farm boy? *R. Geyer, St. Joseph County.*

The education of the twentieth century farmer. *J. Elder, Putnam County.*

Agricultural education. *E. Salisbury, Steuben County.*

Making new soil out of old. *Miss M. Baker, Jackson County.*

Corn. *R. Haymond, Bartholomew County.*

The preparation of the soil, the seeding, and the cultivation of the corn crop.
    H. Heathman, Pike County.

Tree culture. *J. Goble, Hancock County.*

The horse. *P. Pence, Clinton County.*

How to feed and care for poultry for profit. *Mrs. J. Williams, Posey County.*

Conditions of success on the farm. *J. Newton, Starke County.*

The girl on the farm. *Miss M. Osborn, Starke County.*

Our girls and boys—are we living for them? *Mrs. E. Smith, Washington County.*

The relation of parent to child and child to parent. *Mrs. A. Hootman, Lake County.*

Appendix 5

Yearly Attendance at Farmers' Institutes
in Indiana, 1889 to 1931*

Year (Nov.—Mar.)	Estimated Attendance	Year (Nov.—Mar.)	Estimated Attendance
1889–90	not recorded	1910–11	201,580
1890–91	not recorded	1911–12	174,758
1891–92	not recorded	1912–13	225,496
1892–93	not recorded	1913–14	248,293
1893–94	not recorded	1914–15	274,187
1894–95	11,446	1915–16	276,013
1895–96	28,016	1916–17	262,101
1896–97	24,126	1917–18	164,764
1897–98	29,376	1918–19	164,764
1898–99	25,500	1919–20	164,661
1899–1900	27,976	1920–21	165,775
1900–01	29,016	1921–22	191,606
1901–02	37,603	1922–23	179,046
1902–03	34,226	1923–24	160,872
1903–04	59,189	1924–25	180,869
1904–05	74,467	1925–26	170,730
1905–06	129,894	1926–27	175,000
1906–07	175,785	1927–28	175,000
1907–08	195,911	1928–29	158,982
1908–09	215,211	1929–30	162,920
1909–10	203,910	1930–31	161,925
		Total	5,340,944

* *William Carroll Latta,* Purdue University Farmers' Institutes Annual Reports, 1889–1911; *and* Annual Report of the Purdue University Department of Agricultural Extension, *1912–31.*

Appendix 6

Poems Written by William Carroll Latta

Poems to His Grandchildren

Henry Keith at Three

Henry Keith's a lad of three,
A sturdy growing boy is he.
His father's pride, his mother's joy,
Is this big lusty growing boy.

Where sister leads he follows too.
What Carol does he tries to do;
Up ladder steep, down cellar stair,
He goes with her 'most everywhere.

In Carol's shoes on Carol's skates,
This mimic lad displays his traits;
Now on one skate and in one shoe,
But soon this boy will roll on two.

Although these two are full of pranks
Each wants to lead in table thanks.
To keep the peace twixt sister, brother,
Keith prays one meal, Carol another.

May each one with the other vie
Life's wholesome lessons to apply;
In kindly acts strive to excel,
Thus striving on, each will do well.

Though mimic, Keith's original;
No dolls for him his parents tell,
But bottles, nails, he likes full well.
A life career this may foretell.

In sundry ways that are his own,
Some of these days he'll stride alone.
May youthful plays point out his bent
In which his life may well be spent.

December 5, 1928

To Four-Year-Old Carol

I know a blue-eyed girl of four
Who lives in Californy:
The Dutch and Irish and some more,
Her temper is not stormy.

She likes her dad and dolls and toys,
And Keith, her baby brother;
When rest time comes she makes no noise
Because she loves her mother.

She goes to church with dad sometimes
In mild and pleasant weather;
She watches people drop their dimes
And hears them sing together.

When back from church our Carol comes
She helps to get the dinner,
And sets on spinach, milk and plums.
She surely is a winner.

Her grandpa hopes this girl will please
Come back to Injiany,
To play again upon the keys
Of Aunt Mary's piany.

Grandpa would take her to the Park
To ride and swing and teeter,
And have upon the slide a lark
At foot of which he'd meet her.

To Carol at the Age of Five

I know a little five-year old,
Her name is Carol E.
You could not buy her with much gold,
She's not for sale, you see.

Her hair is brown, her eyes are blue;
Her cheeks are pink, her smile is sweet.
She likes to find something to do
With willing hands and flying feet.

She dearly loves to aid her mother
And also likes her dad to please;
She takes good care of little brother
And now and then she helps Louise.

Ere long this girl to school will go,
As other little children do;
Day by day she'll wiser grow
By ever learning what is true.

To make life's pathway smooth and bright,
Just for this little girl of five,—
That she may always love the right,
May friends and parents ever strive.

Her grandpa hopes that this sweet child
Will ever choose the true and good
And thus grow up pure, undefiled,
To gracious noble womanhood.

January 19, 1929

That Lad of Four

In Mountain View there is a lad
Who pleases well his tall slim dad.
He also makes his mother glad,
And sister, too, enjoys the tad.

As dad and sister are away,
Some hours at least, 'most every day,
This four-year-old alone must play
While mother works. Too bad, I say!

But Keith's too big to cry o'er that,
He dons his coat, puts on his hat,
And burrows in a pile of junk.
Some wheels he finds but most is bunk.

He rides his tricycle around
And sees most everything aground.
But when the family sets forth
To see the sights of old New York.

It takes subway, commuter's train,
The "L" and "Tube," home to regain.
Sometimes the ferry boat they ride,
Before return to home fireside.

Excitements vary, never fail;
The daily hours bring trips for mail.
When work is done, the playroom bright
With tots and games is Keith's delight.

When Keith is out, his mother own
Is left to keep the house alone.
Both in, they fill the house with cheer
Till dad and sister do appear.

The twilight hour finds all at home,
In sweet content; let others roam.
Their thanks ascend to God above
Who fills their hearts with peace and love.

December 5, 1929

Carolings

Strange things the children say and do;
Their odd remarks are not a few.
Of Carol's words so sage and queer
Grandpa will jot some down right here.

"By my own self I'll go to sleep."
This big hop toad is "ours" to keep:
"Not ours but God's," her mother said;
"God borrowed it to us" instead?

"I'd rather Mary's 'Cupie' be
Than Grandpa's 'Bossie Calf,'" said she.
She loves her ma, Aunt Mary too
Who held her when she was "brand new."

Her active mind runs on ahead,
As shown one day by words she said:
"Will Keith some day grow bigger, when
He can take care of my children?"

When told her Grandpa R. was dead,
"He'll help God care for us," she said.
She tries to teach "her girls" neatness;
"O Rose! Your bed is such a mess."

'Gainst proposed "lunch" she did demur;
My "usually supper" I prefer.
Her eager mind is quite a rover;
She often says, "Let's talk things over."

Carol's strange words may not long last
Because she'll soon be six years past.
But wiser things we know she'll say
As she grows older day by day.

Grandpa Latta

For Carol's Sixth Birthday
January 19, 1929

A Little Maid of Seven

A little maid of Mountain View
Ofttimes says things that are brand new.
It's very useful to know how
To make things, "well, right here and now."

To dramatize with crayons bright,
Also with pencils, tooth-picks slight;
To make them stand or sit just right,
And act their parts, is her delight.

Good stories, Psalms, she reads aloud,
Which may or may not please the crowd.
At school this maid a blessing asks,
When luncheon follows morning tasks.

She plays the Uke, Piano too;
What else may not this maiden do?
The tunes are, "Row, row, row your boat,"
And Old Black Joe's "I'm coming" note.

Five and Eight

In a rushing, big, wide city,
With no country, more's the pity,
Live a lassie and a laddie
With their mother and their daddy.

Five-year laddie, eight-year girlie,
Growing taller, bigger surely;
And their clothing—what a problem!
For their ma to duly clad them.

Both are playful, finding pleasure
In games wholesome, filling leisure
Hours, fast-flitting, with full measure
Of happiness-rich treasure.

But this sister and her brother,
Daily helping father, mother,
Make parental burdens lighter
And the passing days the brighter.

School for Carol, where she's learning,
Welcome credits, daily earning:
But for Keith, the kindergarten,
Simple truths for him to start on.

May each daily grow more clever:
Success crown each good endeavor.
May joyous life and usefulness
Enable each the world to bless.

December 5, 1930, and January 19, 1931

Untitled

She "Onward Christian Soldiers" tries;
The progress made is some surprise.
The secret of her success lies
In love of work, is my surmise.

Just now with whooping cough she
    whoops,
But guards against infecting groups.
In afternoon she's always glad
To meet the train that brings her dad.

This maiden grows by leaps and spurts,
While short and shorter grow her skirts.
A new-found tooth of second set
Assures her that she'll bigger get.

Her mother—cares increased of late
With family, now, of dollies eight;
Her youngest doll she takes to bed,
And Rose on birthday cake is fed.

I know this seven-year girlie's name;
'Tis Carol Reemtsma, I acclaim.
May she as well play life's great game
With mind, heart, spirit, all aflame.

To Carol and Keith

Grandpa is glad that you are both liking music.
Won't he be pleased when he gets a chance to hear
Carol thrum the piano and Keith blow the clarinet!
Do you suppose Lindy can learn to play on the
trombone or on some other bone?

When Carol the piano plays
And Keith blows on the clarinet
And Lindy gnaws a bone and says
Me too, we'll have a hearty laugh, you bet.

But lest you forget, lest you forget,
'Member that school lessons you must get
So for school work just keep all set
And you will "get there" yet in weather dry or wet.

Then just keep on a'going, girlie, lad,
And you will surely make grandpa, grandma glad.
Then a long pull, a strong pull, a pull all together
And you will be sure to win any kind of weather.

Grandpa is too busy to smooth up this rhyme,
Maybe he can do better when he tries next time.

January 14, 1933

Just Three Lively Youngsters, Nine and Six and One
Just Three Hopeful Entrants in Life's Race to Run

Three bright and happy youngsters, now live away out west.
I've never seen young Lindy, but I do know the rest.
This Lindy takes no schooling because he cannot talk,
But just the same, he's learning on two hind feet to walk.

With Master Keith to teach him, he soon will carry sticks;
And learn, before much older, to do some other tricks.
When playing with the children, he surely has a lark;
You know that he is happy by his quick friendly bark.

Sometimes he gets real lonesome, with children off at school;
Yet he won't go to whining or acting like a fool.
But my! with fun he's brimming, when they come running back,
And if allowed to meet them, he'd do it, lickety smack.

With 'rithmetic and writing, geography and art,
And history and spelling, to give them both a start;
I guess that Keith and Carol, will grow up very wise,
If A's they both keep getting, by their correct replies.

Then hygiene will surely help them both to keep the pace,
In music and in reading, to capture the first place.
With deportment becoming, to his full credit, Keith,
And piano for Carol, they'll earn the victor's wreath.

Ah, this illustrious trio, of girl and boy and dog,
Will keep the Reemtsma elders, both constantly agog,
To guide these frisky youngsters, in study, work, and play,
With feet so widely rambling, along life's upward way.

West Lafayette, Indiana
January 19, 1932

For Carol and Keith Reemtsma and Their Dog, "Lindy."
El Reno, Oklahoma
On the occasion of Carol's ninth birthday.

Poems to Greet the New Year

1921

The husky youngster comes to bat,
In quest of laurels to be won;
And gray-beard twenty doffs his hat
To youthful nineteen twenty-one.

By all past years enriched and blest
and harbinger of good to come;
may this new year prove very best
to you and yours and every one.

1922

To friends who have traveled the old year
  all through,
Glad greetings, well wishes, on reaching
  the new.
Of failures or losses let's make no ado;
But enter with courage nineteen twenty-
  two.

1923

You've served us well, full well we know:
Can you not stay—Ah! must you go?
The clock strikes twelve, adieu, adieu;
Good-bye, good-bye, dear Twenty-two.

But hark! iron tongue and brazen throat
Rend all the air with joyous note:
A New Year born! for you, for me;
Thrice welcome! Nineteen Twenty-three.

1924

Adieu, Adieu! and Welcome Too!
Twenty-three and Twenty-four

Inheritor of annals past
Was 'Twenty-three the best the last:
Its garnered store, a goodly hoard,
On all surpassingly outpoured.

New Year, can you do better still,
And thus our fondest hopes fulfill;
To hearts and homes bring blessings rare,
That peace and plenty all may share?

For answer, look not far away;
Rich opportunity, today,
It's sighted through the new-found door:
Swing wide! We hail you, 'Twenty-four!

1925

Yesterday, Today, Tomorrow

O radiant childhood's morn, thy marvels
In round-eyed wonderment beheld!
Each mirror pool or rippling stream
Allures to splash, swim, fish, or dream.
Each vale, flower-decked, the eye's delight;
Each rising hill or mountain height
A challenge to ascend and see beyond.
Roseate morn, purple eve, and glowing
   noon
Blue sky, bright star, or brilliant moon
All view to charm, inspire. In truth
We say, O glorious day of youth.

O day of work, of eager strife,
When earnest men invest their life
In open field, in city mart,
In learning's hall or mine so dark,
Upon the sea or in the air,
In quest of truth, men everywhere
Strive for gain, for fame, for power.
Some win, some lose; one vict'ry sure
A man's estate all may secure.
O day of strife, O day and hour
Of manhood's prime and manhood's
   power.

O day of rest and retrospect,
Of backward and of forward look.
The memory of manly strife
Warms the heart and cheers the life.
The past secure, some victory won,
No unrest o'er westering sun,
Since Hope looks for a brighter day
And Faith sees shining from afar
The evening and the morning star.
The rapidly approaching night
Shall merge ere long in endless light.

1926

Peace

O thou bright Messenger of Love!
Thou bearer of the olive branch;
May thy glad message, from above,
War-weary souls of men entrance.

Fly swift and far, this orb around;
The Angels' song proclaim again
To this sad world's remotest bound,
Sweet "Peace on earth, good will to men."

From East and West, from South and North,
Men look and long and pray for Thee:
In beauty, garlanded, come forth;
From hate and fear and war set free.

God grant that pulpit, platform, press,
Men so inspire, both near and far,
That high resolve, our souls possess,
To 'stablish Peace, abolish War.

From making instruments of war,
The hand and brain of man release:
Let Art and Science, evermore,
Promote the industries of peace.

Locarno, League, World Court express
The Nations' need, the Nations' quest
For a world-wide abiding peace,
Which, ages long, will make man blest.

E'en now, let Nations all unite
To War outlaw, just Peace enthrone:
And men, of ev'ry hue, delight
To chant, for aye, the Angels' song.

1927
Happy New Year

As changing vibrant New Year's bells
Ring out the Old, ring in the New,
And on the air their music swells,
Our greetings glad fly out to you.

Old Six-and twenty's bounteous store
By Providence so freely given,
Inspires both thanks and hopes for more
Of good, for all in Twenty-seven.

1928
To Twenty-Seven

Before you go, dear Twenty-Seven,
Accept our thanks for blessings given.
Because "Old Faithful" friend you've been
We gladly greet your youthful kin.

To Twenty-Eight

The record fine made by your brother
Leads us to ask from you another.
Your precious moments we shall need.
For kindly word and helpful deed.

Bring sunny hours to cheer us on
To goal achieve ere time is gone:
May all of your months and fleeting days
Inspire our work and songs of praise.

1929
A New Year Meditation

The sands run low, the moments fly,
The gray old year is passing by:
Its notes of joy, of sorrow too,
Things done, undone, pass in review.

In many fields a great advance,
For everyone a larger chance.
Achievements made, predict yet more,
A better world than e'er before.

Since dawning gleams of world-wide peace
Inspire fresh hope that war shall cease,
We'll greet the new year with a song
And join the forward-marching throng.

With test-tube, micro-telescope,
Explore new realms, doors wider open:
Thus seeking truth, more surely find
The tracing of the maker's mind.

And tracing thus, more clearly see
That laws of life and harmony
All blend in one grand symphony—
God's thought of human destiny.

1930
A Better New Year

O, is it true, as some men say,
One can be "better ev'ry way";
That Prophet-Bard in Bible lay,
Foretold a coming "Perfect day"?

Will keeping well the laws of health
Regain, retain, increase the wealth
Of body grace, and vigor, strong,
To fight life's battles with a song?

Can one achieve more open mind,
Yet larger, richer truth to find;
Push back the walls of ignorance
To realms of wider cognizance.

Put all that hinders under ban,
And be a truer "friend to man"?
Then, may the new year better be,
"In ev'ry way" for you and me.

1931
Happy New Year

An ending of December we gratefully
    remember,
With feelings growing tender, the message
    of each sender
Of Merry Christmas greeting.

And as we thoughtful ponder o'er friends
    both here and yonder,
We gladly make rejoinder: may Thirty-one
    be kinder
Than Thirty fast retreating.

But while we're backward glancing,
    the New Year is advancing;
So we, the future facing, do welcome its
    fast pacing
With gladsome Howdy-do, and hearty
    God bless you.

1932
If the Christmas Spirit Abides

If Christmas, gone, in passing on,
Left more of cheer for the New Year
A sweeter song to urge along
Life's toilsome way to brighter day:

Gave greater hope for upward grope
From war, release, for lasting peace;
For larger good, world brotherhood
To free lands, all, of fear's dread thrall:

Helped truth's clear ray illume the way
From error's night to paths of light;
So all mankind may thus possess
A richer need of happiness:

Then Christmas did not come in vain,
But brought a universal gain;
A chance to better live, and do
Yet nobler deeds, in Thirty-two.

1933
Happy New Year

Old Year you've come to journey's end.
New Year we welcome you, our friend,
And in your name a message send.

May God inspire both you and me
To help U.S. keep sober, free,
In Nineteen Hundred Thirty-Three.

1934
Keeping Step

Hooray! Hooray! again Hooray!
The N.R.A. and A.A.A.,
With C.W.A., et-ceter-A,
A strong phalanx in full array
And stately step, are on their way:
But wither bound? What answer, pray?
Aye, there's the rub; for who can say?
This much is sure, we must repay
The Nation's debt, some future day.
But do not yield to blank dismay!
'Gainst these edicts let's not inveigh.
As Prexy's striving for fair play,
So Johnson's arm must have wide say
To banish gloom with hope's clear ray.
By doing thus, perhaps we may
Keep "Old Depression" well at bay.

1935
Thankful Greetings

All who behold in chastened mood,
Life's varied ways with failures strewed,
Who yet believe the world is "good,"
That faith will live and love still give;
That science, youth, will unveil truth
To rend in twain bald error's chain:
Who seek demise of greed and vice,
Help justice, fair, spread ev'rywhere;
Who strive for peace, from fear release,
With prophet's eye, these all descry
Foregleaming rays of better days
For all mankind.

Political, Patriotic, and Other Poems

My Easter Prayer

Thorn crowned and crucified
'Twas thus my Savior died
Third day my risen Lord
Fulfilled His spoken word

He rose for you and me
Gave hope that we shall see
Loved ones gone on before
Who wait on further shore

May Christ arise in me
From sin my soul keep free
Help me someone to win
To life anew in Him

To work from morn till night
In fields for harvest white
To help men choose the right
May this be my delight.

Whither Bound

Oh Ship of State, *our* Ship of State:
So proudly sailing life's high sea;
What winds and waves of cruel Fate
May swerve thee from bright destiny?

Shall beer and wine and ripe old rye
Bestride thy staunch and goodly deck,
Befuddle brain and blear the eye
To reef and rock that cause shipwreck?

"O God of Hosts, be with us yet,
Lest we forget, lest we forget,"
That zenith Star of nation wet,
May soon decline, in gloom to set.

That this sad fate may never be,
May God inspire both you and me,
To help U.S. keep sober, free,
In nineteen hundred thirty-three.

Life Here

A little sun, a little rain,
A little loss, a little gain,
A little joy, a little strife,
And this is Life.

A little work, a little play,
Some kind deed done each passing day,
A few goodbyes, a setting sun,
and Life is done.

Life There

Like swelling bud and opening flower,
We're growing souls for Eden's bower.
The op'ning dawn, the rising tide,
To float our bark to sunlit side.

Glad hands reach out to welcome us
To dwell with them and Jesus Christ.
Celestial day! Free from all strife!
And this, dear friends, is endless Life.

NOTE: *The first two stanzas by an unknown author had the heading "Life." They seemed to end sadly, so I added two of my own. W.C.L.*

The Glorious Fourth

The glorious Fourth is ushered in,
Just as of old, with noise and din.
Feelings of pride well up within
As functions of the day begin.

The noisy son of patriot sire
Disturbs our rest with cracker-fire,
While older folks fan and perspire
And almost wish they were up higher.

We're called upon to celebrate,
Lend patient ear while orate,
Until we come to calculate
That our country is very great.

This opportunity they seize
To make us think we're the whole cheese;
Our ship of state can sail all seas
And safely face untoward breeze.

They call to mind the foreign tea
That our forebears cast in the sea
And thus declared they would be free
From hateful taxes of monarchy.

They fling our starry banner out
And hoist it high with lusty shout.
Let Nations know our courage stout
Can put all earthly foes to rout.

They toast our country's wealth and power
In this, our Independence hour.
Make Nations round us grimly glower,
Think Samuel's pride is turning sour.

They tell of George of hatchet fame,
Who, first in war, in peace the same,
Did the proud English lion tame
And make John's war a losing game.

They think our star of destiny
Will thus always ascendent be
That our fair land of liberty
Will be from danger ever free.

Yet strange enough, with feelings tense,
They would maintain for our defense
With many millions of expense
A fighting force that is immense.

This land of ours they'd isolate:
Let nations round their strifes abate;
They'd have no worries interstate,
Keep us distinct and separate.

Their slogan is "Prepare to fight"
If other nations give us slight,
By force of arms defend our right
E'en tho it bring war's blackest night.

Jingoes decry the men of peace
Who strive to have all warfare cease.
On them anathamas release,
And hope their tribe will not increase.

These men of peace, (Jingoes insist,)
Who'd outlaw war, should soon desist.
They'd like to silence the whole grist
By dubbing each a pacifist.

From Nations' League they'd keep aloof
Nor do they want Locarno stuff.
Of a World Court they have enough;
Would safely keep 'neath our own roof.

Me thinks they're not so very wise.
Our Nation's harm *within* us lies.
Disloyal countrymen arise,
An evil force our laws defies.

We hope we're safe and yet—and yet—
We all do well not to forget
That thirsty hosts, by voting wet,
May cause our sun in shame to set.

With evil forces pressing hard
That would our Nation's course retard.
We do well to be on guard;
Keen vigilance bring our reward.

For this our goodly heritage
Let's thankful be and truly sage,
A ceaseless way on evil wage,
Our country right, not wrong, our gauge.

Eighty-Two?

Eighty-two! Is it true?
If friends but knew—
Friends not a few—
How frosted dew

How whitened hair,
Etched face of care,
How slackened pace
In life's long race;

There friends of mine
Might, I opine,
E'en think it more,
Perhaps a score!

But, could they see
The fun in me
In hours of glee,
They might agree

Yes, even guess,
'Twas twenty less,
Of blunt duress
And happiness.

Friends far and near,
And loved ones, dear;
Your words of cheer
I love, revere.

Each message kind,
As God designed,
Doth lodgement find
In heart and mind.

Thus heartened by
True friendship tie;
With Christ so nigh,
So helped, may I

Though years be few,
Some courage lend.
Prove loyal, true,
To ev'ry friend.

March 10, 1932

To the Dandelion

Dandelion, dandy fellow,
Looking up with face so yellow;
Tho you've come so very early
Still we welcome you most truly.

Dot with gold both lawn and meadow,
Line the walk, invade the garden:
Keep thy pace, thou merry rover,
Sprinkle all the landscape over.

Tho you smile so very brightly,
Yet you make our lawns unsightly.
Crowding out, in many cases,
Weak but struggling tender grasses.

Hostile men will therefore slight thee,
Trample under, dig thee, fight thee;
But you'll laugh at all their labor,
For you still will be their neighbor.

In a trice your feathered lances
You will poise for fresh advances;
Wind-scattered wide, your foes
  outflanking,
Your conquests still will be outranking.

Plucky little dandelion,
Widely planted, deeply rooted,
Holding steadfast thru all weather
Tho spurned, down-trodden,—undefeated.

We would learn a wholesome lesson
From your conq'ring march along
Working in and out of season
To win the vict'ry over wrong.

Forty-One

Your mother says you're forty-one—
Your earthly span is well begun;
But still more years are yet to run
Before life's journey is well done.

So gird your loins for years to come
And thus round out a goodly sum.
Where'er you go, though far you roam,
Do not forget your parents' home.

The latch string's out to ope the door,
With room inside for one or more;
And welcome glad from the heart's core
To bed and food from pantry's store.

Nor is this all as you well know:
There's shelter from the rain and snow,
Both cheer and warmth from fire's glow
And all beside home can bestow.

To Robert, by his father W. C. L.

Fond Memories

No distance can ever
True friendship's tie sever,

And mem'ry, repeating
Events of past meeting,

Give fresh demonstration
By friend and relation

That true hearts still cherish
Kind thoughts that won't perish.

In thanking you duly,
I am yours most truly.

Lafayette, Indiana
March 9, 1933

Four Times Twenty-One

Another mile-stone reached and passed!
Old Father Time moves on so fast
Seems scarce a twelve-month since the last.

What makes each birthday so stand out?
'Tis messages from friends about
Which put all loneliness to rout.

These friends have such a happy way
Of giving kindly thought full play
To signalize each new birthday.

Is't growing old or growing young?
Horizon's doors seem wider flung,
Opp'tunities more thickly strung.

Life's checkered pathway all along:
More chance to right some ancient wrong,
Increase the volume of life's song.

Encouraged thus to carry on
The work of life that's scarce begun
We'll push right on till day is done.

March 10, 1934

Thanks—Many Many Thanks!

To kindly thoughtful comrades, friends,
The undersigned this message sends,
Of grateful sincere hearty thanks,
For cheering note in word and flower
Short-circuiting each wakeful hour,
From those who walk in varied ranks.

Sweet pea and freesia, bright jonquil
The red carnation, stately rose,
Each gave its own peculiar thrill
Inveigling moments of repose
From consciousness of ache or pain.

Rapt gazing on each floral form
With perfumes sweet as honey-dew,
By vagrant zephers gently borne,
Ravished with tints of varied hue
I'll surely soon be well again.

March 10, 1934

Remembered

Though friends by miles are sundered
Their thoughts fly here unhindered
With greetings kindly tendered,
Well wishes heart engendered.

Words spoken, written, printed,
Goodwill express unstinted.
Thanks, friends, for words of greeting
They cheer the hours fast fleeting.

We wish for all full measure
Of heaven's richest treasure;
May God each burden lighten,
Christ's smile each pathway brighten.

As months to years will lengthen,
May hope, faith, courage, strengthen,
To bring to glad fruition
Each laudable ambition.

March 10, 1935

The Little Fire Fairies

*(Suggested by the burning of dry
evergreen wood in an open fireplace
in northern Michigan; and written
for two grandchildren of four and
seven—W.C.L.)*

Twenty little fairies
All blazing in a row.
Come here quickly, dearies,
And watch the fairies grow.

Sprightly little fairies
So very small and good;
Hungry little fairies
Fast eating up the wood.

Pigmy soldier fairies,
With air-guns in full play;
Shooting tiny firebrands
In truly mimic fray.

Frisky little fairies
Go dancing up so high
Through the sooty chimney
To somewhere in the sky.

Hot coals in the fireplace
Are cooling as they die
Leaving only ashes;
How still the ashes lie!

Just a bit of ashes
Is all that's left below.
Why do not the ashes
Up through the chimney go?

They must be too heavy
To with the fairies fly.
If that's not the reason
I'm sure I don't know why.

BEROPAMA
August 7, 1930

Yesterday

O radiant childhood's morn, thy marvels
In round-eyed wonderment beheld!
Each mirror pool or rippling stream
Allures to splash, swim, fish, or dream.
Each vale, flower-decked, the eye's delight;
Each rising hill or mountain height
A challenge to ascend and see beyond.
Roseate morn, purple eve, and glowing
  noon
Blue sky, bright star, or brilliant moon
All vie to charm, inspire. In truth
We say, O glorious day of youth.

Today

O day of work, of eager strife,
When earnest men invest their life
In open field, in city mart,
In learning's hall or mine so dark,
Upon the sea or in the air,
In quest of truth, men everywhere
Strive for gain, for fame, for power.
Some win, some lose; one vict'ry sure
A man's estate all may secure.
O day of strife, O day and hour
Of manhood's prime and manhood's
  power.

Tomorrow

O day of rest and retrospect,
Of backward and of forward look.
The memory of manly strife
Warms the heart and cheers the life.
The past secure, some victory won,
No unrest o'er westering sun,
Since Hope looks for a brighter day
And Faith sees shining from afar
The evening and the morning star.
The rapidly approaching night
Shall merge ere long in endless light.

Beyond

O glorious resurrection morn,
When in wonder mute, and glad surprise,
Responding to God's "Welcome home,"
The earth's redeemed in millions rise,
Our Christ, loved ones, all souls to greet,
A joyous throng, all buoyant, young,
In service blest at Christ's behest;
While myriad choirs make heaven ring
With hulloluiaha to our King.
And heralds bold pierce space untold
To shout again "Good will to men!"
Ye children come, that races, nations, all,
Within one sheltering fold may be,
At home with God eternally.

My Broken Collar Bone

My collar bone, my collar bone!
Ere since it broke my sleep has flown;
Not since when I was fully grown
Has trouble been so much *my own.*

Throughout the day, all through the night,
I find myself in a sad plight.
To be in pain thus is not right
I'd rather wash and scrub and fight.

Four weeks of rest the Doc decrees
While housework piles, up to my knees,
I'd like to send him out to freeze,
This crazy doc with such idees!

What road obstructor I could choke
For "cutting in," the measly bloke!
He should not turn another spoke
Till from all faults he's fully "broke."

If he should come around to croak
Send him below, the fires to stoke,
In hotter clime than Central Mich.
That's pretty near my present wish.

Written on the occasion of an auto
accident in which a sister-in-law
had her collar bone broken on the
return trip from a Thanksgiving
visit to Lafayette—W.C.L.

Appendix 7

Short Stories Written by William Carroll Latta

TWO STREAMS

I

A tiny trickling rivulet from oozy bank or spring starts seaward on its winding way. So weak at first a stone or clod may change its course but gliding, glistening, gurgling, rippling, o'er rock-ledge splashing, it runs on down a smiling valley, fresh greenness spreading, slaking thirst of beast and bird and cheering eye of man with sparkling beauty.

Anon another, then other, and yet other streams unite with major stream which, gathering force with increased volume, pushes on, now quiet-flowing, then a foaming rapids or mayhap a roaring cataract, but tho wide-meandering, ever nears its primal source, the ocean vast.

Tho sometimes by adamantine wall man-curbed and checked, it gathers force, resistless, and plunging down turns mighty wheels of industry and still pursues its onward way.

Sometimes by miasmatic marsh or man-made town polluted, the ever-moving current of this roving stream cleanses, clarifies its liquid depths in full obedience to Nature's law and thus regenerated moves onward still in courage benign.

Sometimes by swollen affluents enlarged, this central stream becomes a mighty sweeping torrent and eating thru its weakened banks spreads destruction wide, disease and death, in its errant flow. But normally it gently flows with hidden strength unmeasured, a mighty artery of commerce, bearing on its bosom wide the stately ships which carry goods of many climates to minister to human needs.

Lending at times its store of liquid water thru man's device it changes burning desert sands to fruitful fields from which as if by magic bounteous crops spring forth the human race to bless. But unheeding all, this mighty stream still onward flows to lose itself at last in ocean's briny depths. Lost? Ah no indeed! Sun-kist and sublimated, it rises in form more delicate than bridal veil, and friendly winds of heaven bear it back to inland hill and vale to oft repeat, through rolling years that into centuries merge, its ministry of good to man.

II

A separate tiny stream of life, love-engendered, heaven sent, of all things animate most weak, slowly gathers strength from its mothers-breast outflowing. At first unconscious as the rivulet, less able to direct its early course, but fed by love akin to love of God, this little human stream soon larger, stronger grows; absorbing wisdom, grace, from varied source, it cheers and charms, enlivens and enriches all within its radiant sphere.

This duly nourished, rightly led, this growing human stream from strength to still more rugged strength advances and thus duly panoplied meets well the buffetings of harsh untoward circumstance, or quick advantage takes of favoring opportunities to render service kind and good.

But sad to tell if wrongly bent, to evil influences a prey, subject to ill-born wrong desire, unable to resist the wiles of things dishonest or impure, this life-stream turbid putrid may become and, in corrupted downward flow, spread moral virus, untold harm, until at last it meets untimely ignominious death.

This need not be; this human stream, unlike the earth-born passive one, has early in its course the power of choice and normally an upward flow. Accepting affluents good and true, rejecting currents base and false, this human stream enlarged, enriched, from sources wholesome, good, pursues its onward upward course, uplifting and beneficent, until at last it flows into the ocean of God's love.

Does this end all? Methinks not so; but rather that this human stream sublimed, ethereal, will carry on in larger realm and higher sphere, some nobler work throughout millenniums of God's unfolding plan.

January 1, 1931

AN AUTOBIOGRAPHY

A few months ago I was a little blind puppy. Although I could not see I could feel and hear and smell and taste. I soon made up my small mind that I was one of several puppies but I did not know what we looked like. I found out that there was a large dog that seemed to be taking care of me. The large dog licked me with its tongue and this made me feel so well that I thought the big dog really did care for me.

About as soon as I came to know anything I began nosing around for dinner as I was getting hungry. I did not know what to call the feeling but I felt it just the same. After poking my nose around for a little while, though I didn't know it was my nose, I felt the warm body of the big dog and would you believe I soon found something sticking out a little from the body of the big dog, something soft and smooth and I began to wonder whether it was good to eat. Then it occurred to my tiny puppy mind to put it in my mouth. I don't know just how it happened but without knowing what I did I must have begun to suck that soft little body which I have since learned is called a nipple or teat. To my surprise and delight something warm came into my mouth that tasted so good that without realizing what I was doing I swallowed it. It so satisfied that hungry feeling that I sucked some more and then some more until that hungry feeling went away for a time. But after a few hours that same feeling came back and this time I knew what to do, so I hunted up that soft nipple that must have had a hole in it because something so good to the taste kept coming out of it while I was sucking at it with my tongue.

In my rolling and crawling about I felt other little bodies that seemed to be much like my little self. They seemed to be acting just about as I was. They were tumbling about and appeared to be nosing around for a soft nipple as I had been doing. At times we little fellows, they call them puppies, would snuggle down together for a nice nap, though I didn't know it was a nap, but I did know or rather feel that it was nice. At such times the big dog, I learned the name dog later, would go away and by the time our nap was over would come back.

After some days of poking around with our noses and feeling about with our little paws, our eyes were opened. Ah, what a sight it was! I found that I was just one of several puppies that looked almost exactly like myself and of the same size. Then too I saw that the big dog looked like us little fellows only much larger. Then the big dog would lie down by us. What a scamper we puppies would have to get hold of those soft nipples with our mouths and we would have a regular family dinner.

Since I have partly grown up and learned a lot of things I have found out that those little tumbling fellows were my brothers and sisters and that the big dog was our mother.

When I was a month or more of age, though I didn't know what a month was, a strange man came and gave something to the man that owned my mother and then the tall man took me away from my mother and my little brothers and sisters. My mother did not want to lose me and she made a harsh noise which I have since learned was a growl. Well, the tall man took me to his home and gave me to a much smaller man that I have since learned is called a boy. Then there was another little man but taller than the boy and dressed differently. I have since learned that this was the boy's bigger sister. My! But I was lonesome for a few days and at night I made noises which the boy and his sister called whining. But this did not last long as they gave me something white to eat that tasted a good deal like what I had been getting from my mother's nipple. I did not know at first what to do with it but I got so hungry that I finally stuck my tongue in it and I found it so good that I began for the first time to lap it. Isn't it funny how we seem so quickly to learn different ways of eating and doing things without knowing just how or why we do it?

Well, this little man—called a boy—and his sister were so kind to me that I soon learned to like them. I wonder and wonder about it. They seem to understand me and I fancy I begin to understand them. How funny it is. I walk on four feet but they walk on two feet and they wear clothes! Yes, it is funny—I just can't understand it—but we do have such fine times playing together. They, the boy and his sister, that is called a girl, seem to enjoy playing just about as much as I do. As I said I can't understand most of it but I am learning every day. Would you believe it! They gave me a name, an airy given name and an aristocratic surname (I wish I knew what those big words mean) and I am so proud! My name is Lindy, Lindy Reemtsma! And I am trying to be a respectable member of the family. But my! What a lot I have yet to learn. But I *am* learning. I already know that the boy is called Keith, and the girl Carol. I know too, by the way they say "Lindy" that they mean one thing at one time and another thing at another time. If they say very sharply "Lindy!" I know that they want me to stop doing something that they don't want me to do.

O dear, I get nearly discouraged sometimes when I see them take something called a book and they get something out of it. If it were just a bone with a little meat on it I could understand, but a book is just clear beyond me.

Then this little boy and girl put on something called wraps and go off to a place where there are other boys and girls—they call it a school. But what is a school? I hope they will take me along some day so I can see what they do. I have heard sometime that a girl called Mary took a lamb to school. Why should not a dog go? Dogs know a lot more than lambs! But I must not complain because they are so good to me. The other day they even let me send my love to their grandpa and grandma and you should have seen my signature on white paper. I bet they can't read it. Some day I want to go out in the country to chase what they call rabbits but I am not old enough yet.

1932

THE SUNBEAM, THE ZEPHYR, THE CLOUD, AND THE CHILD: A FAIRY TALE

A golden sunbeam came sliding down from somewhere and kissed some little plants and lo, violets opened their blue eyes and looked up into the face of the wondering child and smiled.

Another sunbeam kissed a little bush and a lovely rose greeted the child. Another sunbeam came tripping down and kissed some broad-leaved plants, and yellow buttercups greeted the amazed child.

Then still another sunbeam kissed the pretty lake by whose side the child lived in a cozy cottage, and the lake gave a smile, a smile brighter and bigger than a diamond.

Then something fanned the cheek of the child and tossed her bright curls. Before the child could brush back her curls, the Zephyr said, "Sunbeam, let me help you please the child," so the sunbeam and the Zephyr both kissed the lake and it fairly laughed until its face showed thousands of brighter dancing sparkles.

Then the sunbeam thanked the Zephyr, and said, "Let's try again to please this good child." So together they flew up into the top of a great tree with its branches so brown and bare. The sunbeam bestowed warm kisses on the branches while the Zephyr was fanning them and soon hundreds of little green banners fluttered to the delight of the child.

Then the sunbeam looked closely at the happy child and saw that she looked hungry. "We must bring her some food." So the sunbeam kissed and kissed again the brown earth of a field in which a farmer had buried tiny seeds. Soon little needle-shaped pale green shoots began to appear above the ground. Then the Zephyr spoke again, "Sunbeam, I want to help you grow food for the child," and before the sunbeam could reply, the Zephyr flew away, hundreds of miles to the big ocean where it spied a fleecy cloud.

"Come with me, cloud," said the Zephyr, "and help to grow food for a beautiful child."

"I want to go," said the cloud, "but I move so slowly, I fear I cannot get there in time if the way is long."

"It is a long way," said the Zephyr, "but I can help you to move faster." So the Zephyr got behind the cloud and began to push it gently over hill and dale for a long, long time. One day when the sunbeam had begun to fear that the Zephyr had forgotten to keep its promise to help the sunbeam grow food for the sweet child, it looked up into the blue sky in the direction the Zephyr had gone and Lo, a big dark gray cloud was coming slowly toward the field where the little shoots were peeping out of the ground.

"Ah," said the sunbeam, "there is the Zephyr pushing the cloud." When the cloud was right over the field, the Zephyr began blowing a cool breath on the cloud which caused it to weep great tears that fell as rain on the field. Then the tiny green shoots all laughed and said, "We can now grow big and strong to make food for the little child that looks hungry."

After a while, heads of wheat formed at the top of the shoots. Then the farmer came and harvested the wheat and took it to the mill where it was ground into flour from which bread was made for the child. Then other fairies that we have not time to speak of brought other food. So the child ate and was satisfied. Then she began to wonder and to ask questions of the friendly fairies.

"Sunbeam, where did you come from?"

"I came millions of miles from the big round sun to help make you a happy little girl."

"And where did you come from, Zephyr?"

"I came a long way from the wide open spaces of the west because I wanted to help sunbeam make you happy. Do you remember how the lake laughed and sparkled when I kissed it and how the branches of the tree laughed and waved their bright little green banners when I kissed them? Then when I saw that you looked hungry I flew away over the plains and over the mountains to bring the cloud to let its tear drops of rain fall on the brown earth of the field so wheat could grow to make bread for you."

"What good fairies you are to do all these things to make me happy."

Then the child sees that the cloud wanted to speak to her. So the child looked up and said, "And where did you come from, Cloud?"

Then the cloud made a big noise and flash of light and came and frightened the child. When the cloud noticed that the child was frightened, it said, "Don't be scared, little girl. I too, am your fairy friend. I came up out of the big ocean. When the Zephyr told me that the field which was trying to grow wheat for you was thirsty, I wanted to come and give the tiny shoots of wheat a good drink so they could grow big and make wheat for bread to feed you. But I move so slowly that I could not have come in time but for the help of my fairy friend, Zephyr, who pushed and pushed me all the way just in time to help."

For a little while the child seemed to be thinking.

"Did you fairies come all the way from the sun and the wide open spaces and the big ocean to make *me* happy?"

"Yes," said the sunbeam, putting a warm kiss on the child's cheek, "to make you and thousands of other girls and boys happy."

"O thank you, thank you," said the child. Then the child seemed to be thinking again. A questioning look came into her eyes, and she said, "You are all so very kind. What makes you so kind? Did some good god-fairy send you to make the children happy?"

Then the sunbeam and the Zephyr and the Cloud looked at each other and smiled. This time the Zephyr spoke: "Yes, sweet child. There is a king of the fairies who sends us and thousands upon thousands of our brothers and sisters to the earth to make boys and girls happy and help them to grow up to be good men and women. We call this good king God, Jehovah, the Creator of all things. We call Him also our Heavenly Father because He so loved boys and girls, that, hundreds of years ago He sent His Son, Jesus Christ down to this world to show the children how to be good so that sometime they can all go to live with Jesus and His Father for ever and ever."

"And now good bye, little girl," said all three. "We must go so that you can get your sleep and rest, but we will all come again and do many other things to make you and the other children comfortable and happy."

"Good night."

CORNUCOPIA—AN AUTOBIOGRAPHY

I am a cosmopolitan—a world debtor—a world benefactor. I was born in a tiny narrow house without a window. Notwithstanding my humble birth, men traveled thousands of miles to get food for my development. Great ships brought nitrate of soda from Chili and potash from Germany. Railway trains brought phosphates from Tennessee and elsewhere.

The farmers plowed and fitted great fields for me and my brothers and cousins. In one of these fields, the farmer gently covered me in rich soil. The sunlight came millions of miles to warm my earth bed and make me comfortable. Presently a new life began to stir within me. I threw out thread-like rootlets into the soil in search of food as I began to feel hungry. The lowly earth worm and tiniest bacteria helped to make food ready for me. The mighty ocean sent rain thousands of miles to dissolve food so I could drink. You see I cannot eat solid food. I am a great drinker but I drink nothing stronger than water in which my food is dissolved. But I was not yet satisfied so I sent a bright shoot up through an inch or two of soil into the air and sunlight, when lo, the sunbeams kissed my shoot, which was white at first, until it blushed green.

Then I was happy, as I had been born into a plant with roots to drink up food and an upward-growing stem with leaves to breathe the pure air and gather carbon dioxide. Now I was getting food for growth from both air and soil and I grew and grew. Sometimes in warm nights when everything was still the farmer could hear me growing and was glad for the promise of a bountiful crop in the autumn time. Then too I was happy when I began to realize that I could later repay those who had done so much for me. So I kept on growing and rejoicing in the thought that the time was coming when I would cease to be merely a debtor and become a benefactor to both man and beast. As I looked around and saw thousands of my brothers and sisters and cousins covering broad acres, I was delighted to think they and I could help to feed the world. I waved my leaves in very gladness as the gentle breezes kissed me and thus I made music for the farmer boy who was cultivating the field for my benefit.

I continued to grow stronger and taller in the long warm days. When midsummer came, I began to build the same kind of a house in which I had been born the year before. I wish that I could tell you all about this house that I was building. There was no carpenter. This house of mine just grew as I had grown. The walls of my house were somewhat like several thicknesses of paper. As these paper-like walls lengthened to make a long narrow house just like this one in which I was born, a tender and slender shoot or stem began growing up though the center of the house from one end to the other. Presently little milk-white pimples began to form in long rows on the sides of the central shoot or stem.

How pleased I was when I came to understand that each one of these tiny milk-white bodies looking like pimples was soon to grow into the same form that I had when the farmer planted me in his field. Soon, but not just yet, as several wonderful things happened meanwhile. In a few days each one of these little pimple-like bodies began to grow a slender silky thread that pushed its way along between the rows and finally pushed out between the paper walls of the narrow house. They must want something, but what?

I will try to tell you. About the same time that the narrow house began to grow, a flower began to grow, not on the side of my stem like the paper-walled house, but at the top. This flower that I was growing grew as the house grew. When the pretty silk threads had pushed their way out of the narrow house they looked up and saw the feathery flower at the top of my stem and they said:

"Come down to us and we will get acquainted," but the flower, that is called a tassel, said:

"I can't come down but if you will keep looking, I will send down some wee golden grains. You can get acquainted with them."

Just then a wandering breeze stirred the tassel and on came the tiny yellow grains. So pleased were they, these golden grains, to meet their silky neighbors, that they actually kissed them, each one seeking a partner until not a single silky thread was missed. Then the beautiful silky threads laughed and said in a glad chorus:

"Come into our house and help us to grow food for man and beast." This pleased the tiny golden grains as they, too wanted to be useful. So each one went into the narrow paper-walled house and down to one of the milky white bodies, and said,

"I have come to help you grow food for the world." Then, wonder of wonders, those milk-white bodies began to grow into a perfect seed that would make food. Then suddenly I recognized that each one of these seeds was just like I was when the farmer planted me in the rich soil of his field.

Then I realized that by giving up my life as a seed and being born again into a living, growing plant I had, with the help of man, the soil, the air, the sun, the ocean, the mines and the little earthworm, multiplied several hundred-fold.

As I think of the many agencies and forces that have been working in harmony with God's plan to help me grow, I can understand what a world debtor I am and what an obligation I am under to render service.

Then it dawned upon me that the thousands and millions of my brothers would join me in feeding the millions of my own native country and that great shiploads of us would go to nourish the people of other countries. I was truly thankful that in accordance with the wise plans of Divine Providence I could indeed be a world benefactor and a blessing to all mankind. Now good bye, as I must go to help feed the orphans of the Near East. What is my name?

A CHILD'S SOLILOQUY AND QUESTIONS AND A MOTHER'S ANSWER

This is my birthday, my tenth birthday, mother says, and mother ought to know. She must have been here when the stork or the doctor brought me. I have seen pictures of storks bringing babies to homes, so I guess the stork brought me to my mother.

But WHERE did the stork find me? How far did the stork bring me? How long was the stork on the way? How fast can a stork fly?

Mother has told me about little baby Moses being found among the bulrushes by the side of the big river Nile. Did the stork find me in the bulrushes? How far is the river Nile from us? How long did it take the stork to fly all the way from that river Nile to America?

But mother told me on my ninth birthday that I was born right here in this very room. Then did the stork bring me before I was born so I could be born here as mother told me? But how could the stork find me before I was born? Maybe the doctor brought me. He was here when I was born—mother has told me. But where did HE find me? WHEN did he find me?

Maybe the story man who makes the pictures of the stork's bringing babies could tell me all about it, but he is not here. The stork is not here. The doctor is not here. But my mother is here. Yes, but she is busy making my birthday cake and it is to have ten little candles on it. But I just can't wait any longer.

"Mother, I want to know more about my first birthday. Will you tell me?"

"Yes darling, I think you are old enough now to learn more about it but I am busy now. This evening I will try to answer your questions. Go now, and put that pretty pink dress on your big doll Rosemary so she may look well at the dinner table. Then you dress yourself and help little brother get ready. It will soon be dinner time."

"Now, Esther, I will try to explain about your first birthday. But first, let us go into the kitchen and learn something about the egg. This egg is supposed to be fertile. If it were put under a setting hen or in a box called an incubator, where it could be kept warm and if it were turned first on one side and then on the other every few days a little chick would begin to grow inside the shell and in three weeks the chick would hatch. That is, it would break open the shell and come out of it. We might say that the chick was born the day it was hatched; but the chick began to grow three weeks before. Being born then means coming out of a shell like a little chick or coming out of a warm nest which is called a womb. The little kitten or lamb or pig or calf or a baby boy or girl comes out of such a nest. When a kitten or a little baby girl comes out of the warm nest we say it or she is born. But life and growth begin in the case of the child about nine months before it was born."

"O! Now I know, mother! The stork did have time to bring me to you. He found me in a nest like the Princess found little Moses in a basket?"

"No, dear, that is a pretty story about the stork bringing babies to their mothers but it is not true. Let us now open this egg. If it is fertile, we will find something wonderful. There, Esther, do you see that grayish white spot?"

"Yes, I see it, mother, but that isn't a chick; it doesn't even look like a chick."

"Not so fast, daughter. Did I not tell you that the chick would grow about three weeks before it would hatch or be born? That little spot is called an embryo, which means that it has life and can grow. That little cell or embryo has two parts. One part is called an ovum. The other part is called the sperm. The ovum was formed in the body of a hen and is the mother part of what could become a chick after uniting with the sperm which is the father part of the embryo. You have seen the rooster cover the hen in the chicken yard, haven't you?"

"O yes, mother, many times, but wasn't the rooster fighting the hen?"

"No, dear, they were mating. In this way the sperm passed out of the body of the rooster into the body of the hen. By some attraction, which only our heavenly Father understands, the sperm found its way to, and united with, the ovum, to make the embryo, this little grayish spot that you see."

"If instead of breaking this egg, I had put it in a warm place to remain there for three weeks this tiny embryo would have grown into a downy chick like those you have often seen running after their mother in the chicken yard. In like manner the sperm and the ovum come together in the body of the cow or the ewe or the married women. When this union occurs in the body of the woman, the embryo moves into the warm nest called the womb, and there, nourished by the blood in the arteries of the mother, it begins to grow, and it grows and grows from a tiny cell like this which you see in the egg."

"But this embryo in the body of the ewe grows into a little lamb and the embryo in the body of the cow grows into the little calf while the embryo in the body of the married woman grows into a lovely little child which we call a baby. In about nine months after the embryo forms, a little baby will grow from the tiny cell to an infant weighing from five or six pounds to eight or ten pounds. In these nine months the embryo or fetus, as it is usually called, has grown so much that it nearly fills its nest under the mother's heart. The last few months of this period, the fetus becomes quite active and stretches out its little legs and pushes against the sides of its nest. I think it must begin to feel crowded. Perhaps it wants to get out and thus be born. Perhaps the walls of this warm nest grow tired of this pushing of the baby's legs. If these walls could think as well as they can feel I fancy they would say this fetus or baby is getting so big that we must get rid of it. At any rate the nest begins to get smaller and smaller crowding the baby out of its warm nest through a narrow passage until the baby is finally pushed clear outside of the mother, and we say the baby is born. Every normal baby, however, began to live and grow about nine months before it was born. You see, then, Esther, that you are really ten years and nine months old today."

"O, Mother, I am glad that the stork did not bring me to you. He might have become tired flying over the mountains and dropped me and I would have been killed before I was born. How much nicer and safer to be with you before I was born as I have been ever since I was born. One more question, Mother, before I go to bed. Aunt Ellen's baby has a long dress, and Aunt Sue's baby has a short dress. Did I have a long dress, or a short dress, when I was born?"

"You had no dress at all and no clothes when you were born. Remember, you were in a warm nest before you were born—so warm that you did not need any clothing. But your mother was expecting you to be born and she knew you would need clothing after being born, so for several weeks she was busy making warm soft clothes for her baby girl. When you outgrew your baby clothes, you were given larger garments and your baby dresses—several of them—were carefully laid away as your father and mother were hoping that someday you would have a baby brother for your playmate. The Lord who is so good and kind to everybody permitted your brother Eddie to come and grow just as you came and grew."

"Some day when he is older, we will tell him about his first birthday. Now darling, it is time to go to bed but don't forget to thank Jesus who was also born as you were, for your father and mother and all your kind friends."

"In a few days, I want you to tell me the story of your growth from a tiny cell to a fully developed baby girl when you were born, ten years ago today. Can you remember it?"

"O yes, mother, I don't think I could forget it. Good night, mother."

"Good night, dear."

Appendix 8

Armed Guard Sailors Who Served aboard the SS *W. C. Latta* during World War II*

Avanzato, Charles Paul
Black, Donald
Blum, Wallace Lee
Bowden, Donald Edward
Browder, Tom Smith
Burri, Fred Williams
Busch, Edward J.
Campbell, Arman B.
Chasse, Jean Normand
Felts, William John, Jr.
Fink, Loren Durell
Galati, Robert
Gesek, John William, Jr.
Givens, Robert Latimer
Grieser, Donald Francis
Jankowski, Vincent Charles
Johnston, Thomas Harvey
Jones, Floyd Wilson
Kauffman, Ewing M.
Kerr, Robert James
Kieffer, Charles Herbert
Kingsley, William Louis
Ksiazek, Francis Joseph
Luttrell, Robert Gene
MacPherson, Peter
Martin, Winford McFarland
Massie, Orville, Jr.
Meleski, Lawrence Andrew
Miller, Gerald Marvin
Misiaczek, Edward John
Muscoreil, Lawrence Joseph
Nicholson, Clarence Edward

O'Brien, Kenneth Nile
Page, Stanley Guy
Paine, Cedric Kingsley
Pedersen, Edward Albert
Pendleton, Victor Dennis
Perryman, Arthur Eugene, Jr.
Personette, Harold Cecil
Phillips, Burke
Pizzurro, Lawrence Paul
Pringle, Kenneth Charles
Putt, Samuel William
Race, Robert Junior
Robinson, Fredrick, Jr.
Robinson, Ralph Andrew
Rosati, Albert Augustine
Safford, Lyle Russell
Schulz, Leland William
Searles, Clarence Thomas
Silva, Edmundo Tiexeira
Sterling, Conway Grafton
Talaska, Richard Walter
Tangring, Carl Eric
Trombly, Robert Edward
Turner, Bernard Edward
Ugalde, Edward Joseph
Volker, Russell Frederick
Warner, Raymond Herman
Water, Billy R.
Waugh, Harper E.
Weter, Billy Ray
Wright, William Earl
Yurcich, Steve Frank

* *The names of the crew members who served aboard the SS W. C. Latta were drawn from various declassified reports obtained from the National Archives at College Park, Maryland.*

Notes

Abbreviations

LSL   Life Sciences Library, Purdue University,
Lilly Hall of Life Sciences, West Lafayette, Ind.

SC   W. C. Latta Collection
Special Collections, Purdue University Libraries,
Stewart Center, West Lafayette, Ind.

TCHA   W. C. Latta Collection
Tippecanoe County Historical Association, Lafayette, Ind.

CHAPTER ONE
The Education of William Carroll Latta: His Early Years

1. *Pittsburgh Gazette,* 29 October 1795.

2. *Pittsburgh Gazette,* 15 February 1796.

3. Robert H. Latta, "The Latta Collection," vol. 1, branch 1 (1940). Unpublished manuscript at the Rare Book Section, U. S. Library of Congress, Washington, D.C. Manuscript reviewed and summarized by Ken Mueller.

4. Ibid.

5. Dave O. Thompson and William L. Madigan, *One Hundred and Fifty Years of Indiana Agriculture* (n.p., 1966), 12.

6. *An Illustrated Historical Atlas of Noble County, Indiana* (Chicago: Andreas & Baskin, 1874), 354–55.

7. Ken Mueller, "The James T. Latta Update," in *The Latta Genealogy Newsletter* 6 (Winter 1998): 5. Available online at: http://www.latta.org/.

8. James Albert Woodburn, "Men of Mark in Indiana" (1905–6), Manuscripts Department, Lilly Library, Indiana University, Bloomington, Ind. Indiana University describes this source as "consist(ing) of biographical questionnaires filled out by the subjects or their representatives at the request of James Albert Woodburn." The material quoted here was drawn from a survey completed by William Carroll Latta on 30 April 1906.

9. Richard Patten Dehart, *Past and Present of Tippecanoe County, Indiana* (Indianapolis, Ind.: B. F. Bowen, 1909), 952.

10. Woodburn, "Men of Mark in Indiana," W. C. Latta survey, 30 April 1906.

11. Ibid.

12. All statistics regarding the Latta farm were drawn from the U.S. Bureau of the Census, Indiana, Noble County, Perry Township, Ligonier Post Office (Washington, D.C., 9 June 1860).

13. William Carroll Latta, Purdue University Personnel Records, 1882–1935.

14. National Normal University, "Twenty-fifth Annual Catalogue" (National Normal University, [1880]), 61.

15. "Township Histories. Turtle Creek Township." In *The History of Warren County, Ohio* (Chicago: W. H. Beers Co., 1882; reprint, Mt. Vernon, Ind.: Windmill Publications, 1992), 481.

16. National Normal University, "Twenty-fifth Annual Catalogue," 61.

17. Warren County (Ohio) Historical Society, letter to Frederick Whitford, 18 September 2003. This letter contained various historical information regarding National Normal School during the time that William Carroll Latta attended classes there.

18. "Township Histories. Turtle Creek Township," in *The History of Warren County, Ohio*, 481.

19. Warren County (Ohio) Historical Society, letter to Frederick Whitford, 18 September 2003.

20. National Normal University, "Twenty-fifth Annual Catalogue," 61.

21. William Carroll Latta, "Some Problems of the Rural Community Church" (n.p., n.d.), 2.

22. William Carroll Latta, Michigan Agricultural College transcripts, 1874–77.

23. Phyllis Webster, e-mail to Frederick Whitford, 18 August 2003. This correspondence contained information from Paul Cheney, nephew to William Carroll Latta, about visits by students from Michigan Agricultural College to Maple Ridge Farm during this time.

24. "A Michigan Farmer: Something about a Pioneer in Blooded Stock Raising" (newspaper clipping, n.p, [1881]). Private collection of Phyllis Webster, who is a great-granddaughter of Amos Wood. She provided many of the newspaper clippings dealing with the Wood family and the Ingham County Farmers' Club. Many of these were part of family scrapbooks. The newspapers at that time were the *Ingham County News* and the *Ingham Democrat*. The newspaper clippings were mostly undated and not sourced.

25. Newspaper clipping (n.p., n.d.) from Phyllis Webster. See note 24 above.

26. Ibid.

27. Amos Freeman Wood, "History of Ingham County Farmers' Club" (newspaper clipping, n.p., n.d.). This was a newspaper account of a speech presented by Amos Wood at the Ingham County Farmers' Club meeting held at Maple Ridge Farm in December 1898.

28. "Historic Ingham Farmers Club Bows to Rapidly Changing Times" (newspaper clipping, n.p., December 1936).

29. From a paper read by Eunice Brewster Wood to the Ingham County Farmers' Club in November 1906.

30. Ibid.

31. Ibid.

32. Eliza Melton, "Old Club Friendships." This was a speech read at the Ingham County Farmers' Club meeting, 13 April 1918.

33. Myra Wood Cheney, "Ingham County Farmers' Club History." This was a paper read by Myra Wood Cheney on the Michigan State University campus on the occasion of the club's fortieth anniversary in 1912.

34. William Carroll Latta, letter to Amos and Eunice Wood, 1878, regarding showing livestock at the Michigan State Fair. **SC**

35. "Historic Ingham Farmers Club Bows to Rapidly Changing Times."

36. Michigan State University, master of science degree recipients (n.d.), Office of the Registrar, Michigan State University, Lansing, Mich.

37. William Carroll Latta, "Feeding Value of Ensilage" (master's thesis, catalog no. 115 251 THS, Michigan State University, 1882).

38. Ibid.

39. Woodburn, "Men of Mark in Indiana," W. C. Latta survey, 30 April 1906.

40. Ibid.

CHAPTER TWO

Building an Agricultural University: Politics, Vision, and Perseverance

1. Purdue University, Board of Trustees meeting minutes,12 April 1866, vol. 1, 29.

2. Purdue University, Board of Trustees meeting minutes, 28 August 1866, vol. 1, 37.

3. Ibid., 41.

4. Purdue University, Board of Trustees meeting minutes, 9 April 1867, vol. 1, 47.

5. James Roger Wood, "Science, Education, and the Political Economy in Indiana: A History of the School of Agriculture, Agricultural Experiment Station, and Department of Agricultural Extension at Purdue University to 1945" (Ph.D. diss., Purdue University, May 1993), 51.

6. Purdue University Reamer Club, *A University of Tradition: The Spirit of Purdue* (West Lafayette, Ind.: Purdue University Press, 2002), 4; Robert W. Topping, *A Century and Beyond: The History of Purdue University* (West Lafayette, Ind.: Purdue University Press, 1988), 74 and 76.

7. Topping, 78.

8. Purdue University, Board of Trustees meeting minutes, 10 March 1874, vol. 1, 142.

9. W. M. Hepburn and L. M. Sears, *Purdue University: Fifty Years of Progress* (Indianapolis: Hollenbeck Press, 1925), 59. Sometimes this class total includes one graduate student, which would bring the enrollment to 65 students (Topping, 84).

10. Jack Edward Walters, ed., *The Semi-Centennial Alumni Record of Purdue University* (West Lafayette, Ind.: Purdue University, May 1924), 15.

11. Frederic H. Weigle, *Purdue University Alumni Directory: 1875–1934* (West Lafayette, Ind.: Purdue University, 1934), 515; Topping, 75, 84; Founders Park plaque on the Purdue University campus, West Lafayette, Ind.; and Eunice Trotter, "Pioneers to Be Honored," *Lafayette (Ind.) Journal and Courier,* 23 April 1994.

12. *Purdue University Annual Register,* 1876–77, 29. The *Annual Register* was the university's listing of classes, professors, and areas of study. In 1894, this publication was renamed the *Annual Catalog.*

13. James Roger Wood, 77.

14. *Purdue University Annual Register,* 1874–75, 10.

15. Purdue University, Board of Trustees meeting minutes, 16 June 1876, vol. 1, 243.

16. *Purdue University Annual Register,* 1879–80, 12.

17. Ibid., 21.

18. *Purdue University Annual Register*, 1880–81, 27.

19. *Purdue University Annual Report,* 1876, 4.

20. Purdue University, Board of Trustees meeting minutes, 16 June 1876, vol. 1, 243.

21. Purdue University, Board of Trustees meeting minutes, 22 October 1878, vol. 1, 355.

22. Ibid.

23. Ibid.

24. *Purdue University Annual Report,* 1879, 16.

25. James Roger Wood, 74.

26. *Purdue University Annual Report,* 1881, 77.

CHAPTER THREE
The College Professor: Fulfilling a Dream of Teaching

1. William Carroll Latta, "Culture and Agriculture" (newspaper clipping, n.p., [1890s]).

2. William Carroll Latta, *Outline History of Indiana Agriculture* (West Lafayette, Ind.: Epsilon Sigma Phi [Alpha Lambda Chapter], Purdue University, and Indiana County Agricultural Agents Association, 1938), 339.

3. Announcement of William C. Latta's appointment as professor of agriculture at Purdue University, *Indianapolis News,* 30 August 1882, p. 2, col. 5.

4. Horton Budd Knoll, *The Story of Purdue Engineering* (West Lafayette, Ind.: Purdue University Studies, 1963), 362.

5. *Purdue University Annual Report,* 1883, 59.

6. Ibid., 24.

7. *Purdue University Annual Report,* 1882, 61.

8. *Purdue University Annual Report,* 1883, 60.

9. *Purdue University Annual Register*, 1884–85, 31.

10. William Carroll Latta, "The Agricultural College: Its Missions and Needs." Speech delivered before the Annual Agricultural Convention, Jan. 1884. *Thirty-Third Annual Report of the Indiana State Board of Agriculture,* 1883, vol. 25, 207.

11. *Purdue University Annual Register,* 1883–84, 19.

12. Ibid., 28.

13. Ibid., 30.

14. Ibid., 20.

15. *Purdue University Annual Register,* 1884–85, 31.

16. William Carroll Latta, form letter, 6 November 1900. Letter book, 3 February 1900 to 23 November 1900, 843. This letter along with many others written by Latta and cited in this book are contained in a set of ten letter books located in the W. C. Latta Collection, Special Collections, Purdue University Libraries, Stewart Center, West Lafayette, Ind.

17. *Purdue University Annual Register,* 1887–89, 61.

18. *Purdue University Annual Register,* 1895–96, 91.

19. *Purdue University Annual Catalog,* 1900–01, 107. Until 1894, the publication that contained information about classes, professors, and areas of study was titled the *Annual Register.* Beginning with the 1894–95 academic year, this publication was renamed the *Annual Catalog.*

20. William Carroll Latta, letter to Mr. B. F. Magee, 3 July 1894. Letter book, 23 March 1894 to 5 January 1895, 247. **SC**

21. William Carroll Latta, letter to Mr. C. W. Garfield, 25 April 1896. Letter book, 13 November 1895 to 3 August 1896, 844. **SC**

22. William Carroll Latta, letter to Mr. O. H. Martz, 17 December 1895. Letter book, 13 November 1895 to 3 August 1896, 249. **SC**

23. William Carroll Latta, letter to Mr. A. B. Minor, 28 March 1894. Letter book, 23 March 1894 to 5 January 1895, 44. **SC**

24. William Carroll Latta, letter to Mr. J. B. Fitch, 29 March 1894. Letter book, 23 March 1894 to 5 January 1895, 52. **SC**

25. William Carroll Latta, letter to Mr. R. F. Trambell, 14 July 1894. Letter book, 23 March 1894 to 5 January 1895, 285. **SC**

26. William Carroll Latta, letter to Mr. D. B. Johnson, 15 March 1902. Letter book, 9 December 1901 to 10 June 1902, 756. **SC**

27. William Carroll Latta, letter to Laura E. Rigmey, 2 August 1902. Letter book, 10 June 1902 to 4 December 1902, 220. **SC**

28. William Carroll Latta, letter to Mr. E. C. Mercer, 22 April 1904. Letter book, 30 November 1903 to 3 August 1904, 772. **SC**

29. William Carroll Latta, letter to Wm. F. Davis, 19 May 1904. Letter book, 30 November 1903 to 3 August 1904, 843. **SC**

30. William Carroll Latta, letter to Aaron Turley, 21 November 1901. Letter book, 15 July 1901 to 9 December 1901, 852. **SC**

31. Charles S. Plumb and William Carroll Latta, "Course of Instruction, Equipment and Method of Instruction in the School of Agriculture" (Purdue University, 1893), 3–4.

32. Ibid., 55.

33. Almon Mace, "Farm Equipment, Breeds of Live Stock, Farm Economy, Stock Breeding" (unpublished notebook, [1901]). This notebook contains classroom notes taken by Mace while he was a student at Purdue University.

34. *Purdue University Annual Report,* 1884, 36.

35. Knoll, 369.

36. *Purdue University Annual Report,* 1884, 38.

37. *Purdue University Annual Report,* 1883, 78.

38. William Carroll Latta, letter to editor, 31 January 1901. Letter book, 23 November 1900 to 13 July 1901, 388. **SC**

39. *Purdue University Annual Catalog,* 1895–96, 88.

40. *Purdue Agriculturist* 1, no. 7 (June 1907): 57.

41. Ibid.

42. Purdue University, faculty meeting minutes, 14 March 1884, 235.

43. Purdue University, faculty meeting minutes, 1 May 1882, 137.

44. Purdue University, faculty meeting minutes, 10 December 1883, 209.

45. *Purdue University Annual Register,* 1879–80, 46.

46. Ibid.

47. Ibid.

48. *Purdue University Annual Register,* 1883–84, 52.

49. Purdue University, faculty meeting minutes, 8 March 1892, 14.

50. Purdue University, faculty meeting minutes, 29 April 1892, 21.

51. Purdue University, faculty meeting minutes, 6 June 1892, 33.

52. Purdue University, faculty meeting minutes, 31 May 1883, 185.

53. Ibid.

54. *Purdue University Annual Catalog,* 1898–99, 97.

55. Purdue University, Board of Trustees meeting minutes, 2 January 1888, vol. 2, 288.

56. Purdue University, Board of Trustees meeting minutes, 31 January 1888, vol. 2, 292.

57. Purdue University, Board of Trustees meeting minutes, 18 April 1888, vol. 2, 307.

58. Knoll, 364.

59. *Purdue University Annual Report,* 1902, 40.

60. *Purdue University Annual Report,* 1900, 31.

61. Purdue University, "Questions and Answers about the School of Agriculture" (brochure, 1901). **SC**

62. William Carroll Latta, form letter to the agricultural press, 13 July 1904. Letter book, 30 November 1903 to 3 August 1904, 933. **SC**

63. William Carroll Latta, letter to Amos Ragle, 17 January 1901. Letter book, 23 November 1900 to 13 July 1901, 321.

64. Purdue University, Board of Trustees meeting minutes, 12 June 1907, vol. 3, 261.

65. *Purdue Agriculturist* 2, no. 1 (October 1907): 4.

66. Ibid., 3.

67. William Carroll Latta, letter to Professor T. L. Lyon, 24 May 1901. Letter book, 23 November 1900 to 13 July 1901, 808. **SC**

68. *Purdue Agriculturist* 2, no. 4 (January 1908): 5.

69. William Carroll Latta, Purdue University Personnel Records, 1882–1935.

70. William Carroll Latta, letter to James H. Smart, 28 May 1894. Letter book, 23 March 1894 to 5 January 1895, 233. **SC**

71. William Carroll Latta, Purdue University Personnel Records, 1882–1935.

72. Ibid.

73. James Roger Wood, 174.

74. Ibid.

75. Ibid.

76. *Purdue University Annual Catalog,* 1907–08, 69.

77. Knoll, 362.

78. Latta, *Outline History of Indiana Agriculture,* 340.

CHAPTER FOUR

The Field Researcher: Using Science to Answer Agricultural Questions

1. *Purdue University Annual Report,* 1888, 6.

2. Purdue University, Board of Trustees meeting minutes, 30 January 1888, vol. 2, 290.

3. William Carroll Latta, "Calendar of Events Preceding and During the Evolution and Growth of the Indiana Agricultural Experiment Station" (unpublished manuscript, [1930]), 1.

4. William Carroll Latta, "The Indiana State Board of Agriculture: A Historical Sketch" (unpublished manuscript, [1930]), 5.

5. Ibid, 19.

6. Ibid, 23.

7. *Indiana State Board of Agriculture Annual Report*, 1852, 213.

8. *Indiana State Board of Agriculture Annual Report*, 1854, 392.

9. Latta, "The Indiana State Board of Agriculture," 22.

10. Plumb and Latta, "Course of Instruction," 11.

11. *Purdue University Annual Report*, 1874, 37. The revenue reported from the sale of the oats may have included an adjustment, since it totaled seven dollars less than indicated.

12. *Purdue University Annual Report*, 1877, 14 and 19.

13. *Purdue University Annual Report*, 1879, 13.

14. *Purdue University Annual Report*, 1881, 6.

15. *Purdue University Annual Report*, 1883, 80.

16. *Purdue University Annual Report*, 1882, 99.

17. Ibid., 101.

18. *Purdue University Annual Report*, 1883, 81.

19. *Purdue University Annual Report*, 1883, 85.

20. *Purdue University Annual Report*, 1884, 28.

21. *Purdue University Annual Report*, 1879, 16.

22. Latta, "Calendar of Events," 17.

23. Ibid.

24. *Purdue University Agricultural Experiment Station Annual Report*, 1888, 20.

25. Purdue University, Board of Trustees meeting minutes, 15 April 1936, vol. 10, 313; Purdue University, "Purdue Yesterday and Today: 75th Anniversary" (brochure, n.d.).

26. *Purdue University Annual Register*, 1881–82, 49.

27. Purdue University, *The Debris* (student yearbook, 1899).

28. William Carroll Latta, letter to Mr. B. F. Magee, 3 July 1894. Letter book, 23 March 1894 to 5 January 1895, 247. **SC**

29. *Purdue University Annual Report*, 1882, 76.

30. *Purdue University Agricultural Experiment Station Annual Report*, 1889, 20.

31. This list of topics was drawn from the Experiment Station bulletins authored by Latta. See Appendix 3 for a full list of these publications.

32. William Carroll Latta, *Field Experiments with Corn* (Purdue University Agricultural Experiment Station Bulletin No. 39, April 1892), 33.

33. *Purdue University Annual Report*, 1884, 38.

34. *Purdue University Annual Report*, 1886, 12.

35. William Carroll Latta, *Experiments with Nitrogenous, Phosphates, and Other Fertilizers* (Purdue University Agricultural Experiment Station Bulletin No. 2, 1885), 10.

36. William Carroll Latta, *Experiments with Wheat* (Purdue University Agricultural Experiment Station Bulletin No. 4, 1885), 4.

37. William Carroll Latta, *Experiments with Wheat* (Purdue University Agricultural Experiment Station Bulletin No. 12, 1887), 15.

38. Ibid.

39. William Carroll Latta, *Experiments with Wheat* (Purdue University Agricultural Experiment Station Bulletin No. 4, 1885), 12.

40. William Carroll Latta, *Experiments with Oats and Corn* (Purdue University Agricultural Experiment Station Bulletin No. 14, 1888), 19.

41. William Carroll Latta, *Experiments with Wheat* (Purdue University Agricultural Experiment Station Bulletin No. 4, 1885), 7.

42. James Troop, *Report of the Director of the Indiana State Horticultural Experiment Station* (Purdue University Agricultural Experiment Station Bulletin No. 10, 1886), 3. **LSL**

43. Almon Mace, "Data Concerning Experiments in Crop Rotation and Soil Fertilization. Farm of C. L. Mace & Son, Lexington, Scott Co. Ind." This notebook contains notes from experiments conducted by Mace on behalf of Purdue University.

44. Ibid.

45. William Carroll Latta, "Culture and Agriculture."

46. *Purdue University Agricultural Experiment Station Annual Report,* 1896, 7.

CHAPTER FIVE

The Extension Specialist: Taking the University to the People

1. *Purdue University Annual Report,* 1898, 44.

2. Horace Stockbridge, letter to Indiana farmers, January 1889. In J. A. Arthur, *Spotting of Peaches and Cucumbers* (Purdue University Agricultural Experiment Station Bulletin No. 19, 1889), 11.

3. *Purdue University Agricultural Experiment Station Annual Report,* 1893, 11; and *Purdue University Agricultural Experiment Station Annual Report,* 1899, 9.

4. H. E. Young, "25 Years of Extension Work in Indiana: Historical Narrative and Achievement Summary" (Purdue University, 1939), 5.

5. William Carroll Latta, "The Story of Farmers' Institutes" (unpublished manuscript, [1930]), 66.

6. Ibid., 5–6.

7. Ibid., 7.

8. Ibid., 15.

9. Ibid., 17.

10. *Indiana State Board of Agriculture Annual Report,* 1883, 94.

11. Latta, "The Story of Farmers' Institutes," 22.

12. *Indiana State Board of Agriculture Annual Report,* 1887, 68.

13. Ibid.

14. William Carroll Latta, letter to Mr. J. H. Beattey, 10 April 1894. Letter book, 23 March 1894 to 5 January 1895, 116. **SC**

15. Latta, "The Story of Farmers' Institutes," 61.

16. William Carroll Latta, letter to Mr. S. Carson, 4 February 1896. Letter book, 13 November 1895 to 3 August 1896, 568. **SC**

17. William Carroll Latta, "Personal Record of William Carroll Latta," in the Epsilon Sigma Phi, Alpha Lambda Chapter, *Book of Annals* (n.p., 24 September 1928).

18. William Carroll Latta, letter to Mr. J. M. Welborn, 13 November 1901. Letter book, 15 July 1901 to 9 December 1901, 787. **SC**

19. William Carroll Latta, "Report on Farmers' Institutes: 1889–1893" (1893), 6. In *Purdue University Farmers' Institutes Annual Reports, 1889–1911* (n.p., [1911]). The Farmers' Institutes annual reports written by Latta are bound together in this book that is located in the W. C. Latta Collection, Special Collections, Purdue University Libraries, Stewart Center, West Lafayette, Ind.

20. Latta, "The Story of Farmers' Institutes," 42.

21. William Carroll Latta, "Brief Outline of the Farmers' Institute Work in Indiana," 31 March 1896. Letter book, 13 November 1895 to 3 August 1896, 810. **SC**

22. William Carroll Latta, letter to William Mitchell, 29 March 1894. Letter book, 23 March 1894 to 5 January 1895, 50. **SC**

23. William Carroll Latta, letter to Luther Dennell, 26 December 1895. Letter book, 13 November 1895 to 3 August 1896, 313. **SC**

24. William Carroll Latta, letter to Mr. E. H. Collins, 21 February 1900. Letter book, 3 February 1900 to 23 November 1900, 103. **SC**

25. William Carroll Latta, letter to Virginia C. Meredith, 21 February 1896. Letter book, 13 November 1895 to 3 August 1896, 664. **SC**

26. William Carroll Latta, letter to Mr. F. M. Grant, 7 September 1899. Letter book, 18 July 1899 to 2 February 1900, 120. **SC**

27. William Carroll Latta, letter to Mr. W. S. Ratliff, 20 June 1896. Letter book, 13 November 1895 to 3 August 1896, 936. **SC**

28. William Carroll Latta, letter to chairmen of Farmers' Institutes, 10 March 1900. Letter book, 3 February 1900 to 23 November 1900, 210. **SC**

29. William Carroll Latta, letter to Mr. Jas. Haslet, 7 July 1894. Letter book, 23 March 1894 to 5 January 1895, 257. **SC**

30. William Carroll Latta, letter to Professor C. C. Georgeson, 2 November 1894. Letter book, 23 March 1894 to 5 January 1895, 523. **SC**

31. William Carroll Latta, letter to Virginia C. Meredith, 21 February 1896. Letter book, 13 November 1895 to 3 August 1896, 664. **SC**

32. William Carroll Latta, letter to Virginia C. Meredith, 31 March 1894. Letter book, 23 March 1894 to 5 January 1895, 61. **SC**

33. William Carroll Latta, letter to Mr. A. E. Swope, 18 November 1895. Letter book, 13 November 1895 to 3 August 1896, 35. **SC**

34. William Carroll Latta, letter to Mr. C. B. Benjamin, 22 December 1903. Letter book, 30 November 1903 to 3 August 1904, 154. **SC**

35. William Carroll Latta, letter to editor, *The (Scottsburg, Ind.) Democrat,* 27 November 1899. Letter book, 18 July 1899 to 2 February 1900, 603. **SC**

36. William Carroll Latta, letter to Mr. D. M. Lett, 27 December 1899. Letter book, 18 July 1899 to 2 February 1900, 770. **SC**

37. Latta, "Report on Farmers' Institutes: 1889–1893," 9. In *Purdue University Farmers' Institutes Annual Reports, 1889–1911.* **SC**

38. William Carroll Latta, letter to F. C. Donald, 4 September 1894. Letter book, 23 March 1894 to 5 January 1895, 389. **SC**

39. William Carroll Latta, letter to D. G. Edwards, 24 November 1894. Letter book, 23 March 1894 to 5 January 1895, 618. **SC**

40. William Carroll Latta, letter to Mr. C. F. Daly, 27 May 1896. Letter book, 13 November 1895 to 3 August 1896, 899. SC

41. William Carroll Latta, letter to Ticket Agent, City Office, Pennsylvania Railroad Co., 7 August 1899. Letter book, 18 July 1899 to 2 February 1900, 28. SC

42. William Carroll Latta, letter to Mr. E. T. Winn, 31 October 1899. Letter book, 18 July 1899 to 2 February 1900, 443. SC

43. William Carroll Latta, letter to James Riley, 21 November 1899. Letter book, 18 July 1899 to 2 February 1900, 565. SC

44. William Carroll Latta, letter to Mr. W. F. Evans, 10 December 1895. Letter book, 13 November 1895 to 3 August 1896, 189. SC

45. William Carroll Latta, "Attend the Farmers' Institute at Orleans, Dec. 17–18," 5 December 1894. Letter book, 23 March 1894 to 5 January 1895, 723. SC

46. William Carroll Latta, letter to Mr. B. F. Biliter, 27 October 1899. Letter book, 18 July 1899 to 2 February 1900, 415. SC

47. William Carroll Latta, letter to Laura G. Day, 28 October 1901. Letter book, 15 July 1901 to 9 December 1901, 656. SC

48. William Carroll Latta, Tippecanoe County Farmers' Institute: Annual Report of Officers, [December 18, 1899]. Letter book, 18 July 1899 to 2 February 1900, 721. SC

49. Published presentations can be found in *Indiana State Board of Agriculture Annual Report,* 1888–1907. These reports are located at the John W. Hicks Undergraduate Library, Purdue University, West Lafayette, Ind.

50. William Carroll Latta, letter to Amos B. Lantz, 15 August 1899. Letter book, 18 July 1899 to 2 February 1900, 69. SC

51. William Carroll Latta, "Putnam County Farmers' Institute," 13 December 1895. Letter book, 13 November 1895 to 3 August 1896, 226. SC

52. William Carroll Latta, letter to Mr. C. E. Hatch, 30 January 1904. Letter book, 30 November 1903 to 3 August 1904, 402. SC

53. Latta, "The Story of Farmers' Institutes," 56.

54. William Carroll Latta, "Report on Farmers' Institutes" (1896), 8–11. In *Purdue University Farmers' Institutes Annual Reports, 1889–1911.* The Farmers' Institutes annual reports written by Latta are bound together in this book that is located in the W. C. Latta Collection, Special Collections, Purdue University Libraries, Stewart Center, West Lafayette, Ind.

55. William Carroll Latta, letter to Dr. E. H. Collins, 6 December 1899. Letter book, 18 July 1899 to 2 February 1900, 658. SC

56. William Carroll Latta, letter to Mr. I. M. Miller, 28 December 1895. Letter book, 13 November 1895 to 3 August 1896, 322. SC

57. William Carroll Latta, letter to Mr. W. H. Fry, 27 November 1901. Letter book, 15 July 1901 to 9 December 1901, 916. SC

58. William Carroll Latta, letter to Mr. J. H. Beattey, 30 April 1894. Letter book, 23 March 1894 to 5 January 1895, 187. SC

59. William Carroll Latta, letter to Prof. W. Hayes, 19 April 1901. Letter book, 23 November 1900 to 13 July 1901, 711. SC

60. William Carroll Latta, letter to Robert L. Birch, 13 July 1901. Letter book, 23 November 1900 to 13 July 1901, 996. SC

61. William Carroll Latta, letter to Postmaster, 5 May 1904. Letter book, 30 November 1903 to 3 August 1904, 807. **SC**

62. William Carroll Latta, letter to Geo. Smith, 28 March 1904. Letter book, 30 November 1903 to 3 August 1904, 686. **SC**

63. William Carroll Latta, letter to Mr. C. B. Benjamin, 22 December 1903. Letter book, 30 November 1903 to 3 August 1904, 154. **SC**

64. *Purdue University Annual Report,* 1909, 46.

65. *Indiana State Board of Agriculture Annual Report,* 1901, 615.

66. William Carroll Latta, "Report on Farmers' Institutes" (1902), 6. In *Purdue University Farmers' Institutes Annual Reports, 1889–1911.* The Farmers' Institutes annual reports written by Latta are bound together in this book that is located in the W. C. Latta Collection, Special Collections, Purdue University Libraries, Stewart Center, West Lafayette, Ind.

67. William Carroll Latta, letter to Mrs. S. O. N. Pleasants, 11 February 1896. Letter book, 13 November 1895 to 3 August 1896, 606. **SC**

68. William Carroll Latta, letter to Mr. J. Sherfick, 12 December 1895. Letter book, 13 November 1895 to 3 August 1896, 224. **SC**

69. William Carroll Latta, letter to Chas. E. Himmel, 3 January 1901. Letter book, 23 November 1900 to 13 July 1901, 249. **SC**

70. William Carroll Latta, letter to Mrs. J. C. Erwin, 25 July 1900. Letter book, 3 February 1900 to 23 November 1900, 445. **SC**

71. William Carroll Latta, form letter to editors of Indiana newspapers, 25 October 1900. Letter book, 3 February 1900 to 23 November 1900, 778. **SC**

72. Latta, "The Story of Farmers' Institutes," 52.

73. Virginia Meredith's comments were included on page 345 of Latta's *Outline History of Indiana Agriculture.*

74. Young, 26.

75. Latta, "The Story of Farmers' Institutes," 58.

76. Latta, "Report on Farmers' Institutes" (1896), 4 and 8. In *Purdue University Farmers' Institutes Annual Reports, 1889–1911.* **SC**

77. William Carroll Latta, letter to Mr. D. W. Hubbell, 17 December 1895. Letter book, 13 November 1895 to 3 August 1896, 253. **SC**

78. *Purdue University Department of Agricultural Extension Annual Report,* 1912, 11.

79. William Carroll Latta, letter to Theo. Romine, 24 February 1904. Letter book, 30 November 1903 to 3 August 1904, 527. **SC**

80. William Carroll Latta, "Report on Farmers' Institutes" (1906–07), 42. In *Purdue University Farmers' Institutes Annual Reports, 1889–1911.* The Farmers' Institutes annual reports written by Latta are bound together in this book that is located in the W. C. Latta Collection, Special Collections, Purdue University Libraries, Stewart Center, West Lafayette, Ind.

81. James Roger Wood, 115.

82. *Purdue University Annual Report,* 1915, 47.

83. *Purdue University Annual Report,* 1910, 48.

84. *Purdue University Annual Report,* 1911, 42.

85. Latta, "The Story of Farmers' Institutes," 65.

86. Charles Louis Lang, "A Historical Review of the Forces that Contributed to the Formation of the Cooperative Extension Service" (Ph.D. diss., Michigan State University, 1975), 169.

87. Purdue University, Board of Trustees meeting minutes, 25 April 1923, vol. 5, 637.

88. Knoll, 362.

89. William Carroll Latta, "Report on Farmers' Institutes" (1894), 8. In *Purdue University Farmers' Institutes Annual Reports, 1889–1911*. The Farmers' Institutes annual reports written by Latta are bound together in this book that is located in the W. C. Latta Collection, Special Collections, Purdue University Libraries, Stewart Center, West Lafayette, Ind.

90. Young, 4.

91. Latta, "Personal Record of William Carroll Latta."

CHAPTER SIX
The Purdue Politician: An Unwavering Belief in the University

1. William Carroll Latta, letter to Dr. C. A. Robinson, 27 March 1894. Letter book, 23 March 1894 to 5 January 1895, 35. SC

2. *Purdue University Annual Report,* 1901, 32.

3. William Carroll Latta, letter to Mr. S. Sutton, 29 June 1896. Letter book, 13 November 1895 to 3 August 1896, 953. SC

4. William Carroll Latta, letter to Mr. H. C. Vestal, 18 May 1896. Letter book, 13 November 1895 to 3 August 1896, 883. SC

5. Latta, "Report on Farmers' Institutes: 1889–1893," 12. In *Purdue University Farmers' Institutes Annual Reports, 1889–1911*. SC

6. William Carroll Latta, letter to Hon. S. Jett Williams, 17 December 1894. Letter book, 23 March 1894 to 5 January 1895, 826. SC

7. Latta, "Report on Farmers' Institutes" (1894), 1. In *Purdue University Farmers' Institutes Annual Reports, 1889–1911*. SC

8. Ibid., 16.

9. Latta, "Report on Farmers' Institutes" (1896)," 36. In *Purdue University Farmers' Institutes Annual Reports, 1889–1911*. SC

10. William Carroll Latta, letter to Mr. D. B. Johnson, 16 October 1899. Letter book, 18 July 1899 to 2 February 1900, 359. SC

11. William Carroll Latta, letter to Virginia Meredith, 18 July 1901. Letter book, 15 July 1901 to 9 December 1901, 43. SC

12. William Carroll Latta, letter to Mrs. J. W. Bates, 4 January 1900. Letter book, 18 July 1899 to 2 February 1900, 822. SC

13. William Carroll Latta, letter to the editors of *Indiana Farmer,* 21 December 1900. Letter book, 23 November 1900 to 13 July 1901, 185. SC

14. William Carroll Latta, letter to Naomi De Vilbiss, 11 October 1900. Letter book, 3 February 1900 to 23 November 1900, 702. SC

15. William Carroll Latta, letter to editor of the *(Indianapolis) Journal,* 19 October 1900. Letter book, 3 February 1900 to 23 November 1900, 747. SC

16. William Carroll Latta, letter to Mr. G. W. Borrell, 24 November 1900. Letter book, 23 November 1900 to 13 July 1901, 12. SC

17. William Carroll Latta, letter [recipient's name is illegible], 18 November 1899. Letter book, 18 July 1899 to 2 February 1900, 552. **SC**

18. William Carroll Latta, letter to Mr. B. F. Biliter [of the *(Huntington, Ind.) Guide]*, 26 July 1900. Letter book, 3 February 1900 to 23 November 1900, 449. **SC**

19. William Carroll Latta, letter to Mr. J. H. Gwaltney, 28 December 1900. Letter book, 23 November 1900 to 13 July 1901, 205. **SC**

20. William Carroll Latta, letter to Hon. Fremont Goodwine, 29 January 1901. Letter book, 23 November 1900 to 13 July 1901, 370. **SC**

21. William Carroll Latta, letter to Hon. J. C. Murphy, 25 February 1901. Letter book, 23 November 1900 to 13 July 1901, 521–22. **SC**

22. William Carroll Latta, letter to Hon. J. W. Parks, 25 February 1901. Letter book, 23 November 1900 to 13 July 1901, 519. **SC**

23. William Carroll Latta, letter to Mr. O. A. Somers, 1 March 1901. Letter book, 23 November 1900 to 13 July 1901, 545. **SC**

24. William Carroll Latta, letter to Cal Husselman, 30 January 1901. Letter book, 23 November 1900 to 13 July 1901, 374. **SC**

25. William Carroll, letter to Mrs. W. L. Berryman, 18 February 1901. Letter book, 23 November 1900 to 13 July 1901, 483. **SC**

26. William Carroll Latta, letter to R. P. Daggett and Co., 6 June 1901. Letter book, 23 November 1900 to 13 July 1901, 841. **SC**

27. William Carroll Latta, letter to "Friend" [former students in the Winter Short Course], 20 July 1901. Letter book, 15 July 1901 to 9 December 1901, 71. **SC**

28. William Carroll Latta, letter to Mrs. James A. Mount, 2 April 1901. Letter book, 23 November 1900 to 13 July 1901, 676. **SC**

29. William Carroll Latta, letter to Charles E. Butler, 1 August 1902. Letter book, 10 June 1902 to 4 December 1902, 215. **SC**

30. William Carroll Latta, letter to Mrs. Oliver Cline, 5 February 1901. Letter book, 23 November 1900 to 13 July 1901, 406. **SC**

31. William Carroll Latta, letter to Nellie S. Kedzie, 16 March 1901. Letter book, 23 November 1900 to 13 July 1901, 618. **SC**

32. William Carroll Latta, letter to Nellie S. Kedzie, 26 March 1901. Letter book, 23 November 1900 to 13 July 1901, 660; William Carroll Latta, letter to Nellie S. Kedzie, 23 April 1901. Letter book, 23 November 1900 to 13 July 1901, 730. **SC**

33. William Carroll Latta, letter to Virginia Meredith, 15 July 1901. Letter book, 15 July 1901 to 9 December 1901, 10. **SC**

34. William Carroll Latta, letter to Virginia Meredith, 18 July 1901. Letter book, 15 July 1901 to 9 December 1901, 43. **SC**

35. William Carroll Latta, letter to Virginia Meredith, 31 July 1901. Letter book, 15 July 1901 to 9 December 1901, 164. **SC**

36. William Carroll Latta, letter to "Dear Madame," 11 August 1901. Letter book, 15 July 1901 to 9 December 1901, 269. **SC**

37. William Carroll Latta, "The Woman's Conference at Purdue," 17 August 1901. Letter book, 15 July 1901 to 9 December 1901, 303. **SC**

38. William Carroll Latta, letter to Laura G. Day, 22 July 1901. Letter book, 15 July 1901 to 9 December 1901, 63. **SC**

39. William Carroll Latta, letter to Mr. B. F. Biliter, 2 November 1901. Letter book, 15 July 1901 to 9 December 1901, 699. **SC**

40. Ibid., 700.

41. William Carroll Latta, letter to Hon. Christian Holler, 9 August 1902. Letter book, 10 June 1902 to 4 December 1902, 278. **SC**

42. William Carroll Latta, letter to Mr. J. J. W. Billingsley, 6 October 1902. Letter book, 10 June 1902 to 4 December 1902, 529. **SC**

43. Ibid., 530.

44. William Carroll Latta, letter to Mrs. C. M. Thomas, 8 December 1903. Letter book, 30 November 1903 to 3 August 1904, 63. **SC**

45. Purdue University Reamer Club, *A University of Tradition: The Spirit of Purdue* (West Lafayette, Ind.: Purdue University Press, 2002), 14.

CHAPTER SEVEN
Moral Obligations and Civic Responsibilities: A Life of Service

1. Charles M. Sheldon, *In His Steps,* 1896. This work was originally published by *The Advance,* a weekly religious magazine. Due to a problem with the copyright, it became part of the public domain and subsequently has been published in many formats by numerous publishers.

2. William Carroll Latta, "The Rural Church" (unpublished manuscript, n.d.), 1.

3. William Carroll Latta, "The Country Church—Its Weakness, Its Importance, Its Opportunity, and Its Rehabilitation" (unpublished manuscript, 1930), 1.

4. William Carroll Latta, "Concerning the Rural Church" (unpublished manuscript, n.d.), 1.

5. Latta, "The Rural Church," 1.

6. William Carroll Latta, "Some Problems of the Rural Community Church" (unpublished manuscript, n.d.), 1.

7. William Carroll Latta, "Rural Church Merging for Efficiency" (unpublished manuscript, n.d.), 1.

8. Ibid., 2.

9. Ibid., 3.

10. Ibid., 4.

11. Ibid., 5.

12. Latta, "Concerning the Rural Church," 1.

13. William Carroll Latta, "The Church as a Factor in Agricultural Extension" (unpublished manuscript, n.d.), 1.

14. Latta, "The Rural Church," 1.

15. Latta, "The Church as a Factor in Agricultural Extension," 2.

16. Latta, "Some Problems of the Rural Community Church," 4.

17. Latta, "The Rural Church," 1.

18. Latta, "The Church as a Factor in Agricultural Extension," 1.

19. Latta, "Concerning the Rural Church," 1.

20. Latta, "The Church as a Factor in Agricultural Extension," 1.

21. Ibid.

22. William Carroll Latta, letter to George I. Christie, 19 April 1928. **TCHA**

23. George I. Christie, note to William Carroll Latta, [April] 1928. **TCHA**

24. Helen Hand, note to William Carroll Latta, 20 April 1928. **TCHA**

25. Clyde W. Warburton, letter to William Carroll Latta, 3 December 1934. **TCHA**

26. William Carroll Latta, "The Extension Department and the Rural Church" (position paper, [1934]), 2.

27. William Carroll Latta, "Report of the Conference of Rural Community Church Pastors" (unpublished manuscript, 1935), 1.

28. Ibid., 2.

29. Ibid.

30. Oakel Fowler Hall, "A Tribute to a Distinguished Hoosier Ruralist," *Purdue Alumnus* 23, no. 4 (January 1936): 12.

31. *Lafayette (Ind.) Journal and Courier,* 22 January 1936. This is a newspaper clipping about Latta's accomplishments found in the W. C. Latta Collection, Special Collections, Purdue University Libraries, Stewart Center, West Lafayette, Ind.

32. *New York Christian Advocate,* 29 January 1936. This is a newspaper clipping about Latta's accomplishments found in the W. C. Latta Collection, Special Collections, Purdue University Libraries, Stewart Center, West Lafayette, Ind.

33. Civic Improvement Association of Tippecanoe County, Ind. (by-laws, n.d.).

34. William Carroll Latta and F. Williams, "Report of Committee on Policy and Program [of the Tippecanoe County Civic Improvement Association]" (unpublished manuscript, n.d.), 2.

35. Albert Ferris, letter to William Carroll Latta, 10 March 1935. **SC**

36. *Lafayette (Ind.) Journal and Courier,* 22 January 1936. See note 31 in this chapter.

37. Ibid.

38. Ibid.

39. YMCA of Lafayette, Ind., "Fiftieth Anniversary, Young Men's Christian Association (Lafayette, Ind.)" (unpublished manuscript, October 1939).

40. William Carroll Latta, letter to Mr. E. A. Ford, 4 December 1899. Letter book, 18 July 1899 to 2 February 1900, 642. **SC**

41. William Carroll Latta, "Concerning Gifts to the YMCA," fundraising letter to potential donors, December 1932. **TCHA**

42. William Carroll Latta, fundraising letter to members of the Purdue University staff, 1935. **TCHA**

43. YMCA of Lafayette, Ind., Appreciation Book (booklet, n.p., n.d.).

44. E. R. Brown, note to William Carroll Latta, [1925]. This note was written on a proposal called "Organization," a YMCA document concerning women's membership.

45. William Carroll Latta, letter to general secretary of the YMCA in New Castle, Ind., 9 November 1925. **TCHA**

46. YWCA of Lafayette, Ind., "History of the Young Women's Christian Association" (unpublished manuscript, n.d.), 81.

47. YMCA of Lafayette, Ind., board meeting minutes, 9 June 1932. These minutes contain the letter that was read to the board by Flora W. Kern.

48. YMCA of Lafayette, Ind., Appreciation Book.

49. YMCA of Lafayette, Ind., board meeting minutes, 29 April 1930.

50. Ibid.

51. Ibid.

52. E. R. Brown, letter to Lena Baer, 24 February 1941. **SC**

53. Wesley Foundation (West Lafayette, Ind.), constitution and by-laws, 8 January 1919, 1.

54. Fremont E. Fribley, "Why Indiana Methodists Are Interested in Purdue University" (booklet, n.p., n.d.), 4.

55. Wesley Foundation (West Lafayette, Ind.) constitution and by-laws, 8 January 1919, 2 and 5.

56. Wesley Foundation (West Lafayette, Ind.), "Statement Concerning the Wesley Foundation," 13 December 1920. **TCHA**

57. Ibid.

58. Zora M. Smith, et al., letter to William McKenzie, 30 April 1921. **TCHA**

59. Latta, "Some Problems of the Rural Community Church," 3.

60. Latta, "Personal Record of William Carroll Latta."

61. Ibid.

62. "Community Leader Passes," *The Christian Community,* 21 March 1936.

63. Latta, "The Rural Church," 1.

CHAPTER EIGHT

The Private Life of William Latta: A Time Away from Campus

1. Purdue University, Board of Trustees meeting minutes, 1 August 1883, vol. 2, 152.

2. William Carroll Latta, letter to Mrs. J. C. Erwin, 30 August 1899. Letter book, 18 July 1899 to 2 February 1900, 107. **SC**

3. William Carroll Latta, letter to Mrs. James A. Mount, 13 October 1900. Letter book, 3 February 1900 to 23 November 1900, 711. **SC**

4. Knoll, 362.

5. Records from the Trinity Methodist Church, Lafayette, Ind.

6. Information about Eveline Orchards in this section was drawn from Alfred H. Perrin, "Seventy-Five Years of Eveline Orchards History: 1910–1985" (unpublished manuscript, 1985), 4.

7. Ibid., 3.

8. "Eight Weeks' Journey Made by Prof. Latta," *Purdue Exponent,* 15 September 1925.

9. Henry Reemtsma, "Changes" (unpublished autobiography, n.d.), Chapter 10, p. 5.

10. "Youthful Sports Enjoyed by Prof. W. C. Latta, Age 75," *Purdue Exponent,* 26 September 1925.

11. Paul Cheney, report for ninth-grade English class, May 1927.

12. "Prof. W. C. Latta, Pioneer in Agricultural Education, Expires at 85; Famous Farm Leader" (obituary), *Lafayette (Ind.) Journal and Courier,* 23 December 1935. The original poems written by William Latta are found in the W. C. Latta Collection, Special Collections, Purdue University Libraries, Stewart Center, West Lafayette, Ind.

13. Edward C. Elliott, note to William Carroll Latta, [1929]. **SC**

14. William Carroll Latta, note to E. H. Cherrington, 27 December 1932. **SC**

15. William Carroll Latta, letter to Carol Reemtsma, 26 September 1926. The letters that Latta wrote to his grandchildren are in the W. C. Latta Collection, Special Collections, Purdue University Libraries, Stewart Center, West Lafayette, Ind.

16. William Carroll Latta, letter to Carol and Keith Reemtsma, 26 August 1926. **SC**

17. Ibid.

18. William Carroll Latta, letter to Carol Reemtsma, 1 January 1926. **SC**

19. Ibid.

20. William Carroll Latta, letter to Carol Reemtsma, 26 September 1926. **SC**

21. Ibid.

22. Ibid.

23. William Carroll Latta, letter to Carol Reemtsma, 11 April 1927. **SC**

24. Ibid.

25. William Carroll Latta, letter to Carol and Keith Reemtsma, 29 July 1928. **SC**

26. Alta Latta, letter to Carol Reemtsma, n.d. **SC**

27. The original short stories written by William Latta are found in the W. C. Latta Collection, Special Collections, Purdue University Libraries, Stewart Center, West Lafayette, Ind.

28. Epsilon Sigma Phi, Alpha Lambda Chapter, handwritten note in a file titled "Professor Latta," 24 December 1935.

29. Editorial, *Lafayette (Ind.) Journal and Courier,* 23 December 1935.

30. "Prof. W. C. Latta, Pioneer in Agricultural Education, Expires at 85; Famous Farm Leader" (obituary), *Lafayette (Ind.) Journal and Courier,* 23 December 1935.

31. Epsilon Sigma Phi, Alpha Lambda Chapter, typed page in a file titled "Professor Latta," 27 December 1935. The "Club Department" probably referred to 4-H.

32. Mary Latta, letter to Epsilon Sigma Phi Fraternity in care of Professor W. Q. Fitch, December 1935. In an Epsilon Sigma Phi, Alpha Lambda Chapter, file titled "Professor Latta."

33. Mary Latta, letter to Hazel [no last name given], 12 January 1965. This was written when Mary Latta was living in Asheville, N.C. Private collection of Kim Sharpe.

CHAPTER NINE
Lasting Tributes: The Man Remembered

1. "Forty Years Service at Purdue," *Purdue Exponent,* 9 April 1922.

2. James Noel, letter to William Carroll Latta, 11 April 1922. **SC**

3. William Carroll Latta, letter to James Noel, 12 April 1922. **SC**

4. D. Chambers, *The American Shropshire Registry Association—The First One Hundred Years* (American Shropshire Registry Association, 1984), 8.

5. William Carroll Latta, letter to Mr. C. T. Mattingly, 7 June 1901. Letter book, 23 November 1900 to 13 July 1901, 850. **SC**

6. Chambers, *The American Shropshire Registry Association,* 8.

7. Ibid., 33.

8. Julia M. Wade, letter to William Carroll Latta, 12 December 1934. **SC**

9. Farmers' Institutes speakers of Indiana, letter to William Carroll Latta, 21 October 1910. **SC**

10. Ibid.

11. Information about payments made to Robert Grafton was found in a file titled "Latta Portrait File" ([1930]), which was located in the records of Epsilon Sigma Phi, Alpha Lambda Chapter, at the Purdue University Agricultural Administration Building, West Lafayette, Ind.

12. Purdue University, program for the unveiling of the William Carroll Latta portrait on Latta's eightieth birthday, 9 March 1930. **SC**

13. "A Timely Tribute to Prof. W. C. Latta," *Purdue Alumnus* 18, no. 7 (April 1930): 11.

14. Skinner's comments are found in the program for the portrait ceremony held on Latta's eightieth birthday, 9 March 1930. **SC**

15. Ibid. Latta's comments are also found in the program for the portrait ceremony held on Latta's eightieth birthday, 9 March 1930. **SC**

16. William Carroll Latta, thank-you note to portrait program attendees, [March 1930]. **SC**

17. Epsilon Sigma Phi, Alpha Lambda Chapter, meeting minutes, 13 January 1937, 2. In records of Epsilon Sigma Phi, Alpha Lambda Chapter, at the Purdue University Agricultural Administration Building, West Lafayette, Ind.

18. The advertising brochure is in Epsilon Sigma Phi, Alpha Lambda Chapter, file titled "Latta's *Outline History of Indiana Agriculture.*" In records of Epsilon Sigma Phi, Alpha Lambda Chapter, at the Purdue University Agricultural Administration Building, West Lafayette, Ind.

19. Epsilon Sigma Phi, Alpha Lambda Chapter, financial statement, 4 October 1938. In records of Epsilon Sigma Phi, Alpha Lambda Chapter, at the Purdue University Agricultural Administration Building, West Lafayette, Ind.

20. Leroy E. Hoffman, letter to Indiana vocational agriculture teachers, 16 October 1938. In Epsilon Sigma Phi, Alpha Lambda Chapter, file titled "Latta's *Outline History of Indiana Agriculture.*" In records of Epsilon Sigma Phi, Alpha Lambda Chapter, at the Purdue University Agricultural Administration Building, West Lafayette, Ind.

21. Reemtsma, "Changes," Chapter 10, p. 7.

22. "The Launching of the *W. C. Latta*" (article, n.p., 30 April 1944).

23. Ibid.

24. "U. S. Liberty Ship Honors Purdue Educator," *Lafayette (Ind.) Journal and Courier,* 29 April 1944.

25. Ibid.

26. Albert A. Rosati, phone interview by Frederick Whitford, 5 December 2003.

27. Lawrence J. Muscoreil, phone interview by Frederick Whitford, 18 December 2003.

28. William L. Kingsley, phone interview by Frederick Whitford, 13 December 2003.

29. Larry Sullivan, phone interview by Frederick Whitford, September 2003. Larry Sullivan is the grandson of James Latta, William Carroll Latta's younger brother.

30. "Latta Cited as Father of Farmers Institutes," *Lafayette (Ind.) Journal and Courier,* 7 December 1962.

31. Tom Turpin, "Latta Games: Rules and Regulations" (n.p., n.d.). Provided by Professor Tom Turpin.

32. Ibid.

33. This information was provided by Professor Tom Turpin.

34. Eunice Trotter, "Pioneers to Be Honored," *Lafayette (Ind.) Journal and Courier,* 23 April 1994.

35. Quoted from the plaque located in Founders Park on the Purdue University campus in West Lafayette, Ind.

36. Ibid.

CHAPTER TEN
Epilogue: A Legacy of Caring and Commitment

1. Oakel Fowler Hall, "A Tribute to a Distinguished Hoosier Ruralist," *Purdue Alumnus* 23, no. 4 (January 1936): 12.

2. K. E. Beeson, letter to Bertha Latta and Mary Latta, 15 February 1936. **SC**

Sources

Abbreviations

LSL   Life Sciences Library, Purdue University,
             Lilly Hall of Life Sciences, West Lafayette, Ind.

SC   W. C. Latta Collection
             Special Collections, Purdue University Libraries,
             Stewart Center, West Lafayette, Ind.

TCHA   W. C. Latta Collection
             Tippecanoe County Historical Association, Lafayette, Ind.

Adjutant General of Ohio. *Roster of Ohio Soldiers in the War of 1812.* 1916.
    Reprint, Baltimore, Md.: Genealogical Publishing Company, 1968.
Alvord, Samuel E. *Alvord's History of Noble County, Indiana.* Logansport, Ind.: B. F. Bowen,
    1902.
Announcement of William C. Latta's appointment as professor of agriculture at Purdue
    University. *Indianapolis News.* 30 August 1882, p. 2, col. 5.
Beeson, K. E. Letter to Bertha Latta and Mary Latta, 15 February 1936. **SC**
Berick, R. H. *History of La Grange County, Indiana (Eden Township).* Chicago: F. A. Battey
    & Co., 1882.
Brown, E. R. Letter to Lena Baer, 24 February 1941. **SC**
———. Note to William Carroll Latta, [1925]. Written on proposal called "Organization,"
    a YMCA document concerning women's membership. **TCHA**
Carson, Rachel. *Silent Spring.* Boston: Houghton Mifflin Co., 1962.
Chambers, D. *The American Shropshire Registry Association—The First One Hundred Years.*
    American Shropshire Registry Association, 1984.
Cheney, Myra Wood. "Ingham County Farmers' Club History." Paper, 1912. Private
    collection of Phyllis Webster.
Cheney, Paul. Report for ninth-grade English class. May 1927. Private collection of Phyllis
    Webster.
Christie, George Irving. Note to William Carroll Latta, 1928. **TCHA**
Civic Improvement Association of Tippecanoe County, Ind. By-laws, n.d. **TCHA**
"Community Leader Passes." *The Christian Community.* 21 March 1936. **SC**
Cowles, Albert. *Amos Freeman Wood.* Lansing, Mich.: Michigan Historical Publishing
    Assoc., 1905.
Dehart, Richard Patten. *Past and Present of Tippecanoe County, Indiana.* Indianapolis:
    B. F. Bowen, 1909.
Editorial. *Lafayette (Ind.) Journal and Courier.* 23 December 1935.
Elliott, Edward C. Letter to William Carroll Latta, 7 May 1935. **SC**

Epsilon Sigma Phi, Alpha Lambda Chapter. Meeting minutes and records, 1930–38.
In records of Epsilon Sigma Phi, Alpha Lambda Chapter, at the Purdue University
Agricultural Administration Building, West Lafayette, Ind.

Ferris, Albert. Letter to William Carroll Latta, 10 March 1935. **SC**

"Forty Years Service at Purdue" (short biography of William Carroll Latta).
Purdue Exponent. 9 April 1922. **SC**

Fribley, Fremont E. "Why Indiana Methodists Are Interested in Purdue University"
(booklet). N.p., n.d. Wesley Foundation, West Lafayette, Ind.

Gordon, Bettie. Phone interview by Frederick Whitford, 5 September 2003. Bettie Gordon
is the granddaughter of James Latta, William Carroll Latta's younger brother.

Hall, Oakel Fowler. "A Tribute to a Distinguished Hoosier Ruralist." *Purdue Alumnus* 23,
no. 4 (January 1936). **SC**

Hand, Helen. Note to William Carroll Latta, 20 April 1928. **TCHA**

Hepburn, W. M., and L. M. Sears. *Purdue University: Fifty Years of Progress.* Indianapolis:
Hollenbeck Press, 1925.

"Historic Ingham Farmers Club Bows to Rapidly Changing Times" (newspaper clipping).
N.p., December 1936. Private collection of Phyllis Webster.

Hoffman, Leroy E. Letter to Indiana vocational agriculture teachers, 16 October 1938.
In Epsilon Sigma Phi, Alpha Lambda Chapter, file titled "Latta's *Outline History
of Indiana Agriculture.*" In records of Epsilon Sigma Phi, Alpha Lambda Chapter,
at the Purdue University Agricultural Administration Building, West Lafayette, Ind.

Illustrated Historical Atlas of Noble County, Indiana, An. Chicago: Andreas & Baskin, 1874.

Indiana Historical Bureau. "Indiana Governors' Portrait Artists and Governors Painted."
Website containing information about Robert W. Grafton and the Indiana governors
he painted: http://www.statelib.lib.in.us/www/ihb/govportraits/govartists.html.

Indiana State Board of Agriculture. Annual Reports. 1852–54 and 1883–1907. At the
John W. Hicks Undergraduate Library, Purdue University, West Lafayette, Ind.

Kessler, Sherman. Phone interview by Frederick Whitford, 2003. Kessler is a 1935
graduate of Purdue University and was a member of the Purdue Board of
Trustees from 1973–88.

Kingsley, William L. Phone interview by Frederick Whitford, 13 December 2003.

Knoll, Horton Budd. *The Story of Purdue Engineering.* West Lafayette, Ind.:
Purdue University Studies, 1963.

Kriebel, Robert. *The Midas of the Wabash: A Biography of John Purdue.* West Lafayette, Ind.:
Purdue University Press, 2002.

Lafayette (Ind.) Journal and Courier. 23 December 1935–23 April 1994.

Lang, Charles Louis. "A Historical Review of the Forces that Contributed to the Formation
of the Cooperative Extension Service." Ph.D. diss., Michigan State University, 1975.

Latta, Alta. General correspondence, n.d. **SC**

Latta, Mary. Letter to Epsilon Sigma Phi Fraternity in care of Professor W. Q. Fitch,
December 1935. In an Epsilon Sigma Phi, Alpha Lambda Chapter, file titled
"Professor Latta." In records of Epsilon Sigma Phi, Alpha Lambda Chapter,
at the Purdue University Agricultural Administration Building, West Lafayette, Ind.

Latta, Mary. Letter to Hazel [no last name given], 12 January 1965. Private collection
of Kim Sharpe.

Latta, Robert H. "The Latta Collection," vol. 1, branch 1, 1940. Unpublished manuscript
at the Rare Book Section, U. S. Library of Congress, Washington, D.C. Manuscript
reviewed and summarized by Ken Mueller.

Latta, William Carroll. "The Agricultural College: Its Missions and Needs." Speech delivered
before the Annual Agricultural Convention, Jan. 1884. *Thirty-Third Annual Report
of the Indiana State Board of Agriculture,* 1883, vol. 25. John W. Hicks
Undergraduate Library, Purdue University, West Lafayette, Ind.

———. "Agricultural Education: Its Practical Value." Speech delivered before the
Annual Agricultural Convention, Jan. 1883. *Thirty-Second Annual Report
of the Indiana State Board of Agriculture,* 1882, vol. 24. John W. Hicks
Undergraduate Library, Purdue University, West Lafayette, Ind.

———. "A Brief Account of the Organization, Growth and Work of the Indiana
Experiment Station." Unpublished manuscript, [1930]. **SC**

———. "Calendar of Events Preceding and During the Evolution and Growth of the
Indiana Agricultural Experiment Station." Unpublished manuscript, [1930]. **TCHA**

———. "The Church as a Factor in Agricultural Extension." Unpublished manuscript, n.d.
TCHA

———. "Concerning the Rural Church." Unpublished manuscript, n.d. **TCHA**

———. "The Country Church—Its Weakness, Its Importance, Its Opportunity,
and Its Rehabilitation." Unpublished manuscript, 1930. **TCHA**

———. Cover letter to "Report of the Conference of Rural Community Church Pastors,"
held 26 April 1935 at Purdue University, West Lafayette, Ind. **TCHA**

———. "Culture and Agriculture" (newspaper clipping). N.p., [1890s]. Private collection
of Phyllis Webster.

———. "Evolution and Development of Agricultural Investigation Prior to the
Organization of the Experiment Station." Unpublished manuscript, [1925–35].
TCHA

———. *Experiments with Corn.* Purdue University Agricultural Experiment Station
Bulletin No. 23, 1889. **LSL**

———. *Experiments with Corn and Oats.* Purdue University Agricultural Experiment
Station Bulletin No. 55, March 1895. **LSL**

———. *Experiments with Nitrogenous, Phosphates, and Other Fertilizers.* Purdue
University Agricultural Experiment Station Bulletin No. 2, 1885. **LSL**

———. *Experiments with Oats and Corn.* Purdue University Agricultural Experiment
Station Bulletin No. 6, 1886. **LSL**

———. *Experiments with Oats and Corn.* Purdue University Agricultural Experiment
Station Bulletin No. 14, 1888. **LSL**

———. *Experiments with Wheat.* Purdue University Agricultural Experiment Station
Bulletin No. 4, 1885. **LSL**

——— *Experiments with Wheat.* Purdue University Agricultural Experiment Station
Bulletin No. 12, 1887. **LSL**

Latta, William Carroll. *Experiments with Wheat: Crop Rotations.* Purdue University
Agricultural Experiment Station Bulletin No. 16, 1888. **LSL**

———. "The Extension Department and the Rural Church." Position paper, [1934]. **TCHA**

———. "Feeding Value of Ensilage." Master's thesis, catalog no. 115 251 THS, Michigan
State University, 1882.

———. *Field Experiments with Corn.* Purdue University Agricultural Experiment Station
Bulletin No. 39, April 1892. **LSL**

———. *Field Experiments with Corn and Oats.* Purdue University Agricultural Experiment
Station Bulletin No. 50, April 1894. **LSL**

———. *Field Experiments with Wheat.* Purdue University Agricultural Experiment Station
Bulletin No. 27, 1889. **LSL**

———. *Field Experiments with Wheat.* Purdue University Agricultural Experiment Station
Bulletin No. 32, July 1890. **LSL**

———. *Field Experiments with Wheat.* Purdue University Agricultural Experiment Station
Bulletin No. 36, August 1891. **LSL**

———. *Field Experiments with Wheat.* Purdue University Agricultural Experiment Station
Bulletin No. 45, August 1893. **LSL**

———. General correspondence and papers, 1894–1935. **SC**

———. General correspondence and papers, 1925–35. **TCHA**

———. "Historical Sketch of Purdue University Experiment Station from 1887 to 1932."
Unpublished manuscript, [1932–35]. **SC**

———. "Indiana Farmers' Institutes from Their Origin in 1882 to 1904." Unpublished
manuscript, 1904. In *Purdue University Farmers' Institutes Annual Reports,
1889–1911.* N.p., [1911]. **SC**

———. "The Indiana State Board of Agriculture: A Historical Sketch." Unpublished
manuscript, [1930]. **TCHA**

———. Michigan Agricultural College transcripts. 1874–77. At the Michigan State
University Office of Registrar, Administrative Building, East Lansing, Michigan.

———. *Outline History of Indiana Agriculture.* West Lafayette, Ind.: Epsilon Sigma
Phi (Alpha Lambda Chapter), Purdue University, and Indiana County Agricultural
Agents Association, 1938.

———. "Personal Record of William Carroll Latta." In the Epsilon Sigma Phi,
Alpha Lambda Chapter, *Book of Annals.* N.p., 24 September 1928. In fraternity
records located at the Purdue University Agricultural Administration Building,
West Lafayette, Ind.

———. Poems. Unpublished, [1920–35]. **SC**

———. "A Project for Rural Church Rehabilitation." Unpublished manuscript, n.d. **TCHA**

———. *Purdue University Farmers' Institutes Annual Reports, 1889–1911.* N.p., [1911]. **SC**

———. Purdue University Personnel Records. 1882–1935. In Purdue University
personnel files, Freehafer Hall, West Lafayette, Ind.

———. "Report of the Conference of Rural Community Church Pastors."
Unpublished manuscript, 1935. **TCHA**

———. "The Rural Church." Unpublished manuscript, n.d. **TCHA**

———. "Rural Church Merging for Efficiency." Unpublished manuscript, n.d. **TCHA**

Latta, William Carroll. Secretary's Report of Farmers' Institute Meeting. [1920s]. **TCHA**
———. Short Stories. Unpublished, [1930–35]. **SC**
———. "Some Problems of the Rural Community Church." Unpublished manuscript, n.d. **TCHA**
———. "The Story of Farmers' Institutes." Unpublished manuscript, [1930]. **TCHA**
———. "To the Civic League of LaFayette, Indiana." Unpublished manuscript, n.d. **TCHA**
Latta, William Carroll, and W. B. Anderson. *Field Experiments with Corn, Oats and Forage Plants.* Purdue University Agricultural Experiment Station Bulletin No. 64, April 1897. **LSL**
———. *Field Experiments with Wheat.* Purdue University Agricultural Experiment Station Bulletin No. 61, August 1896. **LSL**
———. *Field Experiments with Wheat.* Purdue University Agricultural Experiment Station Bulletin No. 72, August 1898. **LSL**
Latta, William Carroll, and Alta Wood Latta. Marriage certificate. 10 July 1879. **SC**
Latta, William Carroll, and F. Williams. "Report of Committee on Policy and Program (of the Tippecanoe County Civic Improvement Association)." Unpublished manuscript, n.d. **TCHA**
"Latta Cited as Father of Farmers' Institutes." *Lafayette (Ind.) Journal and Courier.* 7 December 1962.
"Latta Ship Nameplate to Honor Ag Pioneer." *Lafayette (Ind.) Journal and Courier.* 4 December 1962.
"The Launching of the *W. C. Latta*" (article). N.p., 30 April 1944. Private collection of Kim Sharpe.
Mace, Almon. "Data Concerning Experiments in Crop Rotation and Soil Fertilization. Farm of C. L. Mace & Son, Lexington, Scott Co. Ind." Unpublished notebook, 1905–31. Private collection of James Turley.
———. "Farm Equipment, Breeds of Live Stock, Farm Economy, Stock Breeding." Unpublished notebook, [1901]. Private collection of James Turley.
McKinney, Judy Kirkpatrick. Phone interview by Frederick Whitford, 2003.
Melton, Eliza. "Old Club Friendships." Speech read at the Ingham County Farmers' Club meeting, 13 April 1918. Private collection of Phyllis Webster.
"A Michigan Farmer: Something about a Pioneer in Blooded Stock Raising" (newspaper clipping). N.p., [1881]. Private collection of Phyllis Webster.
Michigan State University. Master of science degree recipients. N.d. Michigan State University Office of Registrar, East Lansing, Mich.
———. Transcripts of William Carroll Latta (from Michigan Agricultural College), 1874–77. At the Michigan State University Office of the Registrar, Administrative Building, East Lansing, Michigan.
Mueller, Ken, "The James T. Latta Update." In *The Latta Genealogy Newsletter* 6 (Winter 1998). Available online at: http://www.latta.org/.
Muscoreil, Lawrence J. Phone interview by Frederick Whitford, 18 December 2003.
National Normal University. "Twenty-fifth Annual Catalogue." National Normal University, [1880]. Warren County Historical Society, Lebanon, Ohio.
New York Christian Advocate. 29 January 1936. **SC**

Noel, James. Letter to William Carroll Latta, 11 April 1922. **SC**

Pence, Mervill Olleo. Unpublished autobiography, May 1965. Private collection of Hugh B. Pence.

Perrin, Alfred H. "Seventy-Five Years of Eveline Orchards History: 1910–1985." Unpublished manuscript, 1985. Private collection of Phyllis Webster.

Peterson, John B. "History of Agronomy Department." N.p., n.d. At the Purdue University Department of Agronomy, Lilly Hall, West Lafayette, Ind.

Pittsburgh Gazette, 29 October 1795–15 February 1796.

Plumb, Charles S. *A Note on Two Inferior Fertilizers.* Purdue University Agricultural Experiment Station Bulletin No. 32, 1890. **LSL**

Plumb, Charles S., and William Carroll Latta. "Course of Instruction, Equipment and Method of Instruction in the School of Agriculture." Purdue University, 1893. At the John W. Hicks Undergraduate Library, Purdue University, West Lafayette, Ind.

"Prof. W. C. Latta, Pioneer in Agricultural Education, Expires at 85; Famous Farm Leader." Obituary. *Lafayette (Ind.) Journal and Courier.* 23 December 1935.

Purdue Agriculturist, June 1907–January 1908. In Special Collections, Purdue University Libraries, Stewart Center, West Lafayette, Ind.

Purdue Exponent, 9 April 1922–26 September 1925. In Special Collections, Purdue University Libraries, Stewart Center, West Lafayette, Ind.

Purdue University. *Agricultural Experiment Station Annual Report.* 1888–96. **LSL**

———. *Annual Catalog.* 1894–1908. In Special Collections, Purdue University Libraries, Stewart Center, West Lafayette, Ind.

———. *Annual Register.* 1874–94. In Special Collections, Purdue University Libraries, Stewart Center, West Lafayette, Ind.

———. *Annual Report.* 1874–1928. In Special Collections, Purdue University Libraries, Stewart Center, West Lafayette, Ind.

———. Board of Trustees meeting minutes. 12 April 1866–15 April 1936. Office of the Purdue University Board of Trustees, Hovde Hall, West Lafayette, Ind.

———. *The Debris* (student yearbook). 1899. **SC**

———. *Department of Agricultural Extension Annual Report.* 1912–31. **LSL**

———. Faculty meeting minutes. 1 May 1882–26 April 1893. In Special Collections, Purdue University Libraries, Stewart Center, West Lafayette, Ind.

———. Founders Day Banquet Program. 6 May 1933. Sixty-fourth anniversary of the founding of the university, sponsored by the Purdue Alumni Association. In Special Collections, Purdue University Libraries, Stewart Center, West Lafayette, Ind.

———. Personnel records of William Carroll Latta, 1882–1935. In Purdue University personnel files, Freehafer Hall, West Lafayette, Ind.

———. Program for the unveiling ceremony of the William Carroll Latta portrait, held at the Faculty Lounge in the Purdue Memorial Union on Latta's eightieth birthday, 9 March 1930. **SC**

———. "Purdue Yesterday and Today: 75th Anniversary." Brochure, n.d. Tippecanoe County Historical Association, Lafayette, Ind.

———. "Questions and Answers about the School of Agriculture." Brochure, 1901. **SC**

Purdue University Reamer Club. *A University of Tradition: The Spirit of Purdue.* West Lafayette, Ind.: Purdue University Press, 2002.

Reemtsma, Henry. "Changes." Unpublished autobiography, n.d. Private collection of Phyllis Webster.

Roof, George W. "The Early Village School." *Albion (Ind.) New Era.* 16 January 1918.

Rosati, Albert A. Phone interview by Frederick Whitford, 5 December 2003.

"Sheep Growers Honor Latta at Gala Meeting." *Purdue Alumnus* 22, no. 4 (January 1935). In Special Collections, Purdue University Libraries, Stewart Center, West Lafayette, Ind.

Sheldon, Charles M. *In His Steps,* 1896. In the public domain.

Smith, Zora M., et al. Letter to William McKenzie, 30 April 1921. **TCHA**

Stockbridge, Horace. Letter to Indiana farmers, Jan. 1889. In J. A. Arthur, *Spotting of Peaches and Cucumbers,* Purdue University Agricultural Experiment Station Bulletin No. 19, 1889. **LSL**

Sullivan, Larry. Phone interview by Frederick Whitford, September 2003. Larry Sullivan is the grandson of James Latta, William Carroll Latta's younger brother.

Thompson, Dave O. *A History: Fifty Years of Cooperative Extension Service in Indiana.* N.p., [1962]. **LSL**

Thompson, Dave O., and William L. Madigan. *One Hundred and Fifty Years of Indiana Agriculture.* Written for the Indiana Sesquicentennial Commission. N.p., 1966. **LSL**

"A Timely Tribute to Prof. W. C. Latta." *Purdue Alumnus* 18, no. 7 (April 1930). In Special Collections, Purdue University Libraries, Stewart Center, West Lafayette, Ind.

Topping, Robert W. *A Century and Beyond: The History of Purdue University.* West Lafayette, Ind.: Purdue University Press, 1988.

"Township Histories. Turtle Creek Township." In *The History of Warren County, Ohio.* Chicago: W. H. Beers Co., 1882; reprint, Mt. Vernon, Ind.: Windmill Publications, 1992. Available online at: http://www.rootsweb.com/~ohwarren/Beers/IV/tct/0480.htm. Transcription provided by Arne H. Trelvik, 15 June 2003.

Triplett, Randall. "A Brief History of the Lafayette Indiana Young Men's Christian Association." Unpublished manuscript, April 1975. YMCA, Lafayette, Ind.

Troop, James. *Report of the Director of the Indiana State Horticultural Experiment Station.* Purdue University Agricultural Experimental Station Bulletin No. 10, 1886. **LSL**

Trotter, Eunice. "Pioneers to Be Honored." *Lafayette (Ind.) Joural and Courier.* 23 April 1994.

Turpin, Tom. "Latta Games: Rules and Regulations." N.p., n.d. Provided by Prof. Tom Turpin.

U.S. Bureau of the Census. Indiana, Noble County, Perry Township, Ligonier Post Office. Washington, D.C., 9 June 1860.

———. Michigan, Ingham County, Vevay. Washington, D.C., 4–5 June 1880.

———. U.S. Agricultural Survey for Noble County, Indiana. 28 July 1870. Indiana State Archives, Indianapolis, Ind.

U.S. Department of Agriculture. "Indiana Crop and Livestock Statistics: Historic Crop Summary, 1866–1969." No. H74–1, June 1974. Indiana Agricultural Statistics Service, West Lafayette, Ind.

"U.S. Liberty Ship Honors Purdue Educator." *Lafayette (Ind.) Journal and Courier.* 29 April 1944.

U.S. Merchant Marine. "Liberty Ships Built by the United States Maritime Commission in World War II." Website: http://www.usmm.org/libertyships.html.

U.S. Navy. "Armed Guard Center Report of Materials Furnished to Armed Guard Units." 19 June 1944. Third Naval District Office of Port Director. National Archives and Records Administration, College Park, Md.

———. "Report of Voyage from August 10, 1944, to September 6, 1944." 7 September 1944. Third Naval District Office of Port Director. National Archives and Records Administration, College Park, Md.

———. Ship movement cards for the SS *W. C. Latta.* 25 May 1944–25 August 1946. National Archives and Records Administration, College Park, Md.

Wade, Julia M. Letter to William Carroll Latta, 12 December 1934. **SC**

Walters, Jack Edward, ed. *The Semi-Centennial Alumni Record of Purdue University.* West Lafayette, Ind.: Purdue University, May 1924. **SC**

Warburton, Clyde W. Letter to William Carroll Latta, 3 December 1934. **TCHA**

Warren County (Ohio) Historical Society. Letter to Frederick Whitford, 18 September 2003.

Weigle, Frederic H. *Purdue University Alumni Directory: 1875–1934.* West Lafayette, Ind.: Purdue University, 1934.

Wesley Foundation (West Lafayette, Ind.). Constitution and by-laws, 8 January 1919. **TCHA**

———. "Statement Concerning the Wesley Foundation." 13 December 1920. **TCHA**

———. "The Wesley Cornerstone" (booklet). N.p., 1942. In a file titled "Wesley Foundation at Purdue." At Archives of DePauw University and Indiana United Methodism, Roy O. West Library, Greencastle, Ind.

Wood, Amos Freeman. "History of Ingham County Farmers' Club" (newspaper clipping). N.p., n.d. Newspaper account of a speech presented by Amos Wood at the Ingham County Farmers' Club meeting held at Maple Ridge Farm, December 1898. Private collection of Phyllis Webster.

Wood, Eunice Brewster. Paper read by Eunice Brewster Wood to the Ingham County Farmers' Club, November 1906. Private collection of Phyllis Webster.

Wood, James Roger. "Science, Education, and the Political Economy in Indiana: A History of the School of Agriculture, Agricultural Experiment Station, and Department of Agricultural Extension at Purdue University to 1945." Ph.D. diss., Purdue University, May 1993.

Woodburn, James Albert. "Men of Mark in Indiana." 1905–6. Manuscripts Department, Lilly Library, Indiana University, Bloomington, Ind.

YMCA of Lafayette, Ind. Appreciation Book (booklet). N.p., n.d. **SC**

———. Board meeting minutes. 7 October 1913–9 June 1932. At the YMCA, Lafayette, Ind.

———. "Fiftieth Anniversary, Young Men's Christian Association (Lafayette, Ind.)." Unpublished manuscript, October 1939. **TCHA**

———. "Subscriptions to the YMCA Building Fund." Ledger entry, 1902. **TCHA**

Young, H. E. "25 Years of Extension Work in Indiana: Historical Narrative and Achievement Summary." Purdue University, 1939. **SC**

Index